THE *Environment* AND CANADIAN SOCIETY

THE *Environment* AND CANADIAN SOCIETY

Edited by Thomas Fleming
University of Windsor

ITP® Nelson
an International Thomson Publishing company

Toronto • Albany • Bonn • Boston • Cincinnati • Detroit • London • Madrid • Melbourne •
Mexico City • New York • Pacific Grove • Paris • San Francisco • Singapore • Tokyo • Washington

I⃝TP™
International Thomson Publishing
The ITP logo is a trademark under licence

Published in 1997 by
I⃝TP Nelson
A division of Thomson Canada Limited
1120 Birchmount Road
Scarborough, Ontario M1K 5G4

Canadian Cataloguing in Publication Data

Main entry under title:
    The environment and Canadian society

Includes bibliographical references and index.
ISBN 0-17-604920-7

    1. Human ecology—Canada.   2. Environmental policy—Canada.
3. Environmental protection—Canada. I. Fleming, Thomas, 1951–

GF511.E58   1997   304.2'8'0971   C96-990106-2

Publisher and Team Leader	Michael Young
Acquisitions Editor	Charlotte Forbes
Senior Production Editor	Bob Kohlmeier
Developmental Editor	Dianne Horton
Production Coordinator	Brad Horning
Assistant Art Director	Sylvia Vander Schee
Cover Design	Liz Harasymczuk
Interior Design	Sharon Foster
Senior Composition Analyst	Alicja Jamorski

Printed and bound in Canada
1 2 3 4   (BG) 99 98 97 96

Dedication

This book is lovingly dedicated to my wife, Patricia O'Reilly,
to our children, Patrick, Tom, and Kate,
and to the shores of Georgian Bay,
in whose waters may our grandchildren and their children play.

CONTENTS

Preface   *ix*
Acknowledgments   *xi*

Chapter 1   Understanding the Environment   *1*
Raymond A. Rogers, York University

Chapter 2   Depletion of Renewable Resources   *13*
Alistair J. Bath, Memorial University of Newfoundland

Chapter 3   Agriculture and Ecology   *43*
Ian McQuarrie, University of Prince Edward Island

Chapter 4   Canadian Water Resources and Management   *59*
Isobel W. Heathcote, University of Guelph

Chapter 5   Arctic Contaminants and the Environment   *85*
Nancy C. Doubleday, Carleton University

Chapter 6   Our Cities, Our Air, Our Health: Perspectives on Urban Air Quality
    and Human Health   *105*
Monica Campbell, Metropolitan Toronto Teaching Health Units

Chapter 7   Global Warming   *133*
F. Kenneth Hare, University of Toronto

Chapter 8   NAFTA: Potential Environmental Impact   *151*
George H. Crowell, University of Windsor

Chapter 9   Public Participation and Environmental Planning   *171*
G. Keith Warriner, University of Waterloo

Chapter 10   Solid Waste   *201*
Douglas Macdonald, University of Toronto

Chapter 11   Environmental Management   *219*
Dixon Thompson, The University of Calgary

Chapter 12   Green Politics and the Rise of the Environmental Movement   *251*
Robert Paehlke, Trent University

Chapter 13   Turning the Medicine Wheel: Aboriginal Land Claims and the
   Environment   *275*
Thomas Fleming, University of Windsor

Chapter 14   Is Sustainable Forestry Community Forestry? A British Columbia
   Perspective   *291*
Duncan Taylor, University of Victoria

Chapter 15   New Directions in Environmental Concern   *313*
Melody Hessing, Douglas College

Contributors   *333*
Index   *337*

PREFACE

A few days before Canada Day, 1996, the Ontario government approved a plan that would allow cutting of more than one-third of the old-growth pine forests of the Temagami area, near North Bay. The government also decided to permit mining to resume after an absence of 24 years in the region. The minister responsible for natural resources claimed that these government actions would increase environmental protection for the area and, of course, create jobs.[1] Many of you who are reading this book have perhaps never seen this beautiful crucible of life in Northern Ontario. Perhaps you will never see it in your lifetime. But that does not mean that it is not worth protecting, or that its value is diminished because you may not be able to travel to see it. We understand the beauty of the Mona Lisa and recognize that it may be only once in a lifetime that we travel to the Louvre to see it. But we assume a kind of guardianship, a human need to protect for present and future generations those things that replenish the soul. In the case of the Temagami area, a living, irreplaceable wonder that is part of our unique Canadian heritage and contemporary life was put at risk. History teaches us—from the Alaska pipeline through to the decline of the East Coast fisheries—that when private gain is endorsed over forests and streams, over plant life and wildlife, over air and human life, we often find that treasures of nature are lost to us forever.

This collection is a pioneering effort to address many of the pressing issues that confront us in an environmentally challenged world. While there exist many technical works on the state of the environment, few address environmental issues in the context of the social-policy issues they raise. By this I mean that environmental concerns cannot be isolated from the societal impacts they have. We are becoming increasingly aware that environmental issues often have global implications. The efforts of cities in Canada to deal with environmental pollution, for example, may lead to conflicts with rural regions. Similarly, rural regions, in their use of various chemical agents, may find themselves affecting the lives of city dwellers.

This book attempts to provide readers with a balanced view of many of the environmental issues that now occupy our attention as a society. In planning the book we attempted to provide a solidly grounded introduction to a variety of key areas. Beginning with a general introduction to understanding the environment, the book proceeds to examine a variety of issues. The authors explore the depletion of renewable resources and its implications for the quality of our lives. Similarly, water resources, agriculture, and air quality are the subject of analysis both on a scientific and a cultural basis. Global warming and the effect of Arctic contaminants on our environment are two chapters that have far-reaching implications for our quality of life. The effects of the North American Free Trade Agreement (NAFTA) and public participation in the environmental planning process are examined, illuminating the impact both of international regulation and of local input on shaping the path Canada takes in managing its environmental resources. In another essay, the by-products of our consumer society and the challenges presented in terms of waste management are analyzed. A framework for environmental management is developed in another contribution. The historical development of what has been called "green politics" and the rise of the environmental movement are traced in an illuminating contribution to our knowledge of the origins of contemporary environmental politics. The book also explores the clash between aboriginals and developers, as well as the challenges presented in attempting to develop sustainable forestry practices. The book ends with a look forward at some of the newest developments in environmental concerns.

The contributing authors are from across Canada, reflecting a diversity of approaches and opinions. The topics they explore represent vigorous scientific, legal, and policy examinations presented in language that is accessible to readers. This accessibility reflects the approach that guided the development of the book—to provide a solid introduction to the many areas of concern for the environment that Canadians feel, in terms that are eminently understandable. The book addresses the need for more widely available Canadian-based scientific material. The authors also reflect the interdisciplinary nature of the task that the book undertakes. They work in various disciplines—the sciences, law, sociology, biology, chemistry, economics, health sciences, environmental studies, geography, and agriculture. Their chapters present our most current scientific understanding of the various environmental issues that confront Canadian society in the late 1990s.

NOTES

1   Unland, Karen. 1996. "Temagami Logging, Mining Approved." *The Globe and Mail.* June 29: A1.

ACKNOWLEDGMENTS

The more one edits collections of readings, the more one becomes convinced of their value and of their complexity. This book originated in my own interests in the environment and in educating university, college, and general audiences about the nature of the various crises that confront us on the environmental horizon. Reflecting on the fate of various animal species, I wondered how one could reach the young minds who one day will be positioned to mould our ideas, approaches, and policies of the future. Who would have accepted, other than as lunacy, the idea a decade ago that one day the seemingly inexhaustible cod of the oceans off Nova Scotia and Newfoundland would be depleted? In the 1990s, though we have established blue-box (and now grey-box) recycling in major Canadian cities, it was my opinion that the momentum of the environmental movement was fading fast in the economic crises in the 1990s.

There have been a number of persons who have made a tremendous contribution to this volume of Canadian readings in the environment. First, I would like to thank Scott Fleming for his initial support and guidance on the project. His input proved crucial in assembling the contributors. Dianne Draper of the University of Calgary graciously recommended various contributors, and this greatly helped in assembling the book.

At the University of Windsor, President Ron Ianni has vigorously supported the development of academic programs and research on the environment. Vice-President, Academic, William Jones has provided strong support for environmental programs within the university and in the wider community. Their vision was a foundation that supported the initiation of this book. My academic colleagues have also given freely of their time and advice, and I owe them a debt of gratitude. They are Neil Gold, Leigh West, Deb Gustavsen, Muhammad Shuraydi, Subhas Ramcharan, Barry Adam, Gerald Romsa, Steve Baron, and Barry Clark. I would also like to thank Dean Kate McCrone, Faculty of Social Science, who has been supportive of my efforts in this area of critical inquiry.

The editorial staff at ITP Nelson were a pleasure to work with, and I admire their professionalism and patience on a long and oftentimes complex project. They are Charlotte Forbes, Michael Young, Bob Kohlmeier, Sylvia Vander Schee, and Brad Horning. A special thanks to Dianne Horton, who as developmental editor did a splendid job of assisting with the editing tasks and with author queries.

I would also like to thank the reviewers who commented on the manuscript at various stages in its development. Among them were C. Emdad Haque, Brandon University, and Gordon McIntyre, Vancouver Community College.

Finally, I should like to thank my family, who were very supportive of my efforts: my wife, Patricia O'Reilly, and my children, Patrick, Tom, and Kate.

THOMAS FLEMING
Georgian Bay, Ontario
July 1, 1996

NOTE: Readers wishing further information on data provided through the cooperation of Statistics Canada may obtain copies of related publications by mail from Publications Sales, Statistics Canada, Ottawa, Ont. K1A 0T6, by calling 1-613-951-7277 or by calling toll-free 1-800-267-6677.

C H A P T E R   1

Understanding the Environment

Raymond A. Rogers

Faculty of Environmental Studies
York University

This book presents a wide range of environmental issues of concern to Canadians. Each chapter attempts to outline the complex relations and perspectives surrounding these issues, as well as point to their global significance politically and ecologically. An essential component of environmental issues is the conflicting agendas or interests—whether between various participants or between participants and regulators—that complicate attempts to resolve these concerns.

In terms of "understanding the environment," it is important to distinguish between problems and issues. A problem does not necessarily involve conflicting interests and can be resolved in a relatively straightforward manner, whereas conflict is endemic to most environmental issues, which in turn require a complex policy process to deal with them.[1] This conflict has not only to do with economic interests versus environmental interests, but also with differing values and ethics as they relate to nature and human identity. Because of the general pervasiveness of these conflicts, environmental policy-making necessarily emphasizes the importance of integrating a range of perspectives.

What links the discussions of environmental issues in this book is the common thread of contrasting views of environmental stakeholders and the various frameworks and processes that try to deal with these differences. In attempting to understand the environment, then, it is important to recognize that there is no single form of understanding that can be emphasized above any other necessarily and that there is no single environment to which understanding can be applied. When we examine the range of perspectives present in an environmental issue, it is apparent that these contrasting points of view are linked to the social location of those involved and, more broadly, to the historical forces of particular cultures and where groups or individuals fit within those historical contexts.

In response to these contrasting interests and viewpoints, public institutions set up various processes and frameworks, ranging from local municipal initiatives that deal with a specific issue affecting comparatively few participants, through national agendas that coordinate regional approaches, to international regulations that attempt to address increasingly complex environmental concerns in a cross-cultural debate of global proportions. As Keith Warriner states, these processes and frameworks were organized to allow for greater involvement by the public in decision-making, with matters of environmental planning and dispute resolution being among the most prominent areas of increased citizen participation.[2]

Along with the challenge of dealing with a range of points of view, there is also a general recognition that environmental issues have become increasingly complex in these ways:

- in biophysical terms
- in regulatory jurisdictions
- in the expanding range of participants

In biophysical terms, environmental issues intermingle to create a more complex and uncertain biophysical reality that science has difficulty assessing. For example, there is an obvious biophysical connection between the threat of global climate change and deforestation because photosynthesis is directly connected to the conversion of carbon dioxide into oxygen. Relating the overall effects of deforestation and, say, automobile use is central to understanding climate change, but the growing number of variables involved makes forecasting the effects increasingly difficult. The predictability of biophysical processes is essential to environmental policy-making—so that exploitation and pollution levels can be determined—but the increasing unpredictability of the natural environment undermines this policy goal. Kenneth Hare discusses the scientific uncertainty surrounding global warming and the effect on policymakers who had to be persuaded that global warming was a serious issue.[3]

The increasing biophysical complexity leads to an inevitable crossover in terms of regulatory jurisdictions. Issues related to global climate change involve urban planning, forestry policy, transportation policy, international relations, industrial strategy, to name a few. Policy-making therefore attempts to link regulatory frameworks that in the past operated separately. At the same time, this process brings together information from different disciplines and government departments that are not necessarily compatible. To create an integrated policy that can address the multiple aspects of the issue requires a new kind of accommodation that is both difficult and time-consuming to achieve. In Chapter 4, Isobel Heathcote says about management of water resources:

> Another feature of water management in the future will be decision-making in a climate of scientific uncertainty and public debate. As the issues grow more complex, there is less agreement about what is clearly "right" and what is "wrong." Increasingly, we will see multi-stakeholder decision-making with government as one of many partners.[4]

This attempt at integrated policy-making is complicated by the wide range of participants with a stake in the issue. To use the example of global climate change, stakeholders include oil and gas companies, urban community groups concerned with the effects the automobile has on quality of life, public transportation advocates, road builders, migrant farmers in Brazil, agribusiness interests, aboriginal people in rain forests, and so on. If policy-making is to be successful, these interests need to be consulted. When there is a profound difference in the political and economic power of participants, as well as in point of view, creating a workable environmental policy may involve challenging these unequal power relations.

An early example of this increasingly complex view of environmental policy-making is set out in the *World Conservation Strategy* (1980). The WCS defines conservation as having three objectives: maintaining essential ecological processes and life-support systems, preserving genetic diversity, and making sustainable use of resources. To reach these objectives, the WCS says, the conservation strategy must be linked to a strategy for peace, a strategy for a new international economic order, a strategy for human rights, a strategy for overcoming poverty, a world food supply strategy, and a population strategy.[5] What is important to recognize here is that the fulfilment of the biophysical objectives of conservation leads into a complex sociopolitical project involving a range of other important societal issues. Canadian geographer Bruce Mitchell outlines six perspectives that are essential if environmental policy-making objectives are to be achieved globally:

> These six perspectives—sustainable development, Third World concerns, ideologies, integration, intangibles, uncertainty—are all central in resource management, and deserve explicit attention by resource analysts. The value of resource analysis research is likely to be diminished if these fundamental aspects are not recognized and addressed in our research.[6]

Although, as Mitchell states, the value of policy-making will be diminished if these perspectives are ignored, their inclusion makes for a process that is unwieldy, convoluted, and open to conflict and breakdown. And by the time the policy process has finally produced a result, circumstances may have changed and it may not apply to new realities.

I have used global climate change and the World Conservation Strategy as evocative examples that highlight the complexity of environmental policy-making, but these same realities are present in more locally based issues. This complexity is linked to both the perspectives involved and the processes used to deal with the differences in perspectives.

PERSPECTIVES AND PROCESSES IN ENVIRONMENTAL POLICY-MAKING

In the last thirty years, Canadian society has undergone a massive transformation in the way governments, businesses, and individuals approach environmental concerns. This recent history has significant ramifications for the way Canadian society deals with environmental issues, and these approaches have to be viewed within the broad context of modernity.

The history of modern society has been linked at the beginning with the expansion of mercantile capitalism in 16th- and 17th-century England. Accompanying the expansion of economic activity, societal frameworks began to institutionalize market economy relations supporting this expansion, a process that intensified during the Industrial Revolution, as technological development led to exponential expansion in economic activity. Despite various countermovements—such as the right to vote, trade unionism, socialism, and feminism—the institutionalization of the structures that support market economy have continued to the present day. The current call for "privatization, deregulation, and free trade" in the name of economic globalization is the latest incarnation of the institutionalization of economic growth.

Within this historical context, environmental concerns can be seen as another countermovement that tries to address some of the negative ramifications of market economy. In general, the institutions that deal with environmental concerns are the same institutions that historically have been the facilitators of economic growth. In the last thirty years, therefore, institutions that were concerned with *economic growth, efficiency,* and *utility* are now engaged in a project centred on *valuing the noneconomic.* Whereas economic concerns remain paramount in most sectors of society, environmental policy-making focuses on noneconomic information related mainly to biophysical processes involving pollution and depletion. This noneconomic information provides the benchmarks for measuring the possible negative ramifications of economic activity, rather than promoting efficiency and utility.

This transformation is evident in the resource management perspectives in forestry and fishing in Canada. Whereas the main purpose of forestry and fishery departments throughout most of this century was to support economic exploitation of Canada's "riches," nowadays departments struggle to adapt their mandate to deal with environmental problems and the altered expectations of the forestry and fishing industries—as well as the wider environmental movement — who are concerned with the ravages of overexploitation. In Chapter 14, Duncan Taylor says of the conflict between economic interests and ecological limits in British Columbia forests, it requires a

> debate over the extent to which current trends toward a global liberal trade policy and a North American economic market fly in the face of the ability of resource communities to maintain themselves.[7]

Taylor points out that often the project related to valuing the noneconomic conflicts with economic growth within the government department itself or in the overall government platform. As one who spent twelve years as a commercial fisherman in Nova Scotia, I can say that an analysis of the ecological disaster in the fishing industry reflects a similar conflict between economic growth and conservation. It is clear that, in the face of the fishing moratorium, fishing communities will not be able to "maintain themselves." A significant aspect of the federal government's failure to manage the fishery was its inability to adjust from being an institutional support to economic growth to being a guardian of conservation.

Whereas sectoral management by various government departments was suited to supporting economic growth, these same institutions have great difficulty dealing with the complexity of resolving environmental issues. This has been referred to as "jurisdictional gridlock" and has created a perspective that acknowledges, as Ron Doering states:

> that current government institutional arrangements are wholly inadequate to meet the challenge presented by modern environmental problems. The professional literature abounds with analyses which concludes that present systems of governance (and the "bureaucratic mind") cannot cope with today's global ecological crisis.[8]

Doering goes on to recommend a radical restructuring of the policy process in ecosystem planning, which can take this complexity into account and overcome the narrow sectoral approach of past policy-making. This same kind of recognition is also built into initiatives like integrated resource management, the environmental assessment process, and the multistakeholder round-table approach.

When policy processes are initiated to deal with these situations, they become, by definition, interdisciplinary because of the contrasting points of view that have to be taken into account. Whereas in the past, hydrologists dealt with hydrologists, biologists with biologists, and bridge engineers with other bridge engineers, the complexity of environmental problems that flow from one jurisdiction to the other requires a more complex process to integrate these perspectives. Because of these realities, a more complex relationship between expertise and the policy process emerges. As Dixon Thompson states in Chapter 11:

> Sound and objective scientific descriptions of environmental problems and ways to solve or avoid them are the first steps in effective environmental management.... They must also be translated into terms and formats readily understood by other disciplines and public decision-makers.[9]

> They must also be translated into terms and formats readily understood by other disciplines and decision-makers.

What is evident in the history of environmental policy-making is that, as the complexity of environmental issues intensified, policy responses had to become complex to deal with these realities. As Ian MacQuarrie argues in Chapter 3 about the ecological effects of modern agriculture: "[W]orld hunger has not been banished by the new technologies, and pollution problems abound ... [and] the goal of a sustainable, 'environmentally friendly' farming is still far in the distance."[10] In *A New Century for Natural Resources Management* Richard Knight and Sarah Bates claim that the time is past for technical fixes by experts, and argue that what is required is a "more integrated, holistic approach" that focuses on the "social values" that inform policy-making. There comes a point when this increasingly complex policy-making process not only has to resolve issues, it seems it has to "solve history" if it is to be successful. The process has become so all-encompassing in its recognition of the social and political roots of environmental issues that there is a sense it has to challenge some of the basic assumptions under which modern society operates. In Chapter 6, Monica Campbell comes to the following conclusion when she discusses the underlying difficulties affecting the air quality issue: "It may be that we collectively must accept a lower standard of living, as defined by the consumption of material goods, and exchange it for a higher quality of life ..."[11]

In terms of introducing some of the main themes addressed in this book, there is a contrast between the increasingly complex responses to environmental policy-making that focus on the integration of a range of perspectives, and those theorists and practitioners who argue that this complexity requires us to challenge the very assumptions of the "development mentality" of modern economy, which Robert Paehlke describes in Chapter 12 as "the central tension within the contemporary environment movement."[12] This contrast in approaches raises the question: Is environmental policy-making indeed concerned with resolving issues or with solving history?

An example of these contrasting points of view can be seen in Bruce Mitchell's and Donald Worster's perspective on the sustainability debate. Mitchell states:

> When the environmental movement was reaching its initial peak in the late 1960s a situation developed in which those concerned about protecting the natural environment became the opponents of those concerned with economic development and growth. This polarization of views led to many confrontations between the two groups.... [A]s time went by, those supporting environmental quality issues created a credibility problem for themselves by consistently opposing development.... During the 1980s, a significant shift in thinking appeared. The idea was presented that sustained regional economic growth and ecological integrity were complementary. This idea appeared at the core of the World Conservation Strategy ...[13]

Worster refers to the same transition in the relations between conservation and development, but from a very different perspective:

> Back in the 1960s and 1970s, when contemporary environmentalism first emerged, the goal was more obvious and the route more clear before they became obscured by political compromising. The goal was to save the living world around us, millions of species of plants and animals, including humans, from destruction by our own technology, population, and appetites. The only way to do that, it was easy enough to see was to think the radical thought that there must be limits to growth in three areas—limits to population, limits to technology, and limits to appetite and greed. Underlying this insight was the growing awareness that the progressive, secular materialist philosophy on which modern life rests ... is deeply flawed and ultimately destructive to ourselves and the whole fabric of life

on the planet.... Since it was so painfully difficult to make this turn, to go in a diametrically opposite direction from the way we had been going, however, many started looking for a less intimidating way. By the mid-1980s such an alternative, called 'sustainable development,' had emerged. First it appeared in the World Conservation Strategy ...[14]

These contrasting descriptions of the same period in the history of the environmental movement present conservation, on the one hand, as a regulatory problem, and on the other, as a social and cultural project that requires a profound redefinition of the relationship between humans and the rest of nature.

In other words, the kind of humans we are in historical–cultural terms and the way we understand environmental problems are closely connected. As Robert Paehlke argues in Chapter 12: "Only within a dialogue about the details of everyday economic and social life and about the environmental values that are most important can necessary changes be understood, let alone achieved."[15]

When we consider that environmental problems often have their origin in the dominant perspectives and priorities of modern society, we are confronted with the perception that these same dominant economic, technological, and scientific realities that inform life in Canada, for example, play a large role in setting the parameters of the way environmental issues are discussed. As Alistair Bath states in Chapter 2: "While we may think or want to think that wildlife management is done for wildlife, it is all done for people."[16] Of course, some "people" have more power than others and this has to do with their social location within the dominant structures of modern society. This is clear with regard to aboriginal issues in Canada, as discussed by Tom Fleming in Chapter 13:

> It is not surprising that governments do not wish to acknowledge, other than in a superficial manner, the legitimacy of native land claims. Governments and corporate interests have a close relationship in modern society. If native land claims were settled in favour of aboriginal groups, the potential economic loss to the government and corporations seeking to exploit land resources would be inestimable.[17]

This kind of recognition raises issues about the relationship between knowledge and power. Who decides what information is important as it relates to a particular issue, and to what use is that knowledge put? The round-table approach to environmental issues—which Canada has played a leading role in developing—is an acknowledgment of this complexity, and an attempt to incorporate the complexity of environmental issues into an information-gathering and decision-making process. The round-table process can create the temporary illusion that those sitting at the table are on a "level playing field," whereas there is a profound difference in the economic and political power of the participants, and can lead to agreements like the North American Free Trade Agreement, which George Crowell describes in Chapter 8 as a "huge, complicated body of trilateral law ... designed so that it can hardly do otherwise than to increase and to accelerate the far-reaching damage to the environment that has already been occurring."[18]

These manifold ways of understanding the environment are reflected in the way various perspectives define what is meant by "conservation." As Melody Hessing points out in Chapter 15 with regard to alternative approaches to environmental issues, radical ecofeminism challenges "the joint oppression" of women and nature by patriarchy "as the primary source of their subordination."[19] These kinds of concern link environmental degradation to the parallel feminization of poverty that has occurred in some cultures as patriarchy joins forces with modern economy. This leads, for example, to commonly held grazing land in some African countries to be privatized in men's names as new forms of commodity production reorganize land tenure and replace earlier forms of pastoralism.

Nowhere is this contrast in approaches to environmental issues more apparent and troublesome than in the negotiations between "developed" countries of the Northern Hemisphere and "underdeveloped" countries of the Southern Hemisphere as regards conservation in the context of such global concerns as population growth, climate change, oceans policy, and deforestation, or with the sustainability debate more generally. The contrasting ways of "understanding the environment" and defining what "conservation" means in these discussions is a social and cultural debate, as much as it is an economic, technological, and scientific one. In Chapter 5, Nancy Doubleday highlights this problem in her discussion of the Arctic:

> The global challenge ... [is] our capacity to think ecologically about development and environment, and to design decision-making processes capable of accommodating ecological thinking as something qualitatively different from existing approaches to blending environment and economics.[20]

In the discussion about knowledge and power, Duncan Taylor sets out the contrast to the two perspectives that I have described in terms of resolving issues or solving history:

> Inspection of two waves of environmentalism taking place in the 1960s reveals each in its own way to be inimical to the realization of participation's full potential. Recent developments in Green political thought, emphasizing the concept of emancipation, are introduced as being potentially important to the next stage of public participation's evolution.[21]

Public participation may therefore require not only consultation and interdisciplinary approaches to policy-making, but also a challenge to the interests and power relations that generated the environmental problem in the first place. The complexity of environmental policy-making may therefore have to address the complexity of the historical process if it is to challenge the seeming intractability of many environmental problems.

NOTES

1   Ramsey, Hungerford, and Volk. 1991. "A Technique for Analyzing Environmental Issues." *Journal of Environmental Education*.
2   Chapter 9.
3   Chapter 7.
4   Chapter 4, p. 82.
5   IUCN, UNEP, and WWF. 1980. *World Conservation Strategy*. Gland, Switzerland: Introduction.
6   Bruce Mitchell. 1989. *Geography and Resource Analysis*. New York: Longman & Wiley, p. 306.
7   Chapter 14, p. 306.
8   Ronald L. Doering. 1991. *Pathways: Toward an Ecosystem Approach*. Ottawa: Ministry of Supply and Services, p. 19.
9   Chapter 11, p. 220.
10   Chapter 3, p. 52.
11   Chapter 6, p. 127.
12   Chapter 12, p. 262.
13   Mitchell, 1989, p. 302.
14   Donald Worster. 1994. "The Shaky Ground of Sustainability." In *Global Ecology: A New Arena of Political Conflict*, Wolfgang Sachs, ed. London: Zed Books, pp. 132–33.
15   Chapter 12, p. 261.
16   Chapter 2, p. 15.
17   Chapter 13, p. 285.
18   Chapter 8, p. 152.
19   Chapter 15, p. 322.
20   Chapter 5, p. 103.
21   Chapter 14.

QUESTIONS FOR DISCUSSION

1.   Pick a Canadian environmental issue and identify the groups or participants involved.

2.   Divide the participants into regulators and users. Does any participant or group fit into both categories (regulator and user)?

3. Identify the jurisdictions (municipal, provincial, federal) that the regulators are in charge of, and assess whether there is any overlap.

4. Identify resource users and the uses they make of the resource. What are the underlying values and beliefs that inform these uses?

5. What, if any, is the conflict between the various users?

6. What is the conflict between regulators and users?

7. Identify various strategies to overcome the conflict among regulators, between regulators and users, and among users, as conditions apply.

8. Use this approach to compare a range of approaches to Canadian environmental issues as a series of group projects and presentations.

SUGGESTED READINGS

Brown, L. 1995. *The State of the World.* New York: Norton.

Chatterjee, P., and M. Finger. 1994. *The Earth Brokers.* New York: Routledge.

Chopra, K., G. Kadekodi, and M. Murty. 1990. *Participatory Development.* London: Sage.

Clark, C. 1990. *Mathematical Bioeconomics.* New York: Wiley.

Heilbroner, R. 1985. *The Nature and the Logic of Capitalism.* New York: Norton.

Livingston, J. 1981. *The Fallacy of Wildlife Conservation.* Toronto: McClelland & Stewart.

———. 1994. *Rogue Primate: An Exploration of Human Domestication.* Toronto: Key Porter Books.

McCay, B., and J. Acheson. 1987. *The Question of the Commons.* Tucson: University of Arizona Press.

McEvoy, A. 1986. *The Fisherman's Problem: Ecology and the Law in the California Fisheries, 1850–1980.* New York: Cambridge University Press.

———. 1987. "Toward an Interactive Theory of Nature and Culture: Ecology, Production, and Cognition in the California Fishing Industry." *Environmental Review* 11(4): 289–305.

Mitchell, B. 1989. *Geography and Resource Analysis.* 2nd ed. London: Longman.

Rogers, R.A. 1994. *Nature and the Crisis of Modernity: A Critique of Contemporary Discourse on Managing the Earth.* Montreal: Black Rose Books.

———. 1995. *The Oceans Are Emptying: Fish Wars and Sustainability.* Montreal: Black Rose Books.

Sachs, W., ed. 1992. *The Developing Dictionary.* London: Zed Books.

———. 1993. *Global Ecology.* London: Zed Books.

Shiva, V. 1989. *Staying Alive.* London: Zed Books.

Taussig, M. 1980. *The Devil and Commodity Fetishism in South America.* Chapel Hill: University of North Carolina Press.

Williams, R. 1980. *Problems in Materialism and Culture.* New York: Verso.

World Commission on Environment and Development. 1987. *Our Common Future.* New York: Oxford University Press.

World Conservation Strategy. 1980. Gland: UNESCO, FAO, and IUCN.

World Conservation Union, United Nations Environment Programme, and World Wide Fund for Nature. 1991. *Caring for the Earth.* Gland.

Depletion of Renewable Resources

Alistair J. Bath

Department of Geography
Memorial University of Newfoundland

THE ISSUE IN CONTEXT

Renewable resources are those resources that can rejuvenate themselves, can reproduce, and if managed on a sustainable basis could theoretically last forever. This chapter begins with a definition of a renewable resource that should include a big "if." Wild life (two words) including trees, fish, and animals is potentially renewable; however, if humans harvest too many trees, hunt too many animals, or trawl too many fish, such renewable resources can be exploited, some to extinction. The heath hen, a species believed by early settlers too abundant to waste a shot on, is now extinct. The passenger pigeon, another renewable resource, is gone. Billions of these birds existed; so numerous were they that they blocked out the sun for minutes. Humans, with much less technology than we have today, destroyed this species in a very short time. The last quarter of a million birds were killed in only four years, the last one shot in 1900. The great auk, a large bird with no defence mechanisms on land, was on its way out as early as 1785. On June 3, 1844, the last known nesting pair were killed, and their single egg thrown into the sea. The plains grizzly has been driven to the mountains, the eastern cougar exterminated except for a small remnant population in Florida, and the wolf persecuted by whatever means available. Do we learn that renewable resources are not necessarily renewable unless they are carefully managed? The northern cod off Newfoundland, the endless fishery resource, is no longer there, a moratorium in place since 1992. Wildlife should be a renewable resource but it must be managed by a human population that is willing to place a value on the conservation and sustainable management of the resource.

This chapter focuses upon large carnivores, specifically the wolf (*Canis lupus*), the brown or grizzly bear (*Ursus arctos*), and the mountain lion (*Felis concolor*). Why are we discussing large carnivores in a chapter on the depletion of renewable resources? From a human perspective, the wolf, the bear, and to a lesser extent the mountain lion have elicited a multitude of myths and values. These human values have shaped the management of these species over time. Indeed, resource management, which is a political decision-making process, has been driven by public attitudes, beliefs, and values. Large carnivores have experienced resource management approaches from exploitation to preservation over time. Examining the problems of managing large carnivores provides us with an example of a renewable resource that has been severely depleted and managed from different perspectives.

Fear of large carnivores has led to their extermination in many areas of the world; today, attitudes toward these species are changing and these large carnivores have become the sexy charismatic megafauna that more people feel are worth protecting. Management of large carnivores seems to be more a sociopolitical issue than a biological one. Having a supportive public is a key element to successful management of these large carnivores.

From an ecological perspective, if we can protect habitat and landscape linkages for the large predators at the top of the food chain, we will protect many other species and ensure biodiversity. Our record of managing wildlife sustainably, as stated earlier, has not been good; our management of large carnivores is not much different. Bear, wolf, and mountain lion numbers and their habitat have been reduced dramatically through predator circle hunts, poison programs, and excessive killing campaigns, even within our national parks, yet such large carnivores still exist in Canada. While large-scale poisoning programs and wars on these predators have been significantly reduced, to effectively protect these carnivores will require a great deal more effort. The bears, wolves, and mountain lions are still threatened due to habitat loss and poaching, both of which are on the increase. The proposed endangered species legislation being debated in Canada may not go far enough to protect habitat and ensure the long-term viability of species like the large carnivores.

The context for our discussion of the depletion of large carnivores is within wildlife management. Wildlife management like any resource management issue is driven by human wants, needs, values, and perceptions. While we may think or want to think that wildlife management is done for wildlife, it is all done for people. Increasing, decreasing, or keeping wildlife numbers stable is done for human uses, sometimes more consumptively related (e.g., hunting, fishing) and sometimes less so (e.g., wildlife photography, wildlife viewing). Our management of large carnivores has, more than any other wildlife, been significantly affected by public perceptions and attitudes. Attitudes, many based on myths, have driven management of the large carnivores. Each of these large carnivores has seen its habitat and numbers reduced significantly. Initially, complete extermination of large carnivores was practised; today, efforts are being made to establish carnivore conservation areas (CCAs) and recover predators, in some cases with active reintroductions.

Wildlife management has also evolved from its primary focus upon the biological nature of the species toward a better understanding of habitat and prey–predator relationships. The field continues to change with recent emphasis placed upon the human component of the wildlife management equation. This latter aspect has been labelled human dimensions in wildlife resources (HDWR). HDWR research focuses upon an understanding of public attitudes, beliefs, knowledge, and behaviours associated with fish and wildlife. There is a strong tie between HDWR research and conservation education. An understanding of this human component of wildlife management is an integral part of successful carnivore management.

THE LOSS OF LARGE CARNIVORES
THROUGHOUT HISTORY

Since the arrival of settlers in Canada and in North America generally, there has been a war against the large carnivores. The wolf, the bear, and the mountain lion represented the untamed and evil wilderness that needed to be conquered and subdued. These large predators were perceived as competitors with humans for the same resources—livestock, deer, caribou, and moose, for example. Livestock and defenceless animals like deer and moose had to be protected, and people had to feel they could walk outside safe from the vicious creatures that many described as beasts of waste and desolation. Protection of livestock and large ungulates (hoofed animals) meant one thing: the extermination of large carnivores.

For many years, as Canada and the rest of North America were settled, humans enjoyed a one-sided vendetta against these large carnivores. Perhaps the animal most hated and persecuted was the wolf. And while the wolf still generates much more polarized public attitudes than bears or mountain lions, if behaviour is considered one aspect of attitudes, as sociopsychologists suggest, all three species have been targeted throughout history for extermination and all have seen their numbers and habitat reduced significantly. The eastern Canadian cougar, for example, which is probably exterminated, was listed as early as 1946 as extinct; the Florida panther may be a remnant population struggling to survive amidst four-lane highways and continued urban expansion.

Focusing our discussion on the historical relationship between humans and wolves will illustrate the general attitude and approach that has been taken toward large carnivores. "He [the wolf] was the Devil, red-tongued, sulfur-breathed, and yellow-eyed; he was the werewolf, human cannibal; he was the lust, greed and violence that men saw in themselves" (Lopez, 1978). From the arrival of the first European settlers to at least the early 1980s in Canada, the primary management technique was exploitation with the objective of complete extermination. Some may argue that such a management approach still exists in Canada, citing the 1995 killings of many wolves in southern Alberta, the wolf control efforts in the Yukon, and the lack of interest by agencies to effectively protect the wolf and other large predators. Development continues unabated along the eastern rockies, the heart of large carnivore habitat in Canada.

POACHING AND HABITAT DESTRUCTION

Fear of large carnivores, especially wolves, certainly has played a role in the overbearing attitude humans have taken over the animal. European folklore has not helped. Stories of humans being stalked and eaten by wolves were rampant. In North America, however, there has been only one documented attack by a wild wolf on a human and this attack, in 1942, was believed to have been by a rabid animal. Humans have remained afraid of wolves, however, and the sad truth is humans kill what they fear. Wolves have been tortured and killed with pits, corrals, deadfalls, icebox traps, edge traps, steel traps, fish hooks, ring hunts, hamstringing, lassoing, den hunting, aerial shooting, professional hunting, bountying, and poisoning with everything from strychnine to cyanide.

The learned attitudes from children's stories and media coverage have fanned the heated debate about wolves. Little girls dressed in red are in danger of wolves; little pigs and other livestock certainly are threatened; and some humans may be werewolves in disguise; hence everyone is in danger. "All wolves in literature are creations of adult minds, that is, of adult fears, adult fantasies, adult allegories and adult perversions" (Lopez, 1978). Some hunters believe wolves kill their moose or deer; careful examination of the types of animals taken by wolves versus humans suggests there is very rarely any overlap. While wolves are opportunistic killers and will kill healthy adult animals, weak and young animals make up the bulk of a wolf's diet. The defenceless ungulates, though, were perceived to need protection from these bullies of the woods. Hence wolves were killed wherever and whenever possible. In a 1921 book on wildlife conservation in Canada (Hewitt, 1921), it was clearly stated that within Algonquin Provincial Park in Ontario, wildlife was protected, but park rangers shot wolves whenever possible.

Part of the problem in carnivore management has been media coverage of the large carnivores. The wolf, for example, has always received a bad press. Headlines such as "Wolves menace children," "Girl, 12, climbs tree to escape wolf pack," "Three-legged wolf terrorizes Ontario area," "Bulldozer driver attacked by wolf," and my favourite, "Farmer fends off wolf by grabbing its tongue," have not done the image of the wolf any good. Wolves were perceived as destructive to livestock, ungulate populations, and a threat to human safety. Thus, many believed that wolves, with no apparent use on earth, should be eliminated, and so the onslaught began and continued for many years until populations were severely depleted in Canada and eliminated from many other parts of the world. The era of this predominant wolf hatred could be summarized by one trapper's statement: "The only good wolf is a dead wolf."

Various practices were available to resource managers to implement a goal-oriented wolf policy that focused on extermination. Bounties were probably the oldest predator management tool, having been used to control wolves for more than a thousand years. A bounty was a financial award offered to an individual who brought a certain part of the wolf (e.g., ears, tail) to authorities. While the method was never proven to be effective, it continued in some parts of Canada until the mid-1970s. Inflammatory numbers of wolves were estimated killed during the bounty years, not all of which were probably wolves. German shepherd pups at birth look a lot like wolves and were used by individuals to collect the bounty. Trappers also took parts of the wolf to several counties to claim bounty, resulting in one wolf being recorded killed several times. Wolf bounties in Canada may have been offered as early as the 1700s; by 1900 all Canadian provinces with wolves had bounties and the bounty system continued as late as 1972 in Ontario. A 1972 National Film Board of Canada film by Bill Mason, *Death of a Legend*, which included heart-tugging pictures of wolf pups trying to howl and a slow-motion stiffening of a large black wolf that had been shot, was effective in stopping the bounty in Ontario.

Details of the bounty system and poisoning campaigns may add the necessary background to the issue. Wolves were killed in Canada throughout the 1800s and 1900s. Newfoundland had introduced a wolf bounty in 1839 and wolves became extinct there only 90 years later (Dodds, 1983). In Nova Scotia and New Brunswick bounties were not needed, as wolves were nearly extinct by 1870 (Cameron, 1958). Large sums of money were paid by the Ontario and Quebec governments for wolves; in Ontario more than $2 million was spent to kill wolves between 1925 and 1972 while in Quebec more than $1 million in bounty was spent to kill 8542 wolves. In some counties a supplementary bounty also existed. In the western provinces, the conflicts between wolves and other large carnivores and ranchers have existed for many years and still remain. Manitoba had bounties as early as 1878 (Stardom, 1983; Slough et al., 1987). The bounty system emerged in Saskatchewan and Alberta slightly later, in 1899 (Pimlott, 1961). In British Columbia, where bounties were introduced in 1900 (Pimlott, 1961), more than 9205 wolves were taken between 1909 and 1955 (Tompa, 1983); livestock associations supplemented these bounties.

While the persecution of wolves and other large carnivores continued, a meeting of concerned biologists and managers was held in Calgary in 1954. This conference was an important step in Canadian predator conservation; Alberta and B.C. ended their bounty systems that year (Pimlott, 1961; Gunson, 1983; Tompa, 1983) and Saskatchewan in 1949 (Slough et al., 1987; Stardom, 1983). Manitoba didn't follow suit until 1965. In Canada's north, bounties persisted much later and still today controversial control programs occur; bounties ended in the Yukon in 1971 but not until 1975 in the Northwest Territories. More than 10 100 wolves were bountied in the N.W.T. from 1924 to 1943 (Heard, 1983) and 2796 in the Yukon. Interestingly, while the wolf continued to be hunted, killed, and exterminated in Canada until 1975, it was given federal protection in Minnesota in 1974 (Van Ballenberge, 1974).

Bounties were only one method of wolf control. Perhaps the most effective way to kill wolves and several nontarget species at the same time was poison. Poison was widely used through the 1900s and received little public opposition until the 1960s. Lacing carcasses with poison, which were then dumped on frozen lakes, was common practice and many wolves were killed in this manner. No good hunter or livestock operator would go by a carcass without spiking it in hopes of killing a wolf or two. A variety of poisons have been used against wolves. Strychnine, which affects the central nervous system, received widespread use against carnivores in the U.S. as early as 1834 (Young and Goldman,

1944). Ungulate carcasses were poisoned with strychnine in 1877 to kill wolves even inside Yellowstone National Park, the world's first national park (Weaver, 1978). Ironically, wolves were actively reintroduced into Yellowstone National Park in 1993, more than 100 years later. The Hudson's Bay Company used strychnine to prevent wolves from killing horses in the upper Athabasca Valley in the late 1850s (Spry, 1963). Lacing bison carcasses with the poison during the 1860s and 1870s in Alberta killed many wolves (Rodney, 1969). By 1890, the number of wolves on the Canadian Prairies had been drastically reduced (Cluff and Murray, 1993). Other carnivores, such as bears and mountain lions, were also targets of these poisoning campaigns.

Strychnine continued to be used in Western Canada from 1952 to 1956 to control rabies (Ballantyne and O'Donoghue, 1954). In more northern areas poison was used to enhance ungulate populations, a reason still offered today for wolf control in North America. Poisoning occurred throughout the wolf range in Canada. Strychnine was used from 1950 to 1965 in Manitoba (Stardom, 1983), from the mid-1930s to 1980 in Saskatchewan (Wiltse, 1983; Seguin, 1991), for several years in Ontario before being banned in the 1970s (Kolenosky, 1983), and in Quebec for several years, though it was limited in 1971 to white-tailed deer wintering yards. An effort to bring back widespread poisoning in Quebec in 1972 was met with public opposition and the plan was cancelled by the Quebec government (Banville, 1983). In the Yukon and N.W.T. strychnine continued to be applied to baits into the 1980s. While the Quebec population opposed more poisoning in 1972, the public in the Whitehorse area in 1982 and 1983 demanded more wolf control, and strychnine bait poisoning was done (Hayes et al., 1991). A single carcass laced with the poison could kill many wolves; in May 1956, 68 wolves were killed with a single carcass poisoned near Lady Gray Lake, N.W.T. (W.A. Fuller personal communication in Cluff and Murray, 1993). Poison programs were permitted in Canada's national parks as late as 1959. Massive poison programs and random lacing of carcasses are no longer legal in Canada, though certain poisons may be used in special circumstances. For example, the use of sodium monofluoroacetate (also known as Compound 1080) is inserted in domestic sheep collars to kill specific problem wolves or coyotes. British Columbia has been using this poison since 1949, preferring it to strychnine or cyanide because of its higher toxicity (Tompa, 1983).

Wolves have also been taken by aerial shooting, an effective means of killing large numbers in a short time. Ethically, it has been argued that this may be the fastest method of killing wolves, thus minimizing pain and suffering; these two factors are often stated by animal rights groups concerned about the welfare and humane treatment of individual animals. Radio-collared wolves have been used to locate other pack members to allow for the killing of several animals; this practice has been severely criticized by the public. Perhaps one of the most controversial wolf shooting events in Canada took place in northern British Columbia in 1987. After more than 1000 wolves had been killed in the Kechika and Muskwa wolf control regions, public opposition across Canada was so great that the B.C. government suspended its program. The program was adopted to enhance ungulate numbers and, unlike wolf control programs in the Yukon, human hunting had not been suspended for two years before wolf control was put into effect. Implementing wolf control in the Yukon has been much more successful than in B.C. and Alaska due to intensive public involvement and the restriction of any hunting for two years before the actual control. Wolf populations have been shown to recover from such efforts relatively quickly, and currently in Canada the wolf is not considered threatened or endangered.

BIOLOGY AND POPULATION MANAGEMENT

To provide a better understanding of the large carnivores and for successful management of these predators, it is necessary to look at some of the important biological aspects of these species. An important piece of the management equation is knowing the size of a population and whether it is increasing, decreasing, or remaining stable. Deciding this is often more difficult. With large carnivores like wolves, grizzly bears, and mountain lions, it is difficult to estimate populations since these species are wide-ranging and have large home ranges. For example, home ranges for male grizzlies near Yellowstone National Park have been documented as large as 5374 square kilometres. Therefore population estimates are usually quite broad.

Studying these large predators involves catching individual animals, radiocollaring them, and then tracking them by radiotelemetry. Radiotelemetry is used to identify size of home ranges, areas where prey may have been killed, and possible numbers in the area. Traditionally wolves have been captured using leg hold traps or snares; in open areas, darts fired from a helicopter or plane have been successful. Recent controversy over the use of leg hold traps even for scientific studies may require scientists to explore other ways of trapping wolves live. In an effort to address this issue, wildlife biologists in Poland have experimented with trapping wolves using nets and *fladry*, a Polish word for ropes with red strips of material hanging down. This technique has been effective in keeping wolves in the area, since they seem to be afraid of the red strips of material and will not cross a fladry line. Wolves are chased into a bottleneck and eventually into nets where they can be immobilized. Monitoring wolf movements using radiotelemetry through the night can show biologists whether the pack has made a kill; upon finding the prey species, further data can be gained on its condition. Tracks can provide estimates of the numbers of animals in the pack and possibly the area.

Bears have also been trapped with leg hold traps and snares, but it is more common to use baited culvert traps, which the bear enters and a door closes behind it. Capturing bears with darts fired from the ground has been done but requires careful planning and attention to safety. Using a capture/recapture technique, biologists can get information and estimate population numbers in the area.

The most effective way of capturing mountain lions is with dogs, which chase and tree the lion. The animal then can be darted and lowered for examination and radio-collaring. As the large carnivores (wolves, bears, and mountain lions) have large home ranges and exist at low densities, accurate estimates of populations and trapping of individuals is difficult. Often population estimates are broad; for example, wolf estimates in British Columbia are 6000–12 000 animals. Because males (especially bears and mountain lions) have larger home ranges than females, they are more likely to be caught in traps. This needs to be considered when calculating estimates and planning management strategies. The condition of large carnivore populations depends upon a healthy prey base, a large expanse of wilderness, and protection from humans.

WOLVES

The wolf is a social animal existing in packs of approximately eight to ten individuals; pack size differs according to size of home ranges and prey base. For example, in Northern Canada wolf packs that migrate with the caribou tend to have larger home ranges, be larger in size, and can be up to twenty animals. Perceptions of marauding packs of fifty individuals are purely that, perceptions. Wolf packs establish territories, which they defend against other packs. Generally wolves tend to kill coyotes within their territory, but there are cases in Canada (e.g., Riding Mountain National Park, Manitoba) where coyotes and wolves have been found sharing the same territory.

Wolves are not as large and menacing as people perceive; human dimensions research has shown that the public believes wolves are much larger and heavier than they actually are (Bath, 1991). The male wolf averages 36–52 kilograms but can range from as small as 20 kg to as large as 80 kg. Females are slightly smaller. Males reach sexual maturity at age three, females at two. Within a pack usually only a single pair (the dominant alpha pair) will breed. The social hierarchy is well defined and subordinates choose not to mate with each other. Litters average six to eight pups. All individuals within the pack help raise the pups; the survival rate of pups depends upon ungulate numbers. Contrary to popular tales, wolves do not survive on mice during the winter but prey on large ungulates like moose, caribou, deer, elk, and sometimes musk oxen and bison. Smaller game such as rabbits, hares, and beaver can supplement their diet. In Europe, domestic livestock can be a large part of the wolf's diet. Because the wolf preys on large game animals and occasionally livestock, it is perceived as a threat and competitor with man for the same resources. While opportunistic killers and capable of killing healthy animals, wolves typically prey on calves and older and sicker individuals within the herd; human hunters in contrast usually take the large males within the herd. Prey–predator relationships may exhibit a dynamic equilibrium, meaning that wolves and the prey base can exist at high numbers until both crash to low numbers. There are cases, however, especially in multipredator/multiprey situations, where wolves can keep an ungulate population at a low level and drive it to extinction. It is in such cases that wolf control has been practised and been successful in recovering ungulate numbers.

While wolves may live sixteen years, usually they survive not more than ten years in the wild. Humans are their greatest predator, but grizzly and black bears have been known to scare wolves off carcasses and occasionally kill pups. Wolves have relatively large home ranges and, while not showing preferences for a particular type of habitat, they are attracted to road development.

GRIZZLY BEARS

Unlike the wolf, bears are not social animals. Males and females come together to mate, and male bears are a threat to newborn cubs. Home ranges are considerably larger than those of wolves, and bears of course are much bigger than wolves. Grizzly bears can weigh between 146 and 382 kilograms. They are omnivorous (meaning they will eat the same kinds of things as humans), but tend to eat mainly plants and vegetation; however, diets are seasonal. In the spring, bears concentrate on newborn calves, in the summer on rodents and spawning trout or salmon, and in late summer on berries—the most important food—along with nuts, herbs, and grasses. Approximately 200 species of plants make up roughly half of a bear's yearly intake of food.

Adult male bears are territorial and will defend a large area containing a few females against other males. A female's home range is considerably smaller than a male's, but it can still be up to 1000 square kilometres. While wolf populations can recover quickly after control efforts because of their breeding characteristics, grizzly bears have a slow reproductive rate and are sensitive to human impact. Females do not usually breed until they are six or seven years old, and then they breed only every three years. In areas of good habitat, such as parts of Sweden and Norway, bears have been documented breeding every two years and having twins and sometimes triplets. In North America breeding frequency is every three years, and more than two cubs are rare. Due to the late age of breeding and the fact that it occurs every three years, bear populations can be sensitive to human hunting. Minimum viable populations (MVP) of bears have been estimated at 400 bears to ensure an adequate gene pool. As habitat shrinks and islands are created, genetic diversity can be threatened.

Grizzly bears prefer open areas, alpine tundra, alpine meadows, and occasionally dense cover for shelter. The bear, originally a plains animal, has been driven to the mountains by human encroachment. Increased road construction into wilderness areas and continued logging threaten the habitat of the great bear. Unlike wolves, confrontations between humans and bears do occur and are on increasing. Many of these confrontations involve a sow with cubs; a sow will charge a hiker if she feels threatened. Bears in contact with humans are often destroyed and unlike wolves, bears cannot sustain controlled killing. The loss of only a few reproductive females in a small population can be disastrous.

MOUNTAIN LIONS

The name "mountain lion" is an unfitting one for this big cat and reflects the very recent and much reduced range of the animal, which is also known as puma, cougar, and panther. This carnivore has not elicited the same emotions as wolves or bears from the public, even though it is much more dangerous to humans than wolves or bears. Mountain lions have attacked several children and adults in the past few years in British Columbia and other western provinces and states.

Mountain lions are heavier than wolves; males of between 67 and 103 kilograms have been recorded, females at 36 to 60 kg. Like the other carnivores, mountain lions have relatively large home ranges; a single cat may require 103 to 518 square kilometres. Home ranges shift in size seasonally. Summer ranges are larger and tend to expand as elk and deer migrate to higher summer ranges; winter ranges contract as deer move down into sheltered valleys.

Males breed at three years, females at two to three years. Females need to establish a home range before breeding. Litters average three or four kittens, which stay with the female for up to two years. Females can breed at any time during the year and reproduction seems to be food dependent. If kittens are killed, often the female will come into estrus again. Mountain lions feed mainly on deer and elk but have been known to take hare, porcupine, beaver, and small mammals. Lions have learned to adapt to their environment. The best example of this perhaps is the Florida panther, which utilizes swamps, wooded river valleys, and lowlands, as well as dense coniferous forests and high mountains.

Legal mountain lion hunting occurs in all western states and provinces and is a sought-after commodity. Although lions have no natural predators other than man, they are sometimes killed by their prey. A female lion in Wyoming, particularly good at killing bull elk, was eventually killed when an elk's antler punctured her lungs. Like bears and wolves, mountain lions need an abundant prey base, protection from human persecution, and space.

POPULATION DISTRIBUTION

GRIZZLY BEARS

The survival of grizzly bears, wolves, and mountain lions in Canada is not due to lack of trying to eliminate all the large carnivores, but more to our small human population. Historically the distribution of grizzly bears included the western half of North America; as early as 1948 most populations in the lower

FIGURE 2.1
Distribution of the Grizzly Bear in Canada and the United States, 1983–84.

Current North American range is approximately 4 601 000 km². Historical (c. 1800) distribution was about 10 000 000 km².

Source: P. Paguet and A. Hackman, *Large Carnivore Conservation in the Rocky Mountains: A Long-Term Strategy for Maintaining Free-Ranging and Self-Sustaining Populations of Carnivores,* World Wildlife Fund, 1995.

48 contiguous United States had been extirpated (see Figure 2.1). In Canada the plains grizzly has been driven to the mountains and can be found today in parts of the ranges from the coast of British Columbia to the eastern slopes of the Rockies in Alberta. Grizzlies can also be found in the Yukon Territory and in the mountains west of the Mackenzie River in the Northwest Territories. Within the provinces, development pressures have limited the bear to the eastern foothills of the Canadian Rockies. In southwestern Alberta, grizzly bear range has been compressed into a narrow strip of land 30 to 60 kilometres wide between the continental divide and the Prairies to the east (Carr, 1989). This population of grizzly bears in Canada is connected to two of the highest densities in North America south of Alaska: the Flathead Valley in British Columbia and Montana, and in Glacier National Park, Montana, which borders Waterton National Park in Alberta. Estimating the number of bears in these regions is difficult as bears have large home ranges and are active for only a few months of the year. Biologists have estimated grizzly bear numbers in the Montana, Idaho, and Wyoming system at 500 to 900. The current Alberta population is put at a similar number on provincial lands, with approximately an additional 215 in the national parks and 90 between the parks and the United States border. In British Columbia there are between 6000 and 12 500 grizzlies. With such broad estimates of populations, management of grizzly bears in Canada is difficult.

Based on estimates, the grizzly bear in Canada was listed vulnerable by the Committee on the Status of Endangered Wildlife in Canada (COSEWIC) in 1992. It was listed as threatened in the lower 48 contiguous states under the Endangered Species Act in the U.S. in 1975. Status for the species in both countries has remained the same, despite the continued human developments and expansion into prime habitat. Vulnerable and threatened status in Canada and the United States respectively means that the species is at risk but not under immediate threats. A designation of endangered is more serious, implying there are immediate threats to the species that could lead to decline to nonviable levels. Loss of habitat—as much as 98 percent in the lower 48 states—hunting, defence kills, illegal kills, garbage, and improved access into wilderness areas have all contributed to the depletion of this renewable natural resource and its status in Canada and the United States. Recent research in Banff National Park suggests that grizzlies have been seriously affected by development in some of their best habitat (Gibeau, 1993). For example, bears avoid roads independent of traffic volume (McLellan and Shackleton, 1988); research in British Columbia suggests that habitat near roads is used even less frequently during log hauling (Archibald et al., 1987).

Perhaps the biggest threat in Canada to our grizzly bears is loving the bears to death. There is a direct relationship between the number of bears being designated problem bears and removed and the increased number of visitors to the national parks. Even our northern national parks like Kluane National Park have been forced to remove bears that have harmed or might harm humans (Leonard et al., 1990). While cases are increasing of predation bears (bears that have targeted humans as prey and pulled people out of their tents at night), most of the confrontations between bears and humans to date are surprise encounters on a trail often involving people getting too close to a sow and her cubs.

Humans have also been hurt because of their lack of knowledge of bear behaviour. A bear biologist in Yellowstone National Park told me of a man who put a sandwich in the driver's seat of his car, watched the bear crawl in, shut the door, and ran around to the front of the car to take a picture of the bear and his spouse in the front seat. There are also incidents of people putting honey on a child's head to take a picture of the bear licking the honey off. The message is: Visitors in national parks do not behave appropriately around bears and the result is always a dead bear. Feeding of bears and such incidents have reduced dramatically in Canada and the United States and the days of begging bears along the side of the road, at least in Yellowstone National Park, are gone. In Canada, we still see signs warning visitors not to feed or approach bears. Addressing the misconceptions about bears and teaching appropriate behaviour in bear country are important steps to protecting the species. Successful management of bears is more about people management than bear management.

WOLVES

No other large carnivore and perhaps wild animal has experienced such hatred and complete and purposive killing as the grey wolf. Wolves were once found throughout Canada and the United States with the exception of the Queen Charlotte Islands and Prince Edward Island (Paquet and Hackman, 1995). Wolves have been eliminated from most of the lower 48 contiguous states, large areas of southern British Columbia, the southern Prairie provinces, Southern Ontario, southern Quebec, the Maritime provinces, and Newfoundland. (See Figure 2.2.) In the United States the wolf is considered endangered in most of the lower 48 states and threatened in Minnesota where a population of approximately 2000 animals currently exist. In contrast, in Canada there are large numbers of wolves (approximately 40 000) and the species is not listed as endangered. Unlike in the United States, it is not illegal to shoot a wolf in Canada, and many provinces have liberal hunting seasons on the animal. In the western Rockies from Banff National Park to Yellowstone National Park, there may be as many as 200 wolves (Paquet and Hackman, 1995).

Wolf control programs have taken place in Western Canada for a variety of reasons. Where ungulate numbers are low, wolves can drive a species toward extinction or to a point where recovery is difficult. This is called a predator pit. While indeed several factors may cause a decline in ungulate populations, wolves can be one factor. Wolf control programs that have been implemented in Canada, mainly in northern British Columbia and the Yukon, have been hotly debated by all segments of the population, including biologists. Fundamental to many of the arguments are the reasons behind the controlled hunt. In the Yukon, for example, wolf control is carried out to allow recovery of ungulate

FIGURE 2.2
Distribution of the Wolf in Canada and the United States, 1983–84

Current North American range is approximately 9 831 000 km². Historical (c. 1700) distribution was about 16 700 000 km².

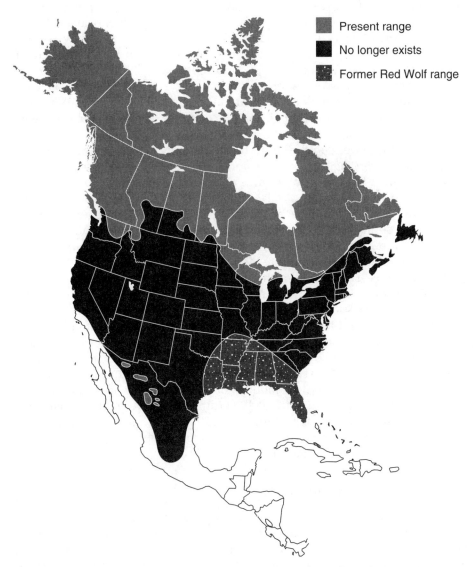

Present range
No longer exists
Former Red Wolf range

Source: P. Paguet and A. Hackman, *Large Carnivore Conservation in the Rocky Mountains: A Long-Term Strategy for Maintaining Free-Ranging and Self-Sustaining Populations of Carnivores,* World Wildlife Fund, 1995.

populations, which have been driven to low numbers. Hunting of these ungulates has to have stopped for two years before any wolf control. In contrast the helicopter wolf hunt in British Columbia was carried out without halting ungulate hunting. It was met with considerable opposition. While killing of any wolf may not be acceptable to some individuals, the wolf control efforts in recent history have not had the objective of the past: extermination. Wolf numbers are simply being reduced to give ungulate numbers an opportunity to pull out of the predator pit. That said, it was interesting that in southern Alberta in 1995, government officials, hunters, trappers, and ranchers were reported to have shot or poisoned approximately 50 percent of the population. Such behaviour is reminiscent of the bounty days, and in reading the article "Killing Season in the Rockies" from the *Canadian Geographic* magazine, I found myself repeatedly checking that it was dated 1995. Such management of wolves should make us all reconsider the title of this chapter and the question of whether we truly learn anything from the past.

Wolves exist in lower densities than bears and may be more easily displaced by human activities (Paquet and Hackman, 1995). And unlike grizzly bears, the destruction of their habitat is not as large an issue as controlling the direct persecution of the species. Still today wolves are perceived as evil and shot on sight, especially by those in rural areas. Three-S management is practised in many parts of wolf country: shoot, shovel, and shut up. Residents will take management into their own hands. Highway traffic has become a more common cause of death, especially in the west where increased use of the national parks has led to more collisions. For example, the fencing of the Trans-Canada Highway through Banff National Park, while reducing collisions of cars with elk, has led to an increase of collisions with wolves and coyotes. The fences have created microhabitats between the road and the fence that are ideal for small rodents, and this has attracted species like coyotes and to a lesser extent wolves. Roads also provide access, and like those of grizzly bears, wolf densities seem to be limited by road density. Paquet (1993) found that humans were the cause of 98 percent of wolf deaths in the eastern foothills of the central Canadian Rockies and of these, 65 percent were related to roads. Fortunately, wolves replace their numbers easily because they reach sexual maturity early and have large litters (Paquet and Hackman, 1995). In comparison to grizzly bears, wolves can withstand relatively high levels of mortality.

MOUNTAIN LIONS

The distribution of the mountain lion was once the largest of any land mammal in the Western Hemisphere, ranging from the tip of Chile in the south and across North America from the Pacific to the Atlantic Ocean (Paquet and Hackman, 1995). See Figure 2.3. Unlike the wolf and bear, the mountain lion has not generated much public debate, but human behaviour toward this large carnivore has been the same: depletion and predator controls. The historic range of mountain

FIGURE 2.3
Distribution of the Mountain Lion in Canada and the United States, 1983–84

Current North American range is approximately 3 983 000 km². Historical (c. 1600) distribution was about 18 900 000 km².

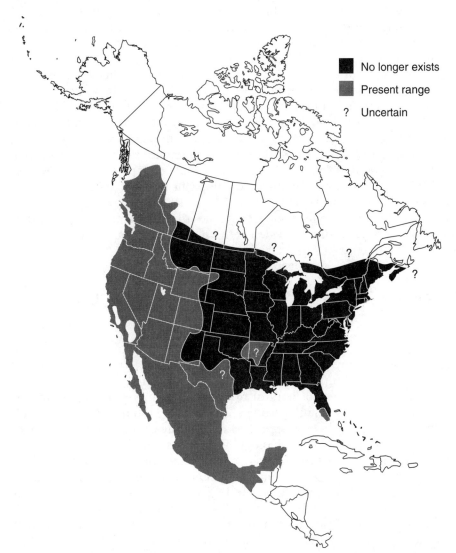

Source: P. Paquet and A. Hackman, *Large Carnivore Conservation in the Rocky Mountain: A Long-Term Strategy for Maintaining Free-Ranging and Self-Sustaining Populations of Carnivores*, World Wildlife Fund, 1995.

lions has been reduced by approximately 50 percent. In Canada, there are two distinct populations, one in the east, which is considered endangered and is probably extirpated, and one in the west, which is not listed. If the mountain lion no longer exists in Eastern Canada, then the total population is confined to Alberta and British Columbia. Viable lion populations also exist in the western United States. Contrary to proposed wolf recovery in Yellowstone National Park, natural recovery of mountain lion populations was met without a murmur from the general public. This is interesting considering that mountain lions are far more dangerous to humans than wolves and there is documented evidence that they have attacked and killed children and adults. Due to increased sightings of mountain lions on hiking trails and the potential for attack, the Park Service in Olympic National Park in Washington state and several other western parks have posted signs warning parents to keep their children close by while hiking.

Within Alberta the mountain lion is on the "blue list," meaning that the species is at risk but not immediately (Paquet and Hackman, 1995). Mountain lion populations appear to be stable in Western Canada and may be slowly increasing in the western states. The best way of conserving the animal seems to be to provide adequate protection and conserve its prey base, mule deer populations and their habitats. Mountain lions occur at all elevations in the west but prefer mixed wood and coniferous vegetation (Paquet and Hackman, 1995). Like wolves and grizzly bears, they avoid roads. Minimizing logging roads and providing linkage corridors are essential to prevent further depletion of this renewable resource.

WORLDWIDE ATTITUDES TOWARD LARGE CARNIVORES

Understanding predators and their relationships with humans is an issue not only in Canada but in many other parts of the world. The International Union for Conservation of Nature and Natural Resources (IUCN), an organization for the research and management of natural resources, has three working groups for large carnivores: a wolf specialist group, a bear specialist group, and a cat specialist group. The groups have representatives from many countries and each team shares its information about the biology, techniques, and management of the species in its particular country. This global perspective and cooperation helps to ensure the survival and successful management of these species. In Canada, there are large expanses of wilderness areas and, generally speaking, few people; yet large carnivore recovery is difficult. Globally, there are many areas where wolves and bears exist in areas of high human densities. The nature of the carnivore management problems differ, but threats to the populations are similar. While mountain lions do not exist outside North America, the IUCN cat specialist group examines other cats, such as tigers, lions, leopards, and to a lesser extent lynx. Several examples of international large carnivore issues are discussed below.

WOLF RECOVERY IN MONTANA

The United States, with a human population several times larger than Canada's, was more effective in eliminating large carnivores. With populations of wolves exterminated in many parts of the United States, active recovery has been required. The U.S. Endangered Species Act, developed in 1968 (Canada still lacks any equivalent, though a bill is under review), requires that fish and wildlife agencies attempt to recover endangered populations. Wolves, for example, are being allowed to recover in the northern Rockies.

Glacier National Park, Montana, is one area identified in a Rocky Mountain Wolf Recovery Plan developed by the U.S. Fish and Wildlife Service for natural wolf recovery. Natural recovery means that wolves that naturally migrate into the park and surrounding area are protected. Glacier National Park borders Waterton National Park in southern Alberta. In the early 1990s wolves appeared in the Glacier area and were heralded by U.S. biologists as the Magic Pack because they apparently appeared from nowhere. In fact, they emerged from southern Alberta and southern British Columbia. Unfortunately, just like magic, they all disappeared several months later when they crossed the 49th parallel back to Canada. In Canada, they were killed, because wolves are not legally protected or endangered and they know only ecosystem boundaries, not international boundaries. Ecosystem management was not occurring. Within the last few years, wolves have again naturally recolonized northern Montana and have learned that living in the United States may be safer.

WOLF RECOVERY IN YELLOWSTONE

Canadian wolves have also played an important role in a more active wolf recovery effort in Yellowstone National Park. A natural wolf recovery is occurring in northern Montana (wolves dispersing from southern Alberta and British Columbia are establishing packs); however, the many roads and human settlements and the open country of northwestern Wyoming make such natural recovery highly unlikely in Yellowstone National Park in the immediate future. An active wolf reintroduction took place there; the program was a reintroduction, not an introduction, because wolves historically existed in the park until they were eliminated through a predator eradication program in the early 1930s. Times have changed from the days when the wolf was seen as the beast of waste and desolation to today when it is a symbol of wilderness and the missing link in an ecosystem that has been described as the Serengeti of North America. To put wolves actively into an ecosystem with large numbers of elk (30 000 approximately), moose, deer, bison, bighorn sheep, bears, coyotes within the park, and free-ranging domestic livestock just outside, remains a challenge. "Ranchers Howl in Protest," read the newspaper headlines. Wolves from southern Alberta and northern British Columbia were darted, radio-collared, and transported to Yellowstone for soft release into the park. To minimize the chance of their heading directly back to Canada, these wolves were released into accli-mation pens. This soft release appears to have been successful: wolves have denned inside the park and are utilizing areas of it. As of July 1996, there were about 45 wolves, including pups, in the Yellowstone ecosystem. Many visitors have seen the wolves, thus enriching their recreational experience.

WOLF RECOVERY IN EUROPE

Large carnivores need large expanses of wilderness, a prey base, and protection from humans. In many parts of Europe, however, wolves live close to human populations and livestock. One wolf pack lives only 35 kilometres from Rome. Indeed, in some areas of Europe the wolf's diet may consist of at least 30 percent domestic livestock, unlike in North America where livestock are not part of a wolf's diet and losses are extremely low. The public interest in wolf recovery by some and fear by others, however, is similar. A conference on European wolf movements took place in Neuchatel, Switzerland, September 17–20, 1995, and delegates heard about wolf recovery in Switzerland and other areas from biologi-cal and sociopolitical perspectives. For example, wolf restoration is also being explored in the Scottish Highlands. Wolves exist in Portugal (c.150), Spain (1500–2000), Italy (c.300), Slovenia (<10), Croatia (<20), Greece (300–500), Poland (c.850), Germany (c.5), Slovakia (c.350), Hungary (<50), Romania (c.2500), and Bosnia–Hercegovina (c.400). And between 80 000 and 120 000 wolves exist in the C.I.S. (former Soviet Union) with some 15 000 animals in the European part (Promberger and Schroder, 1993).

Livestock depredation, loss of habitat, and lack of legal protection for the wolf are the main issues facing wolf managers in Europe. And while the issues are similar to those in North America, the magnitude of the problems is different. For example, a pack of eight animals occupying the Maritime Alps at the French–Italian border killed 36 livestock in 1993. (The French government, which has decided to protect wolves, paid 57 200 francs, about $15 960 Canadian, in compensation.) In 1994, wolves killed 98 sheep and injured 24, 21 of which died later. (Compensation was F200 000, about $56 000 Canadian.) Between January and early June 1995, 50 sheep had been killed and 24 injured (Promberger and Schroder, 1993).

After years of persecution and bounties, wolves in Croatia are now under full legal protection. They were removed from the list of game species in the new "hunting law" of 1994, and on May 17, 1995, they were put under the "nature protection law." Harming the wolf is now a crime with fines up to the equivalent of $49 000 Canadian. Legal protection alone is not enough; managers need to develop plans to win public support and tackle compensation issues. In an effort to bring the public on side in predator management the author is currently involved in studies of public attitudes about wolves in Portugal and Poland, bears in Sweden and Norway, and poaching in the Kamchatka region of Russia. Such human dimensions studies will offer managers baseline data on the public's knowledge, attitudes, concerns, and willingness to make tradeoffs, which can be addressed through education and lead to the success of future carnivore management plans.

BEARS WORLDWIDE

The illegal killing and transport of bear parts in Canada to Asian markets contributes to the overall threat to bears in the world. Bear biologists and managers from 19 countries met at the IUCN Bear meeting in Mora, Sweden, 11–14 September 1995, and the overwhelming message was that bears, regardless of species (brown, black, polar), are increasingly threatened through poaching for bear gall bladders and through destruction of their habitat. These human activities are encouraged by worsening economic conditions and the lack of enforcement to stop them. The continued loss of suitable habitat for bears is resulting in isolated pockets of bears surrounded by development and a gradually shrinking genetic diversity.

While 9000–12 000 brown bears exist in northeastern Siberia and genetic diversity may not be an issue there, only 80–90 brown bears exist in the eastern Carpathian mountains in Poland; such small numbers may be genetically unstable. In the Kamchatka region of Russia, close to the eastern Asian markets, a dramatic increase in the trade of bear parts has been observed. Isolated pockets of relatively high bear densities exist in the southern portion, but these are surrounded by low population densities, apparently caused by poachers from nearby settlements. A recent study by the author and a Russian scientist of public attitudes toward poaching and brown bears in this region will provide better information about the amount of poaching, bear parts trading, and knowledge of and attitudes toward the bear. Preliminary results suggest positive attitudes toward bears and suggest also that illegal trading of parts may be less serious than initially anticipated. The next step will be to address public concerns and integrate them into a management plan for the brown bear in this region.

Small bear population numbers and poaching and livestock losses attributed to bears are also problems in Canada. As few as 50 grizzly bears may exist in Banff National Park, Alberta, once a stronghold for the species. Some of the largest black bears in North America can be found on Newfoundland and in Riding Mountain National Park, Manitoba; both provinces have reported poaching. Brown and black bears have also been poached in Alberta and British Columbia. How extensive is the problem is a matter of debate. Law-enforcement agencies have limited funds to fully assess and address the problem. Bears poached in Canada are destined for Far Eastern markets, where prices for gall bladders are sometimes as high as $112–280 Canadian per gram. In Canada, three jurisdictions (Nova Scotia, Quebec, and N.W.T.) still permit the trade and possession of bear parts taken legally. Recently, environmental groups, particularly the Animal Alliance of Canada, have campaigned for an end to the trade of bear parts in Canada. At a meeting of Canadian law-enforcement officers in early 1996, the consensus emerged that the illegal trading of bear parts in Canada is not a serious problem.

_____■_____

HUMAN DIMENSIONS IN WILDLIFE RESOURCES

Understanding large carnivore management and preventing the loss of large carnivores will require the public to put a value on the conservation of these species. To some individuals, that value may be a consumptive one, a desire to hunt or trap a bear, wolf, or lion. To others, it may involve merely viewing or photographing these creatures. To others, it may be just knowing that carnivores exist and enjoying the thrill of camping in bear country, or hearing a wolf howl in the dark of night. Whatever value humans place on the large carnivores, their successful management will require public support, a big challenge, given that each species elicits strong emotions. Aldo Leopold, the founder of wildlife management, stated in the early 1900s that deer management is more about managing the people than managing the deer. Large carnivore management is definitely more a sociopolitical issue than a biological one.

Human dimensions in wildlife resources research can help managers address, in a scientific manner, the sociological significance of the issue. Such research can identify attitudes, beliefs, and behaviour of the entire resource constituency, can help target educational programs to specific weaknesses in knowledge, and can help managers more effectively balance the viewpoints of the various stakeholders. By understanding and addressing public concerns, the public can be integrated into the decision-making process. Wildlife management, however, should not become a popularity contest and the public should not dictate wildlife policy. Decisions and management plans are formulated on sound biological data, but managers must realize that the best biologically designed management plan will not be implemented without public support.

Public attitudes toward large carnivores have changed considerably. Most residents in Wyoming, Montana, and Idaho supported wolf reintroduction into Yellowstone National Park and held positive attitudes toward the wolf (Bath, 1991). Approximately fifty years before, the public around the park supported wolf control and predator extermination programs. Research on public attitudes toward wolves in Riding Mountain National Park, Manitoba, found that residents on the park boundary held positive attitudes toward wolves and wanted to see their numbers increased to a stable population. Visitors to our national parks have always been excited about seeing wildlife but are particularly thrilled when they see a large carnivore, especially a bear. Individuals from around the world flock to Churchill, Manitoba, to view polar bears and many go to McNeil River in Alaska to watch grizzlies fishing in a salmon-rich river. Eco-tourism focused on large carnivores is growing immensely.

While bears have always caught the limelight with visitors to Yellowstone National Park, Wyoming, wolves have also become a tourist attraction causing wolf jams that easily match the traditional bear jams of the past. At the International Wolf Centre in Ely, Minnesota, many state residents, nonresidents, and foreign visitors are leaving behind significant dollars that infiltrate the local economies. In Algonquin Provincial Park, Ontario, one of the most popular events is a wolf howl. In late August, more than 1000 carfuls of people of all ages stand in complete silence in the dark in the hopes of hearing wolves respond to rangers who initiate a howl. When they held the first howl, park officials were astonished by the amount of interest it generated; this interest remains exceptionally high. In this same area a private wolf centre was scheduled to be created and operational in 1996; at present wolves in a 15 000-acre enclosure are visited and viewed regularly. Wolves and bears can be economic generators for local economies. But while many people would jump at the opportunity to see a mountain lion, the animal tends to be secretive, so chances of having a natural encounter with one are slim.

POLITICAL INFLUENCE IN WILDLIFE MANAGEMENT

To this point in the chapter, the history of carnivore management and the importance of understanding the human dimension in wildlife resource management have been stressed. In this section we return to the definition of wildlife resource management. Management is a political decision-making process and managing wildlife, a renewable public resource, should involve integrating the entire resource constituency (publics) into the decision-making process. Traditionally, wildlife management, like many other resource management decisions, has been driven by vocal lobby groups who are either very much in favour of certain actions or very much against them. Wolf reintroduction in Yellowstone National Park and its impact on the environment was much debated and was the subject of many congressional hearings. The author testified as an expert witness at one of these hearings discussing the findings of research on attitudes of Montana, Idaho, and Wyoming residents. Wildlife management remains a multifaceted issue comprising biological, sociological, and perhaps most significantly, political aspects.

Wolf control continues to create much controversy, and threats of tourism boycotts were effective in getting Alaska and British Columbia to stop their programs. Again the issue was not a matter of biology but of economics and ethics. In the Yukon, however, a group of concerned individuals produced a wolf management plan through consensus building that did include wolf control in certain circumstances. The process involved all the key players early in the process

---

and gave them the power to tackle the management plan. This is an excellent example of how public involvement, if done honestly and thoroughly, can be successful. Public involvement is about redistributing power from the managers to the public and in the Yukon case, management was turned over to the public. If hunting of ungulates has stopped for two years and data can show that wolves are playing a significant role in depleting ungulate numbers perhaps to extinction, it may be appropriate to institute wolf control. In such cases the goal is not to eliminate wolves but to reduce them in a certain area.

Another politically driven large carnivore issue is that of spring black bear hunting and the selling of bear parts. For some individuals the selling of gall bladders from bears that have been legally taken is an example of fully utilizing the carcass; thus they see nothing wrong with the practice. In Nova Scotia, where the sale and possession of gall bladders is legal, approximately 45 percent of gall bladders from legally harvested bears are sold. Certain environmental groups vehemently oppose such actions and at least one is currently (1996) campaigning to get all Canadian provinces to make it illegal to possess and sell bear parts; this campaign is targeted at Nova Scotia, Quebec, and the Northwest Territories, the three regions in Canada where such actions are still legal. Postcard campaigns by concerned citizens have been aimed not at wildlife divisions and directors, but at the premier of the province and the minister of natural resources. Clearly, this campaign is focused at the political decision-making level.

Other controversial issues in black bear management include the use of bait stations to hunt black bears, a practice in Nova Scotia, for example. "How sporting is it for a hunter to sit in a tree waiting for a hungry black bear to come to a bait station and then shoot it?" cry the environmental groups. On the other hand, hunters claim that hunting over registered bait stations (they must keep their gun in its case on the walk in and out of the bait station) is the most humane method of killing the animal (a close shot and a quick death). In addition, hunters say they can see whether the animal has any cubs before shooting (thus minimizing the orphaning of cubs), and the danger to hikers in the woods at the same time is minimized. In Nova Scotia, where the deer season has traditionally not overlapped the bear season, managers have argued that hunting only over registered bait stations dramatically reduces poaching of deer and makes law enforcement easier: anyone found in the woods with a gun would be a poacher. Tourism departments, outfitters, and economists point to the economic benefits of black bear hunting. A spring black bear hunt in Ontario generates about $30 million. Black bear populations in Canada are much higher than grizzly numbers and can biologically sustain regulated harvesting. Considerable debate continues between those who feel the loss of a single animal is unacceptable and those who realize that the population remains stable. Others fear that the hunting of black bears may set a dangerous precedent and lead to the hunting of grizzly bears, which are more sensitive to hunting pressure.

Managers argue that they use a conservation approach to the renewable wildlife resource, managing populations for the greatest good, for the greatest number, for the longest period of time. Environmentalists would like to see a complete protection of the species (preservation management). No group, not even those whose livelihood is directly affected by conflicts with bears (e.g., livestock operators, beekeepers, berry growers), wants exploitation or extermination of the species. The difficulty for the decision-makers is balancing these various viewpoints and managing the wildlife resource truly for the entire resource constituency based on sound biological data and not for a few widely differing interest groups.

TEAMING UP TO SAVE LARGE CARNIVORES

In Canada, the numbers of grizzly bears, wolves, and mountain lions and their habitats have declined considerably. These large carnivores need space, protection from humans, and abundant prey. They also need public support. Attitudes toward these species have improved, but the public's knowledge about them and the appropriate behaviour toward them remains low. Inappropriate behaviour, such as feeding bears, can lead to problem animals that will need to be removed from the population. If the public does not support carnivore recovery, the best biologically designed management plan will be difficult to implement and the result will be a dead carnivore. For example, a wolf recovery effort in Michigan in the 1980s, without public support, resulted in all wolves being killed soon after their release.

Safe and natural viewing of large carnivores may increase the public's appreciation and understanding of these predators. Moving dumps away from areas where humans and bears are active may help reduce encounters and the negative images of bears in dumps. Yellowstone National Park at one time had a grandstand where visitors could sit and listen to a park interpreter at a dump inside the park discussing grizzly bear behaviour. The dump has been moved more than 80 kilometres away from the park to minimize the association of humans with food, which leads to dangerous confrontations between bears and humans. With increasing visitation to national parks and camping in bear country, there have been more encounters, which often result in bears having to be killed. Educating the public about proper food storage in bear country and appropriate behaviour if a bear is encountered will help prevent injuries to humans and the killing of bears. Encounters could be reduced by requiring hikers to organize themselves in parties of at least four or five; a group of that size makes sufficient noise that a bear moves away before feeling threatened. This practice, already in effect in Yellowstone National Park, could be adopted for our Canadian national parks and wilderness areas. Increasing recreational developments in prime large carnivore habitat directly threaten these populations and increase the likelihood of conflicts.

Each of these large carnivores will occasionally kill livestock, so there should be a way of handling the problem acceptable to the livestock community. In the western states an environmental group, Defenders of Wildlife, pays compensation for livestock losses attributed to wolves. By keeping livestock to a minimum in areas where carnivores abound, losses could be further reduced. Giving livestock/agricultural operators the right to kill problem animals that destroy their operations (e.g., beehives) or animals (sheep, calves) might reduce the number of animals that are killed and not reported to wildlife officials, thus improving the biological data on the population.

Poaching of large carnivores does occur but to what extent is unknown as there are few law enforcement officers and large expanses of land. Single instances of bears found with gall bladders removed are often blown out of proportion and reported as the work of major poaching rings; evidence for such in Canada at the present time is lacking. If prices for bear parts continue to increase considerably, poaching may become a problem. The Audubon Society has posted awards for individuals reporting poaching of grizzly bears in the western states and leading to convictions. Such efforts have produced results. Increasing fines and jail terms makes the risks and costs of poaching greater than the perceived benefits. In the past fines for poaching were as incredibly low as $50 to $500; fines have been increased in many regions to several thousand dollars with jail terms and losses of hunting privileges.

Large carnivores require a large amount of space and their home ranges often cross many jurisdictional boundaries. For example, large carnivores in Western Canada may live part of their lives on national parklands, provincial parklands, Crown land, private land, forestry allotments, and grazing leases. It is essential that the many agencies involved in this region work together and at the ecosystem and political levels necessary to ensure the sharing and coordinating of information and management practices. In the western states some of this has been done through an interagency ecosystem management team with representatives from the many stakeholders in the region. In Canada, a carnivore conservation area (CCAs) concept has been developed (Bath et al. 1988) and advocated by World Wildlife Fund Canada. The concept involves integrating management practices and principles to conserve existing carnivores through a zoning system. The success of implementing the concept lies in the willingness of agencies to share information and work together in ways not done before.

SHARING THE ENVIRONMENT: THE FUTURE FOR CARNIVORES

In Canada, there are still healthy populations of wolves, mountain lions, and grizzly bears, due more to the lack of success in killing them all and to our small human population than to a concerted conservation effort. Of the three large carnivores discussed in this chapter, grizzly bears are perhaps the most vulnerable. Because of their low reproductive rates, a willingness to confront individuals when surprised, and an ever-shrinking habitat, populations should be carefully monitored. The increasing interest in Asia in bear parts for medicine may affect Canadian bear populations. Standardization of wildlife policy and better coordination of enforcement across provincial boundaries are needed to effectively monitor the effects of poaching.

Increasing visitation and recreational development in our national parks, which are the core areas for large carnivores, could threaten these species. Wildlife populations can decrease rapidly; the long list of endangered and extinct species is a gruesome reminder of this fact. In addition, we have as a human race destroyed much bigger wildlife populations with much less technology (e.g., the passenger pigeon, the heath hen, the great auk). If we can protect large carnivores, many other species will also be protected, thus helping maintain biodiversity. If wolves, bears, and mountain lions and their wilderness areas still exist in 2050, it will be a living testimony that we as humans can share the environment and its resources with other top predators.

REFERENCES

Archibald, W.R., R. Ellis, and A.N. Hamilton. 1987. "Responses of Grizzly Bears to Logging Truck Traffic in the Kimsquit River Valley, British Columbia." International Conference of Bear Restoration and Management 7: 51–57.

Ballantyne, E.E., and J.G. O'Donoghue. 1954. "Rabies Control in Alberta." *Journal of the American Veterinary Association* 125: 316–26.

Banville, D. 1983. "Status and Management of Wolves in Quebec." In L.N. Carbyn, ed., *Wolves in Canada and Alaska.* Ottawa: Canadian Wildlife Service, no. 45: 41–43.

Bath, A.J. 1991. "Public Attitudes in Wyoming, Montana, and Idaho toward Wolf Restoration in Yellowstone National Park." Transactions of the 56th North American Wildlife and Natural Resources Conference: 91–95.

Bath, A.J., H.A. Dueck, and S. Herrero. 1988. *Carnivore Conservation Areas: A Potential for Comprehensive, Integrated Management.* Prepared for World Wildlife Fund Canada. Toronto. 104 pp.

Cameron, A.W. 1958. "Mammals of the Islands in the Gulf of St. Lawrence." Ottawa: National Museum of Canada, Bulletin no. 154. 165 pp.

Carr, H.D. 1989. "Distribution, Numbers, and Mortality of Grizzly Bears in and around Kananaskis Country, Alberta." Edmonton: Alberta Forestry, Lands and Wildlife, Research Series 3.

Cluff, H.D., and D.L. Murray. 1993. "Review of Wolf Control Methods in North America." Proceedings of the 2nd North American Wolf Symposium, held 25–27 August 1992, University of Alberta, Edmonton.

Dodds, D.G. 1983. "Terrestrial Mammals." In G.R. South, ed., *Biogeography and Ecology of the Island of Newfoundland.* The Hague, Netherlands: Dr. W. Junk: 509–55.

Gibeau, M.L. 1993. "Grizzly Bear Habitat Effectiveness Model for Banff, Yoho, and Kootenay National Parks." Banff, Alta.: Parks Canada.

Gunson, J.R. 1983. "Status and Management of Wolves in Alberta." In L.N. Carbyn, ed., *Wolves in Canada and Alaska.* Ottawa: Environment Canada, Canadian Wildlife Service, series no. 45: pp. 25–29.

Hayes, R.D., A.M. Baer, and D.G. Larson. 1991. "Population Dynamics and Prey Relationships of an Exploited and Recovering Wolf Population in the Southern Yukon." Whitehorse: Yukon Fish and Wildlife Branch, final report TR–91–1. 67 pp.

Heard, D.C. 1983. "Historical and Present Status of Wolves in the Northwest Territories." In L.N. Carbyn, ed., *Wolves in Canada and Alaska.* Ottawa: Environment Canada, Canadian Wildlife Service, series no. 45: pp. 44–47.

Hewitt, G. 1921. *The Conservation of the Wild Life of Canada.* New York: Charles Scribner's Sons.

Kolenosky, G.B. 1983. "Status and Management of Wolves in Ontario." In L.N. Carbyn, ed., *Wolves in Canada and Alaska.* Ottawa: Environment Canada, Canadian Wildlife Service, series no. 45: pp. 35–40.

Leonard, R.D., R. Breneman, and R. Frey. 1990. "A Case History of Grizzly Bear Management in the Slims River Area, Kluane National Park Reserve, Yukon." International Conference of Bear Restoration and Management 8: 113–23.

Lopez, B. 1978. *Of Wolves and Men.* New York: Charles Scribner's Sons.

McLellan, B.N., and D.M. Shackleton. 1988. "Grizzly Bears and Resource Extraction Industries: Effects of Roads on Behaviour, Habitat Use, and Demography." *Journal of Applied Ecology* 25: 451–60.

Paquet, P.C. 1993. "Summary Reference Document—Ecological Studies of Recolonizing Wolves in the Central Canadian Rocky Mountains." Prepared by John/Paul & Associates for Canadian Parks Service. Banff, Alta.: Banff National Park Warden Service. 118 pp.

Paquet, P., and A. Hackman. 1995. "Large Carnivore Conservation in the Rocky Mountains: A Long-Term Strategy for Maintaining Free-Ranging and Self-Sustaining Populations of Carnivores." Prepared for World Wildlife Fund Canada. Toronto. 53 pp.

Pimlott, D.H. 1961. "Wolf Control in Canada." *Canadian Audubon* 23: 145–52.

Promberger, C., and W. Schroder. 1992. "Wolves in Europe: Status and Perspectives." Proceedings of the workshop Wolves in Europe—Current Status and Prospects, held in Oberammergau, Germany, April 2–5.

Rodney, W. 1969. *Kootenai Brown: His Life and Times, 1839–1916.* Sidney, B.C.: Gray's. 251 pp.

Seguin, R. 1991. "A Wolf Management Strategy for Saskatchewan." Meadow Lake, Sask.: Saskatchewan Parks and Renewable Resources, unpublished report. 14 pp.

Slough, B.G., R.H. Jessup, D.I. McKay, and A.B. Stephenson. 1987. "Wild Furbearer Management in Western and Northern Canada." In M. Novak, J.A. Baker, M.E. Obbard, and B. Malloch, eds., *Wild Furbearer Management and Conservation in North America*. North Bay, Ont.: Ontario Trappers Association, pp. 1062–76.

Spry, I.M. 1963. *The Palliser Expedition*. Toronto: Macmillan Co. 310 pp.

Stardom, R.R.P. 1983. "Status and Management of Wolves in Manitoba." In L.N. Carbyn, ed., *Wolves in Canada and Alaska*. Ottawa: Environment Canada, Canadian Wildlife Service, no. 45, pp. 30–34.

Tompa, F.S. 1983. "Problem Wolf Management in British Columbia: Conflict and Program Evaluation." In L.N. Carbyn, ed., *Wolves in Canada and Alaska*. Ottawa: Environment Canada, Canadian Wildlife Service, no. 45, pp. 112–19.

Van Ballenberge, V. 1974. "Wolf Management in Minnesota: An Endangered Species Case History." Trans. North American Wildlife Natural Resources Conference 39: 313–22.

Weaver, J. 1978. "The Wolves of Yellowstone." U.S. Interior Department, National Park Service, Natural Resource Report no. 14. 38 pp.

Wiltse, E. 1983. "Summary of the Status of Wolves in Saskatchewan." In L.N. Carbyn, ed., *Wolves in Canada and Alaska*. Ottawa: Environment Canada, Canadian Wildlife Service, no. 45, p. 125.

Young, S.P., and E.A. Goldman. 1944. *The Wolves of North America*. Washington, D.C.: American Wildlife Institute. 385 pp.

QUESTIONS FOR DISCUSSION

1. Large predators like wolves, grizzly bears, and mountain lions occasionally kill livestock, and while the numbers overall may be extremely small, such losses can be significant to individual farmers. Should compensation be paid and, if so, how much? Most calf and lamb losses occur in the spring when the market price is low. Should compensation for the calf or lamb be based on the market price it would have fetched in the fall when it would have been sold? What if the animal is a prize bull, the loss of which may affect the genetic strength of the herd? What should be paid: market price, compensation for one year, five years, or more?

2. A store owner said he loses up to 8 percent of his merchandise a year through shoplifting, but he would never think of asking for compensation from the government. Should not livestock owners accept a percentage loss to predators as part of the nature of doing business?

3. People visit national parks to enjoy the outdoors and to see large predators. If these predators can be harmful to visitors, and indeed bear–human confrontations and mountain lion attacks are on the increase, what responsibility, if any, do park authorities have to the visitor?

4. A grizzly sow and her two cubs have been seen near a popular trail in a park leading to a magnificent view of a waterfall. For many visitors it will be their first and only trip

to the park, their first and only opportunity to see a magnificent waterfall, hike a trail, and possibly see a bear in the wild. Seeing bears increases visitors' appreciation of the species and gives pleasure. However, protection of the natural resource should also be considered. Is it fair to close the trail?

Agriculture and Ecology

Ian MacQuarrie

Department of Biology
University of Prince Edward Island

INTRODUCTION

For most Canadians, food comes from the supermarket, and agriculture is about as unfamiliar as astronomy.[1] In our country we take for granted reasonably cheap, safe food supplies and spend little time thinking about how such abundance is produced, or what the environmental implications of the production system may be. However, behind the potatoes in the vegetable bin, or the steak in the meat counter, there are hosts of stories: on technology and land use, food preservation and security, pesticides and additives, processing and pollution, packaging and recycling ... the list is lengthy. Continuing to browse, we encounter science and folklore, tradition and innovation, with many reminders of the central role that food has always played in history. For most people in the past, the connection to the soil was necessarily close—the loss of land usually meant starvation. Paradoxically, it is now more important than ever to understand how the landscape works, because ignorance can affect so many, at a distance, in complex ways.

EFFECTS OF FOOD PRODUCTION

Humans have always changed natural systems to their own advantage, and the change has often been destructive. Other living things were classified as good or bad depending on their utility, or whether or not we saw them as dangerous competitors—the first response by humans to anything new or strange was often to attack. So forests were destroyed for the land beneath, and native grasslands ploughed to produce new crops. As well, our unique ability to manipulate fire has been altering the face of the earth for millennia. Grassland burning in temperate zones is an old agricultural practice; in our time the destruction has been extended to tropical forests. Accumulating experience in domesticating plants and animals, working the soil, and (partly) eliminating competitors were the methods that led to the first agricultural revolution some 10 000 years ago; this revolution continues today, still changing the face of our country and the rest of the world.

While anthropologists still argue about exact dates, North America has been inhabited by humans for 15 000–40 000 years. Aboriginal inhabitants certainly affected the natural world into which they emigrated, for instance by burning grasslands and forests, but the effects were minor compared with those that followed. For good or ill, the invasion of European agriculture followed by its later industrialization has resulted in our present landscape in Southern Canada. It is this much-changed land and its present use that we must examine closely.

Most of Canada is not farmland—only about 7 percent of our land base is capable of significant food production (see Figure 3.1). Yet the majority of Canadians live within an area of past or present farming. Once we leave the city core, our surroundings are usually influenced or dominated by agriculture: we are in a cultural rather than a natural environment. The flora and fauna have been profoundly changed to give us a still-pleasing landscape, but one that is very different from pre-Columbus days.

The nature of the crops produced varies across this vast country, and different methods of production result in a wide variation in environmental (and social)

FIGURE 3.1
Canadian Agriculture Lands, 1991

■ Agricultural lands
▨ Nonagricultural lands

Source: Reproduced by authority of the Minister of Industry, 1996, Statistics Canada, "Canadian Agriculture at a Glance," cat. no. 96-301, October 1994.

impacts. For instance, compare intensive row-crop production of potatoes with extensive cattle grazing on semi-natural forages. Intensive production at present involves massive fertilizer, fossil fuel, and pesticide use, with soil and water degradation often following. The system returns high yields of a low unit-value crop, and also supports processing industries that provide many jobs. So, in spite of environmental problems, economic success makes change difficult. Range-land beef farming has much less visible environmental impact—plant and animal communities are certainly affected, but in more subtle ways, often unnoticed unless species become endangered. Water quality, landscape beauty and serenity, fish and wildlife abundance relate closely to what food is being produced, and by what methods.

Ultimately the consumer, perhaps unwittingly, makes the decisions. Cost, and an increasing awareness of the importance of a healthy diet, are probably the most important forces in the complex food market; these forces through time affect the environment in diverse ways.

Farming is of course in continuous change, with only major successes and failures making the headlines. In other countries collapsing farming has led to massive starvation and emigration. Lack of food and land inevitably lead to social turmoil and increasing poverty, with the associated misery so familiar to us from television. In Canada we have had cycles of land clearing and abandonment, and while families and groups have suffered, we have up to the present been fortunate in having enough good productive farms to allow us to escape from major trauma. Yet the warnings have been there through our brief history:

> … your mad system of cropping, which takes from the land till it will take no more, will testify against you.[2]

CROP PROTECTION AND THE HEALTHY ECOSYSTEM

Any method of farming involves making major changes in the entire ecology of an area. Soil must usually be cleared of the original vegetation—often plant communities that are the product of centuries of growth and interaction—and fast-growing invasive species (weeds) must then be controlled. Fungal, bacterial, or viral diseases always appear; these as well as insects and other pests that delight in the rich new habitat are immediate and perennial problems. The water regime is changed through clearing, drainage, or irrigation. Any plant growth depends on topsoil; this thin layer must be worked for the benefit of a few desired plants or animals, yet maintained against the natural forces of erosion.

Essentially, the entire system has to be manipulated to produce and protect a few species, rather than the many products of nature. This simplification has both costs and benefits. In Canada's past, various types of subsistence farming provided food (with much labour) for low population densities; now industrial farming, with massive inputs of machinery, fossil fuels, pesticides, and fertilizers is the norm. Such farming methods have increased productivity and cheap food, but (as always) at a price to the environment. And how long can this bounty continue? Environmental degradation, hidden or obvious, has been a major reason for seeking alternative agricultural methods with greater sustainability.

As an example, consider how crop protection has changed. Our ancestors tried to keep the crows out of the cornfield with a scarecrow or a few blasts of a shotgun. Now we have sophisticated, programmable electronic bird deterrents, producing disturbing audio signals through a network of weatherproof speakers! The scale of production has changed enormously, and so have the costs and effects.

While noisy bird repellents may annoy the neighbours, no other crop protection issue has been as important, or controversial, as the widespread use of synthetic chemicals—modern pesticides. Humans have battled pests (mainly insects) with chemicals such as heavy metals, or naturally occurring poisons like nicotine, for hundreds of years. Some sort of battle is necessary; estimates are that perhaps half of a crop will be lost without any control. However, the real revolution began in the 1940s with the widespread use of DDT (dichlorodiphenyl-trichloroethane), the first important *synthetic* insecticide. DDT has broad-spectrum, persistent activity; it is also cheap to manufacture and easy to apply. At first glance these seem to be positive attributes. In time, however, such supposed benefits were shown to be harmful: broad-spectrum activity means that many beneficial insects will be affected, while persistence led to the now well-known phenomenon of food-chain magnification.

Also, DDT overuse soon led to the selection of resistant strains of insects— many pests bounced back. Food-chain magnification is closely related to the chemistry of the pesticide. DDT and its organochlorine relatives, with their persistence and fat-solubility, are classic candidates for magnification.

Scavengers and predators at the top of the food-chain accumulated DDT to the point where their reproduction, and thus survival, were threatened. Ospreys, eagles, and falcons are among the many wildlife species that suffered during the DDT days. Populations were driven to low levels from that they are still recovering. The impact on humans, which also store such persistent poisons, has been hotly debated.

DDT and related compounds have been banned or severely restricted in North America since the 1970s; however they are still used in other countries. It is now known that atmospheric transport allows such compounds to achieve a worldwide distribution, and we still have significant concentrations in Canada.

Concern for the health of ecosystems plays out in a very large arena, perhaps far from the daily worries of most of us. However, anxiety about direct effects on

FIGURE 3.2
Percentage of Crops Lost Annually to Pests in the United States

Period	Insects	Diseases	Weeds
1989	13.0	12.0	12.0
1974	13.0	12.0	8.0
1951–1960	12.9	12.2	8.5
1942–1951	7.1	10.5	13.8

Source: D. Pimental et al., "Environmental and Economic Effects of Reducing Pesticide Use," *BioScience* 41:6 (June 1991). Reproduced by permission of the American Institute of Biological Sciences and D. Pimental.

human health has also been a major part of the pesticide debate. In the 1990s this concern became more sharply focused on the endocrine system. Impacts on this system may lead to increased cancer rates, reproductive abnormalities, immune system problems, and other, less easily diagnosed effects such as an increase in learning disabilities.

An interesting example that receives much media attention is the possible long-term decline in average human sperm counts. This hypothesis is supported by evidence from several studies;[3] however, problems in historical measurement techniques make it very difficult to establish trends, let alone ascribe such changes to particular environmental chemicals. It should be noted that great numbers of chemicals, not just a few pesticides, are under suspicion as possible disturbers of the endocrine system. These include components of paints, plastics, cosmetics, and many other widely used products. Synthetic or naturally occurring hormones are obvious objects for study.

The debate may thus be focused on food production and pest deterrence, or much more widely on the use, abuse, and impacts of almost any substance in our chemically dependent societies.

One of the more disturbing chapters in the food and pesticide story has been the widespread development of genetic resistance in pests. Initial successes, particularly in the early days with compounds such as DDT, led to overreliance on chemicals and neglect of traditional farming practices like crop rotation. Resistance developed rapidly as susceptible individuals were knocked out of populations—today several hundred pest species have shown that they can cope with pesticides. Changes in compounds and application strategies may help for a time, but in general many pests are at least holding their own in the race, as may be seen by looking at figures on crop losses.

While chemicals continue to be used, and perhaps overused, it would be a mistake to think that this is the only modern method of crop protection. One major advance is through integrated pest management (IPM): this combines biological and cultivation techniques with a minimum of chemical treatment to control a problem. In effect, knowledge of the pest's biology (in particular, population status) is substituted for sledgehammering it with sprays alone. IPM has been quite successful with crops as diverse as cotton and apples.

True biological control of pests is an old but attractive method because of its specificity and relative freedom from side effects. Pests are attacked with predators, parasites, or disease vectors, and spectacular gains have sometimes been seen. For example, control of prickly pear cactus in Australia has been accomplished with the appropriately named cactoblastis moth. Biological control is most effective with introduced pests, and is useful only in a fraction of cases. It may be impossible to find the appropriate agent, or the control may be so slow that a crop may be lost. Still, research into biological methods is a very active field, and every success story represents a lessening of chemical dependency.

Genetic engineering is making contributions to pest resistance in plants. Selection for resistant strains is probably as old as agriculture, but now the plant's genetic complement can be directly altered by inserting material to produce pest resistance—such transgenic plants literally have a built-in advantage when attacked. An interesting example is seen in the use of genetic material from a strain of Bt (*Bacillus thuringiensis*) to protect potatoes from a serious pest, the Colorado potato beetle (*Leptinotarsa decimlineata*). When the larvae feed on the leaves, the endotoxin derived originally from Bt kills them. Any direct side effects are minimal, although the release of such transgenic plants into the wild may have unpredictable effects. Kahl and Winter (1995) have recently summarized many of the current research efforts involving genetic engineering and crop protection.

In spite of alternatives, chemical use is still with us, and will remain. Prudence dictates caution—using the minimum amounts, taking great care to avoid spills and accidents, targeting pests much more accurately in terms of their life cycles. More than 30 years ago Rachel Carson wrote:

> It is not my contention that chemical insecticides must never be used. I do contend that we have put poisonous and biologically potent chemicals indiscriminately into the hands of persons largely or wholly ignorant of their potentials for harm.... I contend, furthermore, that we have allowed these chemicals to be used with little or no advance investigation of their effect on soil, water, wildlife, and man himself. Future generations are unlikely to condone our lack of prudent concern for the integrity of the natural world that supports all life.[4]

Since those words were written, much of the pesticide research, regulation, and debate have been on which compounds may be used, with what dose rates and type of application. Alternative methods, such as organic farming, which minimize or eliminate pesticides, have become more popular. Training and regulation of applicators have improved greatly. Still, the debate remains intense because so much is yet unknown—for instance, what are the long-term effects of mixes of compounds? We seem to have moved from ignorance to wariness, while maintaining crop production—at a documented cost to other species. Agriculture by definition changes the landscape—many pesticide effects are simply modern instances of such habitat change. Concern for human health is probably the major driving force in keeping pesticide use contentious, while other environmental problems such as declines in bird populations matter to a minority. Rachel Carson would probably find much that is familiar in media coverage in the 1990s!

Agricultural diversity leads to protection complexity. Hundreds of pest-killing ingredients in thousands of formulations are used in crop protection. Pests develop resistance, and new formulations are always needed. Since weeds are always a problem, many herbicides and fungicides are used as well as the better-known insecticides. The application of so many potentially toxic compounds over wide areas provides another area of concern: possible contamination of the water resource.

Streams and rivers may become tainted as their waters move to the sea—usually the alarm and reaction come only after obvious dramatic events such as fish kills. However, it is the water in rock and soil beneath our feet that is of particular interest; this groundwater moves slowly, and contamination may not be suspected because the effects are not readily seen (see Figure 3.3).

Farming affects groundwater in many ways, and contamination by pesticides is not the only concern. For instance, almost half of the improved farmland in Canada is fertilized; water enrichment with nitrogen compounds and phosphate from these fertilizers can be quite significant *(The State of Canada's Environment—1991)*. Still waters may become overenriched and eutrophic, with familiar ecological and economic effects. The buildup of nitrogen (particularly in the form of nitrate) in groundwater, and the relationship of such increases to agriculture, is also a contentious issue, since high levels of nitrate have been shown to have harmful effects on human health. In recent surveys of farm wells in Ontario, 13 percent were found to have nitrate levels exceeding Canadian guidelines for maximum acceptable levels (Linton, 1995). Nitrate contamination may come from many sources other than fertilizer leaching, but increased use of fertilizers has been shown to correlate with increases of nitrate in groundwater (Goudie, 1994). Thus a major practice that has led to greater productivity and cheaper food also has a negative side in terms of human health. A true cost/benefit analysis of fertilizer use is extremely difficult to obtain, but it is clear that this practice is such an integral part of modern industrial farming that it could be changed only with great difficulty.

AFFECTED ECOSYSTEMS IN CANADA

Increasing population pressures and the "export" of industrial agricultural technology are just two of the factors that link land degradation to farming in many

FIGURE 3.3
The Water Cycle

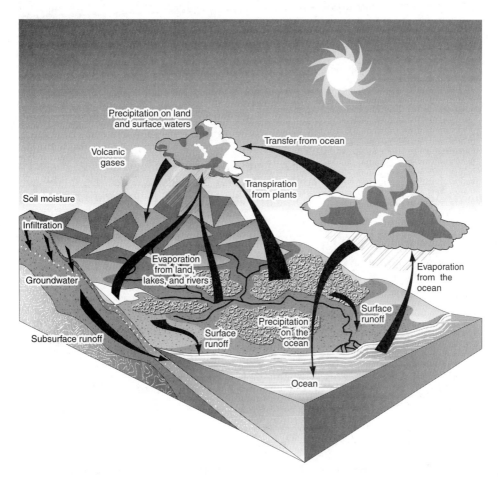

Source: Adapted from Arthur Getis, Judith Getis, and Jerome D. Fellman, *Introduction to Geography,* 5th ed. © 1996 Times Mirror Higher Education Group, Inc., Dubuque, Iowa. All rights reserved. Reprinted by permission.

parts of the world. More food is needed, so the land is pushed harder. Small-scale subsistence farming is displaced with massive projects, often involving forest destruction and land-levelling, river damming and irrigation, the breaking up of grasslands, and in some cases the spreading of deserts. Farmland is also irretrievably lost to pavement as social disruption forces the growth of megacities. Pollution levels increase, and most people leave the countryside for an equally difficult urban existence. While there are bright spots in some countries, world hunger has not been banished by the new technologies, and pollution problems abound.

Technological optimists argue that it does not have to be this way, that for every problem countermeasures exist. For instance, row-crop farming accelerates soil erosion, but this loss can be minimized with better tillage, longer rotations with alternative crops, control of water runoff from the land. Pessimists point out that while this may be true, it is difficult to implement such practices even in sophisticated and stable countries. The goal of a sustainable, "environmentally friendly" farming is still far in the distance.

For instance, the ancient problem of soil degradation and soil loss is still with us in Canada. On the Prairies wind erosion is often the major concern, and management practices such as summerfallowing (allowing the land to lie idle in alternate years) have increased the risk of erosion. Summerfallowing conserves water and allows for better weed control; however, it leads to a decline in the all-important organic content of the soils, and is also related to soil salinization. Thus a practice that is beneficial in some senses is detrimental in the long run.

> The long-hallowed and treasured practice of summerfallowing in a mono-cultural cropping system is perhaps the most singular mismanagement practice that has been in vogue … (*Soil at Risk: Canada's Eroding Future*, Senate Committee Report, 1985)

Wind erosion is also a problem in Central Canada, while in the east water is usually the more significant erosive agent. The complexities of soils, cropping systems, and markets all intertwine to make land degradation a serious and expensive question throughout the country—one estimate suggests that over $1 billion a year is lost in this manner (*A Growing Concern: Soil Degradation in Canada*, Science Council of Canada, 1986).

FARMING: A LIFE OF CONSEQUENCES

Farming abounds in paradoxes. Relatively few people are involved, yet agriculture is economically very important, both in local and export markets. As the number of farms and farmers has declined, productivity has increased tremendously. For instance, a local P.E.I. community history points out that once there were 40 farms in the Stanhope/Cavendish locale (the famous Anne of Green Gables area), while now there are two—but this pair produce more food than the original 40! Farming is romanticized as a healthy outdoor occupation, where hard work and thrift are repaid with independence and family continuity. In reality much farming goes on indoors, in barns and tractor cabs, in noisy and often dangerous and dirty conditions. Accident statistics verify that farming is hazardous. Independence is eroded by the necessity of obtaining off-farm work; even full-time farm families now get more of their net income off the farm than on it.[5] Perhaps the only reality in the stereotype of the farmer is hard work— both male and female farm operators work long hours, keeping their farms going with a variety of part-time or full-time off-farm jobs.

In summary, it is little wonder that in practice farming is not only hard on farmers, it can be hard on the landscape (through pollution and degradation) as well. While a technician can prescribe a proper crop rotation regime for any given situation, economics will dictate whether or not the prescription is followed. The land is often pushed hard—cultivated to the edge of streams, and on slopes that probably should not be tilled at all. Fertilizer runoff from fields or wastes from a feedlot may escape to cause damage downstream. Pesticide use, misuse, and accident all combine to affect lands and waters, to the detriment of their myriad living things. A field of potatoes may be very photogenic in its lush greenness; it is maintained in that state only by the use of much ingenuity, science, fossil fuels and pesticides, hard work ... and money.

THE IMPACT OF THE ENVIRONMENT ON FARMING

Farms and farmers occupy only a small proportion of the Canadian scene, yet food production and processing contribute close to $8 billion to the economy—a sizable share. At present, as usual, almost everything related to food is in a state of change. Fewer farmers, bigger farms, more processing, more diversified diet preferences, shifts in importance within and between sectors—all are occurring within the globalization of the Canadian economy and in an atmosphere of government restraint and deregulation. These realities impact literally every farm in every province.

> Agricultural policy has been a fixture of Canadian public policy since Confederation when the department of agriculture became the first permanent government department to guide an industry that directly touched Barry more than half the Canadian population in 1867. (Barry Wilson, *Farming the System*, 1990)

Much of this policy has been aimed at saving the family farm. The family farm has always been by far the most common operating system in Canada, and governments have created a maze of programs and subsidies designed to preserve this system—with questionable results. Family farms are lost in spite of all the rhetoric. Protection and subsidy drive up food costs. For instance,

---

protection of the dairy industry through a supply management system has helped stabilize this important sector by guaranteeing the producer a fair return on investment. It has also led to comparatively high prices for dairy products on the supermarket shelves. In addition, supply management cannot be maintained under the present state of tariff regulations; this system must be phased out to meet international obligations on trade rules. What will be the impact on the farmers, on the land base, on the environment? Quite possibly harmful in all these cases. The necessity to become profitable in the short term always seems to have negative impacts on the land base; land use is changed, and the land worked harder. Since the farm is in no sense a self-contained unit, impacts are felt at many levels.

Consider another very recent happening that brought farming into the spotlight. In March 1996 the media gave full play to "mad cow" disease in Great Britain: a perceived human health problem, possible destruction of entire cattle populations (the economic consequences of which would affect not only farmers but could push the entire country into a depression), intense political battling were all linked.

The causative agent may be a strange protein known as a prion, or in another sense it may be the entire global, industrialized approach to farming and food that is at fault. It will take years for the outcome to become clear, and consumers' tastes may have been changed indefinitely.

Many nonfarm government policies also impact the farming system, for instance in job creation. As an example close to home, potato processing plant capacity on Prince Edward Island has been greatly increased with enthusiastic government support; this of course brings about more acreage in potato production, more use of marginal lands, more pressure on operators to shorten rotations and skimp on environmental protection. How much of the Island should become a potato patch? How much soil erosion can the land withstand, while remaining productive? There are no obvious answers. Such policy decisions do not get the intensive environmental impact assessments that an industrial plant or major development (such as a bridge) now do; their effects may be much more serious.

SUSTAINABLE AGRICULTURE: AN ACHIEVABLE GOAL?

In the last decade there has been much discussion on creating a more stable, more sustainable agricultural industry—in effect an industry that would be less polluting, would maintain (even enhance) our healthy and attractive landscape, and would be less stressful on farm operators. All of this, of course, while still producing an abundance of cheap and safe food for Canada and the world. A tall order!

In its final report before being abolished by government, the Science Council of Canada identified the principles of sustainable agriculture as follows:

- thorough integration of the farming system with natural processes

- reduction of inputs most likely to harm the environment

- greater use of the biological and genetic potential of plant and animal species

- improvement in the match between cropping patterns and land resources to ensure the sustainability of present production levels

- efficient production, with emphasis on improved farm management and conservation of soil, water, energy, and biological resources

- development of food processing, packaging, distribution and consumption practices consistent with sound environmental management. (*Sustainable Agriculture: The Research Challenge,* Science Council of Canada, 1992)

The list is not necessarily complete; for instance many Canadians expect that farmers will produce not only food but lands for hunting, camping, and other outdoor recreation as well. However, even a brief scan should convince anyone that "sustainable agriculture" as defined is quite different from the present pattern, and that even moving in the *direction* of achieving some of these objectives requires major changes in much of our present society. Integration of farming with natural processes? Reduction of fertilizer use? Removal of sensitive lands from production? Not in my neighbourhood!

Much political will is necessary if any significant advances are to be realized, and the research effort should not be minimized—in many cases it is true to say that we do not know what we are doing, and find out only when catastrophe threatens. We do not need the equivalent of a mad cow scare in Canada.

It is also fair to say that positive steps are occurring. Farms can become more diversified, with additional crops and livestock types—P.E.I. now farms emus as well as potatoes. Wastes from one process can be used as fertilizers or feeds in another. Water and energy monitoring provide useful information in terms of changing practices. Remote sensing technology allows the rapid accumulation and analysis of huge amounts of relevant information on the agricultural world.

Packaging can be made less elaborate and wasteful, and so on. Within each sector, or in terms of any single problem, potential solutions exist.

The major difficulties are in developing the integration necessary if the solutions to individual problems are to lead to a true sustainable agriculture, and in convincing the Canadian public (with the politicians) that the issue is truly important, and worthy of long-term attention and support. Farming is more than food. Now, as in the past, it is a most important landscape designer and environmental quality determiner; these facts are important to all Canadians.

NOTES

1   Only about 3 percent of Canadians are farmers (Statistics Canada, 1991 census).
2   From an 1850 P.E.I. Agricultural Society Report.
3   For instance: *Male Reproductive Health and Environmental Chemicals with Estrogenic Effects,* Danish EPA, 1995.
4   Carson, Rachel. 1962. *Silent Spring.*
5   Statistics Canada.

REFERENCES

For basic environmental and ecological information:
Arms, Karen. 1990. *Environmental Science.* Saunders College Publishers.
Miller, G. Tyler. 1996. *Living in the Environment.* 9th ed. Wadsworth Publishing Co.

For more depth on ecological theory:
Krebs, Charles. 1994. *Ecology.* 4th ed. HarperCollins.

For historical and geographical information on planetary land degradation:
Goudie, Andrew. 1994. *The Human Impact on the Natural Environment.* 4th ed. Cambridge, Mass.: MIT Press.
Johnson, Douglas, and Laurence Lewis. 1995. *Land Degradation: Creation and Destruction.* Blackwell Publishers.

For some Canadian implications:
Fairbairn, Garry. 1989. *Canada Choice: Economic, Health and Moral Issues in Food from Animals.* Agricultural Institute of Canada.
Mungall, Constance, and Digby McLaren. 1990. *Planet under Stress: The Challenge of Global Change.* Oxford University Press.
Statistics Canada. 1994. "Canadian Agriculture at a Glance," CS96–301.

For pesticide/biological control information:
Raven, Peter, Linda Berg, and George Johnson. *Environment 1995.* Saunders College Publishers.

1. It is often suggested that environmental degradation (soil loss, forest loss, species loss) is mainly a modern phenomenon related to industrialization. In point form, list arguments for and against this suggestion.

2. At one time climate was the dominant factor controlling agriculture: crops grown and methods of production were rather different in different parts of Canada due to climatic variation. Is this still true? How much regional variation in Canadian agriculture can still be explained by climate? How have processing and transportation changes affected the basic regional patterns?

3. Agriculture has been called "creative destruction." In the 1990s how much weight would you put on the "creative" term and how much on the "destruction"? In terms of the environment and sustainability, are we gaining or losing? If possible, use local examples in your comments.

4. Why do some people assess the risks from pesticide use as being very low, while others see them as very high? Investigate this in your own class by setting up a questionnaire/interview study. Is there any relationship between knowledge of the pesticide situation and attitudes toward pesticides?

5. Are there any local studies or experiments on biological control of pests going on in your area? How do you define "pest"? Which pests should be targeted for control?

6. Every area in Canada has issues related to water: amounts, quality, changes, pollution, costs. Identify problems in your area and determine if these are locally caused (e.g., untreated sewage), or due to major national or international causes such as acid rain. What kind of report card would you write on water issues in your area or region?

7. Biotechnology (in fact technology in general) is often identified as both a problem and a solution in relation to the *entire* food system, from the beginning of production to final human consumption. Identify an issue in this broad array such as the use of transgenic plants, food irradiation, hormones in milk products, etc. Investigate local attitudes and changes, and make predictions on what you think may happen in the next few years.

C H A P T E R 4

Canadian Water Resources and Management

Isobel W. Heathcote

Institute for Environmental Policy,
Faculty of Environmental Science, and School of Engineering
University of Guelph

THE ISSUES: QUANTITY, QUALITY, AND RESPONSIBILITY

QUANTITY

In many parts of the world, water conservation is a necessity of life. Where water is scarce and expensive, it makes good economic sense to use as little as possible. In Canada, which has 9 percent or approximately 105 000 m^3/sec of the world's renewable water supply serving less than 1 percent of the world's population, water management traditions have grown out of the mistaken perception that Canadian water resources are infinite. In fact, in the heavily populated Canada–U.S. border region, this is far from the truth. For example, over 60 percent of Canada's water resources rise in the north and flow away from the major population centres to the Arctic Ocean. By contrast, more than 90 percent of the Canadian population lives within 300 kilometres of the Canada–U.S. border. The densely populated and industrialized southern parts of Ontario—perhaps a third of the Canadian population (1991 census figures show 10 084 885 Ontario residents against an estimated total Canadian population of 27 719 000)—must rely on the 5000 m^3/sec provided by the Canadian portion of the Great Lakes drainage basin and the Ottawa River. The 35 million residents of the U.S. portion of the Great Lakes Basin impose additional demands on what once appeared a limitless resource.

This intensive use is not reflected in Canadian water policies. In North America, the right to use water has traditionally been awarded at no cost to the user. No Canadian federal or provincial statute currently binds consumers to include water conservation as part of any industrial or municipal program. Instead, water use is governed by a variety of non-legal guidelines and policies. Many of these policies may in fact encourage wasteful use of water by failing to impose realistic prices and by not relating costs to the volume used.

Canadians now are among the world's most wasteful water users, consuming more per capita than any other country except the United States. Canadian water prices are among the lowest in the world: 33 to 50 percent of those in France or Germany, for example, while the per capita consumption on a residential basis is more than double that of those countries. Water rates in most municipalities are in fact set at 65 to 75 percent of the real cost of delivering water and sewage services, so there is little incentive to conserve.

QUALITY

Water is a limited resource that cannot be used and reused without some degradation. The 1985 Inquiry on Federal Water Policy estimated that current municipal water use and related energy requirements could double by 2011. If this occurs, water in even the largest systems may be reused several times before it moves into a downstream body of water. Unless water is returned to the system in its original condition (or better) following use, each withdrawal/use/discharge cycle will result in further deterioration of receiving waters.

Today, the largest Canadian water user by far is the electric power generating sector, which uses more than 26 billion cubic metres a year (1986 figures). Second is manufacturing, at about 8 billion cubic metres a year (including water used in cooling, washing, dilution of wastes, and incorporation into products), followed by municipal withdrawals (water for drinking, washing, lawn-watering, and firefighting) at about 5 billion, agriculture at about 4 billion, and mining at less than 1 billion.

The quality of discharges from industrial and municipal wastewater treatment facilities has improved steadily over the past twenty years. In the pulp and paper industry, for example, effluents now contain about half the suspended solids and one-third the biochemical oxgyen demand discharged in 1970. Petroleum refineries have reduced their discharges of suspended solids by 80 percent, their ammonia by 90 percent, and their oil and grease by 75 percent over the same period. More than 70 percent of Canada's population is now served by sewage treatment facilities, with more than half having sophisticated two- or three-stage treatment available.

At the same time, however, more than 80 percent of Canada's freshwater and saltwater wetlands—which some authors refer to as the "kidneys" of the environment—have been drained for agriculture. And the area of irrigated land continues to grow steadily. In the Atlantic Provinces, Quebec, and Manitoba, only a tiny acreage—less than 10 000 hectares—is irrigated. But in Ontario, Saskatchewan, Alberta, and British Columbia, irrigated acreage has jumped significantly over the past twenty years; each year, those provinces now irrigate 50 000, 90 000, 460 000, and 110 000 hectares respectively.

So while improvements have been made in our ability to treat contaminated water, we are still wasteful water users and our use is increasing steadily. As our population grows, we will have to make significant improvements in our management practices and our usage rates if we are to maintain the standard of supply and quality we have enjoyed in the past.

WATER RESOURCES IN CANADA

The history of water resources issues in Canada is the history of European settlement, land clearance, and management of practical problems of waste disposal and water supply. In the Canadian landscape before European settlement, water flowed freely in rivers and streams down to the lakes and oceans. Where a watershed

FIGURE 4.1

Average Annual Discharges from Canadian Petroleum Refineries, 1972–87

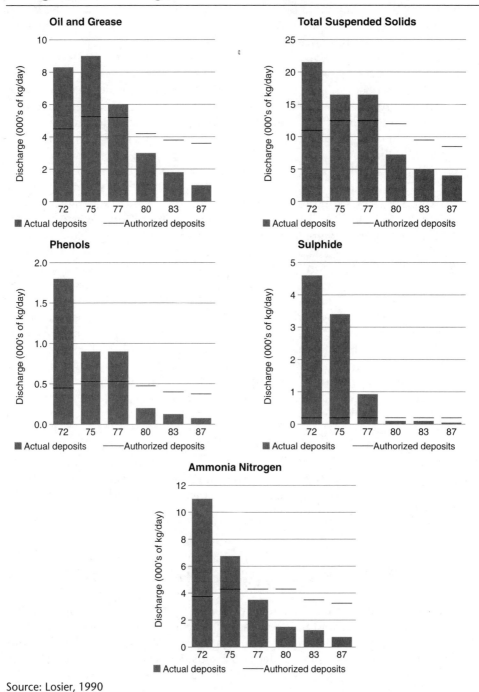

Source: Losier, 1990

The Environment and Canadian Society

(the area drained by a stream system) was densely forested, as was the case in most of Eastern and Western Canada, the stream cut channels through valleys and down slopes, providing corridors for wildlife and human movement. In these forested watersheds, massive stands of timber covered upland slopes, punctuated here and there with the scars of forest fires caused by lightning or careless humans. Under the forest canopy, however, the shade was often so dense that little grew around the base of the largest trees. Fallen trees lay in the thick leaf mould, in itself a natural sponge for rain and groundwater.

The first European settlers wasted no time in clearing and burning trees to ready the land for sowing. Destruction of the forest meant progress, and triumph over the primeval forest threats of wolves and forest fires. It also meant a steady deterioration in the water-holding ability of the forest soils, and gradual lowering of the water table.

With the coming of European settlers in the 18th century, small settlements quickly began to spring up across the country. The dates of these settlements are a tribute to the westward migration of settlers: Montreal 1642; Halifax 1749; Toronto 1793; Winnipeg 1812; Edmonton, as a fur-trading post in 1795, and as a town in 1830; Victoria 1843; Vancouver 1865. In outlying areas, rural settlement was so sparse as to have minimal impact on the landscape (Upper Canada's rural population numbered 14 000 in 1791, while the town of York—now Toronto—probably had fewer than a hundred residents), and was generally well beyond the reach of trade or communication with the urban centre. Around the towns, however, land clearance proceeded rapidly. As streets were paved and buildings roofed, more and more of the landscape became impervious to rainfall, so while streets were easily passable, street drainage created a new form of pollution—storm water runoff.

Arrangements for water supply and waste disposal were primitive in early settlements. Privies and cesspools served for the disposal of human wastes, and drinking water was simply hauled from the nearest creek. Most houses had cisterns—barrels or tanks to collect rainwater—to supply water for washing, and a few had wells. Wealthier citizens could pay carters to haul water to their homes, but home delivery carried no guarantee of quality: the source was still a local stream. By the 1830s, some larger towns had public wells, from which citizens could draw drinking water.

The cholera epidemics of the 1830s drew public attention to rotting garbage and sewage, which produced the foul air believed to cause cholera. Cities introduced daily garbage and sewage collection around this time, and built small drains in the dirtiest areas. Cholera epidemics returned in 1849 and 1854 and threatened again in 1866, by which time medical knowledge and technology were better equipped to combat the problem.

The middle of the century saw the advent of the railway in Canada and from the 1850s rail lines spread rapidly to major centres in the U.S. and Canada, linking water traffic (including that from the Erie Canal, opened in 1825) with upland routes. With the railway came improved communications and accelerated economic growth, and better access to rural areas north and west. Regina was founded as a railway town in 1882, and Vancouver's importance grew significantly when in 1884 it was established as the western terminus of the Canadian Pacific Railway.

The railway had two important impacts on the rate and pattern of settlement. First, railway access greatly increased the rate at which trees could be brought out of logging areas, transported to cities, and from there transshipped to the United States and elsewhere, thus accelerating the speed at which the watershed was stripped of trees. And the establishment of the railway network in turn encouraged the development of industrial centres for the efficient distribution of goods and services. These influences were central to the development of cities like Halifax, Montreal, Toronto, Winnipeg, Edmonton, and Vancouver as heavily populated, industrial centres, with significant local impacts on the land and water.

By the last quarter of the 19th century, most homes still lacked piped water supplies, but continued to draw water directly from streams or from private wells. As the population increased, so did the number of backyard privies and leaking cesspools, and thus the contamination of wells and water supplies throughout the town. In many cities it took a crisis with water supply for fire-fighting to spur the introduction of piped water. In 1874, the city of Toronto numbered 1375 homes with piped water; by 1877 there were more than 4100, and by 1883 more than 16 000.

By the early 20th century, many major cities had sophisticated piped water systems, some with filtration and reservoir storage. More sewers were built, and some cities began to develop sewage disposal plants to ensure that sewage would not come into contact with drinking water supplies. Even into the early part of this century, however, many homes, especially poorer ones, were still served only by backyard privies, and sewers did not exist in many areas.

Chlorination of drinking water and of treated sewage is now known to be one of the cheapest and most effective measures available to control bacterial contamination causing typhoid fever, cholera, and typhus. Yet although chlorination had been known since at least 1900 and was already in place in other cities around the world (London, England, was an early example), Canadian cities were slow to adopt this technology. Much of the impetus for better water and sewage treatment came through the activities of the International Joint Commission, an organization established under the 1909 *Boundary Waters Treaty* between the United States and Canada. Under this treaty, the two countries agreed to cooperate and share information in protecting the quality of their boundary waters, and particularly the Great Lakes. The first task of the commissioners (who are political appointees) was to conduct a survey of pollution in the boundary waters. This study, completed in 1912, revealed widespread pollution in the nearshore areas of the Great Lakes, much of it attributable to uncontrolled discharges from municipal sewers and industry. The commissioners concluded that drinking water drawn from these areas was unsafe for human consumption unless it was treated. The report recommended daily testing of drinking water for bacteriological contamination, treatment of all drinking water supplies, and universal treatment of sewage.

By the mid-1920s, activated sludge plants, which essentially duplicate and accelerate natural degradation processes by encouraging bacterial digestion of wastes, had replaced early sewage disposal facilities in many centres. Not surprisingly, construction of sewage and water works slowed considerably during the Depression years, when public funds were directed more to social services than improving municipal infrastructures.

World War II brought special challenges and opportunities for water management. Shortages of materials and labour for nonmilitary uses were obstacles for major capital projects. On the other hand, wartime demand for chemicals, foodstuffs, armaments, and other supplies created new opportunities for industry. Where once city drains had carried only human waste and water, now the effluvium of countless factories, processing plants, and other industries flowed into the sewers too. The sheer volume of these wastes was staggering: a 1946–49 study by the International Joint Commission showed that, in the Great Lakes overall, the oxygen demand (a measure of the decaying organic matter) of industrial wastes discharged into municipal sewers was equal to the oxygen demand of the untreated sanitary sewage from a population of four million.

In the rural areas, increasing mechanization of farming and the development of new synthetic pesticides and fertilizers had vastly increased farming efficiency and intensified once-diffuse impacts on the land and water. Disposal of human sewage had progressed from privies to septic systems in most areas, although privies can still be found today in many rural areas. As farms became larger and more efficient, management of livestock manures and milkhouse wash water grew steadily more troublesome. And as the Canadian population grew, the demand for farmland also increased: marginal lands on highly erodible slopes were cultivated, and wetlands were drained to create new cropland. Eroded cropland topsoil, and the pollutants attached to eroded soil particles, contributed to the degradation of water quality in lakes and streams. These "nonpoint" pollution sources are particularly difficult to control because they arise over large land areas managed by a variety of landowners.

Today, Canadian watercourses reflect more than two hundred years of European settlement: ongoing pollution from point and nonpoint sources, residual pollution in sediments and biological tissues arising from past practices, and complex interactions among air, water, sediment, and biota for the transportation and metamorphosis of chemical, physical, and biological pollutants. Despite the fact that people have been aware of the significance of water pollution for at least a century, our understanding of the fate and mechanisms of water pollutants, and our ability—or perhaps our will—to reduce our consumption of water remain weak.

POLLUTANTS AND WATER MANAGEMENT OPTIONS IN CANADA

As Canada enters the 21st century, we still boast a wealth of fresh water greater than that of almost any other nation. Eight percent of our territory is occupied by lakes and rivers. Some human activities—for instance, road paving and drainage—have altered natural cycles of infiltration and evaporation. Perhaps more significant, humans have altered the flow of rivers through diversions to serve drinking and irrigation needs, or to generate electricity through hydro power, or both. Some authors consider these diversions to be the most significant threats to Canadian water resources; others believe that sale of water to the U.S. is a beneficial process. There are now 54 major interbasin diversions of water in Canada, employing 613 dams. While most are small, some like the Chicago diversion, at an average annual water transfer rate of 90 cubic metres per second, divert more water away from Canada than flows through many domestic river systems.

More immediate for most Canadians are problems with water supply and water quality. In some centres, particularly those dependent on groundwater, supplies are dwindling rapidly. Communities like Kitchener–Waterloo, Ontario, have led the country in developing water conservation programs to curb demand and manage supplies wisely. Yet in many major urban centres like Toronto, located on the shore of Lake Ontario, the need for water conservation often receives less attention simply because of the apparent abundance close at hand.

Water quality can be affected by many factors, both natural and anthropogenic. Natural water supplies are often affected by the rock formations through which they flow. Typical of this are "hard water" communities like Guelph and Lindsay, Ontario, which are located in areas of limestone rock. Calcium carbonate in the rock is dissolved by the water, creating an alkaline pH (greater than 7) and water containing high levels of dissolved minerals. By contrast, water in the Canadian Shield tends to be more acidic, with less of the natural "buffering" supplied by limestone. Canadian Shield waters are generally considered "soft"—low in dissolved minerals—and, because of their slight acidity, less able to tolerate the effects of acid rain. Other materials in rock can also enter natural waters, including metals like copper and iron, and highly toxic materials like arsenic, uranium, and fluoride.

For most people, however, it is pollutants of human origin that are of most concern and also most controversial. The controversy in most cases arises because the scientific data about a chemical's movement through the ecosystem are contradictory or lacking. Frequently, research on chemical toxicity is conducted on nonhuman organisms such as rats or guinea pigs, or even on bacteria. It is not always easy to extrapolate these results to human impacts. Each type of organism has a unique enzyme system for the detoxification of poisons, and even closely related animals like rats and mice may respond very differently to the same toxin.

Pollutants resulting from human activities can be grouped into several major classifications. Some of these—for instance, nutrients—have been known for longer than others, and there is good consensus as to their sources, mechanisms, and impacts on the environment. Some pollutants, particularly the complex organic molecules used and produced by industry, have only recently been developed. As a result, we have very little information about their behaviour in the natural environment. Certain pollutants like radioisotopes (tritium and radium are two examples) have been known for decades, but their impacts on humans and other organisms are subtle and still poorly understood.

Nutrients are naturally occurring chemicals important for the growth of plants and animals. In the aquatic environment, excess quantities of phosphorus and nitrogen can lead to overabundant growth of algae and rooted aquatic plants. Large volumes of plant material generate considerable oxygen during daylight hours through photosynthesis. At night, however, these plants respire, using up large quantities of oxygen. A water body with excessive nutrient levels is likely to exhibit rich plant growth, including mats or "blooms" of algae visible on the surface of the water, and an exaggerated diurnal oxygen production/utilization curve. This condition is called "eutrophication" from the Greek for "good eating." There are several side effects of eutrophication. Many eutrophic systems exhibit severe oxygen depletion at night, creating conditions inhospitable for fish and other aquatic life, and even fish kills. Another secondary effect is the esthetic (both visual and odour) impact caused by large quantities of rotting vegetation. Eutrophication is considered to be well understood by the scientific community. Both phosphorus and nitrogen must be present for plant tissue to grow, but in freshwater systems usually phosphorus is scarcest, so phosphorus is considered to be the "limiting nutrient" in that when phosphorus supplies have been exhausted, plant growth will cease even in the presence of abundant nitrogen. The reverse appears to be true in many marine systems, where nitrogen is often considered the limiting nutrient.

A variety of water quality constituents provide insight into the *physical condition* and *appearance* of water. Among these are levels of suspended solids (particulate material), alkalinity and hardness, and conductivity (a measure of electrical conductance that reflects the presence of dissolved salts in the water). People have long been concerned about these materials because they can make water look unsightly. In fact, they are often relatively innocuous in terms of human and environmental health. High levels of suspended solids can clog fish gills and impair spawning habitat but do not generally create conditions unsafe for humans. Alkalinity and hardness are related parameters that are generally evaluated for their nuisance potential in pipe encrustation and cleaning difficulties.

Conductivity is sometimes a useful surrogate for the presence of other materials—for instance, in municipal and industrial effluents—but again conductivity levels are seldom of concern for human or environmental health.

Inorganic pollutants, particularly heavy metals, attracted increasing public concern through the 1970s and have remained high on the environmental agenda. Some loadings of metals arise naturally, from the contact of water with ore-bearing rock. In other cases, metals or metal compounds are added during manufacturing or water or wastewater treatment, and are carried through in the effluent to the point of discharge. Sewage treatment plants are designed to remove only nutrients, suspended solids, and oxgyen-demanding (decaying organic) matter. Heavy metals and organic chemicals may adhere to particles in the system but are not truly "treated" or removed in the process.

Nowadays, the vast majority of industries discharge their wastes to municipal sewer systems (about 12 000 in Ontario, compared with about 400 discharging directly to rivers or lakes). This industrial sewer use has emerged as a significant concern in water management, because of the poor capability of sewage treatment plants to remove those compounds. High levels of heavy metals in sewage treatment plant processes can kill off the bacteria necessary for good biological treatment of wastes, and can even pose hazards for plant workers. In many jurisdictions, metal-contaminated sludges from sewage treatment plant reactors cannot be used as agriculture fertilizer because of the risk to human health if metals found their way into food crops. Heavy metals exhibit a range of toxicity in humans and other organisms. Some, like mercury, are highly toxic and persistent in some forms. (Persistent substances are difficult for biological organisms to detoxify and excrete, so their concentrations build up in biological tissues. Larger organisms [such as eagles] must eat many smaller organisms [such as fish], so when the prey's tissues are contaminated with persistent toxins, the predator receives a concentrated dose of toxin, which it in turn cannot easily detoxify or excrete. With time, persistent substances accumulate in an individual, but also become "magnified" in the food chain, such that primary producers [e.g., algae, grasses] may exhibit concentrations not much different from ambient water or soil, but top carnivores may carry severely toxic body burdens of chemicals.)

Other metals, like iron, can create taste problems but are not generally considered a health hazard. A wide range of toxicity, persistence, and toxicological mechanism is present within the range of heavy metals found in water.

Similar concerns exist around *toxic organic chemicals,* many of which are also industrial in origin. Most industrial organics are large complex molecules not easily degraded in sewage treatment facilities. Tens of thousands of these chemicals are in use every year; hundreds of them have been found in fresh-water systems. These compounds may also contaminate sludges, cause worker and process hazards, and pass through the treatment process into the receiving environment. A number of chlorinated organic compounds such as benzene and chloroform are known human carcinogens (cancer-causing agents). A much larger number are suspected carcinogens; in these cases there may be some data

FIGURE 4.2
Mercury Levels in Commercial Fish Samples, Southern Indian Lake, Manitoba, 1971–85

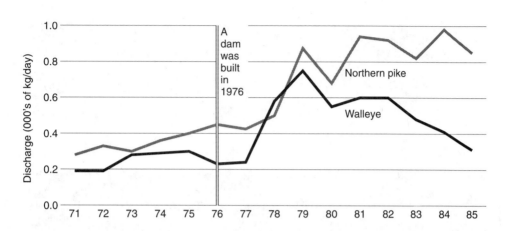

Source: Environment Canada and Manitoba Environment and Workplace Safety and Health, 1987.

from certain animal studies indicating increased cancer rates, but these data may be offset by other, contradictory data. For many chemicals, data on human toxicology are scarce or lacking altogether, so conclusions about "acceptable" levels must be drawn from animal studies and supporting data. Yet, like heavy metals, decisions need to be made about acceptable levels of human and environmental exposure to these compounds, and about acceptable levels of discharge from industries into sewer systems and receiving waters.

There remains considerable scientific and public debate on these issues. In 1994, the Canadian government issued a draft toxics management policy, stating the federal government's intent to manage toxic substances throughout their entire life cycle. A federal policy to address toxic substances certainly seems reasonable, but the draft policy was harshly criticized by nongovernment organizations such as the World Wildlife Fund as being excessively lax. Critics believe that the government's proposed criteria for persistence, bioaccumulative potential, and toxicity are unrestrictive compared with other current initiatives. (In other words, the policy appears to be structured so that only the most obviously toxic offenders, like DDT, PCB, and dioxins, would receive strict controls or phaseouts, while all others, including those of intermediate toxicity and persistence, could freely be used and discharged. Such an approach would allow the federal government to put a policy in place quickly and with little opposition from industry, but would likely provide few if any use restrictions beyond existing levels.)

FIGURE 4.3
The Movement of Toxic Substances in the Aquatic Environment

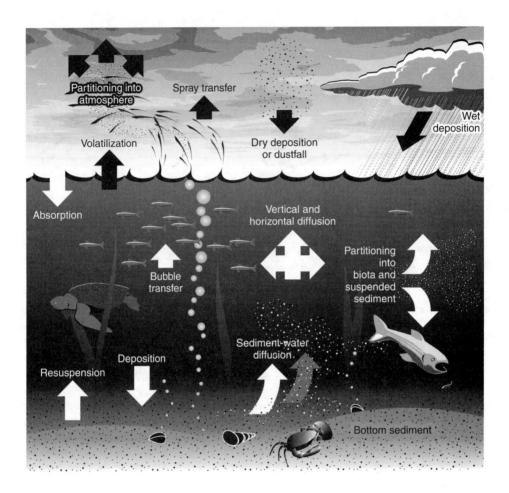

Partitioning into atmosphere

Spray transfer

Wet deposition

Volatilization

Dry deposition or dustfall

Absorption

Vertical and horizontal diffusion

Bubble transfer

Partitioning into biota and suspended sediment

Sediment-water diffusion

Resuspension

Deposition

Bottom sediment

Source: Adapted from Environment Canada, 1990.

A variety of other water pollutants are of interest in determining water quality. *Water temperature* can be a problem where an industry or electric power generating facility discharges hot effluent. Fish populations can be harmed if optimal temperature ranges are not maintained. *Radionuclides*, discussed above, have been identified as sources of concern, especially where uranium is mined or processed. Finally, microorganisms such as *bacteria* and *viruses* are often of concern because of their potential to cause disease. Traditionally, water has been evaluated for bacteriological contamination using a group of "indicator" organisms called fecal coliform bacteria. The fecal coliforms include a wide range of organisms of similar appearance; among them are true disease-causing organisms such as *Escherichia coli*, characteristic of human sewage. But this group also includes innocuous organisms and others, like *Klebsiella pneumoniae*, of uncertain importance. (*Klebsiella* is thought to cause pneumonia-like symptoms in certain industrial settings, but is not believed to cause diarrhea or similar infections as does *E. coli*.) It is now recognized that the presence of fecal coliform bacteria suggests, but does not guarantee, that human illness will result. In an effort to refine bacteriological standards, regulatory agencies are now turning to standards for particular pathogens, including *Pseudomonas aeruginosa*, a cause of human eye and ear infections, *E. coli*, and similar organisms.

In the early 1970s, Germany began to incorporate the notion of precaution or *Vorsorge* into its environmental policies. This principle emphasizes the need for extra care where understanding is incomplete. Some authors have restated this theme as "Better to be roughly right in due time rather than to be precisely right too late." Through the 1980s, this principle was widely adopted in other European countries and in North America, and is still under debate in forums such as the International Joint Commission, a Canada–U.S. body that oversees management of those countries' "boundary waters," including the Great Lakes. It has been particularly important in discussions of the significance of toxic chemical pollution and the need to ban or phase out ("sunset") highly toxic, persistent substances.

INCENTIVES AND CHALLENGES OF GLOBAL WATER MANAGEMENT

Pollution recognizes no boundaries. Canadian ecosystems are linked to the global biosphere through water, air, soil, and biotic pathways. The watershed is now internationally recognized as the preferred unit for water management. Indeed, many countries (notably England, France, Spain, Mexico, China, Argentina, and Venezuela) have adopted the watershed as the basis for regional water management institutions, and recognize the ecological integrity of the watershed unit under their legal systems (Mateo, 1992). In the Toronto waterfront, land use planning activities not originally intended to include an explicit water management component have been realigned to use the watershed as the natural land use planning boundary (Crombie, 1990). Clearly, management on a watershed, or subwatershed, basis will influence, if not direct, water management in the 21st century.

Where a watershed encompasses several municipalities, water management planning poses special problems. Which are the most important pollutant sources? Will differences in local expenditure create inequities in water pricing within a region? Who should be involved in watershed decision-making? In answering these questions, we can look for guidance to France and England, whose watershed management tradition dates back several decades. Even within Canada, the U.S., and Mexico we can find excellent models of watershed management under complex administrative regimes.

Yet where a watershed crosses international boundaries, planning and management challenges become difficult indeed. Now major differences may exist in legal tradition, in jurisdictional clarity, in water use, and in language. Many authors have documented these difficulties, for example Linnerooth (1990) on the Danube River Basin and Kiss (1985) on the Rhine. Although binational water management activities are not a new phenomenon in North America, the advent of the North American Free Trade Agreement (NAFTA) forces us to think in terms of trinational initiatives, with their special challenges and opportunities.

Several important barriers to cooperation exist. None is insurmountable, but awareness of them could certainly facilitate cooperation.

First, language is a fundamental barrier. Canada's two official languages, English and French, are apparent in all official publications and many local and regional ones. Both are taught in most schools from the primary level. By contrast, Spanish is spoken by a minority of Canadian citizens and is available only on a limited basis in the school system. In the U.S., English is the only official language, although Spanish is widely spoken and taught; in that culture, French is the minority language. In Mexico, Spanish dominates, although many professionals and government employees speak English, and English is widely available on television and in print media; French is a relative rarity. An obvious barrier is therefore universal translation of all official documents and other materials into all three official languages. Failure to attend to this seemingly trivial barrier could have significant implications for binational access to information, and thus for bi- or trinational cooperation.

The vast length of the Canada–U.S. border is in itself a barrier, although the binational commissions do provide a mechanism for resolving issues in border regions. This barrier is perhaps best overcome by collaboration on a watershed basis through regional offices of the regulatory agencies.

A further barrier to cooperation is the sensitivity of the federal governments to sharing damning environmental information—to hauling out their dirty environmental laundry in an international forum. These difficulties have always plagued the International Joint Commission and the International Boundary and Water Commission and may be difficult to overcome even with the assistance of the Montreal-based trinational Commission for Environmental Cooperation.

Incentives and disincentives for adequate water management may vary among the countries. This is likely to be particularly true in the case of economic instruments such as taxes, subsidies, and effluent charges, whose structure and impact may differ considerably among trade partners with different levels of economic development.

Finally, lack of political will for environmental reform and collaborative watershed management will remain the obstacle that it has been for over a hundred years. NAFTA appears to demand trinational, collaborative reconsideration of legislation, administration, and progress. Whether that reconsideration will proceed in any meaningful fashion remains an open question and one that may plague NAFTA into the next century.

CONFLICT IN WATER MANAGEMENT ISSUES

Water is often described as the lifeblood of an ecosystem, the pathway that links air to sediment and sediment to biota. Water is essential for human and ecological life. Yet in Canada, the perception of abundance has caused us to take this valuable asset for granted, using it carelessly, pricing it foolishly, polluting it without thought for ourselves or our descendants.

One of the most difficult challenges faced by water managers is therefore persuading individuals and organizations that water must be managed sustainably. In 1991, the (Ontario) MISA (Municipal–Industrial Strategy for Abatement) Advisory Committee observed:

> The traditional assumption of water [in Canada] is that there is always enough, it's always clean and it's always free. Today's reality is that there is not enough, it is not always clean, and it will never again be free.

The Great Lakes Basin is an interesting case in point. Millions of dollars are spent each year in capital and operating costs for water pollution control, but virtually no information exists on the quantity and value of the benefits. Nowhere is this problem more clearly illustrated than in the municipal sector. Some estimates place the current value of Great Lakes Basin (U.S. and Canadian sides) water and sewerage systems at more than $100 billion. Many historical infrastructure investments have been made in response to government-imposed discharge requirements, and much of the capital funding for these systems has come from senior government grants and subsidies. The water and sewerage systems in the Great Lakes Basin now rank among the most advanced in the world, but the benefits of these huge investments are not always clear.

Despite the mountains of data that have been collected by the various agencies over the past ten or fifteen years, very little historical information is available on basin-wide ecosystem conditions in the Great Lakes Basin. Available data comprise detailed information about localized problems and conditions, but efforts to integrate these isolated data bases into a regional framework are rare. Available data have been collected for various and differing purposes, and are difficult to compare across the basin.

Because the available data are fragmented and issue-based, and because people have become complacent about their "limitless" water resources, resolution of water conflicts is becoming increasingly difficult. Scientists disagree about the urgency of the problem, and about whether a problem even exists. Engineers may propose technological solutions without a full understanding of their social and economic implications.

Nickum and Easter (1990) propose a series of solutions for resolving conflict in water management; these may have particular value in developing better water institutions and negotiations in international forums such as NAFTA. Among their solutions are market-based allocation of water; tradeable permits; conflict resolution mechanisms in use disputes; government intervention to delineate rights and duties; collective action by users (perhaps an extension of existing professional/advocacy collaboration); and the establishment of water user organizations at national, regional, and local levels. Of special importance may be local water planning and management, subject to guidance at the federal and state level.

But while the rest of North America is just waking up to the responsibilities and opportunities implicit under NAFTA, public advocacy groups from all three signatory countries are well-advanced in trinational cooperation. Perhaps because these groups are less constrained by diplomatic and administrative protocols, they have rapidly established effective linkages for policy research and advocacy. These groups serve an essential purpose in decision-making. Unencumbered by political baggage, they are free to challenge existing regulatory and administrative structures and develop new agendas for consideration by government. It is important to remember that these groups often have excellent links to jurisdictions outside North America, including Europe and South America, and thus can bring an international perspective that is beyond the capability of most regulators. The importance of this external watchdog scrutiny cannot be overestimated in today's globalized society.

POLITICAL ISSUES IN CANADIAN WATER POLICY

Canada's Constitution was written in 1867 and reflects that era's emphasis on resource extraction and property rights. Under the Constitution, jurisdiction over water management is not clearly articulated, with the result that water management responsibility has historically been split between the federal and provincial governments. The provinces (with their municipalities) traditionally have had primary responsibility for water supply and pollution control through constitutional rights over their own natural resources. In recent years the federal government has taken an increasingly active role in regulation writing and enforcement, but this role may again be reduced under proposed "harmonization" and "regulatory efficiency" initiatives, begun in December 1994.

Canadian water laws have evolved over at least the last hundred years, primarily from public health legislation and related instruments dating from the last quarter of the 19th century. They reflect a paradigm typical of that era, but perhaps less appropriate for modern society, including assumptions that pollution is the inevitable consequence of development; that the environment can absorb some amount of every pollutant; and that it is the task of government to find that "acceptable" level of pollution and set standards at that level. In some jurisdictions, the discharge-permitting system reflects this attitude in granting lifetime discharge permits for each facility, provided that the facility is not expanded or its process changed.

Today, Canadian water policy is a labyrinth of statutes, regulations, policies, and guidelines, administered by dozens of agencies at four levels of government. This abundance of administrative mechanisms creates confusion about who should be writing what laws, and who should be enforcing the laws already enacted. Like many other jurisdictions worldwide, Canada and the provinces are under pressure to streamline this complex system and improve equity and consistency across the country. Under Canadian water law, there is no requirement to manage water resources on a watershed basis. Historically, cross-jurisdictional water management (for instance, mercury pollution in the Wabigoon River and management of binational channels in the Great Lakes System) has relied on federal–provincial or binational agreements. Although these have usually been adequate for the task at hand, they are necessarily short-lived and inconsistent from problem to problem. One of the most important implications of NAFTA for Canadian water policy is therefore that it forces a national consideration of binational and trinational responsibilities. No *ad hoc* working agreements will now be possible without examination of NAFTA rights and responsibilities; the result will likely be more consistency and better repeatability in cross-jurisdictional water management.

There are several key areas of debate in Canadian water resources management. These are discussed in the following paragraphs.

NAFTA AND CANADIAN WATER RESOURCES

The NAFTA provisions most of concern for Canadian water policy analysts relate to the designation of water as a tradeable "good" under the agreement. Although Canadian federal analysts have argued that water is not covered by NAFTA or the environmental side agreement, private analysts (e.g., Linton and Holm, 1993) conclude that the agreements cover "all natural water other than sea water" and not merely bottled water, as has sometimes been suggested. While certain items are specifically exempted, water is not among them: "ice, snow and potable water not containing sugar or sweetener" are considered tariff items in the agreement.

Authors such as Makuch and Sinclair (1993) note that the agreement does not bind the provinces and thus could not be used to enforce provincial environmental laws, which are currently the backbone of environmental protection in Canada. Furthermore, the definition of "environment" in the agreement excludes laws regarding natural resource management, so no enforcement of such laws is possible under NAFTA. Canadian policy analysts therefore fear that the agreement will encourage accelerated extraction of natural resources, including water.

Canadians' greatest fear is that NAFTA will facilitate major water diversions such as the GRAND Canal scheme, a northern diversion/hydroelectric project whose ultimate goal is to generate electricity for sale in the U.S. Accelerated extraction of groundwater for bottled water sale is another major concern. Conservative Canadian analysts, including those at the Fraser Institute in British Columbia, justify water exports to the U.S. on the grounds that the water will be used to irrigate vegetables grown for export back to Canada. Other authors are less optimistic that Canada will reap benefits proportional to the costs of such diversions. At present, there is consensus that major water diversions are an unlikely prospect, if only because of their high cost and complex environmental impacts. Yet it appears clear that if water were to be diverted from a river and reserved for the use of Canadians only, NAFTA would allow the United States to launch a trade challenge to obtain a proportional share of the resource.

MANAGEMENT OF TOXIC SUBSTANCES

Another key area of debate in Canadian water resources management is the need to reduce our use and disposal of persistent toxic substances. Several federal and provincial agencies have recently developed lists of candidate substances for special attention, even bans and phaseouts. The question of which substances are included in such lists depends very much on the criteria proposed for persistence, bioaccumulative potential, and toxicity, and these criteria may differ considerably from one jurisdiction to another.

Criteria for *persistence* often include separate criteria for water, air, soil, and sediment. Persistence is usually measured in half-life, raising the problem of how we account for transport away from a site (e.g., airborne toxics) versus actual chemical degradation, for instance by photolysis. Most programs use half-lives for water, soil, and sediment of 50–56 days. In other words, a compound would be considered "persistent" if 50–56 days after an initial measurement more than half of it remained in a sample.

A second major criterion is *bioaccumulative potential.* Here, the measurement of interest is often bioaccumulation factor (BAF) or bioconcentration factor (BCF), a measure of the tendency of a given substance to accumulate in biological tissue. An understanding of a compound's bioaccumulative potential is typically developed from a large body of experimental evidence relating to the concentration of the substance in the food chain. For instance, the concentration of a substance in fish tissue is compared with that of the substance in the surrounding water. The bioconcentration factor reflects the difference in the two measurements. Bioconcentration factors of 5000 (i.e., 5000 times more of the substance observed in biological tissue than in the surrounding ambient environment) are generally considered to be high, but a number of currently registered (i.e., controlled use) pesticides have BCFs on the order of 1500 to 3000. Ontario has recently developed a candidate substances list for bans and phaseouts that targets substances with BCFs as low as 500.

Finally, toxic substances are evaluated for their *toxicity,* or ability to harm the target organism. The Canadian Environmental Protection Act allows for the designation of substances that "may" cause toxic effects in the long term, but this wording tends to be interpreted more conservatively, as only substances that clearly are now, or may in the short term, cause toxic effects. Other definitions of toxicity use a scoring system to capture the 10–15 percent most "potent" substances that were acutely lethal (i.e., caused death), toxic on chronic exposure (caused long-term sublethal health effects), teratogenic (caused birth defects), or mutagenic (caused changes in genetic material). Other possible measures are liver (detoxification) enzyme induction or enzyme inhibition where no observable disease is present, specific measures such as increased liver weight, behavioural changes, and perceptual changes, endocrine system impairment or disruption, and immune system impairment.

Some authors recommend consideration of the presence, nature, and volume of sources; others believe that such an approach may eliminate some substances that may be of concern now or in the future. Finally, some authors recommend inclusion of substances that are highly toxic but not persistent or bioaccumulative; benzene is probably the most frequently cited example of this. (It is usually argued that more-or-less-continuous releases of benzene, as occur now, probably equate to environmental persistence. The argument against including them in toxics management programs has been that they can be controlled by emissions controls. Yet such controls are currently weak and show little sign of improvement.)

CONTROL OF NONPOINT SOURCE POLLUTION

Through the 1970s and 1980s, Canadian water managers made great advances in controlling pollution from point sources such as industrial discharges. One of the greatest triumphs here was the control of phosphorus discharges, through a combination of product reformulation (particularly detergents) and regulated controls on discharges from municipal and industrial sources. More recently, federal and provincial laws have sought to control discharges of other pollutants, such as biochemical oxygen demand, suspended solids, and inorganic and organic trace substances, from point sources.

It is now apparent that pollution from point sources is only a part—in some areas a small part—of the overall load of pollutants to the environment. In some areas, nonpoint source pollution from agriculture and from urban storm runoff is a highly significant contributor to local and regional environmental degradation. Nonpoint sources are much more difficult to control than point sources, however: they arise over large land areas owned by multiple owners, and their control (although often inexpensive) demands changes in land management practices and human behaviour rather than a simple (if expensive) technological solution.

A further problem with the control of nonpoint sources relates to the long-standing "hands-off" policy of regulators. Agriculture has been a cornerstone of North American economy from earliest times. The legislative framework supporting agriculture strongly reflects the pioneer emphasis on rapid land clearance and settlement, by overriding common law traditions relating to land transfer and resource extraction. An excellent example of this lies in so-called "right to farm" legislation, enacted in both the United States and Canada, which essentially removes the common law right to sue a farmer in nuisance for odour, dust, noise, or similar complaints. In municipalities, historical emphasis on development without explicit concern for the environment has often resulted in land use planning decisions that are good for development but create significant environmental impacts. A good example of this is the street drainage so important in developing urban centres in the early 19th century. Street paving and drainage made for more passable roads, but created a new (storm) sewage stream that has become increasingly polluted with gasoline, oil, particulates, and metals as our society has become more urbanized. And combined sewer systems for the conveyance of both sanitary and storm sewage are now too small for a growing population and must often be "bypassed" without treatment into rivers and lakes. Combined sewer overflow (CSO) discharges are now among the most heavily polluted, yet most difficult to resolve, sources of pollution in Canada's older cities.

The farming community and municipal developers share a concern about these nonpoint sources of pollution, but generally would prefer voluntary cleanup to regulated controls, because of the extent of the problem and the need for controls to be developed on a site-by-site basis. Implicit in this debate is a concern about costs, which may be small in absolute terms relative to major industrial improvements, but which may be onerous for a small farmer or a small municipality with a limited tax base.

HABITAT AND BIODIVERSITY

Traditionally, water managers have been concerned with water alone. Over the past decade, however, managers are realizing that water cannot be managed in isolation. Changes in water quality and flows have important implications for the populations and health of aquatic organisms, especially fish. Dam-building can control flooding and create sustainable power supplies, but will also inun-

FIGURE 4.4
Status of Remedial Action Plans Submitted to the IJC

Lake Superior
⌘ 1 Peninsula Harbour
⌘ 2 Jackfish Bay
⌘ 3 Nipigon Bay
⌘ 4 Thunder Bay
⌘ 5 St. Louis Bay/R.
⌘ 6 Torch Lake
⌘ 7 Deer Lake – Carp Creek/R.

Lake Erie
⌘ 21 Clinton River
⌘ 22 Rouge River
⌘ 23 River Raisin
⌘ 24 Maumee River
⌘ 25 Black River
⌘ 26 Cuyahoga River
⌘ 27 Ashtabula River
⌘ 28 Presque Isle Bay
29 Wheatley Harbour

Lake Ontario
⌘ 30 Buffalo River
31 Eighteen Mile Creek
⌘ 32 Rochester Embayment
◇ 33 Oswego River
⌘ 34 Bay of Quinte
⌘ 35 Port Hope
⌘ 36 Metro Toronto
⌘ 37 Hamilton Harbour

Connecting Channels
⌘ 38 St. Marys River
⌘ 39 St. Clair River
⌘ 40 Detroit River
⌘ 41 Niagara River – Ontario
⌘ 41 Niagara River – New York
⌘ 42 St. Lawrence R. – Cornwall
◇ 42 St. Lawrence R. – Massena

Lake Michigan
⌘ 8 Manistique River
⌘ 9 Menominee River
⌘ 10 Fox River/ Southern
Green Bay
⌘ 11 Sheboygan River
⌘ 12 Milwaukee Estuary
⌘ 13 Waukegan Harbour
◇ 14 Grand Calument River/
Indiana Harbor Canal
⌘ 15 Kalamazoo River
⌘ 16 Muskegon Lake
⌘ 17 White Lake

⌘ Stage 1
◇ Stage 2

This denotes the stage at which documents have been submitted to the IJC for review. This does not denote the extent of progress in an Area of Concern.

Lake Huron
⌘ 18 Saginaw River/Saginaw Bay
⌘ 19 Severn Sound
⌘ 20 Spanish River

date forest and farmland and change riverine habitat for aquatic organisms. And so on.

Increasingly, water resources managers must look to their colleagues in atmospheric science and terrestrial ecology to determine the "best" approach to managing a particular body of water. This demands a new way of working—

across disciplines, across agencies—that is both challenging and rewarding for those involved.

A good example of these new working relationships is to be found in the Remedial Action Plans (RAPs), a program of the binational International Joint Commission for environmental "hot spots" in the Great Lakes. The RAPs require not only professional collaboration across boundaries, but also extensive stakeholder involvement and sharing of results. Perhaps most important, the RAPs require political commitment from all participating jurisdictions, a commitment driven and reinforced by public concern. Another example is the Agroecosystem Profile recently funded by the Great Lakes Protection Fund. The profile is a binational project involving the Great Lakes Commission of Ann Arbor, Michigan; the World Wildlife Fund; Michigan universities; the University of Guelph, Ontario; and Agriculture Canada. The profile will develop a comprehensive data base of environmental conditions (soils, slopes, cropping and tillage practices, water quality and quantity, and environmentally sensitive areas such as wetlands), economic conditions at the local and regional level, applicable legislation and nonregulatory policies, and technical and financial support programs. The project culminated in an Agroecosystem Summit held in the spring of 1996, an opportunity for regulators, scientists, farmers, and agribusiness professionals to share ideas on how best to reduce the environmental impacts of agriculture.

THE ROLE OF THE PUBLIC

A final area of debate in Canadian water resources management relates to the role of the public in decision-making. Current advocacy discussions in Canada, the U.S., and Mexico emphasize an enhanced role for public participation (including information access) in decision-making, both at the local and regional levels. There is general support for harmonization of standards and environmental education across borders, tempered by respect for separate cultures and traditions. There is concern that financing for national and binational environmental projects should reflect the policies and programs of each country, while achieving overall goals of sustainability for the region. Here again, the RAPs are a model of meaningful public involvement in community decision-making.

INITIATIVES IN WATER SUPERVISION

Canada's legal and policy framework for water management has not developed in any systematic or even logical fashion; rather, it is the product of a hundred years of changing perspectives and social forces. The legal systems of the United States and Mexico, Canada's partners under NAFTA, have developed in different directions and may have lessons to teach us about other management approaches.

Under the Canadian Constitution, water resources, like fisheries, forestry, and mineral resources, are provincial responsibilities. The Canadian federal government can and does enact legislation controlling water pollution, but traditionally most water pollution control, flood control, and water supply issues have been dealt with at the provincial level. In the past ten years, the federal government has shown an increasing interest in environmental regulation and enforcement, and at the present time water management is controlled by more than two dozen agencies at four levels of government. In most provinces, there is increasing public scrutiny of water management, and environmental bills of rights such as recently enacted in Ontario (February 15, 1994) may lead to accelerated criticism of Canada's confused legal framework for water management.

In the United States, water management authority has been more clearly centralized at the federal level, with explicit delegation of administration and enforcement to the states. Nevertheless, the United States, like Canada, now has a wide range of water management legislation that complicates enforcement and confuses interpretation. Although some states, like Michigan, have taken steps in recent years to consolidate duplicative legislation, this is more the exception than the rule. Here again, public concern about wasteful and redundant administrative mechanisms may eventually force widespread reform of water management legislation.

Mexico has shown perhaps the greatest initiative in legislative housecleaning, although it too retains a complex body of legislation affecting the environment. The 1976 reforms to Article 27 of the Mexican Constitution set out specific measures governing land use and development, public works, and the division of powers over lands, waters, and forests. Mexican law dating from the early 1970s contains provisions for the protection of human health from environmental effects, and from about 1987, more detailed amendments have been authorized to preserve and restore ecological equilibrium and refine the division of powers among federal, state, and municipal governments. The culmination of these efforts was the General Law for the Ecological Equilibrium and Environmental Protection of 1988. The General Law sets out controls for the protection of natural areas, rational use of natural resources, environmental protection, and social participation. Like the United States, the General Law creates centralized federal regulation but allows for state (regional) and municipal regulation and administration.

All three countries are struggling to incorporate the concept of "sustainable development" into existing regulatory frameworks. Enforcing existing legislation remains a serious concern in all three, but may perhaps be most difficult in Mexico, where social conditions can drive environmental decisions. It is perhaps not surprising that the countries differ in their approach to regulating water quality and quantity: at least three different legal traditions, the Napoleonic Code, the (older, Roman) Justinian Code, and English Common Law underlie the development patterns and controls we now observe in North America. These differences in legal tradition, aside from discrepancies in standards and enforcement, may be the single largest barrier facing trinational legal reform in future.

It is not clear how Canadian water legislation will develop over the next quarter century. Some authors believe that a shift to local (watershed) management would improve management efficiency; others believe that the federal government will play an increasingly important role in the management of truly national, even international, issues like the control of toxic substances; both may occur.

COLLABORATION IN DECISION-MAKING: THE MOVE TO ENVIRONMENTAL IMPROVEMENT

As Canada's economy grows from a resource extraction base to a manufacturing/value-added base to, eventually, a knowledge/expertise base, the problems of and solutions for water management will also change. We are currently living with the heritage of a century or more of polluting activities, and we have not yet learned how to consume less water and to use that water wisely.

There is no question that water management in the future will require collaboration across disciplines, across agencies, and across jurisdictional boundaries. Although Canadians are justifiably nervous about the implications of NAFTA for water management, they are also enthusiastic about the opportunities the agreement will provide for binational and trinational collaboration. To date, binational initiatives have encountered obstacles of language, data compatibility, and political will; under NAFTA, stronger incentives exist to resolve these differences.

Another feature of water management in the future will be decision-making in a climate of scientific uncertainty and public debate. As the issues grow more complex, there is less agreement about what is clearly "right" and what is "wrong." Increasingly, we will see multi-stakeholder decision-making with government as one of many partners. This is a far cry from the paternalistic, behind-closed-doors approach taken by regulators ten or twenty years ago.

Finally, we will see a shift toward the use of technology to monitor and analyze environmental conditions, and even to track compliance with limits on a continuous basis. Although such mechanization needs fewer people to enforce regulations, it also would free workers for technology transfer and technical support. This shift from policing to teaching may signal the beginning of a new role for government in environmental management: a mutually beneficial partnership with industry, agriculture, and municipalities, targeted at continuous environmental improvement and innovative solutions.

REFERENCES

Crombie, David. 1990. *Watershed: Interim Report of the Royal Commission on the Future of the Toronto Waterfront*. Toronto: Queen's Printer.

Kiss, A. 1985. "The Protection of the Rhine against Pollution." *Natural Resources Journal* 25: 613–37.

Linnerooth, J. 1990. "The Danube River Basin: Negotiating Settlements to Transboundary Environmental Issues." *Natural Resources Journal* 30: 629–60.

Linton, J., and W. Holm. 1993. "NAFTA and Water Exports." *Canadian Environmental Law*. Special Report. Toronto: CELA.

Nickum, J.E., and K.W. Easter. 1990. "Institutional Arrangements for Managing Water Conflicts in Lake Basins." *Natural Resources Forum* 14(3): 210–20.

QUESTIONS FOR DISCUSSION

1. Think of a water management problem in your community or province. Discuss the following questions:

   (a) Why is the current situation a "problem"? What beneficial use of the water is impaired or prevented?

   (b) At what point would you consider the problem solved? In other words, what targets should be met to restore the impaired use? The targets you choose could be concentrations of contaminants, water level or flow targets, biological indicators (e.g., number or type of fish species), or similar measures.

   (c) Who is affected by the problem? Who bears the social, economic, cultural, and health costs of the problem? Who reaps the benefits of allowing the problem to continue unabated?

2. Protection of water resources is a personal responsibility for each of us. List five ways that an individual can reduce water use in and around the home. For each, estimate the total volume of water used before and after reductions. Discuss the benefits of and any likely obstacles to implementing these measures.

3. Various countries have adopted the watershed as the basic unit of water management. Discuss how this concept could be applied in managing water resources in your area.

4. How should water be allocated if there is not enough to serve the needs of everyone in a community? Discuss solutions with reference to arid climate countries around the world.

SUGGESTED READINGS

Crombie, D. 1990. *Watershed: Interim Report of the Royal Commission on the Future of the Toronto Waterfront.* Toronto: Queen's Printer.

De Loë, R. 1991. "The Institutional Pattern for Water Quality Management in Ontario." *Canadian Water Resources Journal* 16(1): 23–43.

Dworsky, L.B., J.A. Mauer, and A.E. Utton. 1993. "Managing North American Transboundary Water Resources." Part 2. *Natural Resources Journal* 33(2): 235–539.

Environment Canada. 1991. *The State of Canada's Environment.* Ottawa: Queen's Printer.

———. 1991. *Toxic Chemicals in the Great Lakes and Associated Effects.* Vol. I: *Contaminant Levels and Trends.* Ottawa: Queen's Printer.

———. 1991. *Toxic Chemicals in the Great Lakes and Associated Effects.* Vol. II: *Effects.* Ottawa: Queen's Printer.

Holm, W. 1988. *Water and Free Trade: The Mulroney Government's Agenda for Canada's Most Precious Resource.* Toronto: Lorimer.

Kennett, S.A. 1990. *Federalism and Sustainable Development: The Institutional Challenge in Canadian Resource Management. Alternatives* 17(3): 32–38.

Mateo, R.M. 1992. "Administration of Water Resources: Institutional Aspects and Management Modalities." *Natural Resources Forum* 16(2): 117–24.

Pearse, P.H., F. Bertrand, and J.W. MacLaren. 1985. *Currents of Change: Final Report of the Inquiry on Federal Water Policy.* Ottawa: Queen's Printer.

Smith, W. 1989. "Sustainable Use for Water in the 21st Century." *Ambio* 18(5): 294–95.

CHAPTER 5

Arctic Contaminants and the Environment

Nancy C. Doubleday

Department of Geography
Carleton University

FIGURE 5.1
North American Places Referred to in Chapter 5

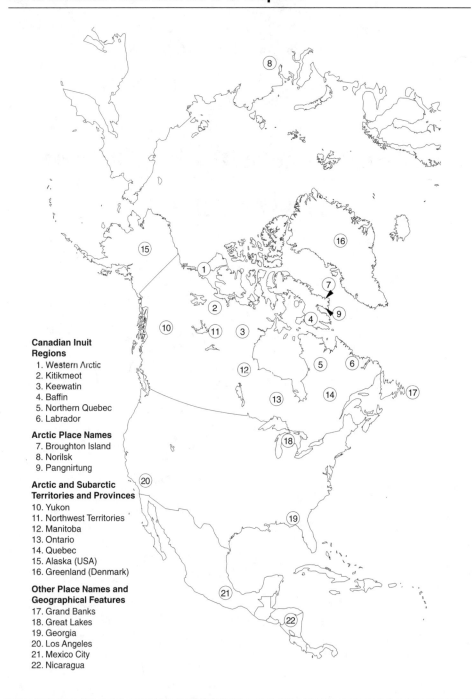

Canadian Inuit Regions
1. Western Arctic
2. Kitikmeot
3. Keewatin
4. Baffin
5. Northern Quebec
6. Labrador

Arctic Place Names
7. Broughton Island
8. Norilsk
9. Pangnirtung

Arctic and Subarctic Territories and Provinces
10. Yukon
11. Northwest Territories
12. Manitoba
13. Ontario
14. Quebec
15. Alaska (USA)
16. Greenland (Denmark)

Other Place Names and Geographical Features
17. Grand Banks
18. Great Lakes
19. Georgia
20. Los Angeles
21. Mexico City
22. Nicaragua

THE ECOLOGICAL HEALTH OF THE ARCTIC

The ecological health of the Arctic ecosystem and the safety of the traditional diet eaten by northern peoples have been called into question by recent scientific findings that the Arctic is being exposed to toxic chemical contaminants. Long-range transport of anthropogenic pollutants from industrial and agricultural regions outside the Arctic has been documented by scientists working in the Canadian Arctic. Significant national and international programs are under way to determine the nature and extent of the environmental and social impacts of these contaminants in Arctic Canada and throughout the circumpolar region. The threat of environmental damage due to pollution generated in other areas further stresses northern peoples, whose lives and societies are already undergoing dramatic changes, including legal settlement of land claims, greater exposure to resource development, and increasing self-government. Uncertainties about the safety of traditional foods, and intense media interest combined with cross-cultural communication issues, have the potential to undermine essential values of the hunting cultures of northern peoples in Canada. The implications for Inuit and for other northern peoples are very serious: the traditional sources of health and strength, the living resources of the Arctic are now also sources of toxic contaminants and concern. For Canadians elsewhere, there are other implications: the industrial world has touched the Arctic and no truly pristine places remain.

EMISSIONS, CONTAMINANTS, AND ARCTIC LIFESTYLES

Two primary types of contamination source affect the Arctic: emissions and effluents from local developments, known as "point" sources; and airborne contaminants deposited far from their origins. Both types are present in the Arctic. But it is not simply the presence of these contaminants that determines that this is an environmental issue. The concern for contaminants in the Arctic is a function of the possible effects of these contaminants on the Arctic ecosystem and on the peoples who live there. In particular, indigenous peoples, such as the Inuit, Dene, and Metis, are vulnerable to the impacts of toxic contaminants as a consequence of their way of life and their direct dependency on wildlife. This section provides a brief introduction to the recent history of development (and hence creation of potential point sources), as well as an overview of Arctic lifestyles, to set the context of the Arctic contaminants issue.

For thousands of years, the circumpolar Arctic Region has functioned as a viable ecosystem that, while subject to extremes of light and dark, cold and warmth, has maintained biological productivity, sustained indigenous peoples, and provided the basis for unique cultures. The Arctic has attracted the attention of Europeans, Americans, Scandinavians, Russians, and many other peoples primarily for the wealth of its natural resources, such as furbearing animals, whales, and other marine mammals, and for mineral, oil, and gas deposits. While the circumpolar states—which include Canada, United States, Russia, Finland, Sweden, Norway, Denmark–Greenland, and Iceland—do not agree totally on the extent and nature of states' jurisdiction in the Arctic, there is general agreement that the Arctic Ocean is an international regional sea. As a consequence of the enhanced ice-breaking capabilities of ships, there has been increasing interest in the Northwest Passage, which separates the Canadian Arctic Archipelago from the mainland, as a potential transportation route between Europe and Asia. At present, supply ships service Inuit communities in the Arctic as well as a few commercial enterprises, such as the Nanisivik mine near Arctic Bay, Northwest Territories. During World War II, military strategists became aware of the strategic value of the Arctic, and military bases were established there. In the Cold War era after World War II, militarization of the Arctic intensified as military planners realized that with the advent of long-range warheads, the shortest distance between Moscow and Washington was over the North Pole. One of the tangible symbols of this intensification of military interest in the Arctic was the creation of the Distant Early Warning Line, more commonly referred to as the "DEW Line," which consisted of a string of bases built across Canada by the United States military at 55° North latitude. With the end of the Cold War, environmental issues have come to the fore in the Arctic; in some cases, such as the disposal of nuclear waste in the Arctic Ocean, information has become available as a direct result of the demilitarization of the region and reduction in national security interests in suppressing information about military activity. Environmental concerns have also been expressed about oil and gas exploration and development, particularly by indigenous peoples who depend upon the living resources of the land and sea. All of these developments have given rise to a general sense of unease as well as specific concerns about environmental impacts.

In the mid-1970s concerns about northern development and the rights of aboriginal peoples of the North led to the creation of the Royal Commission on the Mackenzie Valley Pipeline and to hearings in the North, chaired by Justice Thomas Berger. The hearings were to make northern environmental and aboriginal issues highly visible to Canadians in the south for the first time. The report of the "Berger Commission," as it came to be known, resulted in a moratorium on pipeline construction while extensive research was conducted on the environmental and social impacts of oil and gas exploration and development in general, and pipeline construction in particular. The report can also be credited with educating residents of Southern Canada about aboriginal rights to lands and resources, and in a sense creating a positive climate for the negotiations of Arctic land claims. These events also gave northern peoples confidence in the legitimacy of both their concerns and their rights.

In the past 25 years, attention has been paid sporadically by both scientists and the media to the issue of contamination of the Arctic. In the mid-1970s, awareness of acid rain and its potentially devastating effects in temperate latitudes fuelled public support for study of long-range transport of airborne pollutants like sulphur dioxide. Gradually the connection between atmospheric pollution and ecological effects on aquatic ecosystems, fish reproduction, and temperate forests was understood in scientific terms. With this understanding came various policy and legal initiatives.

One of the research programs associated with these acid rain investigations was the Long Range Transport of Atmospheric Pollutants program conducted in the mid-1970s, which documented the relationship between anthropogenic activity, acid rain, and the phenomenon of arctic haze, first observed in the late 1940s. This discovery was the first indication that the Arctic might not be as pristine as previously believed. Subsequently these early suspicions were confirmed when scientists began to find traces of DDT (dichlorodiphenyl dichloroethylene), and its metabolite DDE, in the fatty tissues of birds and mammals in the Arctic. Initially local sources were suspected. The abandonment of the DEW Line stations, sometimes in a spectacularly destructive manner, raised concerns about these sites as potential point sources for various contaminants, including polychlorinated biphenyls (PCBs). However, no clear single-sources were identified that could account for the patchy distribution of toxic contaminants in the Arctic environment.

In 1985, a report by Wong et al. documented in detail the studies of organic compounds in the Arctic food chain, and questions were raised about the future of Arctic wildlife and, ultimately, about the impacts of contaminants in the Arctic on the indigenous peoples: the Inuit, Indians, and Metis. Subsequently an informal research collaboration among government scientists led to expressions of concern and intensified research. While questions were asked in scientific circles in the mid-1980s, it was not until 1988 when the media made front-page news out of the threat of anthropogenic contaminants to the Arctic, to the wildlife, and to the Inuit, that Arctic contaminants acquired a human face and became an issue of public concern. Science played a significant role, both in the articulation of the problem and in the search for policies to promote action.

THE COMPLEXITIES OF CONTAMINANTS

There are many fields of knowledge involved in coming to an understanding of the Arctic contaminants issue: sources of contaminants; atmospheric transport

---

and deposition mechanisms; uptake by marine, freshwater, and terrestrial ecosystems; metabolism of contaminants by organisms; impacts of contaminants on the health of organisms, including people; the chemistry and physics of biologically active compounds; and the social and cultural understanding needed to move between societies with different languages, values, and concepts.

To begin with a consideration of the contaminants themselves, it is important to recognize that we are dealing only with those resulting from human activity—that is, anthropogenic contaminants—in this chapter. There are many classes of anthropogenic contaminants, including organic contaminants such as PCBs, dioxins, furans, and bornenes, to name a few. Heavy metals like lead, mercury, and cadmium are found in the Arctic ecosystem and occur naturally in the environment. In the Arctic Bay area of North Baffin, for example, narwhal are found to have high concentrations of cadmium in their livers (118 ppm, Wong, 1985). The Nanisivik mine produces lead and zinc, which is associated with cadmium. While the release of heavy metals into the environment can be accelerated by human activities like mining, the cadmium found in the narwhal is most likely due to the naturally occurring cadmium in the environment. Blood tests for cadmium in the human population of Arctic Bay revealed normal levels, but tests for lead showed high levels. Subsequent investigation revealed that those with elevated lead levels were working on engines fuelled with leaded gasoline in inadequately ventilated quarters, and that the higher lead levels resulted from this exposure. This example illustrates the difficulties inherent in interpreting heavy metal exposures and differentiating between exposures due to anthropogenic activity and geological factors.

Man-made organochlorine compounds like DDT and DDE, which were linked to eggshell thinning and reproductive failure in birds and documented by Rachel Carson in *Silent Spring*, are found in birds in the Arctic. This is not really surprising, considering that almost all Arctic birds are migrants that move along the North American flyways every year, collecting contaminants as they travel, and on their wintering grounds in the southern United States, Mexico, and Central and South America. When these and other compounds are found in polar bears, however, there are no simple explanations for the observed exposure levels. Other classes of organic compounds, including furans, dioxins, HCHs (hexachlorocyclohexane), polycyclic aromatic hydrocarbons, toxaphene, and other bornenes and camphenes, are found throughout the food web in birds, mammals, fish, and a host of other organisms.

For example, PCBs were widely used in the 1970s as fillers for capacitors and other electrical components because of their insulating properties. It was believed that these substances were safe and inert. We now know that PCBs are reactive, and are metabolized in living organisms to produce other reactive metabolites. They are lipophilic, which means that they are attracted to fatty tissues, and because they are bound to fat which is largely retained and not excreted from the body, PCBs bioaccumulate. They are not removed from the food chain or food web and bioconcentration is occurring as these substances move from trophic level to trophic level through the food chain. We know that there are potential impacts on health of humans and wildlife, and there are strong suspicions that the presence of these organic compounds in mammals may harm reproductive functions.

Clearly these organochlorines have special reactive properties that make them problematic for living organisms inadvertently exposed, which is not surprising considering that many of these chemicals are deliberately used for pesticides, piscicides, and the like. The affinity of these compounds for lipids means that they bioaccumulate in the food chain. The relationship of organisms to one another in the food chain, coupled with bioaccumulation, leads to bioconcentration, with the highest levels being found in those organisms at the top of the Arctic food chains: the top predators, which in the Arctic are polar bears and humans. But this could happen, and does happen, in other environments as well.

It appears, given our experience with DDT and PCBs, that the rate of growth of the chemical production industry has exceeded the rate of growth of knowledge about the biological effects and environmental consequences of the use of man-made chemicals. As a result, society is in the position of having to learn to understand the impacts of the release of toxic chemicals into the environment after the fact. It also means that there are still many unknowns about Arctic contaminants.

THE ARCTIC SINK

While some contaminants may enter the Arctic environment from local point sources such as abandoned DEW Line sites in Arctic Canada, or smelters at Norilsk in Arctic Russia, the widespread distribution argues for atmospheric transport on a regional, if not global basis, as the most significant delivery mechanism. Essentially, the Arctic is described as a "sink" for airborne contaminants. Biological growth rates are slow due to cold conditions and the lack of light in the winter, implying that the breakdown of these compounds through processes mediated by organisms will also be slower than similar processes of degradation in temperate environments. Once transported to the Arctic, then, these compounds are likely to accumulate and to persist.

A recent paper by Wania and Mackay (1993) proposes a mechanism, based on earlier investigations of pesticides, to account for the accumulation of organochlorine compounds in polar regions, which has been described as "global distillation" by Goldberg (quoted in Wania and Mackay).

In essence this hypothesis flows from the observation that the lighter organochlorine compounds are present in the polar regions at unexpectedly high concentrations, coupled with the knowledge that specific chemical and physical properties of these compounds cause them to condense out of the warmer air masses when they pass over cooler surfaces, with lighter compounds travelling farther before becoming cold enough to condense out. Specific compounds condense out at particular temperatures, and can be revolatized when warmer air arrives to facilitate transport, subsequently condensing on colder surfaces again. This process has been referred to as the "grasshopper effect." When seen within the framework of a global distillation model, this fractionation produces a net northward transfer of lighter-weight organic compounds from southern regions, where these chemicals are produced and used, to colder northern regions, where they are deposited, and offers one explanation for the observation that the Arctic is a "sink" for contaminants. The implications of this are very serious: the Arctic is uniquely attractive to many of the lighter organochlorine compounds because of its temperature regime; therefore continuing and increasing contamination is inevitable as long as these compounds are present in the environment.

The implication of these distribution mechanisms is that the "source" of this problem of Arctic contaminants is in fact many sources, of different types, in different locations. Emissions of toxic contaminants, whether used deliberately as pesticides or emitted inadvertently as smokestack effluents, at any point within the Northern Hemisphere, have the potential to contribute over time to the contaminant burden of the Arctic ecosystem. Clearly, this represents a highly complex challenge for analysis and finding remedies.

The net movement of anthropogenic organics is not simply from south to north. Prevailing winds also play a role in transport of particulate and aerosol materials including contaminants, further complicating the identification of sources. For example, traces of Gobi Desert dust have been found in snow in the Keewatin Region of the Northwest Territories, the central region of the Canadian Arctic, reported by Welch et al. (1991). Meteorology then becomes another essential scientific element of the Arctic contaminant story, introducing an additional source of variability between source and sink.

Understanding how the chemicals move through the ecosystem after being deposited in the Arctic is not a simple matter, even though food chains there are relatively short, because many critical biological links are unknown. This is particularly true in aquatic and marine environments, but the terrestrial environment also has its mysteries. The ecological effects of contaminants in the Arctic are still being diagnosed, but there are concerns about long-term effects on reproduction in polar bears. Exposure levels in Inuit and other aboriginal peoples are also under investigation.

The human health science related to this issue is particularly difficult to use as a basis for medical advice. Clearly the major pathway of exposure is the diet, and equally clearly contaminants are not healthy food supplements. However, aboriginal diets based on traditional or "country" foods obtained by hunting are beginning to be appreciated for their intrinsic health benefits: they are low in saturated fats, high in unsaturated fats, high in vitamins and minerals, and are deeply rooted in cultural and social traditions related to hunting, sharing, and processing that serve important functions within the society in addition to providing for nutritional needs. Moreover, the people are adapted to the diet, and the diet is adapted to environmental conditions. When the factor of the cost of substituting store-bought food for traditional food is introduced, the significance of traditional food is emphasized even more.

In summary, the answer to the question of what makes the Arctic uniquely vulnerable to contaminants is a complex mix of geography, meteorology, ecology, and culture—the same mix that makes the Arctic distinct from many other regions of Canada and, indeed, the world.

TRAVELLING CONTAMINANTS: IMPLICATIONS FOR CANADA

The regions in Canada affected by the issue of Arctic contaminants can be divided into regions of deposition within the Arctic and regions of production, which are generally outside. However, there is a larger national interest, given our commitment to national standards for levels of exposure to toxic contaminants, and that is, the international dimensions of the issue.

On a regional scale, the area within Canada most obviously directly affected by the long-range transport of contaminants into the Arctic is the Arctic itself. There are two territories and four provinces with Arctic or sub-Arctic regions: the Yukon, Northwest Territories, Manitoba, Ontario, Quebec, and Newfoundland–Labrador. Concerns about ecosystem and food chain contamination have been raised at some time in all these regions.

But the Arctic is not the only region with an interest in this issue. Studies have also implicated long-range transport in the accumulation of toxic chemicals in the Great Lakes, which may in turn carry contaminants to the oceans or release them to further atmospheric transport northward. But what of the source regions? Clearly emissions from the south are finding their way northward, and the Arctic is serving as a waste receptacle for contaminants from economic development in other regions. Within a national political economic sphere this is inequitable. However, when the transport mechanisms are considered, and an international view of sources is taken, it is also clear that Southern Canada is itself a way station and recipient of airborne toxic wastes generated in other regions. Some researchers have pointed out, for example, that banning toxaphene in the U.S. has resulted in relocation of the sole American production plant to Nicaragua, which has in turn become a new epicentre of toxaphene use and emissions, which will slowly make their way northward across southern Canada to the Arctic (Bidleman, 1993).

In the short term, there is uncertainty and fear. Demands for action have resulted from the identification of the issue. However, beyond the obvious concerns raised for the direct and immediate impacts of contaminants on ecosystems, and possible implications for the health of Canadians as a result, there are other consequences. In the Arctic, economic losses have been sustained because of the fear of contamination. For example, during the height of the uncertainty about the results of research on contaminants and human health at Broughton Island, in the Baffin Region of the Northwest Territories, hunters and trappers elsewhere in the N.W.T. lost markets for Arctic char. Media reports had caused the export markets to reject the char from fear of contaminants. This is not an uncommon occurrence. In the Shetland Islands, for example, the uncertainties generated by media reports following the Braer oil spill resulted in closure of markets for Shetland seafood, notwithstanding the fact that Shetland fishermen themselves closed the affected areas to fishing and independent quality control monitoring confirmed that the fish taken elsewhere off Shetland were unaffected (Goodlad, 1995).

While by the definition of the problem it may appear that the Arctic contaminants are primarily an "Arctic" issue, it has implications for the rest of Canada as well. Clearly some of the contaminants entering the Arctic ecosystem are travelling across Canada from south to north, if the cold condensation hypothesis is correct. This implies that other Canadian ecosystems may be exposed to these contaminants during transport.

TRAVELLING CONTAMINANTS: GLOBAL IMPLICATIONS

Given that the sources of the contaminants found in the Arctic ecosystem are located in many cases well beyond any recognized Arctic boundaries, Arctic contaminants can be considered to be a global environmental issue, as well as one having regional and national implications.

In the Arctic marine environment, the nature and role of ocean currents is just beginning to be understood. It has been suggested (Shaw, 1994) that the view of the Arctic as a "sink" of final disposal may be incomplete, and that the three major ocean currents flowing out of the Arctic Ocean may provide a route out of the Arctic. These three currents have the potential to influence major international fisheries off Alaska and British Columbia, in the North Sea, and on the Grand Banks in the west Atlantic. One can foresee the implications for international fisheries of the possible contamination of these currents. Two of these three regions are of direct interest to Canadians.

Many of these contaminants are biologically active, and have been implicated in intergenerational effects. Currently there is a major debate as to the implications of chemicals that, although not directly responsible for toxicological effects, may disrupt the endocrine systems of vertebrates and may lead to hormonal effects including loss of fertility in some species (*Science*, 1995).

THE TRADITIONAL DIET AND ARCTIC CONTAMINANTS

During the early period, 1987 and 1988, the issue remained primarily within the domain of science, and consequently was managed without public scrutiny. When the national media picked up the story in late 1988, however, the issue of Arctic contaminants was portrayed as the latest environmental threat story and produced strong public interest. This interest was generated by two dominant concerns: one for northern peoples and environments, much in the tenor of support for the Berger inquiry in the mid-1970s; the other for the death of the myth of the pristine Arctic. As some environmentalists observed, these findings meant that there was now nowhere to escape the ravages of industrial civilization. However, for Arctic indigenous peoples who view the Arctic as home, there never has been.

The very nature of airborne toxic contaminants leads to a sense of vulnerability and helplessness. The challenges to the safety of the wildlife-based food supply undermine the foundations of indigenous culture and identity in the Arctic.

In 1985, a study by Wong noted that "estimates of per capita food production for the Keewatin, Baffin Island and Kitikmeot Regions range from 108 kg (Apex, Baffin Island) to 597 kg (Pangnirtung, Baffin Island) with a mean of 267 kg for the three regions" (p. 3.1). A recent study by Wein and Freeman (1995) of use of traditional or "country" foods among First Nations or Indian peoples in four communities found that "on average, Yukon Indian households used traditional foods over 400 times annually," that is, more than once a day (p. 161). Moose, caribou, and salmon in particular are extremely important in the diet of Yukon Indians. Among Inuit, studies have shown high levels of dependency on country foods as well. Clearly indigenous peoples in the Arctic remain dependent on country food for subsistence, and that dependency cannot be easily changed. Food preferences increase contaminant exposure for Inuit, Indians, and Métis. Substitution of imported "southern" foods would lead to reduction of nutritional benefits, as well as increased cash costs to the indigenous peoples concerned. Given the cash-poor status of communities, substitution of foods that must be bought is likely to lead to increased indebtedness and capital transfers from the underdeveloped North to southern-based corporations. Nor is there any guarantee that such substitutions would be universally accepted in the North.

Further, the values attached to harvesting of country food are complex and extend beyond the need to satisfy hunger. These values are not historical artifacts, as reported by Condon, Collings, and Wenzel (1995), who acknowledge "the economic value of subsistence harvesting and the foods that result from it" but who "emphasize the less easily quantified dimensions of subsistence ideology and its impact upon physical health, psychological well-being, and community integration" (p. 31).

The concerns about safety of the food supply are not unique to the Arctic. Indeed, Health Canada regularly conducts "market basket" studies across Canada to determine, among other things, whether the levels of contaminants contained are within "acceptable levels" or not. One of the differences in the case of the Arctic is that the regular monitoring of country food for contaminants is relatively new. In general, there are no federal inspectors checking caribou carcasses in the same way that meat packing plants in the south are inspected. The social issues of the dependency of culture on traditional diets and ways of life are central issues for indigenous peoples and for responsible government agencies aware of the threat posed by contaminants. The issue is not just the possibility of future health consequences at the level of the individual. Given the interconnections between health of the ecosystem and the health and well-being of communities deeply dependent on wildlife, the threat is no less than a threat to their way of life and to their identity as indigenous peoples.

Environmental organizations and those with an interest in northern issues, such as Ecology North and the Canadian Arctic Resources Committee, have also taken an interest in Arctic contaminants. Within Canada, in general, environmental organizations have not played a significant role to date in the issue of Arctic contaminants. The reasons for this appear to be primarily that indigenous peoples have had the capacity to represent their own interests, that there are significant differences between indigenous peoples and environmentalists as a consequence of the anti-harvesting movement, and that southern-based environmentalists are perceived to lack credibility in Arctic issues.

The impacts on indigenous and other Arctic peoples include economic disbenefits. For example, before the media focus on Arctic contaminants in 1987, some hunters and trappers associations in Baffin had small quotas for commercial sale of Arctic char. Following news reports of contaminants in the diets of Inuit in Broughton Island in Baffin, the Hunters and Trappers Association was unable to sell its char. While in absolute terms, the amount of income lost to the community was small (about $5000) relatively speaking, it was important. It must be remembered that in 1983, the community of 400 people in Broughton Island went from a community income of over $140 000 to less than $25 000, with many people forced on to social security, as a result of the anti-sealing protest and the ban on sealskins by the European Community. Against this background, the economic impacts, both immediate and actual, and long-term and potential, loom much larger.

The economic implications of findings of widespread contamination in the Arctic for fisheries and tourism, both touted as sources of new economic development, are readily understood.

POLICIES FOR CONTAINMENT MANAGEMENT

In the context of long-range transport of atmospheric pollutants, there are two fundamental classes of interests: those associated with the emission of these pollutants into the atmosphere; and those associated with deposition of contaminants from the atmosphere. In the case of the Arctic, science has demonstrated that much of the contamination found there has originated beyond the Arctic, and that which has an Arctic origin in general comes from outside Canada. There are Canadian sources for some contaminants as well, but primarily in terms of local contamination rather than long-range transport. This leads to two different arenas of political activity, one domestic and the other international.

DOMESTIC

Within Canada, the issue of Arctic contaminants involves governments, both federal and territorial, industry, indigenous peoples' organizations (IPOs), and nongovernmental environmental organizations. Scientists working in the various sectors have played significant roles, as have policy analysts. The formal framework for discussion has been provided by the Arctic Environmental Strategy of the Green Plan.

While government has generally dominated the discussion, the clearest and most persistent voices have been those of the people most at risk: the indigenous peoples. Inuit, Indian, and Metis representatives have been drawing attention to this issue for many years, realizing that public concern was essential to any political action. The federal government, together with the governments of the Yukon and the Northwest Territories, have supported multidisciplinary research programs to assess contaminant risks to northerners and to the Arctic ecosystem.

The indigenous peoples' organizations involved include the Inuit Circumpolar Conference, the Inuit Tapirisat of Canada, the Dene Nation, the Metis National Council, and the Council of Yukon Indians, whose First Nations members have subsequently played an important role in the Yukon Contaminants Committee.

Canadian governmental interests have been unified under the leadership of the Department of Indian and Northern Affairs, which has the legal responsibility for land management north of $60°$. Other federal departments involved include Environment Canada, Natural Resources, and Health Canada (formerly Health and Welfare). Canada's Green Plan was driven in part by the Arctic contaminants issue, and most of the funding allocated has been within the Green Plan budget process.

INTERNATIONAL

Given that the scientific understanding that the Arctic contaminants issue is most importantly a problem of long-range transport of atmospheric pollutants across jurisdictional boundaries, and that the Arctic is a region of interest to many nations, an international response is essential to any attempt to address causes and promote solutions. The Government of Finland, the Government of Canada, the Legislative Assembly of the Northwest Territories, and the indigenous peoples' organizations, particularly the Inuit Circumpolar Conference (ICC), strongly advocated the creation of an international forum through which Arctic contaminants and other international environmental concerns in the circumpolar region could be addressed.

International scientific cooperation in tandem with political action led to the signing of the Declaration of Rovaniemi and adoption of the Arctic Environmental Protection Strategy (AEPS) by representatives from the eight Arctic states: Russia, Finland, Sweden, Denmark, Norway, Greenland, Iceland, and Canada. Under the Arctic Monitoring and Assessment Program (AMAP) of the AEPS, these Arctic states are committed to conducting an Assessment of the State of the Arctic Environment, which will be presented to the ministers of the states concerned. (These activities will be considered further below.)

In identifying the interests involved, it is important to recognize that at the point at which these toxic contaminants are released into the environment, they are either released as wastes or unwanted industrial by-products; or deliberately manufactured and applied to the environment, as in the case of pesticides, for their toxicity value. From these circumstances, a number of interests can be determined. In the case of chemicals that are deliberately produced and applied, the interests involved include chemical producers and marketers, agricultural producers, pest control companies, lawn care companies, and individual consumers. In the case of chemicals incidentally released, the interests are much more diverse and include mining, smelting, steel production, manufacturing, pulp and paper processing, oil and gas production, chemical production, and virtually all industrial activities. Incidental emissions are also produced by individual consumers. One has only to think of the smog problems associated with automobiles in major urban centres, such as Los Angeles or Mexico City, to appreciate that relatively small emissions can result in large problems. In short, the interests of industrial society as a whole are also interests of the Arctic contaminants issue, because industrial society is in fact the ultimate source. The problem is further compounded by the fact that this is a transboundary issue, involving source areas and affected areas. Contaminants are being detected in wildlife in Arctic Canada, but not all of the chemicals originate in Canada. Convincing evidence of Eurasian and Russian sources has been presented, but the more important message is not that we are victims of the practices of others, but rather, to paraphrase Barry Commoner, "Everything *really* is connected to everything else."

Toxic contaminants are generally agreed to be undesirable when they appear in remote environments far from home, but we continue to deliberately apply them and other chemicals to crops, gardens, and lawns. The incidental emissions are often seen as a cost of doing business, or of economic prosperity.

For nongovernmental actors, the Arctic contaminants issue has been a major challenge. The organizations most directly and continuously involved have been indigenous peoples' organizations, particularly the Inuit Circumpolar Conference (ICC), the Inuit Tapirisat of Canada (ITC), and the Dene Nation. For them, the contamination of the Arctic is an issue of survival. Concerns range from the immediate, in terms of chronic health issues over the long term, particularly the health and development of children; to the long-term issues of ecosystem health and the survival of communities dependent on hunting and therefore on the health of wildlife. Actions taken by indigenous organizations have included community information dissemination, political action and lobbying—for example, in relation to the AES and Green Plan initiatives—and educational projects. Indigenous organizations have insisted on being involved in the scientific research programs initiated by government, including elements of informed community consent before the funding of research, involvement in the research itself, and timely access to research results in a meaningful form. These conditions have been adopted under the "partnership" principles of Green Plan funding.

Other nongovernmental initiatives also have a bearing on the political development of this issue. For example, the ICC began developing a Comprehensive Arctic Policy in 1983, elements of which are directly relevant to toxic contamination of the Arctic and possible solutions. Under Environmental Issues, this policy states:

> It is urgent that stronger measures be taken, both nationally and internationally, to prevent toxic and persistent substances from entering the Arctic environment and affecting water quality. These substances must be strictly controlled at all stages, from initial production to final disposal. The onus of proving that new substances can and will be used in an environmentally acceptable manner should be on the producer, importer, and user of potentially toxic products.

The concerns expressed demonstrate an awareness that the onus must be shifted to the producer of toxic chemicals to prove it is safe to use rather than leaving it to government regulators to show that harmful effects are within "acceptable" risk levels. Given the limits of our knowledge of the long-term consequences of environmental releases of toxic chemicals, particularly interactions among chemicals, this approach would appear to merit further study.

The limitation that Inuit and other indigenous peoples face in terms of implementing policies for management of toxic substances is directly related to their dependency on governments that have conflicting policy objectives for the Arctic. It remains to be seen what effect the advancement of self-government through initiatives like the creation of Nunavut will have on the advancement of environmentally appropriate policies; but given the long history of Inuit commitment to environmental issues, it is expected that new governmental arrangements will reflect this commitment.

Governments based in Southern Canada have been accused of policies ranging from adverse intervention to benign indifference concerning the Arctic. Clearly the peoples most directly dependent on the land (meaning the land, sea, sea ice, and all the living things) must have the greatest stake in environmental protection and conservation. Even with the power of self-government to some degree, it is difficult to see how Arctic peoples can stem the flow of toxic contaminants into the Arctic without significant levels of international cooperation and coordination.

The Declaration of Rovaniemi and the Arctic Environmental Protection Strategy provide a basis for much of the needed cooperation, but still there are collateral aspects of the problem that lie beyond the mandate of existing efforts. For example, producers of toxic contaminants can move their operations from jurisdictions where they experience stringent regulation of their production methods or products, to other jurisdictions, including the Third World, where it is possible to avoid regulation. While the sources may be moved farther away from the Arctic, the problems of atmospheric contamination due to transport into the Arctic may then be delayed but are not resolved, as in the removal of the manufacturer of toxaphene in the United States to Central America.

The problem of toxic contaminants in general is not new: the fact that the remotest parts of the planet now share in the concern for ecological effects of the use and abuse of these substances is. It is time to face the ecological, economic, and social issues associated with development that depends on inputs of toxic chemicals to survive. It is the view of this author that we must design holistic decision-making processes that serve the interests of the biosphere as a whole. Our contemporary approaches to resolving conflicting interests through economic and political mechanisms are primitive in their capacity to integrate environmental considerations. Environmentally appropriate approaches to development cannot be achieved, in the view of this writer, by simply adding environmental concerns on to the customary processes. Ultimately what is needed in my view is a transformation of the democratic process of making development choices, both domestically and internationally. We need to think more about how to get it right, meaning the attainment of sustainability and ecological integrity, and less about preserving the status quo by paying lip-service to environmental protection.

EDUCATE, REGULATE, ELIMINATE

Concrete steps are being taken through AMAP and the AEPS to support the development of a Protocol on the Long Range Transport of Persistent Organic Compounds under the UN Economic Commission for Europe. If successful, such a protocol could help complete global emissions inventories for chemicals and establish emissions levels and/or rates to control and ultimately reduce the emissions at source.

The broader view is that the chemical burden on the environment is increasing globally because of industry and agriculture and that losses to the environment as a result are inevitable. Most of the chemicals are synthetic, which means that they do not have analogues in the natural environment, and therefore represent "new" substances for the biosphere to detoxify. The fate of these chemicals after release is known only in part, and interactions among chemicals or within living systems are still under investigation. Yet we do not insist on closed cycles in industrial processing, with no losses to the environment. Our thinking remains primitive in regulatory terms. Industry itself has begun to address these shortcomings. For example, the Canadian Chemical Association has developed a voluntary program of certification for "cradle to grave" responsibility for chemicals produced by member corporations. Chemists themselves are developing complex "one pot" syntheses for chemicals to reduce the effluent stream created by chemical production. But these measures represent what is possible under the best of economic and political conditions. States in the former East Bloc lack the capacity to enforce the regulations for environmental protection. Desperation for economic development has created wastelands in countries like Romania that have been the subject of many media accounts of environmental destruction.

Given what we now know of the mobility of contaminants and our awareness of the limitations of our knowledge about their ecological effects, the urgent application of the precautionary principle would seem to be the wisest course: if we do not know the consequences of our intended actions, we should act conservatively to ensure that we stay within the bounds of our knowledge of environmental risk. One way to do this is to reduce, or preferably eliminate, the production and use of toxic substances. At present in Canada, there is a voluntary program supporting the replacement of toxic substances by nontoxic alternatives. Where this cannot be done, we should at least eliminate the emission of toxics into the environment at the source wherever it may be. Technology transfer from the developed to the developing must be seen as an act of enlightened self-interest, rather than a charitable or commercial enterprise.

Where toxic substances are subject to transportation, inadvertent emissions into the environment through spills and other accidents could be reduced by education and better handling. Transnational shipments of toxic contaminants, whether as products or as wastes, must be strictly regulated. Consideration should perhaps be given to prohibiting this traffic altogether and requiring the destruction of unwanted chemicals at source, as it is exceedingly difficult to regulate these shipments. Many examples of toxic dumping in the developing world attest to the problems.

Education for the users of toxic substances remains a critical concern. The promotion of the use of toxics, particularly agricultural pesticides, often subjects uninformed individuals to unnecessary risks in their handling, application, and disposal. Given the mobility of toxic contaminants in the environment, this is a concern for Canadians regardless of where it occurs. This is an occupational health and safety issue, as well as an environmental and ethical one.

It would also seem obvious that we must address development needs urgently in the hope of promoting sustainability of the Earth's living systems. To this end, multilateral cooperation would seem best suited to the challenge of addressing development and sustainability as well as environmental problems. The Arctic Environmental Protection Strategy meets this design requirement, but the implementation of a holistic approach to integration is hindered by the institutional and bureaucratic forms that dictate governmental practice. These forms in turn take their structure from the conventions according to which we organize our understanding of the environment. It is essential that our mode of thinking about environment and development become ecological. Perhaps if it were, we would understand sustainability as an achievable goal and avoid the creation of new complex problems in the environment. Hindsight offers the probability that had we looked at the synthesis, use, and disposal of toxic chemicals from an ecological perspective at the outset, society might have insisted on alternatives to the decisions taken at each step in the growth of this issue. It is possible to learn from the past. While it will take great effort to mitigate and ultimately eliminate the threat of toxic contaminants in the Arctic ecosystem, we may yet avoid even greater problems globally. We will not do this by simply repeating our mistakes through omission and inappropriate action. Our current understanding of the Arctic contaminants issues speaks loudly to the inadequacy of past decisions and demands improvements.

CHALLENGES FOR THE FUTURE

The hazards are real: toxic contaminants may have long-term effects on the health of all members of the Arctic ecosystem, including humans. The Arctic may not be the final sink; despite the slow flushing time of the Arctic Ocean, these contaminants may yet find their way back to the great fishing zones of the Northern Hemisphere, or perhaps even to the industrial regions that produce them. The cumulative effects of increasing contaminant burdens and the potential for adverse interactions among chemicals within living systems are not well understood. The Arctic contaminants challenge is twofold: attacking the sources of toxic contaminants through controls, substitution, or elimination; and mitigating ecological effects from current contaminant loads. The global challenge is to change our way of thinking about making and releasing contaminants that are toxic to life. Domestic and international initiatives are in progress that will ensure that current levels of understanding are at least considered in the assessment of the state of the Arctic environment. Subsequent policy-making, both national and international, will depend on political will. The global challenge remains before us. The critical link between the two is the question of our capacity to think ecologically about development and environment, and to design decision-making processes capable of accommodating ecological thinking as something qualitatively different from existing approaches to blending environment and economics.

REFERENCES

Berger, T.R. 1977."Northern Frontier Northern Homeland: The Report of the Mackenzie Valley Pipeline Inquiry." Canada.

Bidleman, T. 1993. "Workshop on the Analytical and Environmental Chemistry of Toxaphene." Burlington, Ont., Feb. 4–6.

Carson, R. 1969. *Silent Spring*. New York: Crest.

Condon, R.G., P. Collings, and G. Wenzel. 1995. "The Best Part of Life: Subsistence Hunting, Ethnicity, and Economic Adaptation among Young Adult Inuit Males." *Arctic* 48(1) 1–46.

Goodlad, J. 1995. "Effects of the Braer Oil Spill on the Shetland Seafood Industry." Presentation to International Conference on Marine Mammals and the Marine Environment, North Atlantic Marine Mammal Commission, Lerwick, Shetland. April 20–21.

Inuit Circumpolar Conference. n.d. "Principles and Elements for a Comprehensive Arctic Policy," Science, St. Louis Meeting Showcases "Creature Features," vol. 267, 330–31.

Shaw, G.E. 1994. Publication prepared for the European Course on Atmospheres, Grenoble, France.

Wania, F., and D. Mackay. 1993. "Global Fractionation and Cold Condensation of Low Volatility Organochlorine Compounds in Polar Regions." *Ambio* 22(1): 10–18.

Wein, E.E., and M.M.R. Freeman. 1995 "Frequency of Traditional Food Use by Three Yukon First Nations Living in Four Communities." *Arctic* 48(2) (June): 161–71.

Welch, H.E., D.C.G. Muir, B.N. Billeck, L. Lockhart, G.J. Brunskill, H.J. Kling, M.P. Olson, and R.M. Lemoine. 1991. "Brown Snow a Long Range Transport Event in the Canadian Arctic." *Environmental Science and Technology* 25: 280–85.

Wong, M.P. 1985. "Chemical Residues in Fish and Wildlife Harvested in Northern Canada." Ottawa: Northern Affairs Program, DINA, Environmental Studies, no. 46, December.

1. What are the possible types of sources for the toxic contaminants found in the Arctic? List five.

2. Where can Arctic contaminants come from in geographic terms?

3. What are the mechanisms of transport for Arctic contaminants?

4. Draw the life cycle of a toxic organic compound applied as a pesticide in agricultural production of corn, identifying some of the potential links between the cornfield and caribou found in the Arctic.

5. Identify the Arctic states that are participants in the Arctic Environmental Protection Strategy (AEPS) and events or situations that you believe may have encouraged their involvement in the AEPS.

6. Why are indigenous peoples identified as the most vulnerable, yet most supportive of the interests involved in the Arctic contaminants issue?

7. What connections can you draw between your lifestyle and the origins of the Arctic contaminants issue?

8. What local actions can be taken to improve the long-term situation of Arctic contaminants?

9. Can you suggests some candidate projects for "technology transfers" from Canada to source regions that would improve the situation of Arctic contaminants?

10. What connections can be made between international development, sustainability, and the Arctic contaminants issue?

11. What are the implications of the contamination of the Arctic for achieving sustainability in Arctic communities?

12. What elements of the Arctic contaminants issue complicate policy-making?

CHAPTER 6

Our Cities, Our Air, Our Health: Perspectives on Urban Air Quality and Human Health

Monica Campbell

Metropolitan Toronto Teaching Health Units

URBAN AIR QUALITY AND CONCERN FOR HUMAN HEALTH

Air quality and its effect on human health are of particular concern in cities. Settlement patterns have changed dramatically in the last 100 years, so that most of the world's population now live in cities. Consequently, even modest air pollution can be a big health problem because of the large number of persons exposed and potentially at risk. At greatest risk are those with respiratory conditions like asthma, emphysema, and chronic bronchitis, which are worsened by poor air. The number of people with asthma, emphysema, and chronic bronchitis is estimated at 7.5 percent of the Canadian population (Ontario Lung Association, 1991) or two million people.

Concern about asthma and the effects of air quality is increasing in the scientific community. Asthma is a prevalent disease in both adults and children, and morbidity and mortality from it have increased in the last decade in North America (Samet, 1994). Of the many factors that influence its occurrence and severity are such pollutants as tobacco smoke, particulates, nitrogen dioxide, and volatile organic compounds (VOCs) (Samet, 1994). In a recent ecological study in Birmingham, England, children admitted to a hospital for asthma were significantly more likely to live in an area with high traffic flow: more than 24 000 vehicles a day. This level of traffic is comparable with densities on major arterial roads in Canadian cities.

Even healthy individuals who exercise outdoors can suffer ill health from some pollutants, such as ozone, in Canadian cities. With vigorous exercise, such as running or cycling, more pollutants enter the person's lungs than when they are sitting down. Furthermore, with exercise, the person inhales more air directly through the mouth into the lung, bypassing the filtering effect of the nasal passages. Although only a small segment of the population engages in strenuous physical activity, it is important from a policy perspective to ensure that all subpopulations and activity levels can exist without ill health.

In any city, air quality varies enormously depending on the time and place. Except for ozone, levels of vehicle pollutants are highest during the day and in places where traffic is heavy. Each urban resident will experience pollutant levels based on their activity and the microenvironments through which they pass in a given day.

In general, however, as urban intensification continues and population densities increase, more people will come in greater contact with high-traffic areas. With the increased interest in other ways of commuting such as walking, running and bicycling, the number of persons and the degree of exposure to air pollutants and their ill effects are expected to increase.

Another significant issue is the state of research on air quality and its health effects. Researchers are using increasingly sophisticated methods to measure exposure to pollutants. Greater attention is devoted to measuring pollutants known to affect health rather than proxy measures. For example, respirable particulates are increasingly measured rather than total suspended particulates. Acid aerosols, including hydrogen ion, are being measured rather than just sulphur dioxide, which gives rise to acid aerosols (American Lung Association, 1990). By having more precise measurements of the kind of pollutant causing the problem, it is likely that health studies will be better able to demonstrate links between pollutants and illness.

In addition, exposures incurred by individuals are being measured with personal dosimeters. Alternatively, pollutant levels are measured in many microenvironments rather than just at a few fixed monitoring stations in the city. Both these improvements in assessing exposure provide information on the range of microclimates that people typically pass through in a day.

Another research thrust is that scientists are using sophisticated end-points capable of monitoring more subtle changes in the lungs than in the past. As a result, many studies can now demonstrate damage caused by air pollutants at upper end levels in major urban centres throughout North America. While some pollutants, such as ozone and suspended particulates, sometimes exceed air quality standards in Canada's urban centres, of equal concern is whether current air quality criteria properly protect the entire urban population (City of Toronto Department of Public Health, 1993).

While this chapter focuses on the relationship between urban air quality and human health, it also emphasizes that improvements in air quality depend on a good understanding of how *both* urban form and human activity within the city contribute to air pollution. To illustrate these influences, this chapter focuses on air quality in Toronto, but cities throughout Canada and the United States face similar issues.

TRENDS AFFECTING AIR QUALITY

CHANGES IN URBANIZATION PATTERNS

Intense urbanization is a relatively recent but global phenomenon. In 1990, about 10 percent of the world's population lived in cities. By 1986, about 75 percent of the North American population was urbanized (Brown and Jacobson, 1987). In Canada, the vast majority of the population lives in urban and suburban settings, less than 25 percent in rural areas (Mitchell, 1989).

The concentration of so many people on relatively little land has both positive and negative implications for the quality of air in cities. Although compact urban form and high population densities result in lower emissions of air pollutants per capita than less dense habitation (IBI Group, 1990; Paehlke, 1991), the total loading of pollutants emitted to the relatively small urban airshed means that pollutant concentrations can exceed levels known to harm health.

The way we build our cities has a profound influence on the types and concentration of pollutants emitted into the air. Urban form, which entails the structure of the city in terms of density, building massing, and transportation infrastructure, is a critical factor that sets the stage for daily human activity. For example, the nature of the built environment determines whether residents depend on their automobile or on less polluting alternatives, such as walking, cycling, or public transit. In terms of massing of buildings, streets lined with many tall buildings close to each other can create a "canyon effect," impeding the dispersion of pollutants at pedestrian level (City of Toronto Department of Public Health, 1993).

Although urbanization is a century-old phenomenon, it was not until the 1950s that urban form underwent a major change in population density and transportation infrastructure. Mean urban densities in both Canada and the United States fell by 50 percent between 1950 and 1975 (Edmonston et al., 1985). Before the 1950s, most people lived in either densely populated urban centres or in low-density rural areas. With the postwar affluence of the 1950s, suburban housing on larger lots spread well beyond the urban core. Unlike urban centres, in which proximity to work, shopping, and social activities was close, the suburban periphery was mostly homes and the automobile was needed for most of a household's daily activities.

The suburban settlement pattern gives rise to greater use of the automobile, and consequently fuel consumption and vehicle emissions are higher than in urban settlements (Paehlke, 1986). Furthermore, the allocation and frequency of public transit is highly dependent on population density. It is estimated that public transit pays for itself at densities of 6000 persons/km^2 or greater (Metropolitan Toronto Planning Department, 1990). These densities are typical of the urban core of major Canadian cities such as Toronto, Montreal, and Vancouver. At lower densities, rapid transit does not pay for itself and needs a significant subsidy from taxes. Conflict arises when low-density communities, particularly in the suburban periphery, come to expect rapid transit. In reality, as settlement densities decrease, public transit service is relatively sparse and infrequent, which in turn stimulates increased use of the automobile. Figure 6.1 illustrates how vehicle ownership has steadily increased in Canada since 1950, while the use of public transit has decreased.

For most of the world's major cities, the more compact the urban form and the greater the population density, the less fuel consumed per capita (Newman and Kenworthy, 1989). In general, residents of most major American cities consume more gasoline per capita than European cities like Paris and Frankfurt. In Canadian cities, such as Metropolitan Toronto, fuel consumption is midway

FIGURE 6.1
Vehicle Ownership and Transit Use

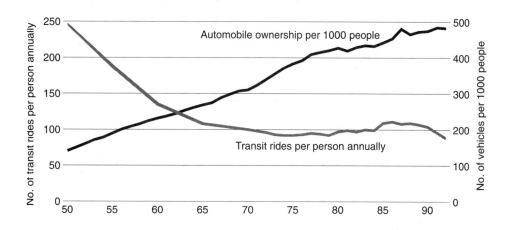

Source: Government of Canada, 1996, *The State of Canada's Environment,* Ottawa, Environment Canada. Reproduced with the permission of the Minister of Supply and Services Canada, 1996.

between San Francisco and Paris, as shown in Figure 6.2. This figure also illustrates how residents in more densely populated cities tend to make greater use of alternatives to the car to commute. For example, in Metropolitan Toronto, about 43 percent of trips to work are done through walking, cycling, and public transit. In contrast, American cities such as Los Angeles, San Francisco, and Chicago, in which urban density is about half of Toronto's, only 12 to 24 percent of trips to work are done on foot, bicycles, and public transit (Metropolitan Toronto Planning Department, 1991; Newman and Kenworthy, 1989).

The size and shape of a city determine its transportation options. Communities with extensive suburban sprawl tend to depend on the private automobile rather than public transit because of logistics and convenience. Public transit can transport people with less fuel and pollution per capita than the automobile. As illustrated in Figure 6.3, one person travelling by car generates about six to eight times as much hydrocarbon pollution as travelling by local bus or train (California Air Resources Board, 1991). Forming car and van pools cuts emissions by of 50 to 75 percent compared with travelling alone in a car (California Air Resources Board, 1991).

FIGURE 6.2
Urban Density Relationships

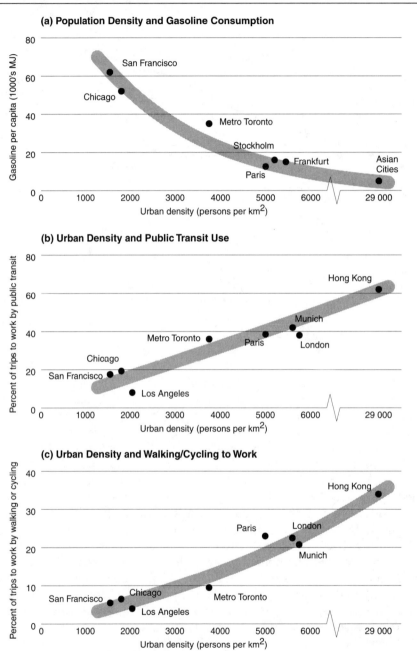

(a) Population Density and Gasoline Consumption

(b) Urban Density and Public Transit Use

(c) Urban Density and Walking/Cycling to Work

Source: Metropolitan Toronto Planning Department, 1990, *The GTA: Concepts for the Future.*
Municipality of Metropolitan Toronto.

FIGURE 6.3
Hydrocarbon Emissions and Transportation Mode[a]

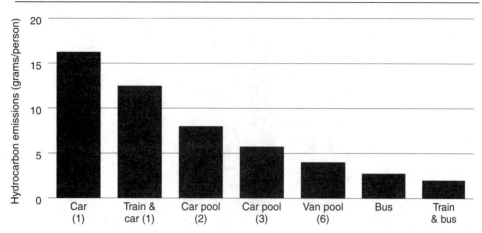

Source: Adapted from *California Air Quality: A Status Report,* 1991, State of California Protection Agency Air Resources Board.

[a] Emissions per person are based on a 20-mile trip.
Numbers in brackets indicate number of persons in vehicle.

CHANGES IN HUMAN ACTIVITIES

While transportation is the main source of air pollutants in most cities, other forms of human activity contribute. Residential heating contributes to carbon dioxide emissions and consequently global warming. Electrical utilities contribute nitrogen oxides (which are precursors of ozone) and sulphur dioxides (which give rise to acid aerosols). In the past, houses and electrical utilities emitted more pollutants because of the common use of sulphur-containing coal and oil, whereas today natural gas and other cleaner-burning fuels are used. In the old days, coal burning was a major contributor of particulates and sulphur dioxides, both of which are harmful to health.

In the last 100 years, major urban centres like Toronto, Montreal, and Vancouver have experienced a decline in industry and an increase in less polluting commercial activity. While historical industrial activity has resulted in current soil contamination due to past air emissions, industry today tends to be a declining source of many common urban air pollutants. Using Toronto data as an example, Figure 6.4 shows that industry is a major contributor of volatile organic compounds (VOCs) and electrical utilities are the major source of sulphur oxides; vehicles are the single largest contributor of nitrogen oxides, carbon

FIGURE 6.4
Metropolitan Toronto Air Emission

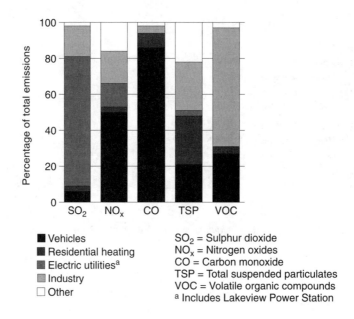

Vehicles
Residential heating
Electric utilities[a]
Industry
Other

SO_2 = Sulphur dioxide
NO_x = Nitrogen oxides
CO = Carbon monoxide
TSP = Total suspended particulates
VOC = Volatile organic compounds
[a] Includes Lakeview Power Station

Source: L. Shenfield, B. Srivastava, D. Yap, and R. Bloxom, 1991, *Environmental Audit of East Bayfront/Port Industrial Area, Phase Z—Atmospheric Environment, Technical Report No. 6* (unpublished report). © Queen's Printer of Ontario, 1991, Reproduced by permission.

monoxide, particulates, and benzene, a human carcinogen. Vehicles contribute 83 percent of all benzene emissions in Canada, industrial sources like petroleum refining and chemical processing less than 10 percent (Dann, 1987).

Other human activities affecting to air quality in cities include commercial activities like dry cleaners, printing shops, and gas stations. These small establishments are distributed throughout the city and emit such toxic substances as perchloroethylene (from dry cleaners), toluene and a variety of other volatile toxics (from printers), and benzene (from gas stations). In addition, the common use of pesticides in homes, workplaces, and institutions contributes to trace air toxics. The use of toxic synthetic chemicals, such as organic solvents and pesticides, became increasingly common from the 1950s after World War II.

CHANGES IN AIR POLLUTION LEVELS

Numerous historical events have demonstrated that elevated levels of air pollutants result in respiratory illness and death. In the Meuse Valley of Belgium, a temperature inversion in 1930 prevented the natural dispersion of industrial emissions from coke ovens, steel mills, and zinc smelters, resulting in 63 deaths due to sulphur dioxide and sulphuric acid mist (Ziegenfus, 1987). In 1948, industrial pollutants in Donora, Pennsylvania, resulted in 20 deaths, as well as headaches, vomiting, coughing, and nausea in 40 percent of the population (Ziegenfus, 1987). In 1952 in New York City, about 250 deaths were attributed to air pollutants such as particulates and sulphur dioxide during a temperature inversion.

Perhaps the most famous historical episode of air pollution occurred in London, during a cold spell in 1952. About 4000 people died within five days of exposure to a "black fog," caused by a stagnant air mass and increased coal burning in power plants and fireplaces. The resultant elevated levels of sulphur dioxide and particulates greatly increased the incidence of bronchitis, influenza, respiratory disease, pneumonia, heart disease, and lung cancer (Ziegenfus, 1987).

With the introduction of pollution control regulations in the 1960s and 1970s in North America and Europe, the levels of particulates and sulphur dioxide dropped considerably, resulting in significant improvements in air quality. Another major improvement was the phaseout and eventual ban of tetraethyl lead in gasoline in 1990 in Canada. Despite these improvements, an estimated 150 million people in the United States breathe air considered unhealthy by the Environmental Protection Agency (Starke, 1990). While death due to air pollution is rare today, scientific monitoring shows that pollution in relatively clean cities with limited industry harms the health of many of the residents, especially the young, the elderly, and those with respiratory problems.

Using Toronto as an example, time trends reveal that, with the exception of lead, pollutant levels did not decrease appreciably between 1980 and 1990. Figure 6.5 shows mean levels in Toronto for nitrogen dioxide, carbon monoxide, ozone, and particulates. All these pollutants are associated with vehicle exhaust. Despite major improvements in emission control technology in new vehicles, these emission reductions have been offset by increases in the number of vehicles and traffic stagnation (City of Toronto Department of Public Health, 1993).

HEALTH EFFECTS OF AIR POLLUTANTS

OVERVIEW OF POLLUTANT TYPES

Urban air contains a large mix of pollutants, which can be grouped as follows:

- Pollutants *directly* emitted into the air with the potential to impair health. This group includes pollutants like carbon monoxide, which are emitted in relatively high amounts, and trace air toxics, like 1,3-butadiene and manganese, which are emitted in relatively low amounts.
- Pollutants emitted into the air that can react with other pollutants, heat, or sunlight to *generate* pollutants capable of impairing health. Examples include

FIGURE 6.5
Trends in Toronto Pollutant Levels

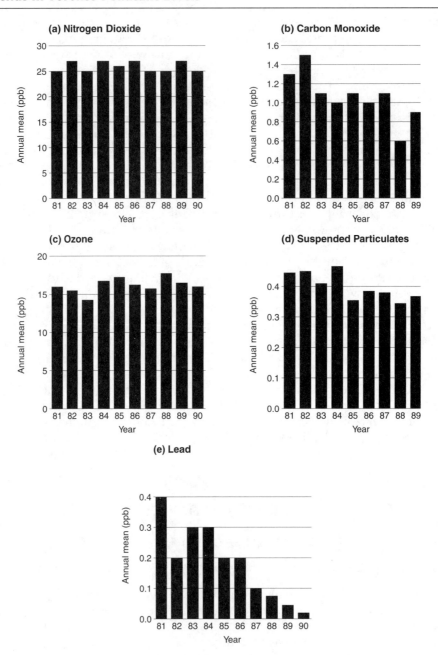

Source: Based on data from the Ontario Ministry of the Environment and Energy, 1994.

nitrogen oxides that are transformed into nitrogen dioxide, which in turn affects health, and nitrogen oxides and VOCs, which in the presence of sunlight give rise to ozone, a potent lung irritant.

- Pollutants with the potential for *secondary* impacts on human health. One example is chlorofluorohydrocarbons (CFCs), for which inherent toxicity to humans is low but which deplete the ozone layer and increase skin cancer. Another example is carbon dioxide, which has no direct health impacts but causes global warming and secondary health impacts like heat stroke in the elderly.

Air pollutants can also be divided into "criteria pollutants" or "air toxics." Criteria pollutants are linked to acute impacts on the respiratory system at elevated exposure levels, and are routinely monitored by provincial and federal government agencies through Canada. Examples of criteria pollutants include ozone, nitrogen oxides, suspended particulates, sulphur dioxide, and carbon monoxide.

Air toxics refers to the many chemicals that occur in air at low levels compared with criteria pollutants. From a public health perspective, both criteria pollutants and air toxics can be toxic, depending on the exposure level. Traditionally, the concern for criteria pollutants has centred on acute or immediate health effects, air toxics on long-term effects, including contribution to body burden of persistent chemicals, potential reproductive effects, and cancer with lifetime exposure. Studies on air toxics have tended to focus on sources of toxics (e.g., studies of diesel-powered or gasoline-powered vehicles) or on specific chemicals (e.g., benzene) and chemical groups (e.g., PAHs, VOCs).

HEALTH EFFECTS OF SELECTED CRITERIA POLLUTANTS

Ozone

People are exposed to a large number of pollutants, and each one fluctuates in concentration throughout the day. It is difficult, therefore, for scientists to fully determine the health effects of individual pollutants and their possible interactions. Nonetheless, recent epidemiological studies of Canadians exposed to a mixture of criteria pollutants previously thought to be without harmful effects have demonstrated health impacts at low levels.

Data from 168 hospitals in Ontario show a significant association between the number of daily admissions for respiratory problems and both ozone and sulphate levels. Most importantly, the investigators did not find a threshold level of air pollutants below which there was no harmful effect, suggesting that even the low levels of pollutants that occur in Ontario's outdoor air are sufficiently high to affect human health. Infants were the most sensitive age group, accounting for about 15 percent of the hospital admissions associated with the ozone–sulphate pollution mix (Burnett et al., 1994). In a parallel study that examined hospital admissions for cardiac disease as well as respiratory illness, Burnett et al. (1995) found a direct relationship between hospital admissions and outdoor sulphate levels. Finally, a study based on pollutant levels in the Toronto region found a strong association between premature death due to respiratory disease and airborne particulates, ozone, and nitrogen dioxide (Ozkaynak et al., 1995). Taken together, these studies clearly show that existing pollutant levels in southern Ontario are affecting the public's health.

Ground-level ozone results from chemical reactions between nitrogen oxides and VOCs in sunlight. Consequently ozone levels are highest in summer and during the afternoon. Although industrial sources (including hydroelectric utilities) in Canada and the United States are major contributors of ozone precursors, vehicles in dense urban centres are also a significant source. Ironically, although vehicles emit ozone-precursors, ozone levels are typically low in high traffic areas because nitric oxide (NO), also emitted from the tailpipe, quickly converts ozone to oxygen and nitrogen dioxide (City of Toronto Department of Public Health, 1993).

Of concern to public health is that the ozone precursors from high traffic areas result in elevated ozone levels in residential low-traffic areas downwind. In one Toronto study, ozone levels at a residential low-traffic site persisted at 50 to 60 ppb for six hours daily during the study period. Upper-end summer ozone levels were expected to affect the lungs of healthy exercising individuals, as well as those with respiratory conditions, based on the health effects literature for ozone (City of Toronto Department of Public Health, 1993).

Ozone is a lung irritant that can damage the structure and function of respiratory tissues. Experiments showed that healthy exercising individuals exposed to ozone at levels as low as 80 ppb for a short period—say, six hours—suffered decreased lung function and athletic performance (Horstman et al., 1988). Ozone can alter respiration rates, leading to shallow, rapid breathing. Ozone at peak urban levels can increase bronchial responsiveness in asthmatics and contribute to wheezing and shortness of breath (Molfino, 1991). Although experiments show that respiratory function returns to normal when elevated ozone exposure stops, at issue is whether the daily peak ozone levels can lead to nonreversible effects. Of particular concern is the extent to which upper-end ozone levels can permanently damage and scar the alveoli (air sacs) in the lung, thereby reducing lung capacity (City of Toronto Department of Public Health, 1993). Preliminary research on deceased young adults from areas in California with high ozone levels indicated unusually high rates of chronic bronchitis and inflammation of respiratory tissues, suggestive of permanent lung damage (CARB, 1991).

Suspended Particulates

In nonindustrial urban centres like Toronto, Montreal, and Vancouver, vehicles are a major source of suspended particulates, including respirable particulates. Suspended particulate levels are highest in Toronto and Montreal and somewhat lower in Vancouver (OMOEE, 1994). Although average suspended particulate levels are below the current air quality criteria, excessive levels do occur at locations throughout Canada. For example, the number of days a year with excessess of suspended particulates at one Toronto location ranged from 26 to 53 between 1988 and 1990 (City of Toronto Department of Public Health, 1993).

Suspended particulates range in size from 0.005 to 100 um in diameter, but particulates 10 um or smaller (i.e., the PM_{10} fraction) are of greatest concern because they can penetrate deep into the lungs, thereby coming in contact with the exchange surfaces of the alveoli and the circulatory system. Suspended particulates can harm health when levels are high enough to overwhelm the normal lung-clearing functions or when the particles may be toxic (e.g., sulphates) or have toxic chemicals adsorbed (e.g., PAHs) (Ziegenfus, 1987). Particulates are associated with trace toxic compounds, some of which are carcinogenic.

Different investigators and jurisdictions use different methods to measure and report suspended particulate levels and their health effects, so it is hard to compare ambient particulate levels in Canadian urban centres with those in the literature associated with harm. Nonetheless, some generalizations are possible. Upper-end particulate levels in Canadian cities overlap with levels in the literature associated with increased incidence of chronic cough, bronchitis, chest illness, and earaches in children (Dockery et al.,1989). Levels of suspended particulates in Toronto and Montreal approach levels in a study in Steubenville, Ohio, which showed an association with daily mortality rates (Schwartz and Dockery, 1992).

In a study in Minneapolis–St. Paul (in which mean particulate levels were about 30 percent higher than in Toronto), respirable particulate levels (PM_{10}) were positively associated with hospital admissions for pneumonia in the elderly (Schwartz, 1994a). Another study of hospital admissions by the elderly in Montreal indicated that both ozone and suspended particulates were associated with urgent hospital admissions due to respiratory illness (Delfino et al., 1994). A similar study in Detroit also found a significant association between respiratory illness in the elderly, including pneumonia, and respirable particulate levels (Schwartz, 1994b).

Suspended particulates are also associated with childhood hospitalization for asthma. In one study of children between the ages of one and four from Hong Kong, hospitalization rates for asthma were strongly associated with ambient levels of suspended particulates (Tseng et al., 1992). In a study of California Seventh-Day Adventists, elevated suspended particulate levels were positively associated with asthma, airway obstructive disease, and bronchitis in non-smoking adults over a six-year period (Abbey, 1991).

Sulphur Dioxide, Nitrogen Dioxide, and Acid Aerosols

Although sulphur dioxides (SO_2) derive primarily from industry, transportation and heating are other sources. In Ontario, for example, 92 percent of SO_2

emissions were produced by industry and 8 percent from local sources such as transportation and space heating (OMOEE, 1994). In the air, SO_2 can be converted to sulphur trioxide (SO_3), which in the presence of water vapour converts to sulphuric acid mist. Other oxides can combine with SO_3 to form sulphate aerosols (OMOEE, 1994).

Nitrogen dioxides (NO_2) derive primarily from vehicles (i.e., the atmospheric conversion of nitrogen oxides emitted directly from the tailpipe). In Ontario, for example, transportation accounts for 61 percent of nitrogen oxide emissions, power utilities and smelters for about 20 percent (OMOEE, 1994).

Although many studies have shown a clear association between SO_2 or NO_2 levels and ill health, several investigators now believe that these primary pollutants give rise to secondary pollutants through atmospheric reactions. These secondary pollutants, known as acid aerosols, are increasingly shown to be correlated to harmful respiratory effects.

Acid aerosols derive from many sources, including the oxidation of sulphur dioxides and nitrogen oxides that results from combustion (American Lung Association, 1990). At present, the measurement of acid aerosols is still under development. Acid aerosols are sometimes expressed as hydrogen ion; but because this entity is reactive and difficult to capture, the measurement of acid aerosols is reserved for scientific studies rather than routine air quality monitoring. This presents some difficulties in linking the health-effects literature on acid aerosols with ambient levels in urban centres.

Nitrogen dioxide levels in most urban centres in Canada are lower than those for which ill effects in healthy adults have been demonstrated in the literature. In contrast, many studies have demonstrated that those with respiratory conditions could be affected by high urban levels of NO_2. Asthmatics and those with chronic obstructive airway disease experience increased respiratory effects, such as decreased lung function and bronchial hyperactivity, at levels similar to peak levels in Canadian cities (City of Toronto Department of Public Health, 1993; Bauer et al., 1984; Bylin et al., 1985).

Similarly, sulphur dioxide levels in most nonindustrial urban centres across Canada are below those shown in the literature to harm healthy individuals. However, peak SO_2 levels overlap with levels shown in some studies to further decrease the already compromised pulmonary function of asthmatic children. For example, in a study of Hamilton school children, ambient SO_2 levels were associated with clinically significant increases in airflow obstruction in asthmatic children (City of Toronto Department of Public Health, 1993; Pengally and Goldsmith, 1988).

It is hypothesized that acid aerosols are responsible for the health effects observed in earlier epidemiological studies of air pollution. While previous studies measured a variety of pollutants, including SO_2 and NO_2, it is now believed that NO_2 and SO_2 were indicators or surrogates of acid aerosol exposure. Many studies have shown respiratory impairment in children during pollution episodes in Canada. In several studies, both ozone and acid aerosol levels were correlated with increased respiratory symptoms. An epidemiological study by Raizenne et al. (1989) observed small decrements in lung function in girls at summer camp in Southern Ontario that correlated with acid aerosol and ozone levels. A study by Ostro et al. (1991) of 200 asthmatics in Denver found that airborne hydrogen ion was significantly associated with several indicators of asthma, including coughing and shortness of breath. In a recent study by Thurston et al. (1994), acid aerosols were positively associated with respiratory and asthma admissions to hospital in Toronto during summertime haze.

HEALTH EFFECTS OF SELECTED AIR TOXICS

Assessing the impact of individual toxics or classes of toxics on human health is difficult because these chemicals are often produced by a variety of sources and occur in conjunction with many other pollutants. In toxicological studies, a single toxicant may be administered to a single species of laboratory animal, providing good evidence of inherent toxicity to this species. Considerable uncertainty is introduced when the results of animal studies are applied to human populations.

The need for using toxicological test results to predict adverse reactions in human populations is recognized, given that toxicants cannot be administered directly to humans, and given that epidemiological studies from workplace exposures to these substances may not be available. However, in extrapolating animal test results to human populations, it is important to recognize that humans may respond to toxicants differently, that coexposure to the multitude of other trace toxicants that humans are exposed to may affect how they handle a particular toxicant, and that the variability in genetic and health status in human populations is much greater than in a given strain of laboratory animals.

Given the enormous variety of trace toxic compounds known to occur in ambient air, and the difficulty of causally linking a specific compound with health outcomes, risk assessment procedures are used to predict the health risk associated with each compound. However, given current limitations in the toxicological and epidemiological data bases available, scientists have greater ability to measure trace toxic compounds than to conclusively assess their health impacts at the relatively low levels of exposures in nonindustrial Canadian cities. Nonetheless, based on the little we do know about toxic compounds that occur in cities, there is cause for concern.

For example, in a study by the Toronto Department of Public Health (1993), 160 trace toxics were identified in ambient air regularly. A quantitative risk assessment was possible for only 23 of these chemicals due to limited toxicological and epidemiological information on the remaining chemicals. As a result of the risk assessment, 14 compounds were flagged as health priorities because average concentrations in Toronto exceeded benchmark levels (i.e., reference concentrations) above which adverse health impact was expected or excess cancer risks

FIGURE 6.6
Benzene Levels in Toronto[a]

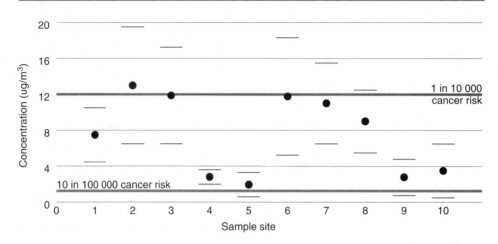

Source: Perry Kendall, *Outdoor Air Quality in Toronto: Issues and Concerns,* 1993, City of Toronto Department of Public Health.

[a] Shows annual mean and standard deviation.

exceeded one-in-a-million. Compounds of priority concern included benzene, chromium, nickel, 1,3-butadiene, cadmium, and a variety of chlorinated solvents. Substances such as benzene and 1,3-butadiene derive predominantly from motor vehicles, while chlorinated solvents derive from commercial/industrial activities. Figure 6.6 shows how benzene levels in Toronto exceed the reference concentration by the United States Environmental Protection Agency associated with an excess cancer risk of one in a million.

Monitoring of Toronto air pollutants reveals that about 25 percent of the 160 substances detected in Toronto's outdoor air have provincial regulatory limits (City of Toronto Department of Public Health, 1993). In the Toronto study, none of the approximately 40 "air toxics" for which regulatory limits exist exceeded the provincial maximum acceptable limits (MALs) at any sampling location. However, several of the 40 chemicals with regulatory limits did exceed health-based reference concentrations at the one-in-a-million excess cancer risk level (City of Toronto Department of Public Health, 1993). As new health-effects studies emerge, it is essential that regulatory agencies review and revise their air quality standards to ensure greater alignment with reference concentrations derived from toxicological and epidemiological studies. Without regulatory reform, the impetus for protecting ambient air is diminished.

URBAN AIR QUALITY ACROSS CANADA

Environment Canada operates a national system of air pollution monitoring stations known as the National Air Pollution Surveillance (NAPS) network, and many provinces have their own monitoring network. To date, most monitoring data still focus on criteria pollutants. The relatively higher cost and technical difficulty of monitoring air toxics has meant that these pollutants are measured less often than criteria pollutants, or that special studies are conducted from time to time. Consequently, it is not possible at present to obtain an accurate understanding of the hundreds of trace toxic compounds that occur in the outdoor air in cities across Canada.

Many air pollution control initiatives have been undertaken throughout Canada in the last two decades, resulting in noticeable improvements in air quality, often in areas of point source emissions, such as from industry. For example, between 1977 and 1989, the mean level of sulphur dioxide monitored by NAPS declined by 52 percent, nitrogen dioxide by 32 percent, carbon monoxide by 63 percent, airborne lead by 93 percent, and total suspended particulates by 44 percent (Environment Canada, 1991). Despite these significant improvements for many major urban centres, reductions in pollutant levels from the transportation sector have been more modest.

CANADIAN AIR QUALITY IN A GLOBAL PERSPECTIVE

Compared with other cities around the world, air quality in Canadian cities is relatively good. While new studies demonstrate increasing evidence of adverse health effects at upper-end pollutant levels in our cities, these effects pale in comparison with those observed in other nations with less pollution control and greater industrial and vehicular emissions. In Athens, for example, the number of deaths is six times higher on heavily polluted days than on those when the air is relatively clean (French, 1990). In Mexico City, where airborne lead levels from vehicles are very high, seven out of ten newborns have lead levels in their blood in excess of World Health Organization norms. Many children in Mexico are born with signs of lead poisoning. Mexico City's three million vehicles are estimated to contribute 80 percent of the city's air pollution (Mumme, 1991).

In eastern European countries, air pollution is clearly linked to a variety of diseases. In the former Czechoslovakia, for example, high air pollution levels are linked to elevated mortality and rates of respiratory disease. In Hungary, children living in polluted industrial regions have twice the incidence of upper respiratory illness as those living in nonindustrial areas. In Poland, the polluted region of Upper Silesia has 150 percent more circulatory illnesses, 30 percent more cancer, and 47 percent more respiratory illness than the national average (French, 1990). Although the severity of health problems in North American cities is considerably less than in less developed nations, air quality continues to be an environmental issue of great importance in all of the world's major cities.

The significance of urban air quality is further realized when considered from an ecosystem perspective in which human health is viewed as fully dependent on the health and well-being of the ecosystem. Not only is clean air vital to minimize the health risk associated with breathing urban air, it is also important to ensure minimal uptake of air pollutants into other parts of the ecosystem, such as soil, water systems, and the plants and animals that make up the food chain. For persistent toxic air pollutants like lead, historical airborne emissions continue to contaminate the environment through their presence in soil. For example, it is estimated that 80 percent of the land area of the City of Toronto has lead levels in the soil higher than the current health-based guidelines recommend (OMOEE, 1994). Consequently, toddlers playing on contaminated properties may continue to be exposed to an environmental contaminant, even though it is no longer emitted directly into the air. Other air pollutants, particularly lipophilic substances such as many pesticides, tend to bioconcentrate in the food chain. In this way, some air pollutants may persist in the environment for a long time, increasing the probability of exposure by both humans and wildlife.

On a global scale, the United Nations Environment Program (UNEP) and the World Health Organization (WHO) operate a worldwide network of air monitoring stations. This network, known as the Global Environment Monitoring System (GEMS), has assessed urban air quality in more than 20 world megacities, which are defined as urban conglomerations with current or projected populations of 10 million or more by the year 2000 (UNEP/WHO, 1994). Globally, population trends show continued urban growth in most of the megacities, leading to increases in many air pollutants and a larger segment of the population exposed. Based on recent GEMS monitoring data, 14 of the 20 megacities assessed have two or more air pollutants that exceed WHO health-based guidelines, and each megacity has at least one major pollutant that regularly exceeds the guidelines. Elevated particulates remain the most prevalent form of pollution. As in Canada, the phaseout of high-sulphur coal and oil has resulted in decreased sulphur dioxide pollution levels; however, vehicle related pollutants like carbon monoxide, nitrogen dioxide, and ozone are still pollutants of major significance in most cities (UNEP/WHO, 1994).

AIR POLLUTION: HUMAN HEALTH AND WELL-BEING

The ability of air pollutants to affect the physical health of people is inter-related with social impacts. Impairments in physical health can translate into impairments in social and economic well-being. For example, people with respiratory difficulties like asthma, emphysema, or chronic bronchitis are more vulnerable to air pollution, resulting in more sick time. For children, this affects their education, and for adults, workplace productivity. For the elderly, air pollution can aggravate respiratory conditions, contribute to increased spending on health care, and generally spoil the quality of life for a significant part of the population.

Another dimension of air pollution and its social effects concerns issues of social justice and equity. In North American cities, industries that pollute are usually located in poor areas. Affluence enables one to live upwind or remote from industrial and vehicular emissions. In one American study, it was found that visible minorities outnumber whites in areas that violate air quality standards. In this study, a breakdown of populations in areas that exceeded federal health standards for two or more pollutants showed 60 percent were Hispanics, 50 percent black, and 33 percent white (Wernette and Nieves, 1992).

When a previously poor neighbourhood is gentrified, the shift in the neighbourhood's socioeconomic status coincides with greater success in minimizing industrial pollution. In some cases, industry is pushed to relocate outside the community. The amount of pressure on polluters to decrease air emissions or relocate depends in part on the extent to which they are the source of jobs for residents. As gentrification proceeds, improvements in environmental quality may conflict with continued industrial employment for longtime residents.

An examination of vehicle emissions and socioeconomic status reveals that the affluent typically have new vehicles with the latest pollution control devices, whereas the less affluent are more likely to use older, more polluting vehicles, which are responsible for a disproportionate amount of air pollution. In Toronto, for example, 10 percent of vehicles produce more than 50% of the carbon monoxide emissions (Healthy City Office, 1991). Among the worst polluters are the oldest vehicles and those not routinely maintained. In this way, those least able to afford vehicles contribute most to air pollution. However, this trend may be offset by the overall greater impact of the affluent who own more vehicles and use them more.

THE COLLECTIVE GOOD AND INDIVIDUAL DESIRES

Air pollution and its control has considerable political significance at the regional and local levels because of its dependence on land-use planning issues. In Ontario, provincial agencies like the Ontario Round Table on Environment and Economy (through its Urban Development Sectoral Task Force, 1992) and the Commission on Planning and Development Reform in Ontario (1993) have documented the need for policies to minimize sprawl and enhance urban intensification. There has been some success in establishing coherent land-use policies at the provincial level but less so at the local level.

Our existing urban form and societal expectations continue to place the automobile at the centre of our transportation systems, and the large suburban lot as our housing ideal. The ecological need for more compact urban form is not supported and perhaps not understood by most of the population. At issue is the interplay between individual wants and the collective good of society. The shift from sprawl to more compact urban form means less personal space and convenience, but greater access to communal amenities and overall quality of life. Without widespread public support for intensification and increased spending on public transit, local politicians will resist the implementation of provincial policies in their communities.

STRATEGIES TO IMPROVE URBAN AIR QUALITY

Urban air quality is a complex issue that requires a variety of coordinated strategies involving government, the private sector, and the general public to work together to resolve. In most major urban centres across Canada, concerns about the health and environmental impacts of air pollution have triggered many improvement initiatives. Some of these are described below.

ECOSYSTEM-BASED URBAN PLANNING

Ecosystem-based planning tries to recognize the city as a settlement within, rather than beyond, the ecosystem. It takes a long-term view of how our cities should look and function, and it recognizes the interconnection of environmental, social, and economic concerns for establishing sustainable, livable communities (Royal Commission on the Future of the Toronto Waterfront, 1991; Symposium on Planning for Sustainable Development, 1989). Provincial policies that call for ecosystem-based planning can be implemented through planning instruments, such as "official plans" at the regional and municipal levels.

Through the use of official plans, each municipality can guide redevelopment and urban renewal so that transit and land-use planning are integrated; new development is based on a mixed-use concept of housing, jobs, shops, and social amenities; and residential intensification is kept remote from significant point sources of pollution, such as industrial zones. In addition, municipal and regional policies and infrastructure planning could ensure greater integration of local and regional public transit systems, an increase in the quantity and quality of public transit services, and an extensive network of bicycle lanes that take into account safety and air pollution concerns. The long-term shift away from car use will depend on the careful interplay of many public and private sector policies that will enable the public to reduce its dependency on the automobile (City of Toronto Department of Public Health, 1993).

REDUCING EMISSIONS FROM VEHICLES

Emissions from vehicles can be reduced in two major ways: by ensuring that vehicles emit less pollutants, and by encouraging the public to use their vehicles less.

Several strategies are available to minimize emissions from vehicles. Federal regulations covering permissible levels of vehicle pollutants need to be continually reviewed in light of new health effects studies, so that revised regulations spur continuous improvement in motor vehicle manufacturing and fuel production. In the meantime, existing emission standards need to be enforced through vehicle testing. Enforcing emission standards would encourage operators to maintain their vehicles through regular tune-ups, and would discourage tampering with pollution control devices.

Another strategy involves research, technology development and use of cleaner fuels. While some alternative fuels—such as ethanol, compressed natural gas, propane, and electric batteries—are still in the developmental stage, others—such as ethanol-blended gasoline—are not. In the United States, reformulated gasoline, such as ethanol blends, are required in areas with significant ozone pollution (Chang et al., 1991). Reformulated fuels can ensure reductions in benzene in gasoline, or sulphur in diesel fuel.

While technology can make vehicles less polluting, it is up to people to reduce their dependency on the car when other forms of transportation are freely available. As the built environment is improved to make public transit, cycling, and other forms of transportation more attractive, there is an opportunity and need to shift public behaviour away from exclusive reliance on the car.

REDUCING EMISSIONS FROM NON-VEHICLE SOURCES

There are many industrial, commercial, institutional, and household sources of air pollutants, each requiring specific strategies for their control. In general, significant industrial point sources are regulated through provincial air standards, guidelines, or site-specific certificates of approval. In Ontario, as in other provinces, the number of trace toxics covered by air quality standards or guidelines is limited, and of those that have regulatory limits, many do not sufficiently protect public health. Consequently, air quality standards need to be reviewed and revised to reflect the most recent health effects research.

In urban centres, greenhouse gases such as carbon dioxide derive primarily from the residential, commercial, and industrial sectors. In Toronto, about 20 percent of carbon dioxide comes from vehicles, whereas 30 percent is from housing, and 50 percent is from commercial and industrial sources (City of Toronto Special Advisory Committee on the Environment, 1991). The Intergovernmental Panel on Climate Change recently proposed short- and long-term strategies to reduce greenhouse gases on a global scale, but many of these measures can be implemented municipally (City of Toronto Department of Public Health, 1993). Possible measures include conserving energy; improving the production efficiency, conversion, and use of energy; enhancing systems for cogeneration of steam and electricity; improving heating and cooling of buildings; and enhancing lighting and appliance efficiency.

Another major category of air pollutants generated in cities is household toxics including pesticides and solvents. There is a need for greater public awareness of their risks and knowledge about alternatives for them. For example, a telephone survey in Toronto found that more than half the respondents used chemical pesticides at their home (City of Toronto Department of Health, 1992). The promotion and use of Integrated Pest Management (IPM) can significantly reduce the quantity of traditional pesticides used in residences, institutions, and businesses (Bio-Integral Resource Centre, 1989).

VISIONING THE IDEAL CITY: ROAD TO THE FUTURE

Ecologicaliy, most of Canada's largest population centres are under stress. Cities are plagued by traffic congestion, air pollution, contaminated soils, a paucity of natural areas, polluted waterfronts, and noise. However, further population growth in our cities is inevitable. The challenge is to make the best use of land and transportation to bring cities in better balance with their natural environment. This will require a major shift from automobile-centred, sprawling communities to development that is compact, centred on pedestrians, efficient in use of energy, and conservative in use of resources. Increasing urban density could make pedestrian life possible again. Perhaps future growth will lead us to car-free zones and the reclamation of green space from the third of the city now taken up by road allowances.

Ecologically, the ideal urban structure is one in which community buildings and activities are concentrated together, and are surrounded by an agricultural and natural zone (hinterland) big enough to handle resource demands and waste disposal needs of the urban core. In the environmentally sustainable urban community, workplaces and homes are close together, and supply lines between the urban core and the hinterland are relatively short, so that energy demands for transportation and resultant air pollution are minimal. Walking, cycling, and public transit take precedence over the automobile, and compact building form and passive solar design minimize heating requirements and resultant air emissions. In the ideal city, vegetation around and within the built environment is abundant, complex, and diverse to soak up carbon dioxide emissions from human activity. The use of indigenous and diverse vegetation is promoted, as opposed to the current dominance of manicured lawns, so that reliance on pesticides is diminished and the amount of trace toxics in the ecosystem declines.

Although all major Canadian cities currently exceed the carrying capacity of their bioregion, there is great opportunity to rehabilitate underutilized lands into vibrant "chunks of city" that take on the characteristics of an environmentally sustainable community. Until we adjust our land use and transportation policies to fit the limitations posed by the natural environment to provide raw resources and absorb the waste products of urban life, issues like air quality and its effects on health cannot be resolved.

Urban planners and politicians need to rethink how we build and move about in our cities, but it is individual values that will drive social change. The sustainability of cities in the global environment requires re-evaluation of humanity's place in the world and a collective deepening of our responsibility to the Earth and future generations. In the end, we must ask ourselves whether the current level of materialism and consumerism can survive the transition to a sustainable world (Brown and Jacobson, 1987). It may be that we collectively must accept a lower standard of living, as defined by the consumption of material goods, and exchange it for a higher quality of life, as illustrated by good health, social well-being, and the long-term enjoyment of a stable ecosystem.

REFERENCES

Abbey, D.E. 1991. Long-Term Ambient Concentrations of Total Suspended Particulates and Oxidants as Related to Incidence of Chronic Disease in California Seventh-Day Adventists." *Environmental Health Perspectives* 94: 43–50.

American Lung Association. 1990. Workshop on Health Effects of Atmospheric Acids and Their Precursors. Co-chairs D.V. Bates and M.J. Utell. Sponsored by the American Lung Association/American Thoracic Society and the Canadian Lung Association/Canadian Thoracic Society. Sante Fe, N.M., March 22–24.

Bauer, M.A., M.J. Utell, and P.E. Morrow. 1984. "0.3 ppm Nitrogen Dioxide Potentiates Exercise Induced Bronchospasm in Asthmatics." *American Review of Respiratory Disease* 129: A151.

Bio-Integral Resource Centre. 1989. *IPM Policy and Implementation.* Berkeley, Calif.

Brown, L., and J. Jacobson. 1987. "The Future of Urbanization: Facing the Ecological and Economic Constraints." *Worldwatch Paper 77.* Worldwatch Institute.

Burnett, R., et al. 1994. "Effects of Low Ambient Levels of Ozone and Sulphates on the Frequency of Respiratory Admissions to Ontario Hospitals." *Environmental Research* 65: 172–194.

———. 1995. "Associations between Ambient Particulate Sulphate and Admissions to Ontario Hospitals for Cardiac and Respiratory Diseases." *American Journal of Epidemiology* 142(1): 15–22.

Bylin, G., T. Lindvall, T. Rehn, and S. Sundin. "Effects of Short Term Exposure to Ambient Nitrogen Dioxide Concentrations on Human Bronchial Reactivity and Lung Function." *European Journal of Respiratory Disease* 66: 205–17.

California Air Resources Board (CARB). 1991. "California Air Quality—A Status Report." Sacramento, Calif.: Public Information Office.

Chang, T.Y., R.H. Hamerle, S.M. Japar, and I.T. Salmeen. 1991. "Alternative Transportation Fuels and Air Quality." *Environmental Science and Technology* 25(7): 1190–97.

City of Toronto Department of Public Health. 1993. "Outdoor Air Quality in Toronto: Issues and Concerns." Perry Kendall, Medical Officer of Health. City of Toronto.

City of Toronto Department of Public Health. 1992. "Use of Pesticides in the City of Toronto." Clause embodied in Report No. 7 of the Board of Health, referred to the Executive Committee by City Council at its meeting July 6–7. Department of the City Clerk, City of Toronto.

Commission on Planning and Development Reform in Ontario. 1993. *New Planning for Ontario.* Toronto: Queen's Printer for Ontario.

Dann, T. 1987. "Benzene in the Ambient Air of Canadian Urban Areas." Pollution Management Division, Conservation and Protection, Environment Canada. July. Ottawa.

Delfino, R.J., M.R. Becklake, and J.A. Hanley. 1994. "The Relationship of Urgent Hospital Admissions for Respiratory Illnesses to Photochemical Air Pollution Levels in Montreal." *Environmental Research* 67(1): 1–19.

Dockery, D.W., F.E. Speizer, and D.O. Stram. 1989. "Effects of Inhalable Particles on Respiratory Health of Children." *American Review of Respiratory Disease* 139: 587–94.

Edmonston, M., M. Goldberg, and J. Mercer. 1985. "Urban Form in Canada and the United States: An Examination of Urban Density Gradients." *Journal of the American Planning Association* 51(2).

Environment Canada. 1991. *The State of Canada's Environment*. Ottawa: Minister of Supply and Services.

———. In press. *The State of Canada's Environment*. Ottawa: State of the Environment Directorate.

French, H.F. 1990. "Clearing the Air." *State of the World 1990*. Worldwatch Institute.

Healthy City Office. 1991. "Evaluating the Role of the Automobile: A Municipal Strategy." A report prepared by the Technical Workgroup on Traffic Calming and Vehicle Emission Reduction. City of Toronto.

Horstman, D., W. McDonnell, and S. Abdul-Salaam. 1988. "Changes in Pulmonary Function and Airway Reactivity Due to Prolonged Exposure to Near Ambient Ozone Levels." Presented at the Third U.S.–Dutch International Symposium on Atmospheric Ozone Research and Its Policy Implications. Nijmegen, Netherlands. May.

IBI Group. 1990. "Greater Toronto Area Urban Structure Concepts Study." Greater Toronto Coordinating Committee, Toronto.

Metropolitan Toronto Planning Department. 1990. "Concepts for the Future GTA." Municipality of Metropolitan Toronto.

Mitchell, R. 1989. "Canada's Population from Ocean to Ocean." *Focus on Canada Series* (cat. no. 98–120). Ottawa: Statistics Canada.

Molfino, N. 1991. "Effect of Low Concentrations of Ozone on Inhaled Allergen Responses in Asthmatic Subjects." *The Lancet*. July 27: 199.

Mumme, S.P., 1991. "Clearing the Air: Environmental Reform in Mexico." *Environment* 33(10): 6–12.

Newman, P., and J. Kenworthy. 1989. *Cities and Automobile Dependence: An International Sourcebook*. Brookfield, Vt.: Grower, Technical.

Ontario Lung Association. 1991. *Lung Facts*. Toronto.

Ontario Ministry of the Environment (OMOE). 1985. "Metropolitan Toronto Emissions Inventory." (Unpublished). Toronto.

Ontario Ministry of the Environment and Energy (OMOEE). 1994. *Air Quality in Ontario: 1993*. Toronto: Queen's Printer for Ontario.

———. 1994. Scientific Criteria Document for Multimedia Environmental Standards Development—Lead. Standards Development Branch. Prepared by S. Fleming and F. Ursitti. Toronto: Queen's Printer for Ontario.

Ontario Round Table on Environment and Economy. 1991. "Urban Development Sectoral Task Force—Final Report." Toronto: Queen's Printer for Ontario.

Ostro, B.D., M.J. Lipsett, M.B. Wiener, and J.C. Selner. 1991. "Asthmatic Responses to Airborne Acid Aerosols." *American Journal of Public Health* 81: 694–702.

Ozkaynak, A., et al. 1995. "Association between Daily Mortality and Air Pollution in Toronto, Canada." Proceedings of the International Society for Environmental Epidemiology. Noordwijkerhout, Netherlands.

Paehlke, R. 1991. "The Environmental Effects of Urban Intensification." Prepared for the Municipal Planning Policy Branch, Ontario Ministry of Municipal Affairs. Toronto.

———. 1986. "Bucolic Mythis: Towards a More Urbanist Environmentalism." Research Paper no. 159. Centre for Urban and Community Studies, University of Toronto.

Pengally, L.D., and C.H. Goldsmith. 1988. "Effect of the Environment on Asthma in Children." Proceedings Session A: Air Quality Research. Environmental Research Technology Transfer Conference. November 28–29. Royal York Hotel, Toronto.

Royal Commission on the Future of the Toronto Waterfront. 1991. "Towards an Ecosystem Approach to Land Use Planning." *Planning for Sustainability*. Minister of Supply and Services Canada.

Samet, J.M. 1994. "Learning about Air Pollution and Asthma." *American Journal of Respiratory and Critical Care Medicine* 149(6): 1398–99.

Schwartz, J. 1994a. "PM10, Ozone and Hospital Admissions for the Elderly in Minneapolis–St. Paul, Minnesota." *Archives of Environmental Health* 49(5): 366–74.

———. 1994b. "Air Pollution and Hospital Admissions for the Elderly in Detroit, Michigan." *American Journal of Respiratory and Critical Care Medicine* 150(3): 648–55.

Schwartz, J., and D.W. Dockery. 1992. "Particulate Air Pollution and Daily Mortality in Steubenville, Ohio." *American Journal of Epidemiology* 135(1): 12–19.

Shenfeld, L., B. Srivastava, D. Yap, and R. Bloxam. 1991. "Environmental Audit of the East Bayfront/Port Industrial Area. Phase 2: Atmospheric Environment." Technical Report No. 6. Royal Commission on the Future of the Toronto Waterfront. Toronto.

Starke, L. 1990. *State of the World.* New York: W.W. Norton and Co.

Symposium on Planning for Sustainable Development. 1989. "Planning for Sustainable Development: A Resource Book." W.E. Rees, ed. Proceedings of a November 1988 Symposium Organized by the School of Community and Regional Planning. Published by UBC Centre for Human Settlements, University of British Columbia.

Thurston, G.D., K. Ito, C.G. Hayes, D.V. Bates, and M. Lippmann. 1994. "Respiratory Hospital Admissions and Summertime Haze Air Pollution in Toronto, Ontario: Consideration of the Role of Acid Aerosols." *Environmental Health Research* 65(2): 271–90.

Tseng, R.Y., C.K. Li, and J.A. Spinks. 1992. "Particulate Air Pollution and Hospitalization for Asthma." *Annals of Allergy* 68(5): 425–32.

United Nations Environment Program (UNEP) and World Health Organization (WHO). 1994. "Air Pollution in the World's Megacities." *Environment* 36(2): 4–37.

Wernette, D., and L. Nieves. 1992. "Breathing Polluted Air: Minorities Are Disproportionately Exposed." *EPA Journal*, March/April: 16–17.

Ziegenfus, R.C. 1987. "Air Quality and Health." In *Public Health and the Environment: The United States Experience*, M.R. Greenberg, ed. New York: Guilford Press, 139–72.

QUESTIONS FOR DISCUSSION

1. How significant a health problem is air quality in Canadian cities?

2. How good is our current knowledge of the health risks of air pollutants and how does this influence our ability to make policies and regulations to control air pollution?

3. What is the cause of air pollution problems in our cities?

4. What can urban residents do to improve air quality? Which actions should be voluntary and which should be mandatory?

5. What are the roles of municipal, provincial, and federal government in improving air quality?

6. Are regulations effective in improving air quality?

7. Is it possible to design or live in a car-free city?

8. How would you envision the ideal city?

Global Warming

F. Kenneth Hare

University Professor Emeritus
University of Toronto

THE QUESTION OF GLOBAL WARMING

There is evidence—which will be discussed later—that mean annual global surface air temperatures have risen since the beginning of the 20th century, while the lower stratosphere appears to have cooled. These are global effects, though their impact has not been uniform. Canada has been among the most affected countries.

Have these changes been caused by worldwide releases of greenhouse gases, of which carbon dioxide from fuel burning is the most prominent? Several of these gases have been rising in global concentration. But there is argument about cause and effect. Is a lasting, pollution-induced climatic change being induced? Or are the observed changes part of a natural fluctuation? Will they continue, and perhaps intensify? Or will they reverse themselves?

Beyond these primary questions are others of a reactive kind. What will the climatic changes do to natural ecosystems, and hence to renewable resources? How will they affect farming, forestry, fisheries, transportation, and energy use? Will they influence human health? Will sea levels rise? Can we devise effective strategies to combat the bad effects—and perhaps profit from the good? Are issues of equity involved?

THE ROOTS OF CLIMATIC CHANGE

Climate can be seen as the generalized behaviour in time and space of the atmosphere, oceans, lakes, and rivers. Terrestrial climate depends on receipts of solar energy, on a compensating return flow of energy to space, on the rate of spin of the earth about its axis, on its orbit round the sun, and on the composition of the atmosphere. All of these are nearly (but not quite) constant. Hence one might expect climate to be stable.

In a sense, climate is only a human idea. Reality is the sequence of weather changes. These consolidate themselves into the notion of climate—experience and expectation of the range of weather characteristic of specific places, seasons, and decades. By analogy with human nature, weather is the fickle mood, but climate the enduring personality.

Present-day fears about global warming arose only thirty years ago, though the roots of anxiety go much deeper. Geologists showed in the 19th century that the world had undergone cold periods in its recent history. Research has since demonstrated repeated warmings and coolings of the entire planet over the past two million years. The most recent cold glacial event ended barely 10 000 years ago, as human beings were about to launch the great experiments of agriculture and urbanization. Since then climates have fluctuated, but within narrow limits. But now there are signs that these limits may be exceeded.

Among meteorologists, it used to be stated as a fact that the climate underlying short-term weather changes was unchanging. Such conservatism was a practical necessity, because weather anomalies tended to make the public believe that lasting change was in progress. A series of hot, dry summers or cold winters usually led to media speculation about change. But the unusual conditions nearly always ended—as did, for example, the droughty 1930s—with a return to more normal conditions. Forecasters expected this, and downplayed the idea that current events portended the future. They were slow to admit—as they have now done—that future climates might indeed be different.

The temperature of the earth's surface, and of the overlying atmosphere, depends on the concentration of certain gases, vapours, and cloud layers. Oxygen, nitrogen, and argon, which make up almost 99.97 percent of dry air, are largely transparent to incoming sunlight, and also to the return flow of earth radiation to space. Certain less abundant gases let the sunshine in, but retard the return flow. These greenhouse gases include water vapour (H_2O), carbon dioxide (CO_2), methane (CH_4), nitrous oxide (N_2O), ozone (O_3), and various pollutants, such as the chlorofluorocarbons (CFCs). Thin though these gases may be, they play a key role in moderating surface climates, because they are globally distributed by the winds. The globe's surface is, on average, 33°C warmer than it would be without the greenhouse gases, which thus make the world habitable to advanced organisms. The natural greenhouse effect has been essential to the human colonization of the earth.

Sixty years ago, however, suspicions arose that carbon dioxide was increasing in amount. These suspicions were confirmed in the 1950s, and in 1957 systematic monitoring of CO_2 began, first on Mauna Loa in Hawaii, and today at numerous stations worldwide. It is now clear that CO_2 increased from 280 parts per million by volume (ppmv) in the early 19th century to 360 ppmv in 1995, and is still increasing at about 1.5 ppmv per annum. More recently observers have detected increases in nearly all the other greenhouse gases. The net combined heating effect is increasing at about 1 percent per annum. Moreover the increases are in most cases traceable to human economic practices—the release of gases from exhaust pipes, farms, furnaces, refrigerators, air conditioners, burning forests, and wastage of soils. Humans are thus adding possibly hazardous components to the beneficial greenhouse gases.

International scientific attention to this issue, and to its possible consequences for human welfare, began to increase in the 1960s. Primary credit must go to the late Roger Revelle, then Director of the Scripps Institution of Oceanography at La Jolla, California, who got the ear of the White House on the subject. Revelle chaired a 1964–65 Presidential Task Force whose report was read all round the scientific world. A colleague at La Jolla, C. David Keeling, had led the international monitoring effort by establishing the Mauna Loa (Hawaii) observatory record (in 1957), and subsequently insisted on sound calibration of the instruments used elsewhere. At first, there was scepticism about the issue's importance. But action by UN agencies, especially the World Meteorological Organization and the UN Environment Programme, led to rapid growth in interest. Throughout the 1980s and into the 1990s the interlocked issues of greenhouse gas releases and global warming dominated debate on the stability of the world's climate—and hence of its living cover.

Moreover, the issue has arrived on the world's political agenda. Global warming has become commonplace in parliamentary debate, editorial comment, the visual media, and the attention of public interest groups. From 1988 on (when a key conference in Toronto followed an economic summit, the G-7) the world's statespersons have been involved—though often reluctantly—in trying to devise world action to combat the effect.

CLIMATIC MODELS

Understanding global warming involves many sciences. Meteorology and climatology are central, but other fields are also crucial—for example the geosciences, ecology, chemistry, oceanography, and soil science. Because a wide measure of uncertainty is inevitable, debate is often heated; the less the certainty, the noisier the argument.

Climatic change presents a difficult paradox. The laws governing atmospheric and oceanic behaviour are well-known, and are largely deterministic; equations can be written down expressing the laws—for example, those of dynamics, radiative exchanges, thermodynamics, and continuity (the conservation of mass). But the equations are formidably nonlinear, which means that they can be solved, if at all, only by numerical analysis—made possible by digital algebra and the electronic computer.

The solutions are often chaotic in the mathematical sense. Climate is a prime example of a system in which the governing laws are known, but are found to allow an almost infinite set of solutions (every day's weather is such a solution). The circulation of atmosphere and ocean, which modulates world climate, shows many enduring characteristics (such as prevailing winds and ocean currents); but it has never exactly repeated itself since the world began, and probably never will.

Since the 1950s scientists have nevertheless learned how to predict short-term changes by means of numerical models (numerical weather prediction) expressing these laws. Broadcast weather forecasts are today largely based on such techniques (which were begun by John von Neumann at Princeton's Institute for Advanced Studies in 1949). In the 1960s other scientists—most notably a group at the Geophysical Fluid Dynamics Laboratory (GFDL), also at Princeton—devised ways of adapting these predictive models to the longer term, i.e., to the description of hypothetical future climates.

Climatic models can be designed on a variety of scales. The simplest are just models of the entire planet's response to the incoming solar radiation. They are spatially zero-dimensional, because they make no distinctions between up or down, south or north, east or west. One-dimensional models allow the earth's response to vary along the vertical. Two-dimensional models portray the response along meridional (i.e., latitudinal) cross-sections, to take account of up/down and north/south differences. And three-dimensional models try to represent conditions in real space, i.e., over the whole earth, and through the entire depth of atmosphere and ocean.

Most vitally, the climatic system—the complex pervaded by climate—can only be effectively analyzed by models that link atmosphere and ocean. Though both domains obey the same laws, and need similar modelling techniques, they have very different time and space characteristics. The atmosphere flows freely, is light and mobile, and has only one spatial boundary, the continental and ocean surface. The ocean, by contrast, is confined by gravity to the ocean basins, and is sluggish in behaviour because water is heavy, and has a high heat capacity. Nevertheless, since 1989 (Washington and Meehl, 1989; Stouffer, Manabe, and Bryan, 1989; Mitchell, Johns, Gregory, and Tett, 1995) we have had models that link the two domains, with increasing reliability as experience accumulates.

What do the models do? Models in this sense are pictures devised by the human mind to resemble reality as closely as possible. Those used in climate studies do the following things:

- They express the governing laws in the form of differential equations: the Newtonian equations of motion, linking forces with momentum changes, which predict winds and ocean currents; gravitation; the conservation of mass and energy (neither can be created nor destroyed); and the laws of thermodynamics.
- They specify realistic external conditions, such as the earth's rate of spin about its axis, the composition of the atmosphere, and the rate of input of solar radiation (miscalled the solar constant).
- They allow for the above conditions to be varied (for example, the doubling of greenhouse gas concentrations, or changes in the solar constant) to allow prediction of future climates.
- They are capable of huge data inputs and storage, because initial states must be adequately defined, and the models then run for the equivalent of decades or centuries—hence an ocean of data has to be objectively analyzed, and then stored in accessible form.

Simple zero-, one- and two-dimensional models can be worked out on the blackboard, or with personal computers. But the three-dimensional models (general circulation models, called GCMs) require powerful computers, long data inventories, a major investment in software, and above all a dedicated and competent staff. It takes years to get such models going. Hence they have been successfully established only in a few centres round the world. Canada's GCMs were devised in Toronto (at the Atmospheric Environment Service), and are now run at the Canadian Institute for Climate Studies in Victoria, B.C., very much as a national facility accessible to the research community.

Because this problem is global, it has from the first been tackled internationally. Atmospheric and ocean scientists have achieved a substantial measure of consensus—and have presented the results to statespersons. Since 1988 coordination of effort has been in the hands of an Intergovernmental Panel on Climate Change (IPCC), under the chair of Bert Bolin from Stockholm. This body presented a major report to the World Conference on Environment and Development in 1992 and has subsequently reviewed its own scientific findings (IPCC, 1990, 1992, 1996), with a further update expected near the turn of the century.

The major findings are:

- Most of the greenhouse gases are indeed increasing globally; the list includes carbon dioxide (about 0.5 percent per annum), methane (0.8 percent), nitrous oxide (0.3 percent), ozone, the chlorofluorocarbons and other synthetics, and water vapour (though the latter is not formally known to be increasing).
- The increases will probably continue, and perhaps accelerate above the 1 percent per annum equivalent increase in heating capacity at present observed.
- A rise of global surface air temperature of 0.3°C to 0.6°C has been observed in the past century, only about half what model predictions imply.

Figure 7.1 shows the actual progress of surface global warming since 1855 based on work by several groups that have consolidated the available observations from sea and land, as far as possible removing biases due to urban heating, and to poor distribution of observations in some parts of the world and in earlier times. The findings are still approximate, and are valid for only the earth's surface; the lower stratosphere (the layer 12–20 km above sea level) is known to have cooled (as predicted by the models).

Figure 7.2 shows an equivalent diagram for Canada as a whole, as estimated by Environment Canada on the basis of 132 quality controlled station records. Evidently the warming has been near 1°C in the past century, about double the global figure. The maximum effect has been seen in a belt from the Yukon across the northern Prairie provinces into the Great Lakes region. Parts of the Atlantic coastal belt, and the nearby Labrador Sea, have experienced none of this warming, and some localities may actually have cooled slightly. Unequal spatial distribution has been a feature of the global warming, and is likely to remain so—a feature that makes the design of countermeasures difficult. The precipitation record (rain plus snow) is shorter, and suggests that recent years have been wetter than earlier in the century.

Moreover, figures 7.1 and 7.2 show that the warming has gone ahead in two spurts—one from about 1910 into the early 1940s, and the second from the late 1970s on. In between the global rise stagnated, and over the Northern Hemisphere there was a significant cooling. There are also large year-to-year

FIGURE 7.1
Global Air Temperatures Relative to the 1961–1990 Mean, 1855 to Present

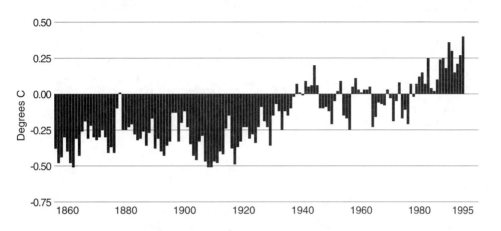

Source: Data produced by the Climatic Research Unit, University of East Anglia, and the Hadley Centre, Bracknell, U.K.

Global surface mean annual air temperature expressed as departures from the 1961–1990 mean value. The curve indicates two main periods of warming, between 1910–1940 and after 1975.

departures from the general curve—some of which are larger than the 100-year trend.

Can such irregularities be reconciled with the theory that increasing greenhouse gas concentrations are responsible? As far as can be judged, the buildup of the effective heating power of the added gases has been fairly uniform in time. The effective gases, moreover, are poorly soluble in water, and hence resist washing out by rain. The world's wind systems distribute them uniformly round the globe, so that their warming effect should also tend to be uniform. Why, then, is the actual outcome so complicated?

The several GCMs available to the IPCC gave varying estimates of the warming to be expected from a doubling of greenhouse gas concentration, expected later in the 21st century. Successive assessments (IPCC, 1990, 1992, 1996) have confirmed that annual global surface air temperature rise should lie within the range 1° to 4°C in the next century—the amount depending on the rate of greenhouse gas buildup, the role of air–sea interactions, and as to how the models handle radiative exchanges, cloud formation, and the form of the earth's surface. No model yet gives fully satisfactory regional detail. The most recent Canadian GCM, for example, shows a very large inland warming for doubled greenhouse gases; but the pattern of warming does not closely resemble the

FIGURE 7.2
Mean Annual Surface Air Temparature, Canada, 1895–1995

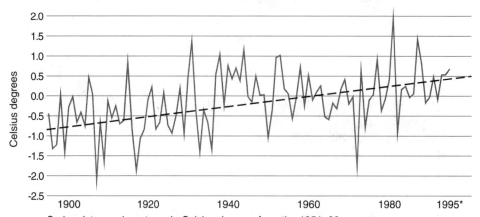

Series data are departures in Celsius degrees from the 1951–80 average.
Dashed line shows linear trend of 1.1 C° over the period 1895–1995.
Mean annual air temperature from a spatially adjusted set of 132 stations, together with the
upward linear trend through the series. Both diagrams are based on deviations from the
1951–1980 averages. The data are complete through December 31,1995.

Mean Annual Precipitation, Canada, 1948–1995

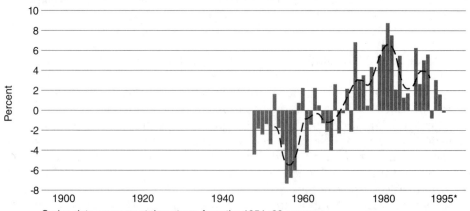

Series data are percent departures from the 1951–80 average.
Smooth curve is a 9-point binomial filter (weighted running mean).
Mean annual precipitation since 1948 over a similar network of stations. The smooth curve
indicates the nine-year trend exhibited by the data. Both diagrams are based on deviations
from the 1951–1980 averages.

Source: Atmospheric Environment Service, Environment Canada. Reproduced with the
permission of the Minister of Supply and Services Canada, 1996.

changes observed so far. The actual global warming also shows such irregularities, and overall is much less than the models predict.

In sum, science presents three main bodies of information about global warming. It has been able, in spite of a poor observational base, to demonstrate an actual warming of the surface of the earth since 1855. Few people challenge this finding, though all agree that it is approximate. Secondly, science has demonstrated the buildup within the atmosphere of the persistent greenhouse gases, and estimated the heating that these should already have caused—more warming, in fact, than has been observed. And thirdly, science has made possible the application of predictive models to future climates.

As shown above, Canada has already been affected by these global changes, and this will continue in the future. But the effect is very unequal in different parts of the country. This, too, is likely to be the case in future, and to be a source of political tensions arising from probable measures of adaptation or avoidance. For example, if it is decided that consumption of coal, oil, and natural gas must be curtailed, Alberta will feel the real brunt of the cutbacks, with British Columbia and Saskatchewan also affected. Impacts on farming will fall very unequally on the Prairie provinces and Ontario. At this time it looks as if spring wheat production on the Prairies may be handicapped by the predicted changes, whereas in parts of Ontario, agriculture may actually be helped. These are the kinds of regional inequalities that cause difficulties in federal politics. It is hard to devise remedies that will please all regions.

ECOSYSTEM IMPACT: RENEWABLE RESOURCES

A century or more of research has demonstrated that ecosystems—plant and animal communities and their physical setting—relate closely to climate; indeed, if the original meaning of "ecosystem" is retained (Tansley, 1935), climate is part and parcel of the global ecosystem. As climate has changed in the past, moreover, vegetation, animal life, and soils have also changed, though not in lockstep. All agree that there is a high degree of interdependence between climate and the world's living cover; but one cannot yet specify exactly what the links should be.

Plant and animal communities get their energy from the sun directly, or from the atmosphere (which delivers solar energy indirectly whenever warm air flows over a cool, plant-covered landscape). Ecosystems store energy, however, at only a small fraction of the power of atmospheric processes. Photosynthesis by green plants (the creation of energy-rich sugars and starches by green tissues) captures less than 1 percent of the incoming sunlight. Direct measurement of climate–plant energy linkages is hence difficult, because of the precision required.

Nevertheless, working models exist (e.g., Melillo et al., 1993) of the potential global productivity of present-day terrestrial ecosystems, i.e., of the capacity of the land plant cover to convert energy into living tissues, and of the possible response to altered climate. Similar attempts have been made to estimate the mass/energy productivity of marine ecosystems, though in this case the conversions take place within ocean waters rather than an air–land interface. From such exercises it may be possible to estimate the impact of impending climatic change on living communities—which to human interests implies also the future availability of renewable resources.

Such research cannot at present detect quantitatively the impact on life of the climatic changes in progress (though major efforts are being made). But one can point to a few major areas of concern:

1. The desert margin continues to plague the public conscience, because in many places—especially in Africa—rising human population puts pressure on the thin soils and scattered vegetation of lands that can in nature sustain only low animal populations, and that allow only subsistence farming (unless irrigation water is available from external sources, as in Pakistan and several Middle Eastern countries). The prolonged desiccation (drying out) of sub-Saharan Africa (Rowell, Folland, Maskell, and Ward, 1995) after the mid 1960s gave rise to fears about desertification, i.e., the spread of desert surfaces into formerly productive land. Rainfall in this zone is monsoon-fed, and is erratic and unreliable. Although conditions have eased in recent years, rainfall returned to pre-1965 levels only in 1994 (World Meteorological Organization, 1995), leading to fears that human misuse might have permanently damaged not only soil and vegetation, but the climate itself. Modelling exercises have not confirmed these fears, and it is possible that monsoon rainfall may be strengthened, not only in Africa, but in southern Asia also. Clear answers to these anxieties will be slow in coming, in spite of major international efforts.

2. Tropical rain forest areas are also under intense economic pressure, leading often to permanent clearance—with the forest replaced by grassy pastures, as in Brazil, or by poorer-quality forest regrowth in areas of shifting agriculture. These pressures cause concern on many grounds: for example, that they are likely to lead to global climatic effects (now seen as unlikely); to altered climates within the deforested areas (quite certain); or to fundamental changes in the removal of soil nutrients, and their transport by rivers (notably the Amazon) into the oceans (already in progress). No single issue has more completely polarized opinion than the fate of these magnificent forests. To countries in Latin America or Southeast Asia with large areas of surviving forest, they appear as resources to be exploited as, for example, Canada has exploited her Pacific rain forests; whereas to many scientists and environmentalists their destruction seems to threaten global well-being. The impact of tropical rain-forest clearance on global warming has been examined by several modelling groups, with ambiguous results. Most

studies suggest substantial effects on temperature and precipitation in the cleared areas, but there is no result firmly supporting the view that the rain forests are crucial to the overall global climate. Further clearance will slightly augment the greenhouse effect. Overall, however, the evidence suggests that global climatic effects will be minor, whereas the effects within the countries clearing their forests are likely to be drastic, and largely hostile (deterioration of soil fertility, water quality, and perhaps rainfall in nearby arid areas, as in Brazil).

3. Of direct concern to Canada is the fate of the remaining Pacific coast rain forest, and the boreal forest. Much of the productive part of this immense stretch of cooler or cold forested land has already been clear-cut or thinned by the forest industries. Conflicts between environmentalist groups and the industry have focused upon native claims to much of this land. Given the high value of the harvestable resources, this conflict is understandable. But model predictions have long suggested that the main impact of global warming will be felt in high latitudes. In Canada the past century, and in particular the 1980s and 1990s, has seen warming in these latitudes. The largest increase in mean annual temperature has been in northwestern forest regions, the Mackenzie Valley and the Prairie provinces. The boreal forest—the evergreen spruce–fir–larch–pine forest extending from Alaska across Canada to Newfoundland—is clearly at risk from the predicted warming. The dominant tree species, which are remarkably hardy, appear well-adapted to the present-day boreal climate (Hare and Ritchie, 1972). But the area over which such climate extends will be driven far north by the expected warming, and the forest area will experience conditions now typical of the northern Great Plains and Great Lakes regions. It is uncertain whether northwest migration of the trees will keep pace with the warming. It is possible (Rizzo, 1991) that the spruce trees so valuable in pulp manufacture will be segregated into small separated areas. Fire is necessary for the renewal of the boreal forest, but the warming may greatly augment the natural burning. Insect damage may also be heightened. A large research program is in progress (the Canada–U.S. BOREAS project) to measure the sensitivity of the forest to impending climatic change; but it does not extend to the design of countermeasures. That will have to come when the present situation has been appraised.

SOCIAL SIGNIFICANCE AND INTELLECTUAL RESPONSE

The threat of global warming has gone, in barely three decades, from scientific awakening in the 1960s to intergovernmental action in the 1990s (or so it is hoped). The ozone depletion scare was even more expeditious, in that hypotheses voiced only in the early 1970s led to the Montreal Protocol, and action to elimi-nate the offending pollutants, in only twenty years. But moves to control human-made climatic change (besides being related to the ozone issue) are far more sweeping in their requirements and impacts on people. To have got this far has been a unique exercise in searching for consensus by determined scientists and environmentalists. Cynics say that nothing has yet been achieved, except a great many extra seat sales on transoceanic flights. But that is unfair to the sponsors of the proposed actions.

Canadian consciousness of this issue has been high, and Canadian scientists have been among the leaders in the consensus-building movement. Perhaps this is because Canada has a very high per-capita energy use, and fossil fuel con-sumption. Perhaps it is because it has already been affected by the warming more than most other countries—and is likely to continue as one of the warm-ing's major targets. As the issue has passed from scientists to diplomats and politicians Canada's stance has become more conservative and cautious. But Canada still appears among the world's most concerned societies.

There are tangible written evidences of this concern. One is the report of a task force on climate adaptation of the Canadian Climate Program (Smit, 1994), which sets out in some detail how Canadian society might respond to the pre-dicted changes. Adaptation is, of course, a possible response to the challenge—a response that admits the likelihood that we cannot avoid the warming. The alternative response, avoidance, will depend on more drastic measures to alter our economic practices, a solution that will hurt us more than it would some other countries. This document is quasi-official, in that the Climate Program Board brings together (and has done so since 1979) most of Canada's govern-ments and some of her academics and private groups in an informal forum. It is a typical Canadian response to the rigidities imposed by federalism.

There are also documents that reveal the breadth of Canada's nongovern-mental response to the challenge. Two books discuss the ethical dilemmas aris-ing from the impending changes (Coward and Hurka, 1993; Dotto, 1993). What intergovernmental issues are involved within Canada? What inequities exist as between provinces? Or between developed and developing countries? Tom Hurka's conclusions end with seven recommendations, all of which have influ-enced the present book. This was an initiative of the University of Calgary's Institute for the Humanities, of which Coward was then director.

A second exercise led by Coward, after his move to the Centre for Studies in Religion and Society of the University of Victoria, was a conference addressing the issues of resource consumption and the environment (Searle, 1995), effec-tively moving beyond the issues of equity into those of conscience and belief. One of those present, David Hallman, was also involved in the preparation of a World Council of Churches study paper, *Accelerated Climate Change* (World Council of Churches, 1993), which reviewed many of the same issues.

But for most students and scholars in the humanities and social sciences, the global warming issue—and its even broader relative, global change—has seemed unfamiliar. It is significant that many of the individuals and institutions who have considered the human response to global warming have been natural scientists or geographers, rather than lawyers, economists, sociologists, historians, or political scientists. The traditional concerns of these latter groups—and their working assumptions—did not stress regard for nature, or for humanity's role as a disturber of natural systems. This has been especially true of economists, who have seen the natural world as the fount of resources on which human enterprises could rely. Such resources could readily be replaced by others, say these economists, if any one of them showed signs of exhaustion. This attitude has been modified by recent experience; but it is still there, even among the most environmentally concerned economists. As against this lurking bias, however, there have been attempts at a more consensual approach—one of them involving the chair of IPCC (Bolin) and a Nobel laureate in economics (Arrow, Bolin, Constanza, Dasgupta, Folke, Holling, Jansson, Levin, Mäler, Perrings, and Pimentel, 1995).

Whatever the outcome of this controversy, the industrialized western powers seem to have admitted that the problems are real, though the degree of commitment varies from power to power. The Canadian public also seems to be aware that global warming has already affected Canada, and is likely to pose problems in the future calling for control. But here, too, the problem appears differently to various groups. Fossil fuel producing or dependent corporations naturally fear efforts to reduce carbon dioxide and methane releases, because the proposed remedies threaten higher costs and future sales. By the same token the problem appears different in Alberta from its image in, for example, Manitoba or Québec. No national consensus has appeared on what Canada should do, though plans exist, and have been presented to international forums. There are suggestions that the issue is receding in public attention in many countries, Canada included. The G-7 leaders meeting in June 1995 in Halifax barely mentioned environmental issues. On the other hand, the dry, hot summer of 1995 created a severe forest fire situation in Manitoba and Ontario. Increased burning of the northern forests has been widely predicted as a consequence of global warming, and already there are voices saying that 1995 was the latest in a series of bad fire years that confirm the prediction. Cause and effect have not yet been demonstrated; but the likelihood remains that further rises in summer temperatures will threaten severe increases in fires.

POLITICAL SIGNIFICANCE AND DEVELOPMENTS

The attendance—and the words—of Prime Ministers Harlem Brundtland (of Norway) and Mulroney (of Canada) at the World Conference on the Changing Atmosphere, held in Toronto in late June 1988, marked the real entrance of global warming on to the stage of world politics. Under the inspired chairmanship of Stephen Lewis, then Canada's Ambassador to the United Nations, the conference issued a powerful manifesto calling for a specific target for reduced CO_2 emissions (a 5 percent reduction by 2005). The manifesto also recognized that the interests of developed and less developed countries differed strikingly. For countries such as Canada, the United States, and the members of the European Union the challenge was to reduce fossil-fuel use, both per capita and in aggregate totals. For the less developed countries, the national agendas were virtually unanimous: *more* development was essential to their emergence from 1988 living standards. If such countries were to cut back on forest clearance, for example, they could do so only if they were in some way compensated. This was also a central message of the World Commission on Environment and Development, chaired by Mrs. Brundtland: that sustainable development, and not retrenchment, would have to be the way out of the wilderness for the poorer nations (WCED, 1989).

The attention of the world community was thus awakened. At the Second World Climate Conference, held in Geneva in 1990, the message was reinforced (the speakers included Lady Thatcher of the U.K., Prime Minister Rocard of France, and King Hussein of Jordan). Both conferences, incidentally, were organized by a quiet Canadian, Howard Ferguson, who had been head of the Canadian Atmospheric Environment Service. In 1988 the World Meteorological Organization (a UN agency) and the UN Environment Programme established an Intergovernmental Panel on Climate Change (IPCC), chaired by Bert Bolin, an eminent atmospheric scientist from Stockholm. The IPCC has since served as the international review agency for all aspects of global warming—the science, the potential impacts, and measures to prevent or adapt to the impending changes. In 1990 the UN General Assembly established an Intergovernmental Negotiating Committee (INC) whose chief task was to draw up a draft Framework Convention on Climate Change. This convention was laid before the 1992 UN Conference on Environment and Development in Rio de Janeiro (UNCED), which was chaired by Maurice Strong. The convention would become binding on the parties after fifty countries had ratified it. This was achieved early in 1994, when Portugal signed. Among the first ten signatories were three small island states (Mauritius, Seychelles, and Maldives) whose territories would be threatened by rising sea levels, a predicted outcome of the warming. The convention is thus in force.

It calls for stabilization of greenhouse gas concentrations at levels that will not harm natural ecosystems, and that will accordingly not reduce further the usefulness of what have previously been seen as abundantly renewable resources. Stabilization, however, calls for inventory, and then for sharp reductions in emissions, especially of carbon dioxide. This at once opens up the difference of interest between developed and less developed countries, and the convention stresses that accommodation between these interests (allowing for the rapid industrialization of some hitherto less developed economies, notably those of southeast Asia) is a cardinal aspect of the convention. It was stipulated that "meetings of the parties"—i.e., of the political representatives of the signatories—would seek such accommodation, as well as receive continued scientific advice from the IPCC or successor bodies.

The first such meeting took place in Berlin in late March and early April of 1995. From it emerged a document called the Berlin Mandate, whose usefulness and implications have yet to be fully assessed. Bonn has been selected as the convention's *siège-social*. But the main achievement was to establish a working process to bring more concrete measures before the next Conference of the Parties (probably in the fall of 1996). The major sticking points remain unresolved. Environmentalists, are, as usual, disappointed at the lack of concrete targets for emission reductions. Canada and the U.S. (whose prior commitment to strong measures had been sceptically viewed) emerged dissatisfied yet not wholly discouraged—in the eyes of the two countries' official representatives.

But one can argue, given the slowness with which democracies crawl toward solutions of internal problems, that it is amazing that the world has got as far as it has on a subject so novel to diplomats and statespersons. That they have done so is a tribute to the scientists who have refused to be discouraged.

CONSENSUS AND UNCERTAINTY: TREATING GLOBAL WARMING

The road to future security is not merely impeded, however, by the claims of competing interests, and by the slowness of the governments to respond to the scientific evidence. Also effective has been the uncertainty of science's findings, and the fact that opinion among individual scientists is not unanimous. Those whose doubts are supported by strong credentials often accuse the IPCC of having created a consensus only among those who have been willing to accept the findings of the numerical modellers, a small élite that, in the view of the critics, claims too much for its collective work. Among the qualified critics are figures such as Reid Bryson, one of the founders of modern climatology, Richard Lindzen, William Nierenberg, and Fred Singer in the U.S.

The impact of this uncertainty on decision-making has been treated elsewhere (Hare, 1989). Persons and corporations whose interests may be injured by action to contain greenhouse warming naturally seize on dissension among scientists, and argue that one should wait for greater certainty before acting. Cost-effective or cost-neutral steps can be taken first, before more challenging moves are attempted.

The sense that Canada should respond cautiously springs more from the nature of the uncertainty than from doubts about the scientific analysis. Characteristically, the uncertainty leads to oversimplification of the issue, and it is this tendency to think in bulk terms about the warming that carries danger with it.

Characteristically, decision-makers and managers think of global warming as a general, slow but steady rise in temperature, perhaps accompanied by changes in rainfall and snowfall. This may be valid in certain regions, and quite wrong in others. For example, there has already been an increase in forest fire losses in Western Canada. Many commentators have blamed this on warmer, drier springs and summers and assume that this will continue as climate warms up. But foresters warn that the rise in fires may have been due to the accumulation of litter and brush in the forests, rather than to climatic warming. On the Atlantic coast, where there has been little or no warming so far, and where sea temperatures may actually have fallen, a rise in temperature might be welcomed, although its possible effect on fish stocks remains hard to predict. The essence of the problem is that global warming is anything but a uniform, simple, and steady process.

The present solar constant, the present composition of the atmosphere, and the present level of human economic activity do *not* create a uniform climate for the earth. The reality is highly complex. Why else would Winnipeg's climate differ so greatly from Vancouver's if these factors did not lead to spatially variable consequences? And why do successive years differ so much from one another? The answer lies in the complexity of the links between the driving factors and the observed outcome. The world reacts to nearly constant forcing in a skittish way that scientific models do a poor job in predicting beyond a few days ahead.

By the same token, any countermeasures that may be designed under the Climate Convention will produce nonuniform effects in both space and time. Some countries, and some future generations, will profit more than others. If, for example, the rest of the world can persuade the tropical countries to conserve much of what remains of their rain forest, who will gain? Most probably it will be the northern countries whose actions probably caused the warming in the first place.

REFERENCES

Arrow, K., B. Bolin, R. Constanza, P. Dasgupta, C. Folke, C.S. Holling, B.-O. Jansson, S. Levin, K-G. Mäler, C. Perrings, and D. Pimentel. 1995. "Economic Growth, Carrying Capacity, and the Environment." *Science* 268: 520–21.

Coward, H., and T. Hurka. 1993. *Ethics and Climate Change: The Greenhouse Effect.* Waterloo: Wilfrid Laurier University Press for Calgary Institute for the Humanities.

Dotto, L. 1993. *Ethical Choices and Global Greenhouse Warming.* Waterloo: Wilfrid Laurier University Press for Calgary Institute for the Humanities.

Hare, F.K. 1989. "Environmental Uncertainty: Science and the Greenhouse Effect." In G.B. Doern, ed., *The Environmental Imperative: Marketing Approaches to the Greening of Canada*. Toronto and Calgary: C.D. Howe Institute.

Hare, F.K., and J.C. Ritchie. 1973. "The Boreal Bioclimates." *Geographical Review* 62: 333–65.

Intergovernmental Panel on Climate Change. 1990. J.T. Houghton, G. J. Jenkins, and J.J. Ephraums, eds. *Climate Change: The IPCC Scientific Assessment*. Cambridge: The University Press.

Intergovernmental Panel on Climate Change. 1992. J.T. Houghton, B.A. Callander, and S.K. Varney, eds. *Climate Change 1992: The Supplementary Report to the IPCC Scientific Assessment*. Cambridge: The University Press.

Intergovernmental Panel on Climate Change. Forthcoming, 1996.

Melillo, J.M., A.D. McGuire, D.W. Kicklighter, B. Morre III, C.J. Vorosmarty, and A.L. Schloss. 1993. "Global Climate Change and Terrestrial Net Primary Production." *Nature* 363: 234–40.

Environment Canada. 1995. "Annual Review (1994)—Historical Perspective." *Climate Perspectives* 16: 2.

Mitchell, J.F.B., J.C. Johns, J.M. Gregory, and S.F.B. Tett. 1995. "Climate Response to Increasing Levels of Greenhouse Gases and Sulphate Aerosols." *Nature* 376: 501–4.

Rizzo, B. 1991. Cited in H. Hengevelt. *Understanding Atmospheric Change*. SOE Report 91-2, Fig. 25. Ottawa: Supply and Services Canada, 1990.

Rowell, D.P., C.K. Folland, K. Maskell, and M.N. Ward. 1995. "Variability of Summer Rainfall over Tropical North Africa (1906–92)." *Quarterly Journal of the Royal Meteorological Society* 121: 669–704.

Searle, R. 1995. *Population Growth, Resource Consumption, and the Environment: Seeking a Common Vision for a Troubled World*. Victoria: Centre for Studies in Religion and Society.

Smit, B. 1994. "Adaptation to Climatic Variability and Change." *Delta* 5(4):1 and 16.

Stouffer, R.J., S. Manabe, and K. Bryan. 1989. "Interhemispheric Asymmetry in Climate Response to a Gradual Increase of Atmospheric CO_2." *Science* 342: 660–62.

Tansley, A.G. 1935. "The Use and Abuse of Vegetational Terms and Concepts." *Ecology* 16: 284–307.

Washington, W.T., and G.A. Meehl. 1989. "Climate Sensitivity Due to Increased CO_2: Experiments with a Coupled Atmosphere and Ocean General Circulation Model." *Climate Dynamics* 4: 1–38.

World Commission on Environment and Development. 1989. *Our Common Future*. Oxford and New York: The University Press.

World Council of Churches. 1993. *Accelerated Climate Change*. Geneva: Programme Unit III of WCC.

World Meteorological Organization. 1995. Figure 16 in WMO Statement on the Status of the Global Climate in 1994. Geneva: World Meteorological Organization.

QUESTIONS FOR DISCUSSION

1. How reliable is one's own experience in assessing the reality of a general climatic warming?

2. Is it true that Canada has already been more affected by a warming than the rest of the world? Can you suggest why?

3. How probable is it that the world will agree to reduce the use and/or production of coal, oil, and natural gas, as required by the Convention on Climate Change?

4. Canada is said to have the highest per capita output of carbon dioxide in the world. Why is this? How could we set about reducing consumption—and what would be the consequences?

5. The future of spring wheat cultivation on the Prairies is threatened by the prospect of future losses of summer rainfall. What alternative crops and/or farming practices might offset this threat?

6. Canada's forest industries seem so far to have been unimpressed by predictions of altered climate in their cutting areas. Is this short-sighted? What threats can you foresee?

7. Can you estimate what the predicted warming will do to leisure activities in Canada?

8. Given that Canada is among the coldest of countries, why should we regard warming as a hazard?

CHAPTER 8

NAFTA: Potential Environmental Impact

George H. Crowell

Department of Religious Studies
University of Windsor

NAFTA: ITS INTENTIONS AND IMPACT

Examination of the provisions of the North American Free Trade Agreement (NAFTA) indicates that this huge, complicated body of trinational law is designed so that it can hardly do otherwise than to increase and to accelerate the far-reaching damage to the environment that has already been occurring. This is not to say that environmental damage is a directly intended result of NAFTA. Rather the environment can be expected to suffer damage as an indirect result of the primary goal of NAFTA, which is to provide greatly increased opportunities for private business enterprises to grow and to profit.

The impact of NAFTA on the environment is unlikely to come suddenly or massively. Nor is the increasing damage likely to be readily traceable to NAFTA alone, since it is only one factor among many that are in the process of contributing to environmental degradation. But it is clear that NAFTA provisions not only do little to prohibit or to inhibit activities that would damage the environment, but also do much to authorize and promote practices that increase environmental destruction.

The environmental issue is obviously highly urgent in the modern world, and could hardly have been overlooked when NAFTA was promulgated. Indeed, the preamble of the document expresses pious concern for "environmental protection and conservation," for "sustainable development," and for "the development and enforcement of environmental laws and regulations." But when it comes to the provisions designed to have real impact on human action, the environment fares badly. The basic thrust of NAFTA, and obviously its fundamental intention, is to promote patterns of investment and trade that overwhelmingly benefit corporations, and especially the largest and most powerful transnational corporations, with minimal concern for its impact on the environment and on human welfare. The enactment of NAFTA, which came into force on January 1, 1994, has—together with the Canada–U.S. Free Trade Agreement (FTA), which came into effect exactly five years earlier, setting precedents for most of the content of NAFTA—brought about a prodigious shift of power away from governments, especially from the governments of Canada and Mexico, and into the hands of transnational corporations.

National governments have not proven themselves to be reliable protectors of the environment, but at least they acknowledge their responsibility in this area. The corporations accept virtually no such responsibility, except when it provides clear, immediate opportunities for profit, or except when it is thrust upon them by governments. Even then many of them do all they can to escape responsibility for the environment. The corporations, as they have come to be structured and institutionalized, with the full support of law, are single-mindedly devoted to the pursuit of profits and growth. In intense competition with each other, the corporations that survive and grow tend to be those that are least scrupulous about the environment and human welfare. With the vast power at their disposal, they constantly work, with a high degree of effectiveness, to shape legal systems to their advantage, and to exert control over governments.

While corporations compete with each other for profits, they also form a community of sorts that cooperates in efforts to control governments and to shape law to their benefit. If, by working together instead of competing, they can make it possible for all of them together to profit and to grow—less at the expense of each other than at the expense of governments, the environment, and human welfare—they set aside their rivalries to pursue these ends. With the huge profits that large, successful corporations accrue, and with our increasing dependence upon them for goods, services, and employment, they have vast resources available to influence governments and to shape law. The enactment of NAFTA is one of their crowning collective achievements.

Before turning to a description of specific ways in which NAFTA can be expected to damage the environment, let us consider where we can find reliable sources enabling us to understand and to evaluate NAFTA, despite its length, complexity, and technicality. Since it was the subject of wildly conflicting claims in the public debate before its enactment, it is not surprising that there was much confusion about it.

THE PROBLEM OF RELIABLE INFORMATION ABOUT NAFTA

How can ordinary people, with no special expertise or training in trade matters, gain adequate, reliable information enabling them accurately to assess this huge, complicated body of law? Is the best approach to go directly to the text of NAFTA itself? It is daunting enough to face the task of reading hundreds of pages. But it is downright exasperating to discover that much of the terminology, even though unquestionably in the English language, is nevertheless incomprehensible. Even after the technical meanings of the terminology have been mastered, however, considerable practical knowledge of trade, commerce, and existing related trade law, and of their social and environmental consequences, past and prospective, are also necessary. In order to assess trade policy, therefore, people need the assistance of experts. But which "experts" are to be trusted?

The need for reliable information on trade policy became especially evident in Canada during the federal election campaign of 1988. The primary issue in this campaign was whether Canada should ratify the FTA, which had recently been negotiated. Under the leadership of Prime Minister Brian Mulroney, the pro-FTA

Progressive Conservative Party (PCs) held a comfortable lead in the pre-election polls until the televised leadership debates of October 24 and 25. In those debates, the Liberal Party leader, John Turner, launched a scathing attack against the FTA, while Prime Minister Mulroney vigorously defended it. Each speaker made sharply differing claims about the probable impact of NAFTA. Apparently the public found Mr. Turner's arguments more convincing, for in the next few days the polls revealed a startling reversal, with the Liberals moving from 25 percent in early October to 37 percent while the PCs dropped from 42 percent to 31percent (*The Globe and Mail*, November 1, 1988, pp. A1, A10).

During the weeks before election day, however, the media were flooded with a barrage of claims and counterclaims about the FTA, including a four-page advertising section placed in the nation's major newspapers, and financed by business interests that stood to profit from the FTA (Hurtig, 1992, pp. 195–200). On election day, November 21, 1988, 53.5 percent of the voters supported the two parties that opposed the FTA, but the PCs, with only 43 percent of the vote, nevertheless won a majority of the seats in Parliament (Orchard, 1993, p. 195). They quickly approved the FTA, and then proceeded during their years in office to negotiate NAFTA as well, giving it final approval shortly before their over-whelming defeat in the election of 1993, when the voters reduced their represen-tation in Parliament to only two members. It is not clear to what extent this represented rejection of the free trade agenda. A 1995 TIME-Environics poll reported 44 percent of Canadians believing NAFTA has hurt the Canadian econ-omy and 34 percent believing it has helped (TIME, November 20, 1995, pp. 26, 29). There is no way of knowing the bases of these opinions, or from this poll what Canadians believe about the impact of NAFTA on the environment. But it appears a great deal of confusion remains about the impact of the free trade agreements.

Where can we turn for reliable analysis of NAFTA? To be realistic, we need to be skeptical of the claims of the profit-oriented business community, including the mainline media controlled by powerful corporate and financial interests. It is well-known that powerful corporations were extremely eager to see the enact-ment of the FTA and NAFTA. It is hardly surprising to have them arguing that the free trade agreements would benefit the public and the environment. But with their primary interest their own profit, we need to be skeptical of their claims. To be more confident of an accurate assessment, we need to turn else-where. Fortunately there are nonprofit public interest groups that have devel-oped sufficient expertise to provide thorough analyses of the free trade agreements in the light of their impact upon human and environmental wel-fare. These include Action Canada Network, the Council of Canadians, the Ecumenical Coalition for Economic Justice, the Canadian Centre for Policy Alternatives, and, especially for insights concerning environmental issues, the Canadian Environmental Law Association.

Could these organizations, which are motivated by deep concern for human and environmental welfare, be unfairly biased against the free trade agreements? I cannot see what interest they could possibly have except to provide accurate evaluations. If the free trade agreements had been designed so that they would benefit the environment, I am sure they would gladly have expressed their approval of them. I have been impressed by the careful, conscientious, scholarly approach that these organizations bring to their task of analysis. We need not accept their judgments blindly, however, because we can check for ourselves their interpretations of particular portions of the NAFTA text. Indeed, I recommend that readers approach this chapter itself with a healthy dose of skepticism, and spend some time comparing its conclusions with the NAFTA text.

Insofar as the limitations of this brief inquiry permit, I shall attempt to provide specific examples showing how key provisions of NAFTA permit abuse of the environment. But first let us consider the extent to which the North American Agreement on Environmental Cooperation, better known as the Environmental Side Agreement (ESA), revises the impact of NAFTA on the environment. When Bill Clinton campaigned for the office of president of the U.S. in 1992, he acknowledged the deficiency of NAFTA with regard to the environment, promising to negotiate a side agreement to remedy this crucial problem. Largely on the strength of Clinton's assertion that environmental concerns were overcome through the ESA, which was completed in September 1993, he was able to push NAFTA through Congress despite strong opposition. Examination of the provisions of the ESA, however, unfortunately reveal that it can be expected to do very little to reduce the environmental damage that can occur through NAFTA.

THE ENVIRONMENTAL SIDE AGREEMENT

For the Environmental Side Agreement to exert a favourable impact on the environment, it would need to have legal standing giving it precedence over the provisions of NAFTA. The most obvious way to accomplish this would have been to include such a provision within the ESA itself. No such provision exists. Under international law, however, in case of conflicting provisions between treaties, the more recent treaty is to prevail. This would normally give the ESA precedence. But NAFTA Article 103(2) gives NAFTA precedence over any other agreement among the signatory nations. Any assumption, therefore, that the ESA would supersede NAFTA, is, at best, doubtful.

Even if it should somehow be ruled that the ESA takes clear precedence over NAFTA, its power to defend the environment is severely limited. The ESA, for example, excludes from its purview statutes or regulations whose primary purpose "is managing the commercial harvest or exploitation of natural ... resources" (ESA, Article 45 2(c)). This renders the ESA useless for challenging numerous activities that are among the most devastating to the environment—such as hydroelectric dams, water diversion projects, uranium mining, clearcutting of forests, and overfishing. Moreover, the ESA cannot be used to impose environmental legislation on any of its parties (i.e., Canada, Mexico, and the U.S.), nor can it be used to compel any of the parties to strengthen its environmental laws (Makuch and Sinclair, 1993, pp. 6–7).

The ESA might be used to pressure a party to enforce its environmental law, but only under severe limitations. The agreement of two-thirds of the parties (presently two of the three nations) is required to bring a charge against one party for failure to observe its own environmental laws. Charges can be brought against a party only for "persistent patterns of failure to enforce environmental laws" (ESA, Article 24(1)), but the meaning of "persistent" is left vague and open to abuse. No institution or individual other than the federal government of each nation—not even a provincial or state government—has the right to initiate charges unless a federal government acts on its behalf. This could encourage the federal government of each nation to collude in overlooking violations in the other nations' jurisdictions. Hearings of charges are to be kept secret unless two-thirds of the parties agree to make them public. Environmental and citizens' groups have no right, except by invitation, to make their concerns heard, nor do they have any right to know, other than the final decisions, what occurred in the hearings. The rules for hearing of complaints allow for delays of nearly four years, during which time the ESA could effect nothing to halt ongoing environmental damage (Makuch and Sinclair, 1993, pp. 7–35).

The Commission for Environmental Cooperation (CEC), which is established by the ESA (Articles 8–21), might conceivably make some constructive contributions to promoting discussion and cooperative, voluntary action on behalf of the environment among our three nations. But its conclusions and recommendations are not binding. Much experience has shown that rigorous enforcement of clearly formulated environmental law is necessary to achieve environmental protection (Makuch and Sinclair, 1993, pp. 21–34).

The ESA is extremely unlikely to function effectively to mitigate the environmental damage of NAFTA. Rather than serving to limit the potential damage, the ESA appears to be designed to avoid interference with the freedoms that NAFTA grants to corporations to disregard or to exploit the environment. I shall now indicate some provisions of NAFTA itself that can be expected to undermine efforts to protect the environment, and may even promote its damage.

NAFTA AND ENVIRONMENTAL LAW

It would not be accurate to say that unlimited freedom to exploit the environment is permitted in NAFTA. Article 104 commits the parties to honour three international and two bilateral environmental treaties, involving trade in endangered species, protection of the ozone layer, shipments of hazardous wastes, and Mexican–U.S. border pollution. These treaties deal with important, but limited aspects of human impact on the environment. In case any of these treaties should become relevant to a NAFTA dispute, the interpretation "least inconsistent" with NAFTA is to prevail. This provision could conceivably dilute the benefits of the environmental treaties, although it appears unlikely to have major negative impact (Swenarchuk, 1993b, pp. 102–4).

NAFTA affirms the right of the parties to establish their own bodies of legislation on environmental issues (NAFTA, Chapter 7, section B, "Sanitary and Phytosanitary Measures," and Chapter 9, "Standards-Related Measures"), and even to establish measures more stringent than existing international standards (NAFTA, Articles 712(1), 905(3)). So far, so good. However, several criteria for environmental legislation are established, and these are designed to reduce the possibilities for environmental concerns to interfere with the activities of profit-oriented businesses. These include the following:

1. Only measures having effect within each party's own territory are permissible (NAFTA, Article 712 (1)). This requirement could, for example, undermine efforts to protect migratory birds and marine life, whose territorial limits extend beyond national boundaries. It could, furthermore, hinder attempts to halt imports of agricultural products with residues of pesticides banned by the importing nation (Swenarchuk, 1993b, p. 112).

2. Environmental legislation must also be subjected to a rather thoroughly elaborated standard of "risk assessment" (NAFTA, Articles 715, 907). The notion, for example, that we should avoid knowingly introducing toxic substances into the environment is rejected by this approach. If there might be an economic benefit that could be calculated to outweigh the risk of releasing toxic substances, the practice must be permitted. Previously existing Canadian law on pesticide use, based on concern for human health and environmental protection, could be subject to challenge because it does not include sufficient consideration for the economic gain that might occur from liberalizing pesticide regulations. The requirement for risk assessment can be used to justify environmental damage on economic grounds. It can go a long way toward giving priority to economic gain over human health and environmental protection (Swenarchuk, 1993b, pp. 113–15).

3. No environmental measure is permitted to have "the effect of creating a disguised restriction on trade between the Parties" (NAFTA, Article 712 (6)), or "an unnecessary obstacle to trade" (NAFTA, Article 904(4)). For example, if one party should ban the use of chlorine-bleached paper within its territory in order to prevent the release of highly toxic pollutants, including dioxins, which result from the manufacturing process, such a law might be successfully challenged as a "disguised restriction on trade" by another party involved in the export of such paper. The long-established General Agreement on Tariffs and Trade (GATT), to which Canada, Mexico, and the U.S. are parties, along with 108 other nations, has a similar provision forbidding any "disguised restriction on international trade." In numerous trade disputes resolved under the rules of GATT, this provision has resulted

in decisions giving priority to profit-seeking business ventures over protection of human health or the environment (Swenarchuk, 1993b, pp. 66–70).

4. It will be very difficult for any party to introduce new environmental legislation unilaterally. When attempting to introduce such legislation, the parties are required to consult thoroughly with each other, attempting to harmonize their legislation with "international standards." Article 724 specifies several organizations that are recognized and acceptable sources of these standards. Notable among them is Codex Alimentarius, an organization operating under the United Nations, and largely controlled by the representatives of the same transnational agribusiness firms that helped to devise NAFTA. None of the specified organizations includes in its procedures consultations with the public or with grassroots environmental organizations. (Swenarchuk, 1993a, p. 199)

It is conceivable that the NAFTA provisions regarding each party's environmental law might result in improved legislation for all of North America, and, as other nations sign on, beyond. Given the necessity to gain agreement from so many jurisdictions and agencies, however, and the restraints on expressing concern for the environment without giving priority to trade, it seems far more likely that very little innovative environmental legislation will be achieved, and that law in this area will gravitate toward the lowest common denominator.

In addition to the difficulties created by NAFTA for enacting and maintaining effective environmental legislation, there are further difficulties in enforcement. While NAFTA affirms the need for each party to "ensure that investment activity in its territory is undertaken in a manner sensitive to environmental concerns," it mandates no effective enforcement procedures. It deplores the practice of reducing or relaxing environmental standards to attract investment, but it states only that parties "should not" engage in such practices. If one party believes another has encouraged investment in this manner, "it may request consultations with the other Party, and the two Parties shall consult with a view to avoiding any such encouragement" (NAFTA, Article 1112). But there are no appeal procedures, and no penalties for violations. This contrasts sharply with the sanctions that are available in case of any interference with investment or trade. Under NAFTA, the rights and privileges of profit-seeking investors and traders are strongly asserted and rigorously enforced. Protection of the environment meanwhile is left to voluntary compliance.

NAFTA, NATURAL RESOURCES, AND CANADA

It is not readily apparent to those of us who lack expertise in trade law which sections of NAFTA refer to natural resources. Chapter 6, "Energy and Basic Petrochemicals," clearly deals with an especially significant category of our natural resources. It is not so obvious, however, that Chapter 3, "National Treatment and Market Access for Goods," includes the entire range of natural resources. Presumably this would include energy resources, but the authors of NAFTA apparently considered energy resources, and especially fossil fuels, so crucial that, despite considerable repetition, they provided a separate chapter concentrating on this matter. Assuming that NAFTA remains in effect, these chapters can be expected to have a profound impact on the environment of Canada. The NAFTA provisions dealing with trade in natural resources may well bring greater environmental damage than those dealing with environmental law.

Throughout its history, the U.S. has sought secure access to the natural resources of Canada through a variety of proposals for free trade, and even through pressure for annexation of Canada. While there has often been strong support within Canada for such proposals, primarily from powerful business interests, there has also been strong resistance from Canadian nationalists and from ordinary people who perceived threats to their well-being. When the Canadian colonies united and gained status as an independent nation through the British North America Act approved by the Parliament of Great Britain in 1867, the first priority of the new nation was to establish conditions necessary for economic independence from the overwhelming influence of its huge neighbour to the south. Under the leadership of its first prime minister, John A. Macdonald, Canada constructed its transcontinental railway, completed in 1886, to make possible commerce among the far-flung provinces and territories, and set up tariffs to protect Canadian industry and resources from domination or control by U.S. interests (Orchard, 1993, pp. 37–51, 69–70).

Despite these efforts to assure economic independence for Canada, pressure for a "commercial union" with the U.S. became the primary issue in the elections of 1891 and 1911, and each time the forces favouring free trade were narrowly defeated after passionately fought election campaigns (Orchard, 1993, pp. 70–80, 83–92, 195). Although Prime Minister William Lyon Mackenzie King rejected the final draft of a far-reaching free trade agreement secretly negotiated with the U.S. in 1948, he and President Roosevelt had in 1935 signed the Canada–U.S. Reciprocal Trade Agreement. This allowed exports of Canadian raw materials to the U.S., and for ownership by U.S. companies of Canadian resources to increase substantially (Orchard, 1993, pp. 93–96).

Such inroads did foreign business interests, mostly American, make that by 1980 they controlled 82 percent of Canadian oil production, having bought out more than 300 Canadian oil producers. In 1980 the Canadian government under Prime Minister Pierre Elliott Trudeau enacted the National Energy Program. This called for the federal government to gain 50 percent control over the oil and gas industries in Canada by 1990. By 1984, Canadian ownership had been increased to 40 percent, despite strong objections from the U.S. government and the U.S. oil industry (Orchard, 1993, pp. 127–29). But when Brian Mulroney became prime minister, his government promptly dismantled the National

Energy Program and proceeded to negotiate the FTA, in which Canada essentially turned over to the U.S. control over its energy and other natural resources.

The same sellout of sovereign national control over natural resources that was imposed on Canada in the FTA has been reiterated in NAFTA, and has also been imposed on Mexico. In these times of rapid depletion of natural resources, renewable and nonrenewable, neither Canada nor Mexico is now permitted to reserve, preserve, or conserve its own resources for its own use. Neither may impose export quotas, minimum prices, or export taxes that would discourage exports to the U.S.. Both must make available their resources at current market prices to U.S. consumers, even though current prices must realistically be expected to be well below replacement prices for future resources. Even in times of shortages, Canada, though not Mexico (Annexes 315 and 605), must continue to provide to the U.S. the same proportion of its supplies that the U.S. used during the previous three years (Swenarchuk, 1993b, pp. 104–5, 110).

Through these provisions of NAFTA, Canadians have obviously lost much of their control over their own economy. But what impact is this likely to have on the environment? If Canadians maintained control over their own resources, would they be likely to use them any more responsibly than the Americans to whom they have surrendered so much control? Canadians have certainly not demonstrated any significantly different level of environmental concern than have Americans. The problem for the environment created by these provisions of NAFTA is that they will greatly accelerate the consumption of Mexican and Canadian resources as they are rapidly diverted to the huge U.S. market. Prices of the resources involved will be kept low, and people of all three nations will participate in hastening the exhaustion of nonrenewable resources such as oil and gas, and in consuming renewable resources, such as forests, at unsustainable rates, that is, more rapidly than they can be replaced.

The problem is especially vivid in the case of energy resources. NAFTA provisions will not only accelerate consumption of polluting, nonrenewable fossil fuels, but will also delay the development and deployment of conservation measures, and of environmentally friendly, alternative energy technologies, especially in the U.S., whose huge economy profoundly affects the directions taken in the much smaller economies of Mexico and Canada. Unfortunately all too few people in North America are aware of the extraordinary possibilities for reducing human impact on the environment from the use of alternative energy technologies that have already been developed, and that are already economically viable, to say nothing of promising new technologies presently under development.

There is no guarantee that, if Canada retained control over its own natural resources, it would ultimately use them more wisely than will be the case under NAFTA. If Canada had been able to maintain its National Energy Program, however, there would have been large additional amounts of money for the federal government, which might have been used to stimulate the development of environmentally sound energy technologies through government subsidies. Not only does NAFTA forbid the re-establishment of the National Energy Program, but its provisions also make it very difficult for any Canadian government, federal, provincial, or local, to subsidize the development of alternative energy technologies. However, NAFTA explicitly permits governments to provide subsidies for oil and gas exploration (Article 608), clearly favouring environmentally damaging energy technologies.

THE CONSEQUENCES OF RESOURCE DEPLETION

WATER

With an abundance of water available, most Canadians tend to take for granted this vital resource, which is obviously crucial for human and environmental well-being. NAFTA treats water as one commodity or "good" among others, subject to the same rules that govern other natural resources. If arrangements should be made for water from Canada to be supplied to the U.S., or possibly to Mexico, no Canadian government, federal, provincial, or municipal, would be permitted to reduce or to halt exports of the same proportion of that water supply sold for use in Canada over the last 36 months, even if a severe shortage should occur in Canada (Article 315). Once the tap is turned on, no Canadian government will be allowed under NAFTA rules to turn it off.

In public debates concerning the FTA (which embodied basically the same rules relevant to water that were later incorporated into NAFTA) and again in the debates about NAFTA, Canadian federal government officials proclaimed repeatedly, and often vehemently, that these agreements could not prevent Canada from retaining full sovereign control over its own water resources. *The NAFTA Manual*, a federal government publication issued in August 1992, maintained, for example, that "NAFTA does not apply to large scale exports of water. As in the FTA, only water packaged as a beverage or in tanks is covered in the NAFTA" (Holm, 1993, p. 19).

Much discussion among legal experts, however, supports the conclusion that, according to the provisions of NAFTA, water exports cannot be limited to amounts that can be contained in bottles or even tanks, however large. NAFTA defines "Goods of a Party" as "domestic products as these are understood in the General Agreement on Tariffs and Trade" (Article 201). The Harmonized Commodity Coding System of the GATT deals with water under heading 22.01: "Waters, including natural or artificial mineral waters and aerated waters, not containing added sugar or other sweetening matter nor flavoured; ice and snow." This item is further clarified by the GATT Harmonized Commodity Description and Coding System Explanatory Notes adopted by the GATT signatory nations in 1986. It states: "This heading [22.01] ... covers ordinary natural water of all kinds (other than sea water). Such water remains in this heading whether or not it is clarified or purified" (Holm, 1993, pp. 2–3). Obviously this definition does not limit water exports to those that can be shipped in bottles or tanks.

The NAFTA Manual states further that the federal water policy of 1987 prohibits "large-scale exports of water, either by inter-basin transfer or diversion." It promises that Canada's NAFTA implementing legislation will state clearly that NAFTA applies only to water in bottles or tanks. Both the policy and the legislation, however, are, under well-established international law, subordinate to the NAFTA text. In any dispute, the NAFTA text would have to prevail (Holm, 1993, pp. 17, 25).

When officials of the Canadian federal government under Prime Minister Mulroney said that "NAFTA does not apply to large scale exports of water," they may have meant that, under NAFTA, Canada would not be required to make such exports of water. If this is the case, their claims may be accurate, although they should have warned the Canadian people that once major exports of water begin, they cannot be cut off.

I say "may be accurate" because there is debate whether Canadian governments under NAFTA can refuse to permit the beginning of large-scale water exports that then would have to be continued. Through a complicated chain of reasoning some experts conclude that, under certain conditions, Canada would be required to yield to U.S. demands for water. They argue, for example, that if a Canadian government should permit construction of a water diversion project near the U.S. border for the benefit of Canadians, U.S. interests would have a right to some of the water, provided they financed the engineering projects necessary to collect and transport their portion of the water to the U.S. (Holm, 1993, pp. 4–5, 23–24). Disagreement over interpretation of NAFTA at this point may continue until NAFTA dispute settlement procedures are used to resolve conflict in some specific case.

Even if NAFTA should, as a result of decisions by dispute settlement panels, ultimately be interpreted to allow Canada to refuse to begin large-scale exports of water, it is unlikely that Canadian governments could indefinitely continue to resist pressures to begin such exports. Many states in the U.S. southwest have experienced severe periodic water shortages, and over wide areas groundwater supplies, subjected to heavy withdrawals, are dropping at alarming rates. Already numerous private business enterprises are pressuring Canadian governments, notably that of British Columbia, to issue permits for exports of water to various locations in the U.S. southwest.

Since the 1960s at least a dozen elaborate proposals for diversion of huge quantities of water from Canada to the U.S., and even to Mexico, have gained support from powerful corporations, engineering firms, and prominent politicians. In order to promote the most ambitious of these proposals—the Great Recycling and Northern Development (GRAND) Canal—a corporation, the GRAND Canal Company (GRANDCO), was formed in 1964. GRANDCO continually urges construction of a huge dam across the mouth of James Bay, at the southern end of Hudson Bay. Behind this dam would be collected 61 percent of the fresh water draining into Hudson Bay. This water would be directed by tunnels and canals into the Great Lakes, and from there through the U.S. southwest as far as southern California, and beyond, to Mexico.

It is beyond human capability to anticipate all the environmental consequences of such a vast undertaking, but from experience with lesser megaprojects, we know that they would be far-reaching indeed. The entire Hudson Bay ecosystem would be exposed to extremely damaging effects from the loss of nutrients and fresh water inflow. A major portion of North American migratory bird populations, with loss of staging and nesting grounds, could be destroyed (Linton, 1993, pp. 28–32). Species of aquatic flora and fauna, transported to distant ecosystems, could wreak havoc in new habitats (Bright, 1995).

Nevertheless, pressure to construct a GRAND Canal system, and other major projects for diversion of water from Canada, is likely to intensify as populations increase in water-scarce regions of the U.S., as water tables continue to fall, and perhaps as global warming brings more frequent episodes of increasingly devastating drought. Pressure could also come from efforts to increase the navigability of the Mississippi River. Already the U.S., which unilaterally controls the water of Lake Michigan despite its integral connection with the rest of the Great Lakes, has reversed the flow of the Chicago River, which used to flow into Lake Michigan at Chicago. Some Lake Michigan water therefore flows now into the Mississippi River drainage basin. When the drought of 1988 lowered Mississippi River levels, halting much barge traffic, pressure was exerted to increase withdrawals from Lake Michigan. In this case, rains relieved the crisis before a decision was made, but obviously in similar situations, pressure will be exerted again. Such pressure would contribute to the case for a GRAND Canal (Linton, 1993, pp. 33–34).

With pressures from numerous sources intensifying, and not least from corporations eager to cash in on lucrative new prospects, some Canadian government probably will eventually yield to the lure of jobs from construction projects and of income from sale of water. Then, apart from complete withdrawal from FTA/NAFTA, there will be no turning back. Regrettable consequences for people and the environment could be quickly evident.

This could be the case even for small-scale exports. Canadian Beverage Corp., based in Vancouver, has recently been shipping some 8200 truckloads of water a year drawn from wells in Tillicum Valley, 10 kilometres south of Vernon, B.C., to the U.S. for bottling, while, apparently as a result, the wells of orchardists in the area have been running dry (Holm, 1993, pp. 62–63). Of greater concern are diversions from B.C. to the Columbia River in the U.S. under the terms of the Columbia Treaty of 1964. During drought in the summer of 1992, U.S. interests were able to withdraw increased water from B.C. reservoirs. The people of Fernie watched in horror as their Koocanusa Lake dropped nearly 10 metres! As a result, with less water for production of electricity in 1993, B.C. imported from

Alberta electricity produced from the burning of coal, notorious for its polluting effects. Under FTA/NAFTA it is unlikely that Canada will ever be able to halt such withdrawals, despite their damaging environmental effects (Holm, pp. 68–75). These cases reveal potentialities for far greater problems from larger water diversions of the future.

If we are to have environmentally sustainable human societies in the future, we will need to live within the constraints set by natural ecosystems. We would need to begin by identifying particular ecosystems, or "bioregions," perhaps on the basis of distinct watersheds. It might be worthwhile to explore the notion that importing or exporting large quantities of resources, such as water, from one bioregion to another is likely to be unsustainable, that is, to cause long-term and perhaps irreversible environmental damage. NAFTA, along with other recent free trade arrangements, has a strong tendency to override such environmental constraints (Linton, 1993, pp. 113–25).

AGRICULTURE

Without agricultural systems based on environmentally sound, sustainable practices, we cannot expect that the human population even at its present level, not to mention the annual staggering global increase of more than three times the entire population of Canada, will in the future have sufficient food. All too few people around the world, especially in the wealthier nations, are concerned about this urgent problem, however, since most take it for granted that modern, industrialized agriculture will somehow adequately supply our needs. But it is this type of agriculture that is especially unsustainable. And it is this type of agriculture that NAFTA promotes.

Chapter 7 of NAFTA, divided into two sections, focuses on agriculture. Section A treats agriculture as a business like others, and food as a commodity to be bought and sold for profit. While section B ("Sanitary and Phytosanitary Measures") allows for legislation protecting "human, animal, or plant life or health," it limits, as mentioned above, the possibilities that such measures could be used to interfere with profit-oriented businesses. The primary impact of Chapter 7 on the environment, however, is likely to be indirect. In providing for elimination of measures—import restrictions, tariffs, supply management, and subsidies for export of agricultural goods—designed to support Canadian family farms, Chapter 7 of NAFTA strengthens the unsustainable industrial model of agriculture.

The institution of the family farm in North America long provided conditions not only for stable family life and supportive rural communities, but also for sustainable agriculture. Farm families had strong motivation to preserve and to improve their soil in order to pass on productive land to succeeding generations. With a variety of animal and plant crops, they were much less vulnerable to pests than modern monocultures, and could manage without pesticides. They would restore the soil with organic plant and animal wastes, as well as through rotating crops, sometimes leaving land fallow. They would save from their open-pollinated crops the seeds that thrive in their own local conditions. They would set aside land for woodlots and plant trees for windbreaks.

But in this century, family farms have come under increasing pressure and even compulsion to conform to the industrial model of agriculture. Lured by the prospect of increasing profitability, family farmers have been induced to accept modern machinery, chemical fertilizers, insecticides, herbicides, irrigation, and hybrid seeds. In the quest for profits, less "competitive" farms have been squeezed out, and the surviving farms have become increasingly dependent on these expensive inputs, supplied by increasingly large and powerful corporations able to demand high prices. Under pressure to achieve "efficiency," farmers have turned increasingly to monocultures, covering huge areas with plantings not only of the same species but even of a single genetic variety developed to produce higher yields, but also requiring high inputs of pesticides, fertilizers, and irrigation. With large quantities of single crops, farmers have become vulnerable to profit-oriented corporate marketers that seek to buy their crops as cheaply as possible and to sell them as expensively as possible (Kneen, 1993).

Squeezed between powerful corporate suppliers of their inputs, and powerful corporate buyers of their outputs, farmers have faced increasing expenses and declining returns. "Profits" have been elusive for family farmers, despite long hours of work by all family members, and the need to supplement farm income with work off the farm. High interest rates since the late 1970s have hastened the closing of many family farms and their incorporation into ever larger units (People's Food Commission, 1980). Canadian marketing boards were set up to protect family farmers by enabling them to get fair prices for their produce. But as a result of NAFTA and the latest version of GATT, marketing boards are being dismantled. Increasing exports of agricultural produce from Mexico and the U.S. into Canada will further undermine the viability of Canadian family farms, forcing them to give way to increasingly industrialized agriculture (Canadian Centre for Policy Alternatives, 1992, pp. 55–61).

Many of the environmental consequences of industrialized agriculture are well-known. They include the following:

1. compaction of soil from use of heavy machinery, which also consumes much nonrenewable, polluting fossil fuel
2. heavy applications of pesticides, dispersing into the environment large quantities of deadly chemicals harmful to many other species, including people, and when rapidly multiplying pests develop resistance, the pesticides are usually applied more often and more heavily
3. use of nonrenewable resource-based chemical fertilizers, which, unlike organic wastes, do not bind well with soil but tend to leach out, requiring ever more applications of fertilizer and causing pollution of waterways
4. resort to irrigation, based on environmentally disruptive water diversions, or unsustainable withdrawals from aquifers
5. heavy soil erosion, greatly exceeding natural replacement rates

As short-term profit considerations of powerful transnational corporations, whose interests are favoured by NAFTA, increasingly come into play in agriculture, damage to the ecosystems on which we depend for our food will probably accelerate.

INTELLECTUAL PROPERTY RIGHTS AND THE GLOBAL EFFECTS OF BIOTECHNOLOGY

Chapter 17, "Intellectual Property," could turn out to have more far-reaching impact on the environment than any other part of NAFTA. It is designed to extend beyond national borders the power of corporations—through patents, copyrights, and trade secrets—to gain profits from their innovations. The corporations that pressed for the measures included in Chapter 17 are also working to get these and even greater advantages extended around the world. How can we assess the potential impact of this chapter? It is difficult enough to foresee the consequences of inventions currently under development, to say nothing of those not yet imagined. Moreover, there is a staggering variety of technologies to consider. Recognizing that we can touch on very few of the issues at stake, let us focus on some aspects of biotechnology, which has potential for profound impact on the environment.

Chapter 17, in its support and encouragement for the rapidly developing field of biotechnology, could have all sorts of unpredictable consequences for the environment, perhaps beneficial, perhaps detrimental. A specific case from 1994 is revealing:

> [T]wo Oregon State University scientists discovered in laboratory tests that a soil bacterium they had engineered to produce the fuel ethanol also cut soil populations of mycorrhizal fungi by more than half. These fungi are essential to nutrient uptake in higher plants. "So if the bacterium had been released," one of the scientists dryly observed, "it could have been a real problem. If the organism survived readily and spread widely, very likely we would be unable to grow crops without a control measure for this organism." Thus far there have been 2258 experimental releases of genetically engineered organisms in the United States alone. (Bright, 1995, p. 16)

Even without this possible disastrous consequence, which was fortuitously detected, would there have been any other unforeseen, perhaps long-term damaging consequences? Suppose the bacterium could have produced ethanol without detrimental consequences. This could provide a less polluting substitute for gasoline from renewable biomass. Much would then depend on the source of the biomass, which itself might be produced in unsustainable ways or used in unsustainable quantities. Furthermore, we would need to ask what environmental effects would be likely to result from placing initiative for such a project in the hands of profit-oriented corporations, which are favoured by Chapter 17 of NAFTA.

It has been reported that genetic engineers in more than sixty-five research programs around the world, supported by corporations like Monsanto and DuPont, are striving, with considerable success, to develop food crops with resistance to particular herbicides, usually their own. Not only will they make money selling the seeds, but they will make more money by selling the herbicides. They are investing much money and devoting much valuable scientific talent to creating herbicide dependence, and ensuring further dispersal into the environment of toxic chemical substances (Fowler and Mooney, 1990, pp. 142–43). Chapter 17 of NAFTA encourages and supports this practice.

Biotechnology is becoming an integral part of industrialized agriculture, from which profit-oriented agribusiness firms benefit, as we have seen, at the expense of the environment. This trend is intensified by Chapter 17 of NAFTA, which includes the requirement that parties must either "provide for the protection of plant varieties through patents," or—and here the jargon is confusing—provide "an effective scheme of protection, or both" (NAFTA, Article 1709:3). The first phrase refers to the patenting of seeds, which is obviously not for "protection of plant varieties" as such, but for protecting the right of business enterprises to benefit from ownership of the germ plasm of plants. The second refers to "plant breeders' rights." This is a slightly less demanding requirement, which involves a monopoly right to market a particular variety of plant. This right can be claimed by those who have introduced some genetic change, however minute, into germ plasm found occurring in nature. The Mulroney government has enacted plant breeders' rights legislation for Canada (Canadian Centre for Policy Alternatives, 1992, p. 39; Swenarchuk, 1993b, pp. 55–56).

The potential impact of these provisions of Chapter 17 can be illustrated by a problem that arose before the advent of NAFTA. Agribusiness firms want farmers to become entirely dependent upon them for their seeds. They seek to convert them from competitors to customers. This is what they hope to gain through plant breeders' rights and patenting of seeds. As early as the 1930s agribusiness firms discovered that they could lure farmers to purchase hybrid corn seeds with the promise of higher yields. And they could make the farmers dependent on them because this hybrid seed would not reproduce. No longer could the farmers gather seed from their own crops for the next year's planting. The marketers of hybrid seeds keep the genetic makeup of their inbred seed strains closely guarded trade secrets, which are now protected in NAFTA (Article 1711). But the growing dependence of farmers on seed companies has brought major environmental problems.

With each seed variety consisting of a single genetic type planted over huge areas around the world, it is virtually inevitable that at least one of many disease and pest organisms that feed on this species of plant, with their extraordinary capacity for rapid and abundant reproduction, will soon evolve new varieties capable of overcoming all resistance in the uniform crop. Already in numerous cases high-yield hybrid varieties of various food species have been destroyed by pathogens, as occurred when corn was hit by a devastating blight in 1970.

In such cases, plant breeders usually resort to seed banks (whose stocks are far from adequate), or return to the traditional areas of diversity where the crop originated, such as remote parts of the Andes Mountains for potatoes, to seek resistant varieties. But each year fewer of the old varieties are available, because more farmers, even in areas of greatest historical diversity, have been converted to use of the new genetically uniform and vulnerable hybrid seed, and fewer farmers save traditional highly variegated, open-pollinated varieties. The very success of agribusiness seed marketers is resulting in the extinction of precious germ plasm, some of which surely contains genes that could be extremely useful for providing any of many useful traits, such as resistance to disease and pests.

So far, plant breeders have managed to find other resistant strains, enabling our major food crops to survive. But their usual practice is to insert resistance with a gene that quickly becomes another easy target for pathogens. When resistance to that gene is overcome, it is thereafter useless. Meanwhile with genetic diversity in our food crops rapidly declining, it may not be long before we face the crisis of losing some species of plant that has long been a major source of human food (Fowler and Mooney, 1990). The promotion of plant breeders' rights and seed patenting in Chapter 17 of NAFTA exacerbates this trend. As agribusiness firms succeed in genetically modifying seeds for food crops so that they provide advantages that induce farmers to invest in them, the process of displacing traditional seed varieties and driving them into extinction will gain momentum. From our human point of view, there could hardly occur any greater environmental disaster.

Much depends on whether agribusiness firms will manage to extend these rights beyond North America. They may not succeed. Resistance against this corporate agenda is increasing around the world (Kneen, 1995). Since the environmental impact on Canada of seed patenting depends largely on whether the extension of Chapter 17 of NAFTA to other parts of the world can be prevented, the more successful this resistance is, the more likely that Canada will be saved from some of the most ominous environmental consequences of NAFTA.

DISPUTE SETTLEMENT AS A POSSIBLE SOLUTION TO NAFTA CONFLICTS

The dispute settlement procedures set up under Chapter 20 of NAFTA do not offer much hope that environmental concerns will have significant weight. Dispute settlement panels are to be chosen from lists of trade experts appointed by each of the nations' federal governments. The five panelists chosen to adjudicate each dispute are to meet in secret sessions. Unless specifically invited, no concerned citizens, or affected workers, or environmentalists are permitted to testify.

It is conceivable that scientific review boards that may be invited to provide written reports "on any factual issue concerning environmental, health, safety or other scientific matters" (NAFTA section 2015) might exert some influence favourable to the environment. But the job of the panels would be to interpret the rules set up by NAFTA. They do not give priority to environmental matters. The hearings would essentially be arbitrations carried out under NAFTA's mandate to promote trade and investment. There is no appeal procedure. This is a radical departure from our democratic public system for the administration of justice.

CHOICES AND FUTURE CONSIDERATIONS

If we human beings are to survive and ultimately to thrive on this planet, we need to establish institutional structures that enable us to live in harmony with each other and with our environment. NAFTA is a major step in the wrong direction. It overrides democratically elected governments, and shifts power into the hands of profit-oriented transnational corporations, giving them increased freedom to exploit the environment and people in order to increase their wealth and power. This examination of the provisions of NAFTA indicates some of the damaging effects that NAFTA can be expected to have on the environment. Further examination would reveal that it can also be expected to have damaging effects on human welfare.

The powerful and dynamic corporations whose interests are promoted by NAFTA have made valuable contributions to meeting human needs of all kinds. But their interests are so narrowly focused on profit and growth for themselves, and so preoccupied with short-term success, that it is dangerous to allow them to dominate our lives and to take advantage of our environment, as NAFTA helps them to do. We need to give priority to institutions that, unlike NAFTA, encourage and support people to recognize clearly the environmental crisis that confronts the human community, and which provide us with resources to work effectively to preserve the environment while also promoting human welfare.

NAFTA has a provision (Article 2205) that allows a party to withdraw from the treaty after providing six months' notice to the other parties. Perhaps Canadians who are concerned about human and environmental welfare should be giving this option serious consideration.

REFERENCES

Canadian Centre for Policy Alternatives. 1992. *Canada under Siege: Three Years into the Free Trade Era.* Ottawa: Canadian Centre for Policy Alternatives.

Fowler, C., and C. Mooney. 1990. *Shattering: Food, Politics and the Loss of Genetic Diversity.* Tucson: University of Arizona Press.

Holm, W. 1993. "Water and Free Trade: Provincial Powers to Prevent Water Export." In *Canadian Environmental Law Association* (1–27, 46–75). Toronto: Canadian Environmental Law Association.

Hurtig, M. 1992. *A New and Better Canada: Principles and Policies of a New Canadian Political Party.* 2nd ed. Toronto: Stoddart.

Kneen, B. 1995. Personal interview. December 19.

———. 1993. *From Land to Mouth: Understanding the Food System.* 2nd ed. Toronto: NC Press Limited.

Linton, J. 1993. "Water Export: Toward an Alternative Ecological Vision." In *Canadian Environmental Law Association* (28–45, 113–125). Toronto: Canadian Environmental Law Association.

North American Free Trade Agreement. 1992. Ottawa: Department of External Affairs and International Trade.

Orchard, D. 1993. *The Fight for Canada: Four Centuries of Resistance to American Expansion.* Toronto: Stoddart.

People's Food Commission. 1980. *Land of Milk and Honey: The National Report of the People's Food Commission.* Kitchener: Between the Lines.

Swenarchuk, M. 1993a. "Environment." In D. Cameron and M. Watkins, eds., *Canada under Free Trade,* pp. 196–202. Toronto: James Lorimer.

———. 1993b. "The Environment and International Trade Agreements: An Overview. The Environmental Implications of NAFTA: A Legal Analysis." In *Canadian Environmental Law Association. The Environmental Implications of Trade Agreements,* pp. 65–132. Toronto: Ontario Ministry of Environment and Energy.

QUESTIONS FOR DISCUSSION

1. Has this chapter fairly and accurately analyzed the potential impact of NAFTA on the environment? To what extent is your judgment on this question informed by evidence from sources other than this chapter, including NAFTA itself?

2. Given our increasingly globalized economy, do we have any choice except to adjust to this reality, which includes NAFTA?

3. If you were participating in writing a North American Environmental Protection Agreement, what primary provisions would you want it to include? How would you want it to be related to NAFTA?

Public Participation and Environmental Planning

G. Keith Warriner

Department of Sociology
University of Waterloo

INTRODUCTION

Participation is the foundation of democracy. Whether all we do is vote or involve ourselves far more actively—by joining a political party, participating in a public demonstration, holding office—a democracy requires the participation of its citizens. The avenues for direct, and indirect, input into state functioning in democracies are myriad, and said to be limited only by an individual's own desires and resources. Still, while the need for some involvement by citizens in the governing process is uncontested, the question of how much or what form has been the subject of debate among political philosophers since the time of Plato. Over the past 150 years or so the trend has been toward greater openness in government with various interest groups gradually making more and more inroads into state functioning (Pierce et al., 1992). But even in our current era of "inclusivity," it is clear that many groups—women, native peoples, ethnic and religious minorities, labour, Quebec sovereignists, to name only a few—often feel they are being denied access to the decision-making process.

Does the public's involvement in environmental decision-making make a difference? In part this is what this chapter is designed to address. To be sure, open, honest, and comprehensive involvement by the public can contribute to both a better and more acceptable project by identifying the concerns of stakeholders, providing information on existing conditions, and helping to create a context for negotiation instead of confrontation, leading to consensus (Connor, 1974). At the same time there is also much that is not right with consultation. Developers, and some resource managers, have been known to express concern over the potential for an intrusive and ill-informed public to block or transform a well-conceived project. By the same token environmentalists and other stakeholders sometimes see the consultation process as nothing more than a public relations strategy designed to deflect opposition (Bruton and Howlett, 1992). The modern era of environmental consultation was ushered in by the passage of the U.S. National Environmental Policy Act (NEPA) of 1969, and in the 25 years or so in which public consultation on environmental questions has been widely employed, its techniques have been refined and honed. There is now a sizable commercial industry in public consultation, and since in most cases the consultation is paid for by the proponent, one course is to hire a professional to navigate the proposal through the tricky waters of public approval. Most of the major Crown corporations in Canada, and other large agencies that themselves are developers, now have their own public consultation staffs. These conditions are not always conducive to the concepts of openness, inclusivity, and impartiality that are supposed to be the cornerstones of effective public involvement.

Attempting to address some of the criticisms of the public involvement process will form an important objective in this chapter, but there is still a larger issue, and that concerns what should be the appropriate level of participation by citizens for meeting democratic objectives (Pateman, 1970, 1979; Press, 1994). Public participation in environmental decision-making is not just about environmental protection, it is also about the far broader issue of how our democratic state should function. As we will later observe, current political theory on the environment tends to view the environment and democracy as mutually sustaining systems. To understand how this symbiotic relationship came about we need to review several important themes in environmental public participation.

DEFINING PUBLIC PARTICIPATION

Citizen participation has been around as long as democracy has existed, but significant social science investigation of it—especially in matters relating to the environment—has occurred mainly since the 1960s. The major areas of review have involved questions about (1) democratic theory, (2) grassroots and community activism, and (3) public involvement techniques. In this work the terms *public involvement*, *public participation*, *citizen participation*, *citizen action*, *political participation* , and *public consultation* have largely been used interchangeably. As the existence of this polymorphic and inexact set of terms implies, the field in public participation has never been well-defined.

Broadly speaking, public participation has to do with how ordinary people communicate their views on social issues to policymakers in a purposeful and organized manner. This can include anything from voting to public demonstration, but in practical terms the areas of interest in public participation research have been limited to the more or less formal and structured mechanisms for providing input on decisions. Stuart Langton (1978: 21) identifies four distinct levels of such citizen involvement: (1) obligatory citizen participation (paying taxes, jury duty, military duty, etc.), (2) electoral participation (voting), (3) government-initiated citizen involvement (government-invited submissions and consultations), and (4) citizen action (citizen-initiated input, collective action, and protest). Each of these four basic forms of democratic participation is described further in Figure 9.1, along with examples and descriptions of the objectives, activities, and groups typically associated with each.

For its part, academic research into public participation has concentrated largely on the third and fourth levels of democratic activity described in Figure 9.1, with particular emphasis on level three. It has been with respect to these levels of involvement that democracy is said to have evolved over the past 150 years. On one level there is citizen involvement initiated by the state. Today this takes the form of the ubiquitous "public consultation" in which policymakers invite the public to communicate on state policy and projects. This essentially

FIGURE 9.1
Categories of Citizen Participation

	Citizen Action	Citizen Involvment	Electoral Participation	Obligatory Participation
Major distinguishing feature	Refers to activities initiated and controlled by citizens for some purpose	Refers to activities initiated and controlled by government for administrative purposes	Refers to activities to nominate and elect representatives or to vote on pertinent issues on a regularly scheduled basis established by law	Refers to activities in which participation is compulsory according to law
Major purpose	To influence decisions of government officials or voters	To improve decision-making and services and develop consensus and support for decisions	To provide stability, continuity of leadership, and a workable consensus for government	To provide sufficient support for government to perform its legal functions
Examples of activities	Lobbying; public education; protest; public advocacy; civil disobedience; class-action suits	Advisory committees; public hearings; goals programs; surveys; hotlines; volunteer programs	Voting; running for office; working for a candidate; volunteering to help a political party	Paying taxes; doing military service; jury duty
Dominant concerns	Organizing effectively; obtaining appropriate information; developing support; raising funds; making maximum political and public impact	Involving more citizens; informing citizens better; broadening the range of citizen representation; maintaining citizen interest; effectively utilizing citizen involvement in decision-making; obtaining necessary funds	Increasing voter turnout; raising funds for a party or candidate	Increasing public understanding of the obligations of citizenship; attracting and retaining capable jurors and military personnel
Typically interested groups	Neighbourhood and community action groups; public-interest and consumer groups; community agencies; individual citizens	Legislative committees; administrative agencies; regulatory agencies	Elected officials; political parties; political candidates	Judges; court officers; military leaders; tax officials

Source: Reprinted with permission from *Citizen Participation in America*, Stuart Langton, ed. (Lexington, Mass.: D.C. Heath, 1978), p. 22. Copyright © 1978 Jossey-Bass Inc., Publishers. First published by Lexington Books. All rights reserved.

"top down" approach by government to learn more about the general public's views on social matters generally reflects the tendencies in Canada and elsewhere toward more open government. Such a trend has been discussed on both practical and ideological grounds (Howell et al., 1987; Johnson et al., 1987; Pateman, 1979). In practical terms, seeking advice on state matters is seen to contribute to responsible state management and bureaucratic efficiency. By this means choices between alternative proposals are informed by knowledge of the public's support before a decision is made. The result is to allow state managers to anticipate the public's objections and incorporate them in management plans.

Ideologically, widespread public consultation by government generally supports a trend toward "participatory" over "representative" democracy (Pateman, 1970; Vincent, 1987). Here the benefits of consultation are more debatable. Increased public consultation can be seen to reflect a move in the direction of direct, or populist, forms of democracy, with its supporters claiming benefits both for society and the individual (Almond and Verba, 1963, 1980). On the other hand critics of greater citizen involvement tend to see it as a potentially virulent and destabilizing force in democracy, which could undermine the duty of elected representatives to serve independently on behalf of constituents (e.g., Satori, 1962; Schumpeter, 1943). What is the point of elections, these critics ask, if the mass public is allowed to define and decide public issues? Thus while increased direct public involvement in state decision-making is a growing trend in society, questions about its legitimacy remain.

The fourth level of citizen involvement in state functioning described in Figure 9.1 has been termed by Langton "citizen action," and is a second area of significant interest to students of public participation. Citizen action refers to citizen-initiated attempts to influence state decision-making, and is largely seen as a "bottom up" or "grassroots" approach to informing public policy. Private citizens seek to increase their efforts to influence directly the policies of the state for several reasons. Foremost is the public's growing distrust of politicians in general and cynicism about the ability of state mangers to handle state affairs competently (Mitchell and Scott, 1987). In the highly charged and controversial arena of environmental management in particular, there are many notable examples of perceived mismanagement around which this public skepticism can develop. At the same time the environmental movement has grown steadily over the past twenty-five years and it now represents a sophisticated and formidable presence in the decision apparatus of the state (Mitchell et al., 1992; McCloskey, 1992). No particular political institution or party speaks for this interest, while over time the movement has maintained much of its early grassroots and activist emphasis (Scarce, 1990). Thus direct citizen-initiated input into policy is increasingly common in today's society,

Overall, the last three decades have seen significant growth in two simultaneously occurring citizen-participation movements (Langton, 1978: 1–2). On the

one hand, citizens themselves are making demands for greater say in state functioning; on the other, officials have moved to allow the state's apparatus to
become more accessible. While not everyone will agree these trends are in the
best interests of democratic functioning, neither are there signs of their diminu-
tion. Indeed the current fiscal crisis of the state and its efforts to offload many of
its traditional responsibilities can only serve to encourage even greater citizen
involvement in the future. All this tends to confirm Gabriel Almond and Sidney
Verba's (1963: 4) famous claim of more than thirty years ago: "[If] there is a revolution going on throughout the world, it is what might be called the participation explosion." These tendencies appear to have reached even beyond what
these early analysts predicted, with public participation today being both socio-
logically and politically one of society's most compelling and exciting features.

THE PROMISE OF PARTICIPATION

"Maximum feasible participation." So stipulated the 1964 U.S. Economic
Opportunity Act, which ushered in the modern era of the public participation
movement (ACIR, 1979). This act, which was the centrepiece of U.S. President
Lyndon Johnson's Great Society was a turning point for the recruitment of all
segments of the population in the administrative planning process (Rosenbaum,
1978: 82). The objectives of the Economic Opportunity Act—and associated acts
that followed, including the National Environmental Policy Act (1969)—reflect
clearly what are now commonly recognized as the objectives of public participation itself. Why participate? What social benefits are being served by having
members of the lay public scrutinize and perhaps alter social programs designed
by professional planners and administrators hired and paid by the public's taxes
to do just that? In answer to this, supporters of participation point out that
increased public involvement in decision-making serves several objectives for
society and individuals both (Verba and Nie, 1972). These include *democratic
objectives*, *policy objectives*, and *intrinsic objectives*, and together represent a continuum of social benefits ranging from the societal to the personal level.

The democratic values of public involvement are both symbolic and practical.
Public participation programs can allow a kind of public input that is reflective
of and important to the continued functioning of democracy (Freudenburg,
1983: 228). Before more widespread participation emerged beginning in the
1960s, the reigning democratic approaches essentially favoured control by the
administrative bureaucracy along with limited public input. This was particularly the case in Canada, where democratic rights have historically been understood to be more constrained than in the United States (Lipset, 1990), and in
which opportunities for public input were largely limited to the formal administrative hearing (Gillies, 1989). In the United States more accessible routes to

involvement have existed for much of this century (e.g., Selznick, 1966; Daneke et al., 1983: 12), but it took until the mid-1960s before participation blossomed in all areas of public policy.

The basis for this change was the emergence of a fundamental redefinition in society's vision of the citizen's role in democracy. For some time theorists of democracy had been questioning both the value and need for public participation. The so called "elite" theories of Joseph Schumpeter (1943), Michels (1958 [1915]), Satori (1962), Robert Dahl (1996), and others (see Pateman, 1970; Walker, 1966) questioned the role played in democratic decision-making by a largely uninformed and apathetic mass citizenry. The immense expansion of the state's administrative units throughout the 20th century, together with the existence of a vast and skilled civil service, had removed any strong necessity for the average person to be active in state planning. At the same time the rise of totalitarian states in which "mass participation backed by intimidation and coercion" came to be linked with dictatorship rather than democracy had sullied participation's image (Pateman, 1970). Finally, studies in political sociology on political attitudes and behaviour had often revealed evidence of the public's lack of interest in politics as well as widespread authoritarianism and antidemocratic beliefs, especially among the lower socioeconomic groups. Hence, in the early 1960s there existed a variety of bases for questioning the benefits of participation, not the least its potential to destabilize the efficient and orderly functioning of the state itself. At the same time it was felt there was sufficient expertise among elites to provide wise public counsel free of the taint of an apathetic and uninformed mass public.

The philosophical challenge to elite democratic theory came through the reintroduction of the classical democratic theory of participation by such "participatory democracy" theorists as Carol Pateman (1970, 1979), Jack Walker (1966), and Peter Bachrach (1967). In part theirs was a return to idealism, with its essential tenet that the ultimate source of government is the people themselves. Thus, in the tradition of the classical theorists reminiscent of Rousseau's *social contract*, every citizen is guaranteed the opportunity to exert influence on the state through political activity, *which is equal to that of all others*. Further, from such rights to participation flow not only opportunity but obligation (Pateman, 1979). As J. S. Mill noted: "[T]he rights and interests of every or any person are only secure from being disregarded when the person is himself able and habitually disposed to stand up for them" (Mill, 1862; cf. Rosenbaum, 1978: 44–45).

This mutuality between the right to participate and its necessity amounts to a crucially defining feature in the maintenance of democracy. First, it is through voluntary association with the state that the individual derives feelings of satisfaction and confidence that government is responsive to his or her own needs and interests. Next, the security of the state benefits from the existence of an involved and committed populace. Finally, participation is liberating, aiding in the discovery of personal self-worth and competency and an avenue to the development of the individual's full capabilities (Bachrach, 1967: 5). Hence, widely achieved, participation defies dictatorship. How can the involved and liberated mass public see it as anything but in its self-interests to defy tyranny? How can the state, directed by and responsive to its citizenry, succumb to the domination of elites?

The articulation of classical democratic theory in the context of public participation helped redefine understanding of the boundaries of civil society during the 1960s and '70s. It is important to emphasize the theory's multiple denouement. The benefits of participation, it is argued, are democratic, policy-related, and intrinsic. Through participation in the affairs of the government, democratic principles of equality and self-government are achieved. On intrinsic grounds participation helps citizens to gain self-confidence through knowledge and understanding of how society functions (Almond and Verba, 1963) while at the same time achieving social solidarity through the formation of group identities and opportunities for face-to-face contact (Cole, 1974). Finally, on practical grounds participation can enhance the quality of decision-making by bringing the broadest possible array of knowledge and experience to bear on a problem, and helping to identify the level of support for various policy options before a decision is made.

THE PROBLEMS OF PARTICIPATION

The conceptual basis in support of the wide application of public consultation in formulating state policy, it must be emphasized, is still only a *theory* about the supposed merits of public involvement. As with most theories, its potential shortcomings should be acknowledged, and we now must turn to the consideration of these limits.

A heuristic device suitable for helping to assess the overall quality of the public involvement process is provided by Sewell and Phillips (1979). Their model is depicted in Figure 9.2. Here Sewell and Phillips suggest that public involvement in decision-making is constituted of three interrelated dimensions: an *efficiency* dimension, an *involvement* dimension, and an *equity* dimension. All three dimensions have implications for meeting the objectives of participatory democracy, but it is rare for any particular public participation situation to achieve maximum public benefit on all three poles at the same time. Normally real public involvement will involve tradeoffs between these factors, and the overall assessment of the promise of public participation in terms of its democratic, policy-related, and intrinsic objectives is provided by identifying its potential shortcomings along each of these continua.

EFFICIENCY

Taking each of the three dimensions in turn, *efficiency* refers to the amount of time, personnel, and other agency resources required for the consultative process

---

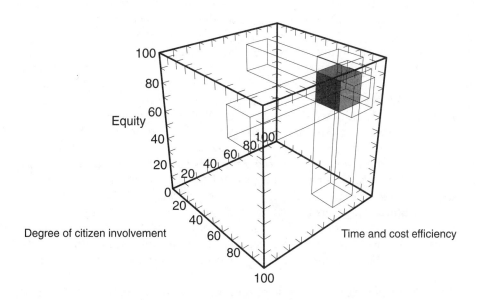

Source: W.R. Derrick Sewell and Susan D. Philips, "Models for the Evaluation of Public Participation Programs," *Natural Resources Journal* 19(2) (1979): 335.

to reach a decision. Democracy is nothing if not unwieldy, and conducting public involvement is expensive and time-consuming. For the public's input to be effective, enormous amounts of information must be distributed, reviewed, and ingested. A famous example of this is the Mackenzie Valley Pipeline Inquiry headed by Justice Thomas Berger from 1974 through 1976. This one-man royal commission examined the potential social and environmental impacts of a proposed pipeline to bring natural gas from the Mackenzie Delta on the Beaufort Sea to Southern Canada and the United States. Formal hearings were held in Yellowknife, Inuvik, Whitehorse, and Ottawa, and then the inquiry visited each of the 35 communities of the Mackenzie River valley to consult with residents. The resulting official record constituted 40 791 pages of transcript in 281 volumes, together with another 1568 exhibits (Berger, 1977: Volume 1, p. 203). Obviously the burden required to review, assimilate, and interpret all this is enormous and beyond the capability of many average citizens. In spite of this, the eventual result from this inquiry was the recommendation that the pipeline not be built, with the process leading up to this decision being since heralded as a watershed achievement demonstrating effective public involvement in environmental planning in Canada.

Nevertheless, as should be clear from this, with public involvement, great technical expertise is often required and much time and patience needed to guide participants from diverse backgrounds through all that must be understood. Further, in environmental matters especially, the affected publics are often widely scattered, necessitating transporting the consultative forum and all personnel to several sites. Finally, years of public participation practice have proven that effective consultation requires both multiple forms of communication and ongoing engagement between parties (Howell et al., 1987). The days are gone when all that seemed necessary was an obligatory meeting between planners and the public and then a decision was made. Well-designed public involvement now gathers information using a wide array of means. In her review of participatory planning techniques, Roesner (1975, 1978) identifies 39 distinct ways in which data from the public can be collected, with each method fulfilling different information needs. No one expects proponents and planners to utilize more than a few of these techniques during any one project, but it is recommended that the consultation should involve several stages, while the commitment to making the public's involvement ongoing has also deepened. Thus, public involvement practice nowdays is more ungainly, time-consuming, and expensive than ever, while also ever increasing as a requisite stage in environmental planning.

At the same time the tremendous expansion of public involvement has not necessarily solved its other practical limitations. Critics have long claimed that many ordinary citizens have no definite preferences (or should have) on many issues affecting them (Dahl, 1996; Nisbet, 1975). Expanding efforts to reach out to the public do little to improve the quality of decisions if there is little to dispute in the first place. Still, the failure of the public to become embroiled in an issue over which it has no strong preference is sometimes cited as evidence of apathy and the inability of ordinary citizens to participate meaningfully in defining and defending their own interests (Rosenbaum, 1978: 48). Another problem is lack of any real means of aggregating and summarizing all the different views managers are confronted with. One only needs to observe a public meeting in action to recognize the difficulty of interpreting, recording, and weighing all the different points of view. Efforts to address this problem range from the application of improved knowledge of small group processes to computer-generated inventory and content analysis (Stankey, 1972; Creighton, 1981; Syme and Eaton, 1989). Nevertheless, so much is missed, misinterpreted, or ignored during normal public participation that it can be a source both of the public's general distrust of the consultative process itself and a basis for the future appeal of decisions.

In addition there are questions about alleged redundancies occurring between the public and state agencies. The bureaucracy of planners and other experts grew in Canada as a principal means of managing effectively the multiplicity of social challenges. Direct public involvement in decision-making can be seen to undermine the authority of these agencies while rendering their pools of talent impotent. The strong emphasis in public participation forums for consensus-based outcomes can lead to undue compromise and decisions made more on the basis of social acceptability than either policy effectiveness or wise resource management.

Associated with such redundancy is public participation's contribution to the demoralization of the public service (Rosenbaum, 1978). It is paradoxical that growth in the public participation movement over the last thirty years may be seen to have undermined the role of professional public service. Early on during the modern era of the participation movement, planners were in the forefront of the social changes it represented, zealously championing the spread of public participation among society's disadvantaged (Sewell and Phillips, 1979: 358). The success of the movement resulted in a transfer of authority from the administrative state to the public at large, and to an important extent made civil servants peripheral to the formulation of policy. Today the public interest movement has all the resources and skills necessary to lobby effectively on its own behalf (Gottlieb, 1993: 314–20; McCloskey, 1992). In acting on this, the grassroots public participation movement is increasingly contemptuous of the administrative bureaucracy for what is deemed its pro-development stance and willingness to defend the *status quo*. Thus, an ironic twist to the participation movement's success has been to put state managers on the defensive while disparaging their role as the servants of the public.

Overall, from the point of view of democracy, the efficiency problems faced by public participation in planning have several negative consequences. The increasing use of public participation in state planning may be more of a force in state destabilization than in improved functioning. Increasing levels of public participation can amount to an unnecessary drain on state resources, while misrepresenting, or failing to represent, important public interests, and compromising the morale of the public service and its ability to make effective and decisive decisions on its own.

EQUITY

Equity problems faced by public participation involve questions of bias produced either by the exclusion of some groups, or the failure of certain points of view to be given credence while others are weighed too much. Equity issues are at the heart of the democratic objective of involvement. What is the point of public participation unless all stakeholders are represented and all positions respected equally? Unfortunately such fairness is not always easily achieved. For the most part, problems faced are systemic within the process of public participation itself, rather than deliberately intended by organizers.

First, it should be noted that only a small proportion of the general public participates at all. The pattern is for the significant majority of the population to be inactive, with a small number of devoted activists being highly involved. In Canada only between about 2 and 4 percent of the adult population belong to an environmental or public interest group (Curtis et al., 1989), while in his study of U.S. political activity Lester Milbrath (1965; Milbrath and Goel, 1977) concludes that about one-third of the population is apathetic or passive, with another 60 percent playing spectator roles, and only the remaining 5 to 7 percent assuming the role of "gladiators" who actively participate. Of those who are prepared to participate in a consultative process, a recent survey of Ontario residents found that nearly 70 percent of the respondents had not attended any forum or public meeting within the last three years, with just 14 percent reporting attending a meeting on an environmental issue. Indeed, for organizers the low turnout that often accompanies the invitation to participate in the planning process is a major source of vexation, with those responsible often heard to wonder how such "public apathy" and "lack of representation" may affect the proposal.

Second, a number of studies suggest that those who do participate are more likely to be come from the middle and upper strata of society (Burch, 1976; Hays, 1987; Van Liere and Dunlap, 1980; Morrison and Dunlap, 1986). Generally, high incomes, educational levels, and occupational statuses are the hallmarks of the participating public. Studies also document the domination of organized economic interests and "social elites" on appointed citizen advisory boards and community voluntary associations (Lorimer, 1972). Thus, low levels of public involvement overall, and the overrepresentation of higher status participants, are two general threats to equity in the public involvement process.

At the same time, it is important to note that the low income, less educated and lower occupational classes of society still do participate in environmental decision-making in Canada. Such people may be underrepresented relative to their numbers in society, but do still often make their voices heard on important environmental issues. Aboriginal groups, for example, have been highly involved in a number of controversial siting and resource management disputes in Canada, including the James Bay hydroelectric project, the Mackenzie Valley pipeline, and logging in Clayoquot Sound on Vancouver Island. In addition, grassroots citizen participation is becoming a force to be reckoned with in the adjudication of many environmental disputes at the community level. Such groups often form over concern for a local contamination problem, while depending almost entirely on volunteers to carry out their work, and placing heavy emphasis on the use of citizen participation techniques to communicate their message. By and large, grassroots environmental groups adhere strongly to principles of democracy in their own organizations, while also being quite representative of the general categories of class and occupation within society. Another notable feature of these organizations is the frequent high level of involvement by women, as founding organizers, leaders, and general members (Freudenberg and Steinsapir, 1992).

Aside from problems of the representativeness of participants in public involvement along such objective social categories as gender, race, schooling, education, and occupation, the process of exclusion may take more subtle forms. One of the best known and long-standing findings on organizational functioning from sociology is Robert Michels' (1958 [1915]) "Iron Law of Oligarchy." Michels was concerned with what he saw as the tendency of even democratic organizations to become bureaucratically ruled by an elite few (an oligarchy) who took over and controlled the upper ranks of the organization. According to Michels, "Who says organization, says oligarchy." This pattern is a consistent finding in the research on environmental public consultation. Most environmental planning and dispute resolution is a protracted affair. Over time, the accumulation of experience, plus long effort and sacrifice, allows participants to become highly knowledgeable about matters relating to the issue, as well as fiercely protective of their position earned within the hierarchy of decision-making. Such people are not easily dislodged from their seats of influence, and in issues of resource planning and dispute resolution it is common to see the whole matter taken over and decided by a small cadre of leaders, with the remainder of the participating public acting as observers or providing tacit support.

A final issue of equity, not unrelated to Michels' law, has to do with the promulgation of the statuses and credentials of some participants in environmental public involvement. This point revolves around how knowledge, and control of knowledge, provides certain parties with a powerful advantage during the course of environmental negotiations (Yearley, 1991; Zehr, 1994; Schnaiberg, 1986). The frequent problem involves the control of scientific evidence, although other forms of knowledge (e.g., legal and administrative) can be similarly used. Thus, it is a typical, and troubling, feature of many environmental controversies that much of the basis for a decision can hinge on who is best able to control the use of scientific data (Latour, 1987). The tendency is for many environmental problems to become reified as mainly scientific problems in need of "correct" scientific answers. Environmental hearings then become arenas where scientists, engineers, and other "experts" rival one another over whose data, or interpretations, are best. Nonexperts and concerns declared nonscientific are marginalized and dismissed. In addition, the collection and ownership of scientific information is an important advantage normally controlled by the proponent in environmental disputes. Environmentalists and the local community are often only in the position to react to data presented to them by the developer collected during the preparation of the development plan. This ownership of data carries with it informal proprietary rights of interpretation, and much formal control over its access. The ability to challenge this taken-for-granted aspect of the environmental hearing, in which the status and centrality of science and its disciples hold sway, has become an important issue confronting public intervenors. While occasional challenges have been successful (e.g., Berger, 1977; Richardson et al., 1993), this veneration of science is still a serious obstacle for which the public involved in environmental disputes is ill-equipped to deal.

On equity grounds, therefore, a variety of conditions stand as challenges to the fulfilment of the promise of public involvement and its democratic goals. Among these is the choice of the bulk of the public not to participate, while those that do participate tend to be the privileged segments of society already close to the mainstream of decision-making. The exception involves the emerging presence of grassroots environmentalism's involvement in local community planning. While a promising trend, such forms of involvement until now have mainly developed over issues of human health risk. The high emotions engendered by such cases caused by immediate threats to person and family are one reason for the stronger than normal inclinations of local populations to become involved in such problems. Grassroots opposition also increasingly occurs in siting disputes over landfills, hazardous waste storage, and other environmental facilities. Thus, there are signs of increasing involvement and representativeness by the public in matters of environmental planning. Still, concerns remain over the potential for systemic problems of bias during environmental consultation in connection with how the public participation process functions and the likelihood of its domination by elites.

INVOLVEMENT

The third dimension on which the overall quality of public participation can be judged is *involvement* and has to do with the level and types of involvement, as well as with the techniques employed and the relations of power between participants. Since this dimension is most associated with the *experience* of involvement, it is also closely tied to participant satisfaction, and is an important factor relating to the intrinsic objectives of public participation overall (Sewell and Phillips, 1979: 354; Checkoway and Van Til, 1978).

The question of who participates has already been addressed from the point of view of representativeness, but there is another issue. For a field of policy analysis that has existed now for three decades, the issue of what is "the public" with respect to research on "public consultation" is probably the most important and least understood concept still to be clarified. What is a *public*? Who *should* participate? The unfortunate tendency within environmental planning has been to confuse the sociological concept of *public* with something else, *mass society*. That is, many consultative exercises attempt to bring in the "representative public," meaning a cross-section of the general population. In environmental planning this tendency is often reinforced by the likelihood of the existence of fairly clear physical boundaries for the zone of concern—for example, a watershed, lake, community, harbour, etc., together with some adjacent region. The objective, therefore, is to attempt to consult with a high proportion of the "affected" population living within this defined geographical zone. In practical terms the definition of the public becomes "everyone in the affected area." When, as often occurs, only a small number of the designated population actually take part in the consultation process, organizers blame "public apathy," and are anxious over the likelihood of the whole issue being hijacked by the few "special interests" that did show up.

Other problems arise out of this confusion over the definition of the public. In order to increase representation, the organizers may decide to conduct a social survey to gauge public opinion on the issues based on a random sample drawn from the entire population. But increasing the level of participation in this way does not increase public participation, simply because neither a population, nor a random sample of one, is necessarily a public. Many other techniques exist to allow organizers to "reach out" to more members of the population in order to increase the levels of participation (see Willeke, 1976), but to the extent to which the recruited individuals feel no real personal engagement in the matter at hand, this is not public consultation. Conversely, anyone interested in participating but not living within the designated boundaries of the region can end up labelled an "outsider" whose views should not count.

Public consultation should not confuse numbers with public representation. The notion of "the public" goes beyond mass society, or numbers. A public exists at the level of shared perceptions and collective identity. Genuine publics replace sheer numbers, or mass society, at the point at which a shared consciousness prevails. In his definitive text *The Sociological Imagination* (1959), C. Wright Mills notes:

> Whether or not they are aware of them, men in a mass society are gripped by personal troubles which they are not able to turn into social issues. They do not understand the interplay of these personal troubles of their milieux with problems of social structure. The knowledgeable man in a genuine public, on the other hand, is able to do just that. He understands that what he thinks and feels to be personal troubles are very often also problems shared by others, and more importantly, not capable of solution by any one individual but only by modifications of the structure of the groups in which he lives and sometimes the structure of the entire society. Men in masses have troubles, but they are not usually aware of their true meaning and source; *men in publics confront issues, and they usually come to be aware of their public terms.* (Mills, 1959: 187; emphasis added)

As this suggests, the best indication of genuine public involvement in environmental planning, as far as anyone can ever really tell, is the level of concern and commitment demonstrated by those who have chosen to take part. This may be a few or many, but how many participate is of little importance, so long as all the affected publics have been notified and given the opportunity to be involved. Publics may be small or large, but defining them in terms of either political or geographic boundaries is a questionable course. A mass outpouring of concern may either reflect a very widely held public—a mass public—or it may represent multiple publics. Hence, for most important environmental issues there exist various publics to be consulted, each in its unique way representing a common framework of understanding.

From the point of view of involvement, this conceptualization of publics has implications for deciding who is involved as well as how they are involved. The advantage of the many techniques for increasing participation in public consultation that now exist is not so much to do with increasing representation, as in helping to identify the diversity of publics. Often a distinction is made between "affected" and "interested" publics (Wengert, 1976). The affected public is that group for which the policy or environmental event has consequence, and it is not limited to those in the immediate physical vicinity of the problem. In pollution cases affected publics are often located well downstream or downwind of the source. In the case of the Chernobyl nuclear disaster, for example, the affected publics spanned continents. Publics may be also affected indirectly due to such things as changes to the economy or employment conditions resulting from new programs, the cancellation of developments, or the need to redirect taxes to pay for environmental remediation. In environmental matters, many of the affected publics have not yet even been born, but they must still be considered when assessing the consequences or plans or projects.

Affected publics are *potential* publics that clearly must be identified and, as far as is possible, notified about the pending issue and consultation plan. In theory the interested, or *real*, public will then come forward. From the point of view of planning for public consultation, however, the presence of the affected, but uninterested, public does not add anything really meaningful to the consultative process, while usually amounting to a significant drain on resources. The strategy for organizers, therefore, should be to invest less in representativeness, and more in attempting to identify real publics with respect to the matter at hand while at the same time providing a forum in which legitimate communication among these agents can occur.

Another issue on the question of publics has to do with the treatment of public involvement participants and the relations of power existing between the organizers and the other parties. Today in Canada public involvement in environmental planning is used in a wide array of institutional settings. It is important to recognize that, by and large, there is still relatively little statutory support for such consultation (Lucas, 1976; Vanderzwaag and Duncan, 1992). The statutory requirements for the most part vary widely across federal, provincial, and municipal levels, but are far from all-encompassing. Formal environmental hearings under the federal Environmental Assessment and Review Process (EARP), as well as provincial environmental assessment and appeal laws, do provide for public participation, but such highly formal proceedings apply in only a small minority of environmental plans and disputes. In Ontario the Provincial Planning Act (1983) and Bill 163 (1994) require a minimum of two public meetings for any zoning change or development covered by regional official policy plans. The recent Ontario Environmental Bill of Rights allows for greater public access to information and new avenues for individuals to challenge development proposals, but does not make public consultation in environmental matters mandatory. Public meetings before municipal councils are required by many municipal official plans, and programs of public consultation may be compulsory under some corporate administrative regulations (e.g., Quebec Hydro). Provincial ministries, including the Ontario Ministry of Natural Resources (MNR) and Ministry of Environment and Energy (MOEE), have often developed their own guidelines on public consultation, but though development proponents are strongly encouraged to follow these, they are not compulsory (Province of Ontario, 1994a, b, c).

Formal efforts to allow input into environmental decisions go well beyond these statutory and quasi-legal requirements, but are not always related to the desire for a full airing of issues among all parties and a decision based on maximum public input. Often participation is merely intended to satisfy minimum legal requirements by government, or build public support for an agency or development proponent's plans, reduce antagonism and avoid confrontations between disputants, provide legitimacy to decisions that have already been made, or reduce the likelihood of appeals (Chekoway and Van Til, 1979: 32; Arnstein, 1969). This can be referred to as the "decide, announce, and defend" approach (Susskind, 1985). In other words, agencies and proponents often use public involvement to achieve their own ends, without any commitment to the transfer or sharing of power with the public. For the goals of public involvement to be genuinely realized some realignment of power between the formal and informal nexus of decision-making is needed.

In a classic work, Sherry Arnstein (1969) proposed a typology for public involvement along the continuum of power. Her scale, known as Arnstein's Ladder, is displayed in Figure 9.3. Arnstein's approach is a direct challenge to a

FIGURE 9.3
Arnstein's Ladder

8	Citizen Control	Degrees of citizen power
7	Delegated Power	
6	Partnership	
5	Placation	Degrees of tokenism
4	Consultation	
3	Informing	
2	Therapy	Nonparticipation
1	Manipulation	

Source: Sherry Arnstein, "A Ladder of Citizen Participation." Reprinted by permission of *The Journal of the American Institute of Planners*, July 1969: 216–24.

model of participatory democracy, while equating public involvement to an administrative device designed to deny the rights of citizenry.

Arnstein's Ladder is a scale of citizen empowerment. For the first two rungs, at levels 1 and 2, participation is merely a guise. The bottom rung identifies the process of *manipulation.* Here the point is simply to allow power holders to educate participants. The public is placed on advisory boards or other committees to flatter and to engineer support. At best the goal is civility; at worst it is nothing more than a public relations game. At level 2, *therapy*, there is minimal progress toward involvement through more intensive application of resources; for example, use of expert testimony, corporate or agency announcements, and the organization of public events. *Informing* occurs at level 3 and is the first minimal step toward legitimate participation. Levels 3, 4, and 5 together represent the broad pattern of *tokenism*, or commitment to communication without of any redistribution of power. Informing, therefore, consists of the one-way flow of information from agency to citizens, without any channel for feedback. Techniques here may include the use of media releases, community newsletters, or "public information" advertisements on radio and television. Level 4, *consultation,* allows for the two-way flow of communication between parties, but without any guarantee that the public's voice will be heeded. Citizens are permitted to comment on decisions, while the decision itself remains in the hands of power holders. Follow-up monitoring by citizens of the consequences of a decision is restricted. Citizens only know that they have "participated in participation," while power holders can show that the requirement to involve the public has been met. Level 5, *placation*, occurs when mediation is arranged between stakeholder representatives and decision-makers. The aim is to appease the public by suggesting that the matter can be reasonably negotiated to the satisfaction of all parties. Placation occurs when power holders retain the right to judge the legitimacy or feasibility of the public's position. The public's influence is mainly dependent on the interpersonal skills of its representatives and their powers to persuade.

The upper three rungs of Arnstein's Ladder represent degrees of actual citizen empowerment. *Partnership*, at level 6, permits real negotiation and bargaining over the effects of the decision. For partnership to occur, the public must usually discover a way to win power from decision-makers. The struggle over power requires the strategic use of resources not available to all citizen groups. Financial resources may permit the group to expand its membership, fund activities, support leaders, pay technicians, lawyers, and community organizers, and conduct research. Social resources, such as a substantial community power base, may provide legitimacy and the potential for mobilization on behalf of the group's cause. *Delegated power,* at level 7, occurs when citizens achieve majority representation on the decision-making body. At this point the citizens take executive control of the decision process, while formal administrative authority remains with a parallel bureaucracy controlled by the state. Finally, level 8, *citizen control*, gives public representatives access to full administrative authority, including control over agency resources, personnel, and management.

Arnstein's Ladder is an early, but still widely utilized, model appropriate for assessing the quality of the involvement process in public participation practice. Is Arnstein's warning still valid today? René Parenteau (1988) examined this question by assessing the formal environmental review process for three Canadian jurisdictions: the federal Environmental Assessment and Review Process (EARP) and the provincial procedures found in Ontario and Quebec. His findings provide only very limited support for a trend toward citizen empowerment in environmental planning. Assessing the findings from 42 environmental review hearings, involving 1948 public participants, Parenteau concludes that only in the case of provincially mandated environmental reviews in Ontario do the procedures reflect any of the upper rungs of Arnstein's Ladder, reaching level 6, partnership. The federal government's procedures under EARP rank lowest of the three jurisdictions compared, achieving level 4, consultation. According to Parenteau, the federal process of public involvement is limited by being mainly a forum for information exchange between the public and decision-makers. The Quebec environmental review procedures are ranked by Parenteau one level higher than the federal procedures, placation, on the grounds that in Quebec citizens are permitted to make recommendations, in addition to exchanging information. The federal and Quebec environmental review procedures, therefore, are ranked as alternative degrees of tokenism on a scale of citizen empowerment.

Additional evidence about the ability of public participation procedures in environmental planning in Canada to meet the objectives of participatory democracy is sparse. But it should be observed that in addition to formal environmental assessment at the federal and provincial levels, there are myriad other opportunities for public involvement at the ministerial, agency, Crown corporation, and community levels, and in certain cases the goal of citizen empowerment may exist. Some evidence exists for instances of enhanced citizen control. In British Columbia consideration has been given to more community-based forestry management through proposals made by a coalition of environmentalists, First Nation members, trade unionists, and businesses (Tester, 1992). Elsewhere in Canada dozens of agreements have been signed between local populations and upper tier governments during the past fifteen years involving co-management in land zoning, parks, and wildlife (Cizek, 1993). In complex, multijurisdictional megaprojects, the trend is toward acknowledging the rights of local populations over the broader concerns of distant consumers, while ensuring greater protection of natural resources, traditional lifestyles, and local communities. Even in the field of federal environmental review, Novek (1995) reports an increasing tendency for the formal environmental impact assessment process to become incorporated into the mainstream of democratic decision-making, and its wider and more effective utilization by a lay opposition.

Despite this evidence, there are still many grounds for skepticism. Here the concerns have less to do with direct manipulation of the participation process, or its corruption by proponents or organizers, as suggested by Arnstein, and have more to do with systemic problems involving the prerogatives of the modern administrative state. Frank Tester (1992), for one, argues that the greater access to the decision process afforded by governments over the past decades has been granted reluctantly, and without any serious willingness of politicians or administrators to redefine the essential *raison d'être* of the state, which is to facilitate the accumulation of private capital. In this regard, nature is still mainly a basis for economic profit, and until such time as the logic of capitalism, in which the rights of private property prevail over those of environmental protection, is challenged, public participation in planning will exist as more of a political rite than a real step toward the redistribution of power. It is this taken-for-granted aspect of society that frames the basis for the still relatively modest levels of participation taking place, and that is responsible for the extent to which the views of those consulted are taken seriously. Gains beyond acknowledging the current state of the public's right to recognition are unlikely to take place.

> For western liberal democracies such pressures to extend the form and content of citizen participation threaten established political and economic arrangements which have constituted liberal democracy for the past 150 years. They also challenge the assumptions about proper human/nature relations which underlie our present political economy. Citizen participation in Canada now proposes to redefine democracy, economic decision making and the taken for granted world ... Government and business interests cannot be expected to welcome such changes. Indeed there are clear indications that governments are making deliberate attempts to relocate the locus for economic decision-making so that it is, by statute, shielded from citizen demands for input and control. (Tester, 1992: 40)

Overall, the involvement dimension relating to the assessment of public participation involves some conceptually thorny issues, which stand as fundamental challenges to the functioning and objectives of public participation in our modern society. The question of publics calls for a basic reassessment of the purpose and goal of participation. Is participation intended mainly to acquire the broadest possible inventory of public opinion in order to arrive at a decision that is the most informed? Or is participation intended to fulfil the realization by some to guide directly the affairs of the state over which they truly care? The question of publics requires this issue to be faced. Until now, administrative procedures appear more to have favoured representation over real public engagement, but it is not clear to what extent this has been intentional because the dilemma of publics is not that widely understood. Finally, the second issue of involvement concerns the real role of participation in state plans. Is it to appease or to empower? If it is the latter, an impartial weighing up would have to conclude that there still is much to be done.

PROSPECTS FOR AN ECOLOGICAL CITIZENRY

Where do we go from here? A number of factors should be considered. First, it must be acknowledged that, even in consideration of all the foregoing qualifications, the success of the public participation movement still puts it within the first rank of social movements in the western societies this century. Emerging strongly during the 1960s and 1970s, participation's success parallels even environmentalism's in terms of the fullness of its assimilation into the affairs of the state. Not all is law, but in Canada today it is the environmental manager who serves in peril for failing to demonstrate public accountability. Where laws and regulations are absent, strong normative expectations still frequently compel the public's involvement. As well, the movement has discovered new forms of enterprise. Comanagement, aboriginal self-management, and community land trusts are all among the recent offshoots of the public participation movement finding their way onto the state's policy agenda. And whether we agree with Tester (1992) or not that the state's commitment to participation is open to question, the reality of government downsizing in the 1990s gives powerful logic to the likelihood of a more involved citizen of the future.

Still, if the first two decades of participation were golden, the last two have been a return to dross. The 1960s and 1970s were heady days in the swing toward participatory democracy. The participation and environmental movements have moved in tandem, and environmentalism's spread from about 1970 served as participation's principal instrument and *raison d'être*. Participation, it is true, pervades every corner of the state from constitutional talks to road building, but many of its major battles have been fought on the environmental front, and it is here that the greatest advances have been made and where most significant developments continue to occur.

How goes environmentalism, goes participation. By Earth Day 1970 it was clear that persistent environmental problems—like pesticide use, industrial pollution, fossil fuel depletion, and population growth, identified by the likes of Rachel Carson, Paul Ehrlich, and others—were not going to be solved easily. Earth Day 1970, in which over 20 million people are said to have taken part, ushered in the full-blown admission of the depths of our ecological crisis (Dunlap and Gale, 1972). With this realization came pressures for new environmental regulations, better enforcement of existing laws, and changes to lifestyles. The public was expected to "pitch in" and do its part to overcome society's latest conflagration. But, while dealing with the environmental challenge was paramount, almost as important was the need to distribute the burden of sacrifice evenly. Robyn Eckersley (1992: 9) reports:

[E]nvironmental problems were originally perceived in the 1960s as a "crisis of participation" whereby excluded groups sought to ensure a more equitable distribution of environmental "goods" (e.g., urban amenity) and "bads (e.g., pollution). This is not surprising given that the early wave of environmental activism was generally seen as but a facet of the civil rights movement in its concern for more grassroots democratic participation in societal decision-making, in this case, land and resource usage. The growth in public concern over environmental problems was thus widely interpreted as being only, or at least primarily, concerned with participatory and distributional issues; that is issues concerning "who decides" and "who get what, when and how."

Yet accompanying this commission was also the view that the source of the dilemma was really just poor planning. During this stage of environmentalism, between 1970 and 1980, there was little tendency while confronting ecological problems to question the basic anthropocentric ethos of the day, assuming that all could be solved by human ingenuity, planning, and technology. At the time the response of scholars was to attempt to extend the mantle of understanding of public participation practice, and theory, and the period of the 1970s through the early 1980s saw the proliferation of books, articles, reports, and conferences in the field. The overriding concern was to improve channels of political communication and discover means to facilitate the achievement of democratic consensus in policy and planning.

While a laudable effort, one disquieting tendency with this work, not apparent at the time, was a predilection toward methodological refinement and applied technique. The technical literature in areas such as social impact assessment, community needs assessment, public consultation, community counselling, and dispute resolution grew steadily during this time, together with a host of case study applications and recommendations to managers on how to conduct a consultation. Given the tendency to view social and environmental problems as amenable to human fixes, it is not surprising that all that seemed required was to find the best model, or set of procedures, in order to allow agencies to incorporate democratic practice into the search for the technical solutions they were confident would eventually emerge.

By the early 1980s the limits to advances of this type appear to have been nearly reached, but in any case, as things began to grind down, environmentalism took another turn, taking participation with it. From the mid-1970s a new era in environmentalism was emerging, a period termed the "crisis of survival" by Eckersley (1992). With increasing understanding of the truly global scale of the environmental crisis, and appreciation of the common fate of all humankind, came the call for the return to a more centralized, authoritarian system of governing. This "survivalist" logic, best exemplified by Robert Heilbroner's (1974) *An Inquiry into the Human Prospect*, saw humanity's hope to be in the reintroduction of a strong and decisive system of authority capable of compelling the necessary constraints to prevent the limits of global carrying capacity being breached (Eckersley, 1992: 13–17). Thus, with conservativism's new ascendancy, much of the outward support and enthusiasm for public participation was lost, and from about 1985 on the number of new books and other scholarly contributions in the field fell sharply.

It is not exactly the case in our current era of the new, more authoritative regimes that the public participation movement has gone to ground, but it does appear that in the period since 1985 the advances that have taken place have principally to do with administrative implementation. Substantial growth has occurred in the wider use of public consultation in most areas of state functioning, with new policies and standards being developed, and considerable expansion occurring in the commercial public consultation industry in response to the growing demand for professional design and facilitation. At the same time, the *major* objective has become efficiency, with the broader vision and hope for participation in democracy that was the defining feature of the earlier era being largely lost. Evidence of this is found in the continuing tendency for public participation to be conceived of largely as an administrative tool in need of application based upon the appropriate mix of technique in order to arrive at an outcome that the public will accept. In suggesting the pattern in modern environmental public consultation to be more show than commitment to power sharing and joint understanding, Parenteau states:

> The public consultation, the aim of which was to involve the parties in the decision and transform it into a collective choice, may thus become a mediation exercise dealing with a project's terms of authorization and implementation. New tendencies make this conclusion inescapable. The agencies responsible for dealing with requests for authorization consistently invite the proponents to carry out their own consultations and the reports of these consultations are added to the file; firms of experts specializing in public consultations are being set up and they are making an arsenal of increasingly sophisticated instruments available to proponents—inquiries, surveys, games, simulations, etc.; interest groups and community institutions affected by the project also carry out consultations, creating structures and mechanisms for conducting direct negotiations with the proponent ... These ... considerations allow us to hypothesize that there has been an important and substantial movement away from the objectives which originally inspired the formulation and institutionalization of the major public consultation procedures. (Parenteau, 1988: 58)

THE MOVE TO EMANCIPATION

What should we now expect? The change that may now be taking place, and that may eventually release participation from its essentially pragmatic focus while reasserting its grander democratic vision, can be referred to as the "emancipation" process and comes to us from Green political thought. It is appropriate to end this chapter with a brief discussion of this new theoretical development, since it may reflect the wave of the future, while also helping lead participation out of its current conceptual void.

"Green theory" owes its birth to the founding of the Green movement in western Europe, particularly in West Germany, during the late 1970s and early 1980s (Tokar, 1987). It developed as a coalition of movements for peace, feminism, ecology, and citizens' initiatives (Galtung, 1986). The Green movement first achieved international prominence in 1983 when the West German Green Party, *Die Grünen*, received 5.6 percent of the popular vote in the 1983 German election and thus obtained parliamentary representation. Since then the term "green politics" has entered the vernacular, and Green parties are a notable, if not dominant, feature of the political systems of most industrialized nations, including Canada.

Green theory has no founding tradition, or principal founding figure. Indeed as Galtung (1986) argues, its only defining characteristic may be the uniformly antiestablishment stance of all the submovements that comprise it, although public participation is one of its pillars. Green theory is an eclectic blend of conceptual debates drawn from across the social, natural, and humanistic sciences. It is not a single theory, but a multifaceted blend of ideas that includes Marxist and post-Marxist thought, critical theory (e.g., Marcuse, Habermas), feminism, and ecology, and that allows its followers to range widely across the spectrum of political philosophy. Adherents to Green thought are sometimes highly divided in their world views and approaches to environmental problems, as in the example of the organization Earth First!, which has experienced a bitter internal quarrel over the use of violent forms of protest by some of its followers (Taylor, 1991).

What little Greens hold in common includes pride in grassroots organization and activism, support for the participatory process, and general rejection of hierarchical relations of control. The so-called "four pillars" of Green thought include *ecology, social responsibility* (including participation), *grass-roots democracy* and *nonviolence* (Coleman, 1994). Green causes include concern over environmental degradation, the arms race, social injustice, Third World poverty, sexism, and the oppression of ethnic and cultural minorities (Eckersley, 1988). Separate ecophilosophies often identified as part of the general Green movement include deep ecology, social ecology, bioregionalism, ecofeminism, and animal liberation.

From the point of view of public participation, the crucially defining concept from current Green theory, in addition to its overall general backing of participation, is that of *emancipation*. For Greens the path to true freedom, and indeed world survival, lies with the principles of ecology. The science of ecology—the "subversive" science, as it was once termed by Paul Sears (1966)—holds the knowledge permitting a fundamental realignment of the human–nature bond. The discovery in the last thirty years of the extent to which our destruction of the environment places humankind and the planet at imminent risk should not simply be seen as grounds for adoption of a "survivalist" mentality by which we attempt to compel more prudent resource use, say Green theorists like Murray Bookchin (1989: 19–39). Rather such knowledge is "liberating" insofar as it compels us to rethink our relationship with nature. The ecological critique of industrialism, it is argued, proves that current efforts to dominate nature, in which humans see themselves as distinct from and superior to nature, will not work (Leis, 1974). Latent within this critique is the potential for both self-discovery and the solution to our global ecological crisis (Eckersley, 1992: 19). Involvement in our individual communities leads to greater knowledge of social and political issues and, through networking locally and globally, an impact on the larger community can be realized. The need to rethink our culture, and its associated economic, social, and political systems, along lines of the new understanding provided by ecology is the first step toward personal enlightenment and self-realization, and it also begins the advance toward real environmental sustainability. Green emancipatory ecopolitical theory may be understood not only as a challenge to current social, economic, and environmental arrangements but as the opportunity to develop new understanding of ourselves and our relationship with the planet. Timothy O'Riordin (1995: 12) provides a cogent overview:

> The success of environmentalism is the loss of its special identity. Think about that. For the past 20 years of so environmentalists have been trying to bully or scare us into reforming our conscience, our behaviour, our society and our economy. They have done this by trying to make environmentalism not a separate science, or teaching material, or political party or social ethos, but *a companion in our day-to-day existence*. The so-called "greening" of society is the attempt to incorporate the cost of living into our economics, the totality of existence into our ethics, and the sharing of the living world into our politics. *When that is properly achieved, we should be emancipated. There should be no separate environmentalism.* [emphasis added]

Thus, the emancipation principle provides powerful food for thought, and it is appropriate that we close this chapter on such a note. This new link between political participation and global survival gives additional meaning to the term freedom. As well, the mutuality of interests between personal liberation, the advance of democracy, and global ecological security proposed by the emancipation cause is quite reminiscent of participation's more idealistic beginnings, and these latest developments in Green political thought may be a step toward reclaiming this lost vision.

REFERENCES

ACIR (Advisory Commission on Intergovernmental Relations). 1979. *Citizen Participation in the American Federal System.* Washington, D.C.

Almond, Gabriel A., and Sidney Verba. 1963. *The Civic Culture.* Princeton, N.J.: Princeton University Press.

———, eds. 1980. *The Civic Culture Revisited.* Boston: Little, Brown and Company.

Arnstein, S.R. 1969. "A Ladder of Citizen Participation." *Journal of the American Institute of Planners,* July: 216–24.

Bachrach, Peter. 1967. *The Theories of Democratic Elitism.* Boston: Little, Brown and Company.

Berger, Thomas R. 1977. *Northern Frontier, Northern Homeland: The Report of the Mackenzie Valley Pipeline Inquiry,* vols. 1 and 2. Toronto: James Lorimer.

Bookchin, Murray. 1989. *Remaking Society.* Montreal: Black Rose Books.

Bruton, Jim, and Michael Howlett. 1992. "Differences of Opinion." *Alternatives* 19(1): 25–33.

Burch, William R., Jr. 1976. "Who Participates: A Sociological Interpretation of Natural Resource Decisions." *Natural Resources Journal* 16(1): 41–54.

Checkoway, Barry, and Jon Van Til. 1978. "What Do We Know about Citizen Participation? A Selected Review of Research." In Stuart Langton, ed., *Citizen Participation in America.* Lexington, Mass.: D.C. Heath, 25–42.

Cizek, Peter. 1993. "Guardians of Monomin: Aboriginal Self-Management of Wild Rice Harvesting." *Alternatives* 19(3): 29–32.

Cole, Richard C. 1974. *Citizen Participation in the Urban Planning Process.* Lexington, Mass.: D.C. Heath.

Coleman, Daniel A. 1994. *Ecopolitics: Building a Green Society.* New Brunswick, N.J.: Rutgers University Press.

Connor, Desmond. 1974. *Citizens Participate.* Oakville: Development Press.

Creighton, James L. 1980. *Public Involvement Manual: Involving the Public in Water and Power Resource Decisions.* Washington, D.C.: U.S. Government Printing Office.

———. 1981. *The Public Involvement Manual.* Cambridge: Abt Books.

Curtis, James E., Ronald D. Lambert, Steven D. Brown, and Barry J. Kay. 1989. "Affiliating with Voluntary Associations: Canadian-American Comparisons." *Canadian Journal of Sociology* 14(2): 143–61.

Dahl, Robert. 1996. "Further Refections on 'The Elitist Theory of Democracy.'" *American Political Science Review* 60: 296–305.

Daneke, Gregory A., Margot Garcia, and Jerome D. Priscoli, eds. 1983. *Public Involvement and Social Impact Assessment.* Boulder, Colo.: Westview Press.

Dunlap, Riley, and Richard P. Gale. 1972. "Politics and Ecology: A Political Profile of Student Eco-Activists." *Youth and Society* 3(June): 379–97.

Eckersley, Robyn. 1992. *Environmentalism and Political Theory.* Albany, N.Y.: State University of New York Press.

Freudenberg, Nicholas, and Carol Steinsapir. 1992. "Not in Our Backyards: The Grassroots Environmental Movement." In Riley Dunlap and Angela G. Mertig, eds., *American Environmentalism*. Philadelphia: Taylor and Francis, 27–38.

Freudenburg, William R. 1983. "The Promise and Peril of Public Participation in Social Impact Assessment." In Gregory A. Daneke, Margot Garcia, and Jerome D. Priscoli, eds., *Public Involvement and Social Impact Assessment*. Boulder, Colo.: Westview Press, 227–34.

Galtung, Johan. 1986 "The Green Movement: A Socio-Historical Exploration." *International Sociology* 1(1): 75–90.

Gillies, J. 1989. "The Role of Advisory Boards in a Water Management Agency." *Water Resources Bulletin* 25(6): 1234–47.

Gottlieb, Robert. 1993. *Forcing the Spring: The Transformation of the American Environmental Movement*. Washington, D.C.: Island Press.

Hays, S.P. 1987. *Beauty, Health and Permanence: Environmental Politics in the United States, 1955–1985*. New York: Cambridge University Press.

Heilbroner, Robert. 1974. *An Inquiry into the Human Prospect*. New York: Norton.

Howell, Robert E., Marvin E. Olsen, and Darryll Olsen. 1987. *Designing a Citizen Involvement Program*. Corvallis: Western Rural Development Center.

Johnson, Donald E., Larry R. Meiller, L.C. Miller, and Gene Summers. 1987. *Needs Assessment: Theory and Methods*. Ames: Iowa State University Press.

Langton, Stuart, ed. 1978. *Citizen Participation in America*. Lexington, Mass.: D.C. Heath.

Latour, Bruno. 1987. *Science in Action*. Milton Keynes, England: Open University Press.

Leis, William. 1974. *The Domination of Nature*. Boston: Beacon.

Lipset, Seymour Martin. 1990. *Continental Divide: The Values and Institutions of the United States and Canada*. Orono: Borderline Projects.

Lorimer, James. 1972. *A Citizen's Guide to City Politics*. Toronto: James Lewis and Samuel.

Lucus, Alistair R. 1976. "Legal Foundations for Public Participation in Environmental Decisionmaking." *Natural Resource Journal* 16(1): 73–102.

McCloskey, Michael. 1992. "Twenty Years of Change in the Environmental Movement: An Insider's Vew." In Riley Dunlap and Angela G. Mertig, eds., *American Environmentalism*. Philadelphia: Taylor and Francis, 77–88.

Michels, Robert. 1915. *Political Parties*. Glencoe, Ill.: The Free Press, 1958.

Milbrath, Lester. 1965. *Political Participation*. Chicago: Rand McNally.

Milbrath, Lester, and M.L. Goel. 1977. *Political Participation: How and Why People Get Involved in Politics*. 2nd ed. Chicago: Rand McNally.

Mill, John Stuart. 1862. *Consideration of a Representative Government*. New York: Harper and Brothers.

Mills, C. Wright. 1959. *The Sociological Imagination*. New York: Oxford University Press.

Mischler, William. 1979. *Political Participation in Canada*. Toronto: Macmillan.

Mitchell, Robert Cameron, Angela G. Mertig, and Riley E. Dunlap. 1992. "Twenty Years of Environmental Mobilization: Trends among National Environmental Organizations." In Riley Dunlap and Angela G. Mertig, eds., *American Environmentalism*. Philadelphia: Taylor and Francis, 11–26.

Mitchell, T.R., and W.G. Scott. 1987. "Leadership Failures, the Distrusting Public and the Administrative State." *Public Administration Review* (November/December): 445–52.

Morrison, Denton, and Riley E. Dunlap. 1986. "Environmentalism and Elitism: A Conceptual and Empirical Analysis." *Environmental Management* 10: 581–89.

Nisbet, Robert. 1975. "Public Opinion vs. Popular Opinion." *The Public Interest* 41: 166–92.

Novek, Joel. 1995. "Environmental Impact Assessment and Sustainable Development: Case Studies of Environmental Conflict." *Society and Natural Resources* 8(2): 145–60.

O'Riordin, Timothy, ed. 1995. *Environmental Science for Environmental Management.* London, U.K.: Addison-Wesley Longman.

Paehlke, Robert, and Douglas Torgerson, eds. 1990. *Managing Leviathan: Environmental Politics and the Administrative State.* Peterborough, Ont.: Broadview Press.

Parenteau, René. 1988. *Public Participation in Environmental Decision-Making.* Ottawa: Ministry of Supply and Services.

Pateman, Carole. 1979. *The Problem of Political Obligation.* Chichester, England: John Wiley & Sons.

———. 1970. *Participation and Democratic Theory.* Cambridge: Cambridge University Press.

Pierce, John C., Mary Ann Steger, Brent S. Steel, and Nicholas Lorvrich. 1992. *Citizens, Political Communication, and Interest Groups.* Westport, Conn.: Praeger.

Poulantzas, Nicos. 1974. *Political Power and Social Classes.* London: New Left Books.

Press, Daniel. 1994. *Democratic Dilemmas in the Age of Ecology.* Durham, N.C.: Duke University Press.

Province of Ontario, Ministry of Municipal Affairs. 1994a. *Comprehensive Set of Policy Statements.* Toronto: Queen's Printer for Ontario.

———. 1994b. *Bill 163: An Act to Revise the Ontario Planning and Development Act for Ontario and the Municipal Conflict of Interest Act, to Amend the Planning Act and the Municipal Act and to Amend Other Statutes Relating to Planning and Municipal Matters.* Toronto: Queen's Printer for Ontario.

———. 1994c. *Bill 26: An Act Respecting an Environmental Bill of Rights.* Toronto: Queen's Printer for Ontario.

Public Participation in Environmental Decision-Making. 1988. Ottawa: Canadian Environmental Assessment Agency, Ministry of Supply and Services.

Richardson, Mary, Joan Sherman, and Michael Gismondi. 1993. *Winning Back the Words: Confronting Experts in Environmental Public Hearings.* Toronto: Garamond Press.

Roesner, Judy B. 1978. "Matching Method to Purpose: The Challenges of Planning Citizen-Participation Activites." In Stuart Langton, ed., *Citizen Participation in America.* Lexington, Mass.: D.C. Heath, 109–22.

———. 1975. "A Cafeteria of Techniques and Critiques." *Public Management* 57(12).

Rosenbaum, Nelson M. 1978. "Citizen Participation and Democratic Theory." In Stuart Langton, ed., *Citizen Participation in America.* Lexington Mass.: D.C. Heath, 43–54.

Satori, G. 1962. *Democratic Theory.* Detroit: Wayne State University Press.

Scarce, Rik. 1990. *Eco-Warriors: Understanding the Radical Environmental Movement.* Chicago: Noble Press.

Schnaiberg, Allan. 1986. "The Role of Experts and Mediators in the Channeling of Distributional Conflicts." In A. Schnaiberg, N. Watts, and K. Zimmerman, eds. *Distributional Conflicts in Environmental Resource Policy.* New York: St. Martin's, 348–62.

Schumpeter, J.A. 1943. *Capitalism, Socialism and Democracy.* London: Geo. Allen and Unwin.

Sears, Paul. 1966. *The Living Landscape.* New York: Basic Books.

Selznick, Philip. 1966. *T.V.A. and the Grassroots.* New York: Harper and Row.

Sewell, Derrick, and Susan D. Philips. 1979, "Models for the Evaluation of Public Participation Programs." *Natural Resources Journal* 19(2): 337–58.

Stankey, G.H. 1972. "The Use of Content Analysis in Resource Decision-Making." *Journal of Forestry* 70: 148–51.

Susskind, Lawrence E. 1985. "The Siting Puzzle: Balancing Economic and Environmental Gains and Losses." *Environmental Impact Assessment Review* 5(2): 157–63.

Syme, G.J., and E. Eaton. 1989. "Public Involvement as a Negotiation Process." *Journal of Social Issues* 45: 87–107.

Taylor, Bron. 1991. "The Religion and Politics of Earth First!" *The Ecologist* 21(6): 258–66.

Tester, Frank J. 1990. "Refections on Tin Wis: Environmentalism and the Evolution of Citizen Participation in Canada." *Alternatives* 19(1): 34–41.

Tokar, Brian. 1987. *The Green Alternative: Creating an Ecological Future.* San Pedro, Calif.: R&E Miles.

Van Liere, Kent D., and Riley E. Dunlap. 1980. "The Social Bases of Environmental Concern: A Review of Hypotheses, Explanations and Empirical Evidence." *Public Opinion Quarterly* 44: 181–97.

Vanderzwaag, David, and Linda Duncan. 1992. "Canada and Environmental Protection: Confident Political Faces, Uncertain Legal Hands." In Robert Boardman, ed., *Canadian Environmental Policy: Ecosystems, Politics and Process.* Toronto: Oxford University Press, 3–23.

Verba, Sidney, and Norman H. Nie. 1972. *Participation in America: Political Democracy and Social Equality.* New York: Harper and Row.

Vincent, Andrew. 1987. *Theories of the State.* Oxford: Basil Blackwell.

Walker, Jack. 1966. "A Critique of the Elitist Theory of Democracy." *American Political Science Review* 60: 285–95.

Wengert, Norman. 1976. "Participation and the Administrative Process." In John C. Pierce and Harvey R. Doerksen, eds., *Water Politics and Public Involvement.* Ann Arbor, Mich.: AnnArbor Science: 29–42.

Willeke, Gene E. 1976. "Identification of Publics in Water Resources Planning." In John C. Pierce and Harvey R. Doerksen, eds., *Water Politics and Public Involvement.* Ann Arbor Mich.: AnnArbor Science: 43–62.

Yearley, S. 1991. *The Green Case.* London: Harper Collins Academic.

Zehr, Stephen. C. 1994. "The Centrality of Scientists and the Translation of Interests in the U.S. Acid Rain Controversy." *Canadian Review of Sociology and Anthropology* 31(3): 325–53.

1. What, in your opinion, should be the role of public input in environmental decision-making? Should the public have a greater say than is currently the case, or less? Why? Be sure to consider the alternative visions for democracy ascribed to by the "elite" and "participatory" schools in this regard. What are the advantages of each of these approaches in terms of achieving environmental quality? What are the limitations?

2. "Representativeness," by which it is felt that a true cross section of the public has participated in the planning process, has long been a preoccupation of public consultation designers. Assess this. For good consultation to occur, is it necessary that those participating reflect a representative sample of the broader community? How likely is it that a representative cross section of community interests, skills, and social categories can be assembled? If turnout to public meetings is small, should organizers be concerned? Is low turnout evidence of "public apathy"?

3. Assemble information on an issue involving public participation in environmental planning within your community (e.g., a landfill siting dispute, environmental hearing, contamination case, or development plan). Follow the public involvement process through stories in the local newspaper, and if possible go to one or more of the open houses or public meetings scheduled to invite public input on this issue. Critically assess the process you have witnessed. Who participates, and how are the positions of the various sides on the issue presented? Is the process fair? Open? Inclusive? Accountable? Overall, does the input of the public influence the formulation of policy in this case? Assess what you have seen with respect to the eight stages of citizen empowerment contained in Arnstein's Ladder.

4. Consensus-based outcomes are the frequent objective of much organized public consultation. Discuss this. How important is it in environmental planning that the disparate sides on an issue come to agree on a final solution? Is such consensus also likely to reflect a solution that is environmentally, economically, and socially the most desirable outcome? Should a major goal of the public involvement process always be to reach agreement?

5. Green theorists see a deeply rooted bond between democracy and environmental stewardship. Discuss this. What is the relationship between environmental stewardship and democracy? How is it that these social thinkers can claim one cannot exist without the other? Do you agree?

6. While public participation in environmental decision-making has become widespread over the past three decades, it still faces many problems and dilemmas. Discuss public participation in the context of environmental policy formulation. What is its vision? Is this vision being achieved? Why or why not? What kinds of impediments cause public participation in environmental decision-making to fall short of realizing its full democratic promise?

C H A P T E R   1 0

Solid Waste

Douglas Macdonald

Environmental Studies Program
Innis College, University of Toronto

THE SOLID WASTE ISSUE

Of all the issues discussed in this book, undoubtedly the one most familiar to Canadians is solid waste—otherwise known as the garbage that every one of us generates, every day. All waste and pollution issues pose essentially the same technical, social, and political problems: (1) How can we generate less quantities requiring disposal? (2) How can we minimize the ecological health effects associated with disposal of the quantities we do generate? (3) How do we divide up the total cost (measured not only in dollars, but also such things as jobs, time, and convenience) of reducing quantities and improving safety of disposal? Solid waste, however, differs from these other issues in two important respects.

First, hazardous waste—discharged in liquid form to rivers, lakes, or sewers, or as air pollution emissions in gaseous or particle form—is, for all intents and purposes, invisible. Once such pollutants are released to the environment, they are both out of sight and, all too often, out of mind. A green garbage bag filled with solid waste, sitting at the side of the street, is very visible and for that reason represents a political and social issue that is much more difficult to ignore. The second difference is that solid waste, unlike all other forms of waste and pollution, is not simply an unwanted by-product of the manufacturing process. A large part of the solid waste produced by Canadians each year consists of *products themselves,* the toasters, cars, and envelopes we throw away when they reach the end of their useful lives, and the manufacture of which is a primary basis of our collective social goal of increasing economic prosperity. To a certain extent, we can reduce or eliminate waste and pollution by increasing efficiency—using a greater portion of the raw materials fed into the manufacturing process so that less remains as waste. In terms of products themselves, however, efficiency is not an answer. We can make them so they can be used again instead of thrown away, or more durable so they last longer, but as long as we live in a capitalist economy that measures success in large part by producing more products this year than we did last, we will continue to generate increasing quantities of solid waste.

We generate so much solid waste because we are affluent. If we want to generate less waste, do we have to make ourselves poorer? Because of this connection between our economic goals and waste, it is impossible to consider solid waste policy without considering impacts in related fields such as employment and international trade. Because solid waste is generated during extraction of resources and manufacture and use of products, it is also directly tied to resource conservation concerns, particularly in forestry and mining. In this respect, solid waste is similar to all other environmental issues—none can be considered in isolation, without consideration of broader social and economic goals. Because solid waste is so visible, and is familiar to everyone, it is an excellent paradigm for almost all environmental politics and policy.

Under Canadian environmental law, solid waste is distinguished from hazardous waste because it is less toxic and is not in liquid form, and thus not easily disposed of by discharge to rivers, lakes, or sewers. (However, what is referred to as "household hazardous waste," such as paints or cleaners, is often in liquid form and poses a problem when it leaks out of landfills.) Different regulatory regimes govern biomedical and radioactive wastes, which present more significant health threats to humans and other species, neither of which are considered here.

A distinction is usually made between "municipal solid waste," which refers to wastes disposed of in municipal landfills, and "solid waste." Solid waste also includes such things as construction and demolition waste, which may go to specially designed sites, and waste generated by mining and forestry, which is not collected and transported to special sites.

Canadians each year generate more than 30 million tonnes of solid waste, or about one-fifth more than the average of other OECD nations (OECD, 1995, p. 77; Cherniavsky et al., 1995, p. 73). Of that, something like one-third is generated by households, one-third by industry, institutions, and commerce, and one-third by construction and demolition (Cherniavsky et al., 1995, p. 73). Twenty times that quantity, or 650 million tonnes,[1] are generated by mining, 14 millions tonnes of manure by farming, and additional quantities by forestry, pulp mills and saw mills (OECD, 1995, p. 78). The latter wastes are largely burned for energy, manure is used as fertilizer, while mining wastes are left on-site. Of the 30 million tonnes referred to above, it has been estimated that in 1992, 67 percent was landfilled, 27 percent recycled, 5 percent incinerated, and 1 percent composted (OECD, p. 78). Not surprisingly, given their populations and state of industrialization, Ontario and Quebec generate the most solid waste, followed by B.C. and Alberta (Canada, 1991, p. 25-5).

Municipal solid waste is generated by residential households; by commercial establishments such as shops, restaurants, and offices; by institutions such as schools and airports; and by industrial firms. That total municipal solid waste stream is, according to Macdonald and Vopni (1992), made up of the following materials:

- wood, paper, and cardboard   35%
- organics   34%
- plastics   8%
- metals   6%
- glass   3%
- other   14%

In many Canadian cities, the municipality is responsible for collecting and disposing of household and some commercial wastes, using either works department staff or through contracts with waste firms; private firms contract directly with higher volume generators, such as industries, for collection and disposal. In rural areas, collection is not provided and households and businesses must make their own arrangements for disposal, often by taking it to a landfill or incinerator operated by the county or township.

Before World War II, little attention was paid to solid waste or the manner of its disposal. In response to economic demand, some metals were recycled and a number of beverage containers, such as milk, pop, and beer bottles, were reused. Regulation by governments, however, was either nonexistent or was limited to municipal by-laws that dictated where garbage could be burnt or buried. In the late 1960s and early 1970s, our present system of environmental regulation was put in place. Responsibility for solid waste regulation, as was the case with air and water pollution, shifted from the municipal to the provincial level. This meant that municipalities (as well as private firms) still collected and disposed of waste but now had to do so in accordance with provincial laws and policies. The most important element of the solid waste regulatory system adopted at that time was the requirement that it only be disposed of in a facility, whether a landfill or incinerator, which had been licensed by the provincial environment department. Waste disposal was no longer readily available at little cost, and attempts by municipalities or private firms to gain such licences, at least in the more densely populated parts of Canada, have become a major source of social conflict. Nobody, it seems, wants a landfill or incinerator in their backyard.

During the 1970s and early 1980s, the primary policy objective was to avoid threats to the health of humans or other species caused by improper solid waste disposal. Some provinces, following the lead of a number of U.S. states, brought in regulations requiring that a certain portion of soft drinks be sold in refillable bottles, but this was the only attempt made to reduce waste quantities. Recycling, when it was done at all, was purely voluntary, with no attempt by municipal or provincial governments to require recycling or foster increased markets for recyclable materials. Provincial environment departments devoted most of their energies to regulating disposal, and solid waste was seen very much as a pollution issue. The inherent connections, sketched above, between solid waste and resource conservation and other social and economic issues, did not form part of the public policy dialogue.

That began to change, however, by the mid-1980s. In response to growing environmental concern by the Canadian public, policy makers developed the concept of the waste management "hierarchy" of options—reduction, reuse, and recycling. This was a set of principles that, it was said, should govern the behaviour of waste generators. These principles have been described by one provincial environment department as follows:

- Reduction: Generating less waste to begin with, such as by consumers avoiding the purchase of disposable goods or by industries changing production processes to generate fewer unusable by-products.

- Reuse: Using an item again in its original form for the same or a different purpose.
- Recycling: Separating or extracting waste materials to meet a market demand, through systems such as a source separation, centralized composting, and waste processing of mixed waste to recover useful materials. (OMOE, 1990, p. 9)

At that time, as discussed below, proponents of burning as a disposal method were making this option seem more attractive by combining energy generation, which was presented as a fourth "R"—recovery. Environmental policymakers in Ontario originally referred to the "4 Rs" but, later in the decade, as incineration fell into disfavour, deliberately dropped any reference to recovery and referred only to three Rs. Other Canadian jurisdictions, however, refer to four. During this period, the hierarchy also had to accommodate composting of organic materials as a management method. As can be seen from above, this is often referred to as a form of recycling. Taken together, reduction, reuse, recycling and—depending upon one's views on incineration—recovery, are referred to as *diversion*—meaning diversion of waste materials from disposal.

On March 10, 1989, Ontario Minister Jim Bradley announced a policy objective of diverting 25 percent of the waste quantity generated in 1987 from disposal by the year 1992 and 50 percent by the year 2000. The same objectives were adopted by the other provinces and the federal government, through the auspices of the Canadian Council of Ministers of the Environment, in October 1989. It is difficult to know the extent to which government policy or changing attitudes contribute to our ability to meet those objectives, since waste generation seems to be affected more than anything else by economic conditions. During the recession of the early 1980s waste generation dropped by something like one-fifth (CIELAP, 1992, p. 7) and presumably a similar change occurred during the recession of the early 1990s. Regardless of the extent to which recession may have contributed, Ontario was able to claim that it had in fact met the 25 percent diversion target by the end of 1992.

Establishing the hierarchy and the specific diversion objectives meant that policy had evolved so that the goal was now twofold—both to prevent pollution problems, such as toxic substances in paint, ink, or cleaners seeping out of landfills and contaminating underground drinking water supplies, and to conserve resources by encouraging reduction, reuse, and recycling. In the late 1980s, as discussed below, solid waste landfills in the more densely populated provinces, such as Ontario or B.C., were beginning to fill up and those living in the immediate vicinity were strongly resisting the creation of new ones. In response, municipal and provincial governments began to do even more to encourage waste diversion, for instance by prohibiting disposal of some readily recyclable materials in municipal landfills. To the extent that the focus of regulatory action shifted from waste disposal to waste diversion, a whole new set of actors were drawn into the policy process—the manufacturers of products.

As can be seen in Figure 10.1, solid wastes are generated at each stage in the process of taking raw materials out of the environment, using them to manufacture products, and then selling those products to individuals, governments, or businesses who then, at the end of their useful life, either throw them away or recycle them. If our only policy concern were pollution, solid waste would be a relatively straightforward issue, since it poses fewer ecological health threats than other forms of waste. Because we are also attempting to conserve resources, however, solid waste policy is complex and faces enormous political difficulties. Despite the fact that our economy is increasingly shifting toward generating and manipulating information and providing various services, the manufacture of products is still a key component of our unquestioned social objective of ever-increasing material wealth. A significant portion of the Canadian economy, in addition, is devoted to the extraction of raw materials such as wood or metals, which are processed to some extent and then exported to other countries. Our purported objective of waste reduction—which can only be achieved by manufacturing fewer products or exporting less raw material—is thus in direct contradiction to our goal of economic expansion. Manufacturing and resource companies and their workers will naturally resist any policy measures that are effective enough to significantly threaten their profit levels or job opportunities.

In the same way, the soft drink industry over the past twenty years has successfully resisted efforts to increase the ratio of refillable bottle to recyclable can sales, simply because cans are less expensive for the industry (Macdonald, 1991). One of the recycling success stories, the increasing use of recycled newsprint, has meant that the raw material for those manufacturers is now found on the streets of U.S. cities, as well as northern Canadian woods, with corresponding implications for plant location and jobs (McRoberts, 1993). As well as these controversies

FIGURE 10.1
Source of Solid Waste

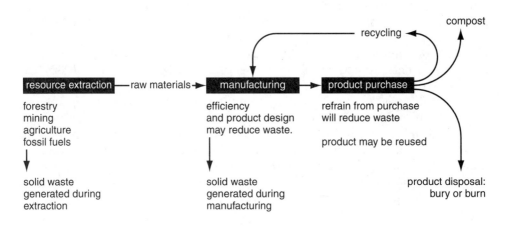

over cost and profit amongst classes or industrial sectors, the issue has implications for both regional and global distribution of wealth. As disposal siting becomes increasingly difficult and more expensive, the economics of transporting waste to far-distant disposal sites become increasingly attractive. As a result, affluent cities in Southern Ontario or along the U.S. Atlantic coast are now shipping solid waste hundreds of miles to the midwest and actively considering options for disposal in Northern Ontario or Atlantic Canada. The rich are externalizing their environmental costs, imposing them upon the poor through the incentive of the jobs that accompany waste disposal and recycling. The primary role of southern nations, or rural parts of Canada, in the global economy is as a supplier of raw materials. We may be approaching the day when the loop is closed, and their role is limited to that of exporting raw materials and then reimporting them as wastes, after they have been profitably turned into products, and enjoyed elsewhere.

Thus we see that solid waste encompasses virtually all of the political issues surrounding environmental management. How do we decide which natural areas, other species, and fellow humans will bear the esthetic, financial, and ecological health costs of waste disposal? How can we bring about internalization of at least some of those costs—that is, convince the waste generators (both big industries and university students who buy food in disposable containers) to change their behaviour in ways they will resist because it will cost them money or time? How do we allocate internalized cost; if we want to divert 50 percent of waste from disposal, which individuals, firms, or towns will pay the price of doing so? In the following pages we will address some of these questions. In terms of disposal, we will examine the two main controversies that have been simmering in Canada and all other industrialized nations during the past decade—the process for siting disposal facilities and the question of whether waste should be incinerated, with or without energy recovery. We will then begin to work our way backward, with a discussion of the major issues surrounding recycling. How can we ensure demand for recyclables and motivate generators to recycle? Who should pay for curbside Blue Box programs: the economy, through revenues from sale of recycled materials; taxpayers; waste disposers; or the manufacturers of the products that end up in the Blue Box?

SOLID WASTE DISPOSAL

As discussed, the social issue of waste disposal is driven primarily by the fact that the question of "where to put the waste," which was once decided by individuals or families alone at relatively low cost, is now decided collectively through a complex system of decision-making by environmental regulators and, on occasions, the courts. Both laws and social convention strongly prohibit littering, and any garbage dump, transfer station, recycling operation, or incinerator must be approved by the state. Disposal capacity has become scarce, relative to our grandparents' time, and like all scarce goods has become expensive and the subject of political conflict. That scarcity would be alleviated if all solid waste were burnt in incinerators, since those facilities, once they have gone through the approvals and licensing process, can operate for many years. Landfills, on the other hand, eventually fill up, and new ones must be sited, thus reminding us that waste disposal is never an out of sight, out of mind process.

SITING DISPOSAL FACILITIES

A municipality or private waste firm wishing to build a landfill or incinerator must not only receive a licence (usually referred to as a permit or certificate of approval) under the basic environmental protection law in that province but also undergo an environmental assessment (under that basic statute or, in some provinces, separate legislation) and, if the land must be rezoned, receive approvals under relevant planning legislation. Both environmental assessment and planning processes are designed to ensure opportunities for participation in the decision-making process by those affected, most notably those living in the immediate area, but also environmental groups pressing for waste diversion as an alternative to disposal. Often, the proposal will be heard by an administrative tribunal, such as the Ontario Municipal Board or Environmental Assessment Board, which operates in a quasi-judicial manner, with lawyers representing all parties and evidence for and against presented by expert witnesses such as hydrologists, toxicologists, engineers, ecologists, or sociologists who have surveyed the surrounding community. Not surprisingly, the process of preparing an environmental assessment, which includes many community meetings, the hearing, and possibly attendant litigation, can often extend over years rather than months.

Environmental assessment is intended to be a technical process, in which social costs and benefits are identified by experts and, based on their findings, decisions then made by impartial actors, either civil servants in the provincial environment department or members of the administrative tribunal. This ideal process can never be realized, however, because data is always incomplete or contested, criteria for evaluation are inevitably subjective (is the air pollution caused by trucks hauling waste to the landfill a greater or lesser environmental impact than the dangers to aircraft posed by gulls attracted to the site?) and some of those affected, such as other species or future generations, cannot be included in the decision-making process. At the same time, a process that arouses bitter controversy and extends over several years will inevitably become explicitly political when it is debated in local or provincial elections. Thus siting decisions are essentially political conflicts between those who will bear the cost of waste disposal (the community surrounding a proposed site) and those who will receive the benefit (the other users of the site and public or private actors who receive revenues generated by the site).

The complexities of the process can be illustrated by a quick review of Metropolitan Toronto waste disposal from 1980 to 1995.[2] At the beginning of that period Metro purchased the Keele Valley landfill, located just northwest of the city, from the private firm that had carried the siting process through the environmental approvals process (although without a requirement for full Environmental Assessment Act approval). Metro acted largely at the instigation of the Canadian Union of Public Employees, which has consistently fought to keep waste management a public, and unionized, process and in response to arguments that revenues from the site should flow to the municipality and not to a private firm. Although Keele Valley was thought to have sufficient capacity for twenty years' use, as the Ontario Ministry of Environment began to close other, older polluting landfills it began to attract waste brought to it by private waste firms throughout Southern Ontario. In 1985 accordingly, Metro was forced to begin a search for another landfill, this time under the EAA. By the time of the 1990 election, it appeared that Keele Valley would have to be closed very soon, and approvals were being sought for interim sites under a ruling by the Liberal government that only EPA, and not EAA, approval would be required. The NDP government, elected that year, began a new site search. The search engendered intense hostility in the regions surrounding Metro, contributing to the NDP's defeat in the 1995 election, and was the subject of litigation by several municipalities fighting to prevent siting of a landfill within their borders. During this five-year period, Metro increased tipping fees to approximately $150 from $18 a tonne, both to generate revenue and to extend the life of the Keele Valley site. Both objectives were achieved. Revenues climbed to generate millions of dollars a year, while much of the waste that had been going there was shipped by private firms to lower-priced landfills in New York state or further south. At the same time, Metro spent considerable time and money on plans to send waste by rail to Kirkland Lake in Northern Ontario, a plan that generated considerable controversy, both there and in Metro, and that was eventually dropped. Although the Metro experience is a somewhat extreme representation, it embodies all of the elements of high-stakes political and commercial manoeuvring that characterize disposal siting throughout North America and Europe.

INCINERATION

Burning solid waste—in apartment building incinerators, at dumps, or as piles of leaves at the curb—has always been attractive, simply because it reduces volume, making at least a part of the total magically disappear. Unfortunately, while parts are dissipated as heat, others remain as air pollution and ash. Because of its contribution to urban smog, waste burning in metropolitan areas was virtually phased out as the modern environmental regulatory regime was established in the 1970s. In the following decade, however, burning reappeared as a policy option, this time touted as a process for generating energy while at the same time meeting waste disposal needs. Like everything else associated with solid waste, it has been the subject of controversy ever since.

Manufacturers of incinerators have since the early 1989s carried out a marketing campaign, pointing to the two main advantages of incineration. It allows recovery of energy from waste before disposal and reduces the need to use valuable land for waste disposal. Critics point to the disadvantages. Air emissions contain pollutants such as heavy metals, hydrogen chloride, and toxic organic compounds, many of which are released from materials such as plastics that would have posed fewer problems had they not been burnt (Smith, 1995). Manufacturers have responded by continually working to improve emission quality by use of scrubbers that capture contaminants before they are released. They also have pointed to air emissions from landfills as representing an ecological health threat analogous to incineration (Gilbert and Bremner, 1995). Critics point to the difficulties of disposing of the materials thus captured, which are classified as hazardous wastes, and proponents point to improvements in our hazardous waste management capabilities. More difficult to resolve is the argument that incineration undercuts diversion policy. Often municipalities contract to provide specified annual quantities of waste to an energy-from-waste incineration facility, which in turn needs them to meet its contractual obligations to energy customers. The result is an incentive for all concerned to ensure that reduction, reuse, and recycling are not so successful as to reduce waste quantities below that contractual limit (CELA, 1995). Finally, critics charge that incineration is more expensive than landfill (CELA, 1995).

Perhaps because of population densities and attendant difficulties in siting facilities, incineration is more widespread in Europe than in North America. In the United States and Canada the arguments set out above are being hashed and rehashed in many cities and towns. Only one jurisdiction, Ontario, has moved to ban incineration, an action that was reversed by the Harris government when it assumed power in 1995. While repealing the incineration ban, that government promulgated a new, stricter regulation governing air emissions—thus implicitly casting the issue as one of pollution and not of resource conservation.

RECYCLING

As discussed, recycling is action taken to use materials in altered form as inputs to the manufacturing process, thus reducing the need for raw materials with their associated resource depletion and pollution. Although it is less desirable than reuse or reduction, it is the major form of waste diversion activity to date. In working to increase recycling, policymakers face two related challenges: (1) ensuring that there is market demand for recyclables, and (2) influencing the behaviour of individuals or organizations as they decide whether to throw away or recycle a given material. Market demand is essential to ensure that recycled materials, such as newspapers or glass bottles, are actually used and do not simply sit for years in storage warehouses. It also provides benefits in the form of financial incentives for recycling and, as discussed below, revenues that can be used to offset the cost of recycling programs. Market demand is ultimately influenced, of course, by the price differential between raw and recycled materials, which is dependent upon both market costs and resource pricing policy in such fields as forestry or mining. Because governments are not willing to use resource pricing for that purpose, a number of other policy instruments, discussed below, have been brought into play. By the same token, the behaviour of those deciding between recycling and disposal will ultimately be influenced by the price differential between those activities. Again, governments could use disposal pricing to establish a clear differential in favour of recycling. Although that has been done to some extent, as discussed below, other instruments are also needed here. Two other issues are discussed in this section—the recycling of organic materials, either directly as food or through composting, and the vexed issue of allocating the cost of curbside recycling programs between product manufacturers and taxpayers.

Since organics constitute something like a third of the municipal waste stream, policymakers intent on preserving landfill space have developed a number of programs to divert them from disposal. In some foodstuffs are collected and used directly as food, either in programs for the urban needy or as agricultural feed, particularly for pigs. Many municipalities have developed programs to offer free backyard composters to their citizens, while some are experimenting with curbside collection of organic wastes, which are then taken to centralized composting facilities.

ENSURING DEMAND FOR RECYCLABLES

To the extent that environmental awareness exists, consumers may deliberately choose products containing recycled materials over those made exclusively from raw materials, with no need for government action, even when the price of the former is higher. During the late 1980s and early 1990s, when environmental concern ranked high in public opinion polls, many products, such as newspapers containing recycled newsprint, were marketed on the basis of their "green" attributes. During that time, governments in Canada and elsewhere began to develop labelling programs to provide consumers with independent, objective information on the environmental attributes of products. The Canadian program, established by the federal government, is known as Environmental Choice. "The federally-funded Environmental Choice programme aims to shift consumer and institutional purchasing towards products and services that conform to environmental guidelines. It is assumed that such a shift in consumer behaviour will provide incentives for industry voluntarily to develop environmentally preferable goods" (Cohen, 1994). In the case of recycling, the intent is to encourage use of recycled materials that, once approved by the program, will allow the manufacturer to display the Environmental Choice logo.

The difficulty encountered by labelling programs is that they are directly analogous to standard setting. Just as it is inherently difficult for regulators to decide what concentration level of a pollutant is "safe," it is difficult to decide what proportion of recycled material merits inclusion in the program. Since both decisions have direct economic implications for the relevant industry, those business interests attempt to influence the decisions being made. In the case of Environmental Choice, industry has insisted that labelling decisions be subject to the same examination of their impact on economic activity, in order to justify their need, as is the case for federal regulations. One analyst has suggested that this business influence has weakened the program: "Government's demand for economic assessments in Environmental Choice decision making indicates that what is to be offered is information on environmentally preferable products that consumers can favour without fear of harming the immediate interests of Canadian industry" (Cohen, 1994, p. 27).

Instead of attempting to indirectly influence purchasing decisions through labelling programs, governments can incorporate requirements for recycled content into their own buying policies. Critics have suggested that governments have not moved forcefully enough to use this potential economic power, but some progress has been made (Pollution Probe, 1991). Governments have also developed programs to help large institutional and industrial purchasers that wish to increase recycled content in their buying.

In addition to such voluntary programs, governments are able to directly regulate, using either law or taxes, to both stimulate demand for recyclables and influence recycling behaviour. A number of European countries, led by Germany, have developed such regulatory programs. The German Packaging Ordinance passed in 1991 "requires that all packaging be made of reusable or recyclable materials and must be reused or recycled. Manufacturers and distributors of packaging are obliged to accept its return after use" (Winfield and Makuch, 1993, p. 6). The law was intended to encourage industry to itself operate collection and recycling systems, which led to the creation of the "Green Dot" system—a label informing the consumer that the product is included in the industry-operated system. A number of U.S. states have enacted legislation requiring use of recycled newsprint in newspapers, while others have introduced taxes on virgin newsprint to achieve the same end (Macdonald, 1994; Aunan, 1993).

In Canada, governments have not directly regulated recycling requirements, but have instead used the threat of regulation to induce voluntary action by industry. The National Packaging Protocol, developed jointly by provincial and federal environment departments, packaging industries, and environmentalists, has used a number of measures to divert packaging wastes from disposal. Between 1988 and 1992, packaging waste sent to disposal in Canada dropped 21 percent, from 5.41 million tonnes to 4.2 million (Macdonald, 1994, p. 27). The Ontario government in 1994 introduced regulatory requirements that large institutional or industrial waste generators develop plans for waste audits and separation, but stopped short of direct requirements for recycling or use of recycled content. Since being elected in June 1995, the Harris government in Ontario has pursued a policy of environmental deregulation, making it extremely unlikely that recycling regulation will be introduced in the province in the near future. Since the election of the Klein government in Alberta in 1993, policy has been moving in the same direction in that province (Macdonald, 1996; Griffiths and Neufeld, 1996).

Driven by deficit concerns and the desire to increase revenue without raising taxes, it is far more likely that provincial governments and their municipalities will use per-bag fees to encourage recycling than the instrument of law. The idea is that if households must pay for every bag of garbage they set out at the curb for collection, they will have an increased incentive to both reduce and reuse and to use Blue Box recycling programs that are provided at no cost. A number of European, U.S., and Canadian municipalities have introduced such systems, and it seems likely that more will do so in the future.

ALLOCATING THE COST OF CURBSIDE RECYCLING

The cost of collecting a tonne of waste and disposing of it in a municipal landfill, including the capital and operating costs of the landfill and operating costs of the collection, is about $50. The net cost of collecting recycled material at the curb, processing, and selling it (after subtracting revenue received from the sale) varies with market conditions, but is about $100 to $150 a tonne (Macdonald and Vopni, 1992). Recycling is more expensive than disposal, simply because more must be done in handling, packaging, and transporting the materials. Those higher costs, for the most part, cannot be offset by sale revenues. Market prices for recycled materials vary over time and differ widely from material to material. By far the most valuable is aluminum, used in the manufacture of recyclable beverage containers, which fetches over $1000 a tonne. Recycled steel can be sold for something like $100 a tonne and glass for about half of that. Over the past decade, the market price for newsprint and other recycled paper has varied from negative (it could not be sold at any price) to as much as $200 per tonne, but, until recently, was usually in the range of $20 a tonne (Chang, 1996). Recyclable sales revenues are unstable and unpredictable and, because the high-price items such as aluminum and steel make up such a small portion of the total volume, cannot match the cost of recycling.

For this reason, curbside recycling has always been subsidized. During the past decade, that subsidy has been the subject of two ongoing policy debates—how much should industrial manufacturers contribute to the cost and, of the remainder, how much should be paid by the local municipality and how much by the provincial government? Curbside recycling was established in Ontario in

1986 as a result of negotiations between the soft drink industry, which wanted a relaxation of regulatory requirements for refillable container sales, and the provincial government, which was willing to accept, in exchange, industrial funding for the Blue Box program. The program was established on the basis of an even three-way split of the cost between the local municipality, the Ontario Ministry of Environment, and Ontario Multi-Material Recycling Inc. (OMMRI), the corporate body established by the soft drink companies to manage recycling (Macdonald, 1991, p. 211). The portion paid by industry declined over time, however. In 1993, the $86 million cost of the Ontario Blue Box program was divided as follows: 33 percent from the province; 39 percent from municipalities; 22 percent from sale of recyclables, and 5 percent from industry (Chang, 1996, p. 8). At about that time, municipalities, faced with declining transfer payments from the province, were increasingly unhappy with the cost of the program and threatening to drop the service. In the fall of 1995, Blue Box funding was ended by the provincial government.

During the early part of the decade, considerable effort was made to build on the "product stewardship" model established by the original contribution of the soft drink industry to the cost of curbside recycling. The term product stewardship refers to responsibility taken by product manufacturers for environmental effects caused by their products after they have been sold and are, for that reason, no longer the legal responsibility of the manufacturer. It is an extension of the legal liability that has always existed for defective products and that is now being extended to products such as cigarettes and handguns. Presumably in an effort to forestall the kinds of regulatory requirements for recycling imposed in Europe, a number of industries, including representatives of grocery product manufacturers and the soft drink industry, developed a program called the Canadian Industry Packaging Stewardship Initiative (CIPSI). Like the European systems, it would be self-administered. CIPSI industries would charge their members a per-tonne fee for packaging materials and use the revenues to contribute to the cost of municipal curbside recycling programs. To ensure that industries participated, provinces would develop "backdrop" regulation that would require that regulated businesses either participate in the CIPSI program or develop their own waste diversion program (Macdonald, 1994, pp. 28–29).

The CIPSI program was advanced for public discussion in Ontario in June 1994, and has been considered as well in B.C., Manitoba, Nova Scotia, and Quebec. In Ontario, the Association of Municipalities of Ontario first rejected the proposal and then, in the fall of 1995, endorsed it. At that same time, however, a group of industries, including beer and automobile manufacturers and the Ontario Waste Management Association, informed the Harris government that they opposed the program. As a result, the provincial government abandoned plans to implement the CIPSI system. Nor has it been adopted by any other province. It has been suggested that beer companies that rely on provincial

FIGURE 10.2
U.S. Consumption of Materials, 1900–1991

support for their refillable-bottle system to keep American beer sold in cans out of the province objected to a system that gave recycling precedence over re-use. Other industries may have been fearful of the cost implications that might flow from such an institutionalization of the concept of product stewardship (Chang, 1996). Since it is obvious that the Harris government will not bring in any new environmental initiatives, there is little reason for Ontario industries to continue to pursue product stewardship funding of curbside recycling.

CONCLUSION

Figure 10.2 provides a depiction of resource consumption in the United States during this century. Quantities have steadily increased, except in times of recession. Undoubtedly the same trend has occurred in Canada and, if data were available, would also be seen in any tracking of solid waste generation. It is difficult to believe that the industrialized nations can continue this expansion of resource consumption indefinitely, or that the planet can provide the resources and waste disposal capacity to allow the ten billion people who will be living here soon to all consume at that level. Something will have to change. Our demand for consumer products, which is presumably related to such things as self-esteem and definitions of happiness, must decline (Durning, 1992). Hopefully, changing attitudes toward solid waste—symbolized by the university student walking to class, her reusable mug swinging from her backpack—will be part of that process.

NOTES

1   For a discussion of solid waste and other ecological effects of Canadian resource extraction, see Paehlke, 1993.
2   A good account is provided in Crooks, 1993.

REFERENCES

Aunan, Lauri. 1993. *A Survey of Recycled Content Laws and Other Market Development Strategies*. Portland, Ore.: National Environmental Law Center.
Canada. 1991. *The State of Canada's Environment*. Ottawa: Ministry of Supply and Services.

CELA (Canadian Environmental Law Association). 1995. *Response to the Proposed Amendment to Regulation 347: The Case Against Incineration.* Toronto: CELA.

Chang, Elfreda. 1996. *CIPSI: An Analysis of Why Packaging Stewardship Has Not Yet Been Implemented in Ontario.* Unpublished manuscript.

Cherniavsky, Ben, Jack Mintz, and Sergio Traviza, in association with Resource Integration Systems. 1995. *Eco-Fees and Tax Policies for Waste Minimization.* Prepared for Environment Canada.

CIELAP (Canadian Institute for Environmental Law and Policy). 1992. *Looking Back and Looking Ahead: Municipal Solid Waste Management in Ontario.* Toronto: Canadian Institute for Environmental Law and Policy.

Cohen, David S. 1994. "Subtle Effects: Requiring Economic Assessment in the Environmental Choice Programme." *Alternatives* 20(4): 23.

Crooks, Harold. 1993. *Giants of Garbage.* Toronto: James Lorimer.

Durning, Alan. 1992. *How Much Is Enough? The Consumer Society and the Future of the Earth.* New York: W.W. Norton.

Gilbert, Richard, and Ray Bremner. 1995. *Overview of Waste Management in the Greater Toronto Area 1990–1997.* Prepared for Ogden Martin Systems Ltd., Mississauga, Ont.

Griffiths, Len, and Richard Neufeld. 1996. "Deregulation in Alberta." *Hazardous Materials Management,* Feb./March.

Macdonald, Doug. 1996. "Environmental Deregulation in Canada." *Canadian Environmental Journal: GreenVIEWS.* Toronto: Spring.

———. 1991. *The Politics of Pollution.* Toronto: McClelland & Stewart.

———, with Nina Lester and Cameron Mackay. 1994. *Taxation and User Fees as Potential Policy Instruments in the Emerging Regulatory Regime of Solid Waste Diversion.* Toronto: York University.

———, and Paula Vopni. 1992. *Overcoming Barriers to Large-Scale Diversion of Municipal Solid Waste.* Toronto: International Council for Local Environmental Initiatives.

McRoberts, David. 1993. "Restructuring the Economy: A Look at the Implications of the Shift to Recycled Materials." *Alternatives* 19(2).

OECD. 1995. *Environmental Performance Reviews: Canada.* Paris: OECD.

OMOE (Ontario Ministry of the Environment). 1990. *Towards a Sustainable Waste Management System: Discussion Paper.* Toronto: Queen's Printer.

Paehlke, Robert. 1993. *Ecological Carrying Capacity Effects of Building Materials Extraction.* Report prepared for Forintek Canada Corp.

Pollution Probe. 1991. *Putting Our Money Where Our Mouth Is: A Review of Environmental Purchasing Policies by Metro Area Municipalities.* Written by E. Schwartzel and J. Haliniak. Toronto: Pollution Probe.

Smith, Kenneth E. 1995. "Municipal Solid Waste: Incineration." In Robert Paehlke, ed., *Conservation and Environmentalism: An Encyclopedia.* New York: Garland.

Winfield, Mark, and Zen Makuch. 1993. *Who Pays for Blue? Financing Residential Waste Diversion in Ontario.* Toronto: Canadian Institute for Environmental Law and Policy.

QUESTIONS FOR DISCUSSION

1. Canada has lots of land to bury waste in. Why should we worry about the issue?

2. Is burning waste a good idea?

3. Is transporting waste for disposal from urban to rural regions a good idea?

4. Should the manufacturers of products such as newspapers and automobiles pay some portion of the costs of the recycling or disposing of them?

5. What are ten things you can do to generate less waste each day?

6. What can governments do to encourage all of us to generate less waste?

7. Will generating less waste mean slower economic growth and fewer jobs?

CHAPTER 11

Environmental Management

Dixon Thompson

Department of Environmental Design
The University of Calgary

INTRODUCTION

This chapter presents the argument that a sound, objective scientific statement about the nature of a problem and a clear description of options for its solution are only the first steps in a much longer process. Scientists must also develop the knowledge and skills to set goals, assess the possible solutions, select the best ones, and ensure that they perform properly. This can be done by applying a defined set of environmental management tools.

Sound and objective scientific descriptions of environmental problems and ways to solve or avoid them are the first steps in effective environmental management. The descriptions of scientific facts must be subjected to peer review and other means of evaluation within the scientific community. They must also be translated into terms and formats readily understood by other disciplines and public decision-makers. That means, refereed journal articles are necessary—but not sufficient. To communicate effectively, scientists must learn to understand the needs of their other audiences and how to deliver the scientific message in a way that can be understood and accepted. This is too important to leave solely to nonscientists such as journalists.

At times, scientists become frustrated with the lack of public response to what they consider obvious problems and their even more obvious solutions. Short of an immediate life-or-death threat such as an epidemic or depletion of the ozone layer, scientists on their own do not have enough credibility to produce an immediate change in society.

To effect the necessary changes, scientists must become much better at synthesizing their results with those of scientists in other disciplines to produce a broad and coherent scientific picture. They must develop the ability to integrate their work into the social, economic, and political context. Perhaps most importantly, they must become much more effective at communicating, especially by being able to explain in simple terms why change is needed. Simply describing the problems and trying to scare society into action is not effective.

The remainder of this chapter then will assume that the scientific description of the environmental problem is no longer the major constraint to its solution, although it is an important first step. The chapter will provide a definition of management, a list of reasons for change (driving forces), a discussion of current environmental management systems, and an outline of a set of environmental management tools. Finally, some of the Canadian and international organizations involved in the development and standardization of the set of tools will be listed.

Scientists do not have to become managers to participate in environmental management, but they often do. The understanding of management and of the set of environmental management tools outlined in this chapter is as important to scientists as the details of their particular scientific discipline. Although scientists can participate directly in environmental decision-making without becoming managers, they will have to know the basics of environmental management and its tools to be effective participants. At the very least, those scientists who participate only by providing information will be more effective if they understand something about the environmental management systems to which they are contributing.

All of this chapter is based upon the assumption that most scientists are willing to try to work to change existing systems from within. However, even those who do not want to work within existing systems, and who advocate rapid and radical change, will benefit from a better understanding of current practices in environmental management.

Scientists, whatever their perspective, need to be prepared to demonstrate why more effective development and application of environmental management tools alone will not be sufficient to deal with all the problems we face.

For example, one problem that more effective environmental management cannot deal with is population growth. With exponential growth of the world's population, no matter how efficient and effective we become, we are doomed to failure. Control of this rapid growth is essential given the environmental damage that it creates. But this solution will lead inevitably to clashes with religious institutions that object to population control. There is no management tool that can influence a fundamental religious belief.

However, effective environmental management is an important short- to medium-term solution. It can help us through the transition to the more fundamental changes that are required.

ENVIRONMENTAL MANAGEMENT

Environmental management can be defined as:

- that group of senior people responsible for decisions about environmental matters
- the physical manipulation of a resource such as forest management, water management, pest management
- the setting and achieving of goals to protect the environment and conserve resources

This chapter will deal with the third definition, in which management includes:

- developing strategic planning
- setting goals

FIGURE 11.1
Evolution of Environmental Science

STAGE	FOCUS	SKILLS
We're O.K.—God and/or technology will provide, not to worry—everything will be just fine.		
Diagnosis and Description	The natural environment	Traditional, reductionist, natural science
Diagnosis and Descriptions	Describing the problems	"
Treatment	The symptoms Supply management at point of origin	Sciences and engineering
Attack	Problems and symptoms Society, people ideologies, lifestyles, consumers, industry, media, the "system(s)," economics, social systems	None, media manipulation, science and engineering, politics, scare tactics, mis- and dis-information, exaggeration
First-Stage Prevention	The source of problems Demand management at point of use	Science, engineering, policy & plans, management, CIA & audits, product assessments
Current-Stage Prevention	Systems, products, processes, planning, management, integrated resource management	Teams, science, engineering, planning, management, policy assessment, accounting, communications, design

FIGURE 11.2
Roles of Environmental Scientists

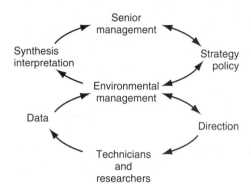

- identifying and organizing the people with skills and knowledge, the technology, finances, and other resources needed
- identifying and assessing the various options for reaching the goals
- assessing risks and setting priorities
- implementing the selected set of options
- monitoring performance for necessary adjustments through feedback

Specific sets of skills and knowledge and very detailed processes need to be developed to make these management steps financially workable. As environmental science matured from its start in the late 1960s, tools were developed and refined to make resource conservation and protection of the environment more effective. Recently those tools are coalescing into a set (or sets) of tools that, used together, enhance the effectiveness of the individual tools.

It was not effective to simply try to inject raw scientific data into the processes of environmental management. The techniques of scientific research were not useful without considerable adaptation. Therefore, environmental scientists had to develop new skills and play a somewhat different role.

On the one hand, environmental scientists must be able to work with researchers and technicians to determine the kind of data required, and to decide the most effective ways of getting it. They guide and, where possible, participate in data collection and research to define the problems and their solutions. Environmental scientists must then process the data into a form that will be useful to decision-makers. Too often what is available is "data rich and information poor." Environmental factors are ignored by decision-makers because they get lost in the data and don't know how to respond.

On the other hand, environmental scientists must also be able to work with senior decision-makers to set, or reset and adjust, goals and objectives when

FIGURE 11.3
Hierarchical Role of Environmental Managers

Level 1	**Top Management** Board of directors, senior managers: Must understand purpose and benefits of environmental management but no need to know protocol or technical details.
Level 2	**Environmental Coordinators** Specialists within certain disciplines responsible for environmental management: Must understand environmental management principles. Must have information collection and interpretation skills. Must understand management protocol and report writing. Must know what top management needs.
Level 3	**Technicians and Specialists** Soil scientists, water specialists, etc.: Must know how to contribute specific services to environmental management. No need to know management skills.

necessary. Then they must guide the monitoring and evaluation to ensure that progress is being made—and must be prepared to adjust solutions to reach those goals.

This is why environmental scientists must have not only refined scientific skills and knowledge, but management skills as well. They need to be able to synthesize the results of research and data gathering from various disciplines; integrate that information into the social, political, and economic context; and then communicate the results of the synthesis and integration to decision-makers.

Environmental managers play a role between that of senior managers and technicians and specialists.

DRIVING FORCES AND THE ENVIRONMENTAL MANAGEMENT SYSTEM

Perhaps the most important step in implementing effective environmental management is convincing decision-makers that it is necessary. Other authors in this text have provided ethical and biophysical arguments about the importance of a healthy natural environment, preserving biodiversity, etc. Unfortunately, those arguments are often not compelling enough to persuade people in governments, institutions, and industry to make substantive changes.

The following list of forces driving change in environmental management apply to a greater or lesser degree to government, institutions, and industry:

- Stricter *criminal* environmental laws and enforcement.
- Strengthened *civil* liabilities on environmental issues. Corporate directors and senior decision-makers can be held personally liable in civil suits for environmental damage.[1]
- Banks and investors are requiring assurance that their loan or investment is not jeopardized because of environmental risks and poor environmental management. Banks and investors will not help finance environmentally risky businesses.
- Employee concerns and personal values change corporate and institutional behaviour.
- Many (but certainly not all) efforts to conserve resources and reduce pollution are cost-effective, so savings are a reason for making changes.
- Customer requirements and the marketplace are leading companies and institutions to change environmental practices.
- Insurance companies and underwriters require information on how environmental risks are assessed and reduced. If risks are reduced, insurance costs go down.
- Other stakeholders (members of the community) often have particular concerns about the impact of local facilities on their health and well-being and therefore influence the local decision-makers.
- Environmental nongovernmental organizations, and through them the public, apply specific pressures for general improvement in environmental management.
- International standards and evolving trade requirements under the NAFTA Parallel Accord and requirements for trade with the European Union are increasingly important factors.
- Industry and institutional associations are publishing environmental policies to be followed by their members.

The importance of these driving forces can change with the particular circumstances of the corporation or institution and do so quickly as external circumstances change.

One of the major driving forces in environmental management is legislation, regulation, and enforcement.

Canadian federal, provincial, and municipal laws, regulations, and bylaws covering the environment are now stricter and carry much tougher penalties. Fines of up to $1 million a day for each day of infraction and jail sentences can be imposed. These penalties can be applied to the senior decision-makers in both the public and private sectors and that threat is a major factor in promoting change.

There are generally three types of offences under the law:

- criminal offences where intent is important and where individuals are innocent until proven guilty
- absolute liability offences, such as traffic tickets, littering, etc., where offenders are guilty unless they can prove innocence
- strict liability offences where intent is important and where it is possible to prove innocence on the basis of having been duly diligent. That is, the accused had acted in a manner consistent with currently accepted practice, which should have prevented the infraction, or had mistakenly believed what were thought to be facts that led to inappropriate action.

Most infractions of environmental laws and regulations are strict liability offences, so a defence of due diligence is possible. The set of environmental management tools discussed later in the chapter is important for a due diligence defence because these actions demonstrate what you have been doing to prevent possible infractions and are evidence of a systematic approach to prevention.

According to a study of Canadian companies, municipalities, and other institutions by KPMG Environmental Services in 1994, fear of prosecution for environmental infractions was the leading force causing executives to change environmental management.

A successful prosecution such as the Bata case in Ontario or the Northern Badger case in Alberta can have major repercussions. The Bata case was a successful prosecution of the Bata Shoe Company for contaminating the environment with toxic materials. The company had delayed spending approximately $60 000 to fix the problem. One corporate official was successful in a due diligence defence but two others were fined. The company was also fined and charged with completing an extensive environmental cleanup costing about $450 000. The judge also imposed a number of other conditions on the company.

This experience immediately raised the level of importance of good environmental management for corporate executives and members of corporate boards of directors. More recently, senior officials in public institutions and governments have become exposed to similar responsibilities.

The Northern Badger case in Alberta resulted in a decision that any funds available in a company in receivership (bankruptcy) must first be used to clean up any environmental problems before funds go to the financial institutions holding the assets of the company. This immediately caused banks to investigate the environmental liabilities of the companies to which they had loaned money, and to require environmental audits of companies seeking loans.

ENVIRONMENTAL MANAGEMENT SYSTEM

The overall environmental management system (EMS), which is used to decide on the use of the environmental management tools, has evolved in the private sector during the past twenty-five years. Recently, steps have been taken by many groups to standardize environmental management systems, so that corporations and institutions have broadly accepted guidelines for effective environmental management.

The British Standards Association was the first to set out guidelines for environmental management systems in their 1994 report BS7750.

The Global Environmental Management Initiative (GEMI), a Washington-based organization of 28 corporations that promotes environmental excellence in business, has published a set of voluntary guidelines for an environmental management system.

The European Union has drafted their guidelines for an Eco-Management and Auditing Scheme (EMAS).

The International Organization for Standardization (ISO = "equal") has approved a guideline for an environmental management system (ISO 14001). Many other countries have similar documents.

In Canada, one of the many information products and guidelines published by the Canadian Standards Association under its environment program is CSA Z750–94, "A Voluntary Environmental Management System." It outlines key elements of an environmental management system and provides practical advice on implementing or enhancing such a system. The CSA states that "the design of an environmental management system is an ongoing, interactive planning process that consists of defining, documenting, and continuously improving the required capabilities, namely: resources, training, information systems, operational processes and procedures, documentation, measurement and monitoring criteria" (Z750–94, p. xi).

The benefits of such an environmental management system are:

- enhanced image and market share
- reduced costs and legal liabilities
- increased profitability
- conservation of input materials

- enhanced access to human resources, financial resources, and locations in which to operate
- improved state of the environment and human health
- increased stakeholder satisfaction and confidence

These benefits are achieved by acting on four key aspects of the environmental management system: purpose, commitment, capability, and learning (see Figure 11. 4).

There has been some difficulty harmonizing the different environmental management systems. The most significant difference lies in the fact that the European Union's environmental management system (EMAS) requires corporations to report publicly on the state of the environment of their operations, and requires an external verification of their environmental management system and the facts in the report—although the role and the qualifications of the verifier are not yet clearly defined. Other environmental management system guidelines do not require reporting or external verification at this time.

ENVIRONMENTAL MANAGEMENT TOOLS

The tools available to an environmental manager working within, or developing an environmental management system, include:

- the list of driving forces (to help introduce changes)
- management structure for environmental issues (decision-making and information flow)
- strategic environmental planning and assessment
- environmental policy statement
- environmental impact assessment (EIA)
- environmental audits
- product and technology assessment (PATA)
- life cycle assessment (LCA) and life cycle costing
- environmental indicators and environmental reporting
- risk management
- economic instruments
- new systems of accounting
- education and training

Recently, these tools have begun to coalesce into an integrated set (or sets) of tools that enhance the effectiveness of the individual tools. The remainder of the chapter defines and describes these tools.

How the tools are applied may vary somewhat, depending on the legal jurisdiction or the circumstances. But for the most part, they are used in the same way, regardless of location of industry or organization activity, accounting methods, or legal instruments.

FIGURE 11.4
The Environmental Management System

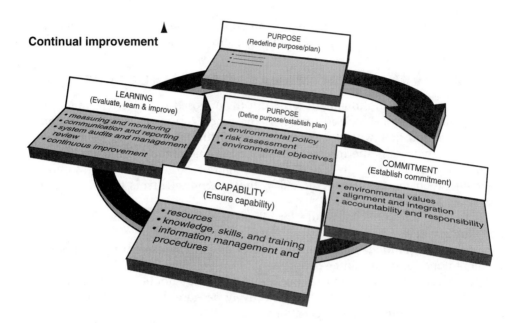

Source: With the permission of the Canadian Standards Association, material is reproduced from CSA Standard, Z760-94, Life Cycle Assessment, which is copyrighted by CSA, 178 Rexdale Blvd., Etobicoke, Ontario M9W 1R3. While use of this material has been authorized, CSA shall not be responsible for the manner in which the information is presented, nor for any interpretations thereof. This CSA material may not be updated to reflect amendments made to the original content. For up-to-date information, contact CSA.

STRATEGIC ENVIRONMENTAL PLANNING AND ASSESSMENT

Strategies are the major longer-term decisions about what a corporation, government, or institution wants to achieve and how it wants to do that. Strategies are for winning the war, tactics for winning the battles. Strategic environmental planning is the use of environmental protection and resource conservation skills and knowledge early in the planning process.

Strategic planning has to do with decisions early in the development of plans, policies, and programs, before specific projects, products, or actions are implemented. If those major early decisions are made without due consideration of environmental factors, then they must be brought in late in the process as an expensive and probably less-than-effective afterthought. Strategic planning is a proactive (before the fact) rather than a reactive (after the fact) process. It requires feedback and information from other tools in the set, especially audits, indicators, and reports.

Strategic environmental assessment is an effort to ensure that environmental factors have been adequately considered in the strategic planning process.

ENVIRONMENTAL MANAGEMENT STRUCTURE

The environmental management structure (as opposed to the environmental management system discussed above) is the organization of decision-making and information flow within a corporation or institution. It is the formal and informal systems for gathering and processing information, reporting, and making decisions. It must be fully integrated with the rest of the organization's management system and effectively linked to the external elements that affect the institution.

There is no one correct structure for all circumstances; each has advantages and disadvantages.

A centralized management structure places all employees dealing with environmental matters in the same department or unit (Figure 11.5a). This produces a stronger, more cohesive unit or department, but it may not be able to influence the activities of other departments as effectively because it is separate from the rest of the organization's daily operations.

A decentralized system places employees dealing with environmental matters wherever they are needed, in direct contact with operations (Figure 11.5b). By being scattered, the environmental management might be less powerful and cohesive, but it could be more effective because of the direct involvement with day-to-day operations.

A modified variation of these basic structures places environmental employees wherever they are needed (decentralized) but has a small but senior management group in a central position in the decision-making system (Figure 11.5c). This structure is often successful because it combines the best features of the two basic structures.

ENVIRONMENTAL POLICY STATEMENTS

The Canadian Standards Association defines environmental policy as the overall environmental intentions and directions of an organization regarding the environment, and as formally expressed by top management.

An environmental policy statement would therefore specify an action or activity that an organization was going to take to reach each goal it set for protecting the environment and conserving resources. Wherever possible, it would also state an expected outcome. Goals would be identified in the strategic planning process

FIGURE 11.5A
Centralized Management and Structure

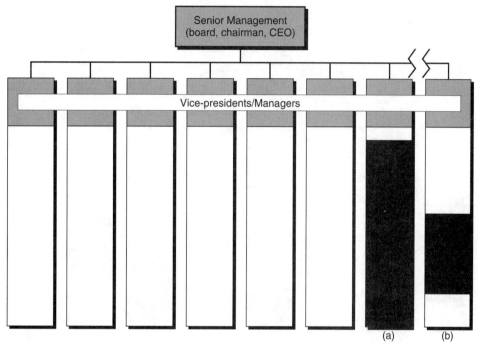

(a) All employees working on environmental affairs in one department
(b) All employees working on environmental affairs in one sub-unit of one department

and would be spelled out in general terms in the organization's mission statement. For example, there could be policies on energy and water conservation, pollution prevention, waste minimization, hazardous materials management, transportation, and the application of the other tools (environmental audits, environmental reporting, impact assessment, etc.).

Figure 11.6 identifies 29 themes that should be addressed in environmental policy statements. Ideally, for each environmental policy, there would be an environmental indicator or indicators to show how well or poorly progress was being made in implementing the policy. The indicators would be presented in an environmental report that would provide feedback to the strategic planning processes and for adjustment of the policies and their implementation.

Policies should be regularly reviewed, updated, and re-endorsed by senior management. Often each policy is backed by one or more detailed practice manuals.

FIGURE 11.5B
Decentralized Management and Structure

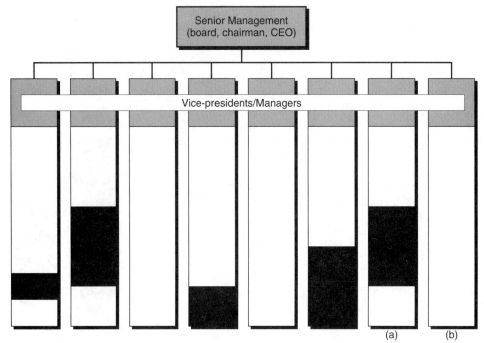

Employees working on environmental affairs spread throughout departments with no one vice-president or manager responsible for them

ENVIRONMENTAL IMPACT ASSESSMENT

This is one of the oldest, most fully developed of the environmental management tools. Figure 11.7 outlines a generic environmental impact assessment process. The main points are that an environmental impact assessment is done before implementing environmental policies or projects in an effort to anticipate and avoid problems. Otherwise, it becomes an environmental audit.

Environmental impact assessments are criticized for involving value judgments (what is critical or significant) and requiring predictions (what environmental impacts are likely to occur if certain actions are taken). The criticisms are valid and work continues to improve the processes. However, the criticisms do not invalidate the tool.

An environmental impact assessment can include social impact assessment, visual impact assessment, and historic resources impact assessment.

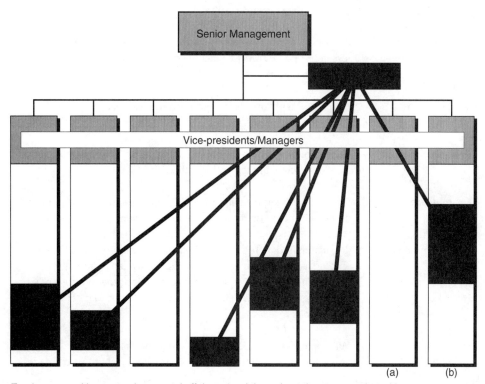

Employees working on environmental affairs spread throughout the company but with a small management group with direct access to senior management coordinating and overseeing work and developing and guiding policy

Class environmental impact assessments are quicker, less expensive reviews of small projects, whose impacts are easily predictable and that do not warrant a full-scale environmental impact assessment. This process basically follows a standard checklist.

Cost/benefit analysis is an important, closely related tool that is often part of an environmental impact assessment. Recently the Alberta government ruled that economic benefits must be considered in environmental impact assessment decisions.

The Government of Canada requires environmental impact assessments of policies and programs, which it terms strategic environmental assessment. When applied to products and technologies, environmental impact assessments are called product and technology assessment (below).

FIGURE 11.6
List of Themes That Are Required to Be Included in Corporate EPSs

REQUIRED TO INCLUDE

Revised Theme	Comments, Dos and Don'ts
Dates and Updating	Important to policy process. Date of most recent version and previous updates must be identified. Explicit commitment to update regularly.
Mission/Vision Statement	Outlines the philosophy or approach used in dealing with environmental issues.
Commitment and Accountability	Signature(s) of senior executives. Must identify officer or committee accountable for implementing policy.
Environmental Goals	The goals drive the environmental policy. An explicit commitment to review and revise these goals must be made.
Legal Commitments	Regulatory requirements must be met. A commitment to meet or exceed legal requirements is part of proactive environmental management. However, for those corporations that are currently challenged to meet requirements, a commitment to meet them is acceptable.
Education and Training	All employees must be educated about the policy and its implications. A commitment to training employees must be made.
Monitoring and Reporting	Environmental indicators must be developed to allow monitoring of commitments made in the policy. Environmental reporting must take place internally to senior executives and directors to ensure they are aware of an organization's environmental status.
Environmental Auditing	Vital to monitor corporate compliance with regulatory requirements and conformity with policy. This is a requirement of environmental management standards. Critical EMS tool.
Emergency Response	Emergency response plans must be in place. Critical EMS tool.
Environmental Scanning	Critical EMS tool. Necessary to ensure effective environmental management. Allows a greater ability to anticipate and proactively address, rather than react to, upcoming changes outside the organization.

(Figure continues next page)

Environmental Impact Assessment	EIA is a critical EMS tool for proactive environmental management.
Strategic Planning	Environmental considerations must be a part of the strategic planning process for effective and proactive environmental management.
Management Responsibility	Environmental appraisal of managers, dedication of resources, and environmental consideration in selection or appraisal of board of directors are sound commitments.
Benchmarking	Corporations should attempt to benchmark themselves against others in their industry. Provides information to use for leadership and continuous improvement.
Waste Management	Waste management provides significant opportunities for financial savings. Hazardous and nonhazardous wastes should be addressed separately. Pollution prevention at source should be the approach used. Follow 3 Rs hierarchy.
Energy Management	Energy management also provides significant opportunities for financial savings. Consider transportation and commuting as well as electricity requirements.
Product and Technology Assessment	Consider the life cycle assessment of products and services as well as products purchased. Include environmental considerations in the product design process. Commit to R & D of appropriate technologies.
Purchasing Guidelines	Important means of minimizing environmental impact of operations. Commit to purchasing environmentally sensitive products.
Risk Management	Perform risk management and/or reduction activities to help minimize risk associated with operations.
Environmental Reporting	Reporting of environmental information to all stakeholders should take place. Closely linked to environmental indicators, monitoring, and environmental auditing. Disclosure of environmental expenditures should be part of this reporting process.

(Figure continues next page)

Legal Concerns	Apply policy to all operations. Do not lower corporate standards in jurisdictions where environmental standards are lower. Be involved with the legislation development process.
Other Business Relationships	Encourage business partners to be environmentally sensitive. If possible, require environmental considerations in contractor selection. Require contractors to follow policy.
Objectives	Objectives should be identified for all commitments made. Ensures that commitments are achievable. Ideally, should lead toward continuous improvement. Should be linked to targets where possible.
Policy on Objectives	There should be a policy to include one or more objectives for each policy commitment.
Policy on Targets	There should be a policy to commit, whenever possible, to specific targets for each of the identified objectives.
Employee Issues	Do commit to employee suggestion and rewards program and whistle blower protection. Ensure all employees are made aware of the policy.
Community Stakeholders	Provide community members with the opportunity for meaningful two-way discussion. Do disclose product hazards.
Advisory Organizations	Do subscribe to industry codes and practices, international protocols and agreements, and environmental management declarations. Work closely with industry associations.
Risk Management	Perform risk management and/or reduction activities to help minimize risks associated with operations.

Source: C. Christopher Ryley, *Corporate Environmental Policy Statements,* The University of Calgary, Calgary, Alta., 1995. © 1995 C. Christopher Ryley.

Analysis of environmental impacts after policies have been implemented or projects constructed are a form of audit and are often called environmental reviews.

The Canadian federal and provincial governments specify the requirements for environmental impact assessments in areas where their legislation applies.

FIGURE 11.7
Generic Environmental Impact Assessment Process

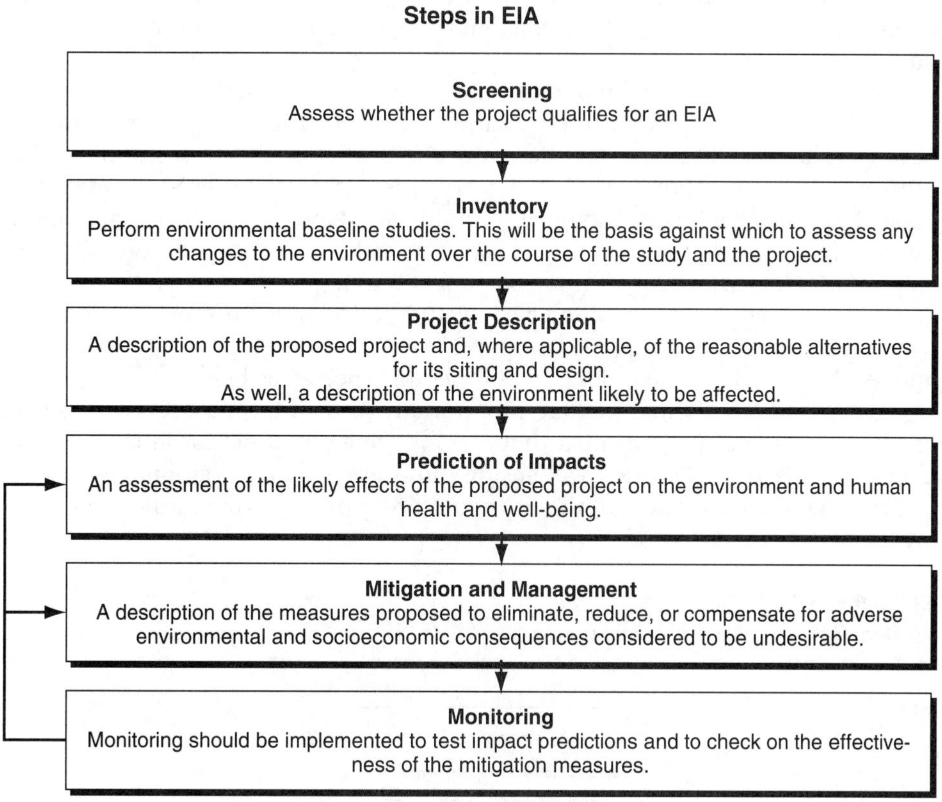

Steps in EIA

Screening
Assess whether the project qualifies for an EIA

Inventory
Perform environmental baseline studies. This will be the basis against which to assess any changes to the environment over the course of the study and the project.

Project Description
A description of the proposed project and, where applicable, of the reasonable alternatives for its siting and design.
As well, a description of the environment likely to be affected.

Prediction of Impacts
An assessment of the likely effects of the proposed project on the environment and human health and well-being.

Mitigation and Management
A description of the measures proposed to eliminate, reduce, or compensate for adverse environmental and socioeconomic consequences considered to be undesirable.

Monitoring
Monitoring should be implemented to test impact predictions and to check on the effectiveness of the mitigation measures.

Municipal governments are working on development of similar processes appropriate to their scale and location. The World Bank has set policies, procedures, and guidelines for international projects.

ENVIRONMENTAL AUDITS

Environmental audits are assessments of five elements of an organization's environmental management:

- the environmental management system
- compliance with laws, regulations, and bylaws
- conformity to the organization's policy and the industry or institution association's environmental policy

- good housekeeping (observations for possible corrective action not covered under compliance or conformity)
- a plan to correct any deficiencies that the audit identified

Audits can be specialized, focusing on a single aspect such as facility audits, property transfer audits, site assessments, waste audits, or compliance audits (laws and regulations only).

Audits must be done every one to three years. The first audit will be difficult, time-consuming, and expensive because of the steep learning curve and the need to gather a data base for the entire life of the facility or institution. The process for subsequent audits will be faster, easier, and less expensive, so the first audit should not be taken as typical. If audits are done on a cycle of more than three years, they are not being done often enough to be a useful management tool. Each audit then becomes more like a first audit.

Audits can tell an organization how well a policy is being implemented and what adjustments are needed. They provide data for development of indicators and can be used as the basis for environmental reports (see below).

Audits can be performed to help monitor environmental impact assessments, or where screening has indicated that a complete environmental impact assessment is not needed. An audit will ensure that the screening decision was correct and provide the feedback that the EIA monitoring process would otherwise have provided.

FIGURE 11.8
Environmental Audit Process

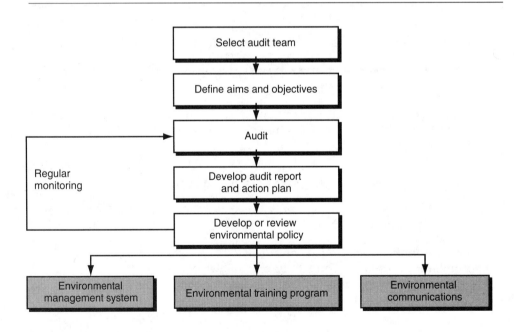

More detailed information on environmental audits and assessments has been published by the Canadian Standards Association in "Guidelines for Environmental Auditing: Statement of Principles and General Practices" (Z751–94), and in "Phase 1 Environmental Site Assessment" (Z768–94).

PRODUCT AND TECHNOLOGY ASSESSMENTS

Like strategic environmental assessment and environmental impact assessment, product and technology assessment (PATA) attempts to predict the adverse environmental, health, and safety impacts of products or technologies over the entire product lifetime and then find means of reducing them to acceptable levels.

Activities that incorporate some of the elements of product and technology assessment and set precedents for it include:

- safety and emissions regulations for automobiles
- health and safety requirements for children's toys, clothing, car seats, etc.
- regulations governing drugs and food additives
- regulations governing the sale and use of pesticides

In addition to concerns about liability, corporations are using product and technology assessment for two purposes

- to improve their products to satisfy consumer demands for environmentally friendly products, giving them a better position in the market
- to assess the products and technologies they buy to reduce their environmental impacts and resource consumption (purchasing guidelines or procurement policies)

Product and technology assessment is the basis for developing product guidelines for people wishing to purchase products that have less impact on the environment. The CSA guideline on product and technology assessment is "Environmentally Responsible Procurement ("Green Procurement" Z766–95).

The average consumer will not be able to do their own product and technology assessment, so the Canadian Standards Association has developed a set of "Guidelines on Environmental Labeling" (Z761–93), which defines the claims that can be made about the environmental characteristics of products. Other countries have developed similar guidelines and the ISO (International Organization for Standardization) is trying to obtain international agreement, but there is still vigorous debate about the details.

Another form of product and technology assessment being developed to assist consumers is Canada's Ecologo program. Products are reviewed by a technical panel. To gain the right to use the Ecologo, the products must be clearly superior to other products on the market on a life cycle assessment (below) basis. The Ecologo can only be held for three years on the assumption that other products will be improving. The Blue Angel program in Germany is similar to Canada's, but some programs in other countries are based solely on the manufacturer's claims without the requirement to verify the claims.

LIFE CYCLE ASSESSMENT AND LIFE CYCLE COSTING

A very important part of environmental impact assessment and product and technology assessment is life cycle assessment (LCA). This examines resource use, production of wastes, energy consumption, and environmental impacts of a product from raw material, production, to final disposal (Figure 11.9). It is also important to do a life cycle costing to determine how cost-effective investments in pollution prevention and resource efficiency improvements are, over the life-time of the system. Life cycle costing attempts to calculate properly amortized capital costs, and the operation and maintenance costs using total environmental cost accounting (below).

Life cycle assessments have been difficult and expensive. At a Massachusetts Institute of Technology conference in late 1993, it was estimated that a comprehensive life cycle assessment would cost $US 100 000. The main difficulty is the availability of appropriate data bases for the environmental stress associated with the use of various materials, processes, and recycling and disposal options. The factors would be different for various locations depending upon energy sources, transportation impacts, disposal and recycling options, etc. Some critics of life cycle assessment say that it is only a subjective public relations exercise because the data and the value judgments are too uncertain. However, with the

FIGURE 11.9
Life Cycle Assessment

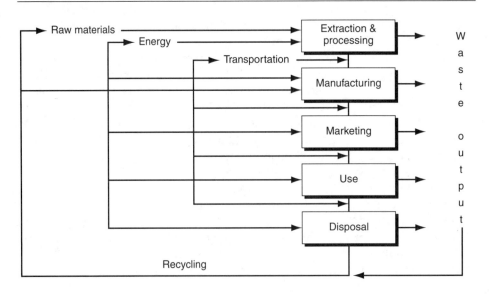

FIGURE 11.10
Canadian Standards Association Life Cycle Assessment

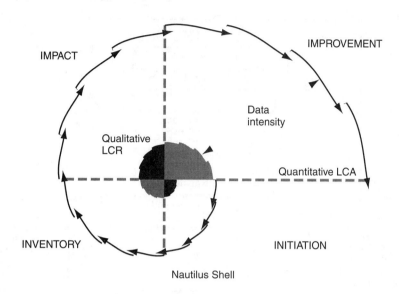

Nautilus Shell

Source: With the permission of the Canadian Standards Association, material is reproduced from CSA Standard, Z760-94, Life Cycle Assessment, which is copyrighted by CSA, 178 Rexdale Blvd., Etobicoke, Ontario M9W 1R3. While use of this material has been authorized, CSA shall not be responsible for the manner in which the information is presented, nor for any interpretations thereof. This CSA material may not be updated to reflect amendments made to the original content. For up-to-date information, contact CSA.

agreements on the methodologies, such as that set by the CSA and the ongoing development of data bases, life cycle assessment will rapidly improve as a management tool.

Once again, the CSA has provided guidelines for this tool: "Life Cycle Assessment" (Z760–94) and "User's Guide to Life Cycle Assessment: Conceptual Life Cycle Assessment in Practice" (PLUS 1107). Figure 11.10 shows the CSA's diagram of a four-stage life cycle assessment: initiation, inventory, impact, and improvement. Figure 11.11 shows these four stages in more detail.

ENVIRONMENTAL INDICATORS AND REPORTING

Environmental indicators are objective and credible measures of the state of the environment and how it is being affected, or a measure of how an organization's

FIGURE 11.11
CSA Life Cycle Model in Detail

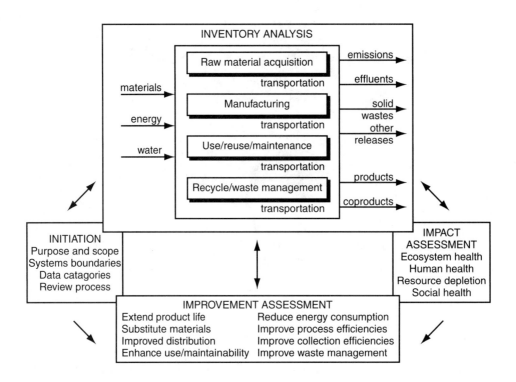

Source: With the permission of the Canadian Standards Association, material is reproduced from CSA Standard, Z760-94, Life Cycle Assessment, which is copyrighted by CSA, 178 Rexdale Blvd., Etobicoke, Ontario M9W 1R3. While use of this material has been authorized, CSA shall not be responsible for the manner in which the information is presented, nor for any interpretations thereof. This CSA material may not be updated to reflect amendments made to the original content. For up-to-date information, contact CSA.

environmental management is reducing its environmental impacts. For a broader picture of overall performance, indicators are collected to describe the state of the environment or to report on an organization's overall environmental performance.

The characteristics of good indicators and the requirements for corporate environmental reports include:

- a discussion of the environmental management system
- quantified performance data

- results of environmental initiatives provided
- inclusion of good news and bad news
- complete reporting of fines, accidents, spills, or excesses
- a letter or foreword by the CEO
- published environmental policies
- established targets
- environmental audit information
- results of waste management programs
- inclusion of a prepaid comment card
- information on community relations
- information on worker health and safety
- description of research and development
- issues clearly defined

Government state of the environment reports (SOER) vary widely with jurisdiction and mandate of the organization producing them, but would follow similar criteria.

Environment Canada and the Organization for Economic Cooperation and Development (OECD) have studied environmental indicators and reporting. The OECD pressure-state-response model (Figure 11.12) requires indicators of the pressures on the environment, of the state of the environment, and of the response of society to change those pressures when the state of the environment is undesirable.

FIGURE 11.12
OECD Pressure – State – Response Framework Model

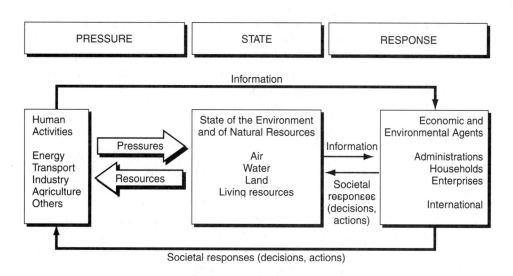

Source: O.E.C.D., Environmental Indicators (O.E.C.D. Core Set), Paris, France, 1994.

Environmental reports are very important for establishing baselines for the development or adjustment of policies, or for baseline data for environmental impact assessments. They provide feedback for strategic planning and for allocation of scarce resources to where they are most needed and would be most effective.

The CSA has started the process of developing guidelines for environmental reporting by publishing "Reporting on Environmental Performance" (PLUS 1131), which was developed in cooperation with the Canadian Institute of Chartered Accountants, the International Institute for Sustainable Development, and the Financial Executives Institute of Canada.

RISK MANAGEMENT

Risk is defined as a hazard that threatens a community or population and the probability that the hazardous event will occur (risk = hazard $\times$ probability).

Risk management includes four basic components:

- risk identification (What hazards threaten the community or population?)
- risk analysis (Can the nature and scale of the hazard be quantified and is anything known about the probability of it occurring?)
- risk management (What can be done to reduce the nature or scale of the hazard and/or its probability, or what should the response be if the event occurred?)
- risk communication (Dialogue with and education of the community or population about the probability and scale of a hazard before it occurs and the consequences and emergency response after the event should the undesirable happen)

For some corporations, risk management is a matter of an emergency response plan and working with their insurance company. Others take a much more proactive position that starts with strategic planning and environmental impact assessment and efforts to establish mutual understanding and trust between the community and the corporation.

ECONOMIC INSTRUMENTS

Economic instruments are incentives, disincentives, and other market adjustments that direct behaviours or internalize costs that would otherwise be borne by the public and future generations or the environment, rather than the party that caused the damage.

Economic instruments include deposit–return systems, effluent and emission fees, tradable emission and effluent fees, disposal fees and recycling credits, feebates (charges for undesirable behaviour that is then rebated to encourage desirable behaviours), subsidies, grants and tax exemptions and credits, user pay pricing, consumption taxes, etc.

NEW SYSTEMS OF ACCOUNTING

New systems of accounting include three different but somewhat related aspects that are currently confused in use of terms and methodologies:

- efforts to identify and account for direct, internal environmental costs and liabilities under current accounting practices (total environmental cost accounting). Revenues and benefits must also be identified.
- efforts to identify all external, but quantifiable, environmental costs and to internalize them (full cost accounting)
- efforts to replace the gross domestic product (GDP) with a more realistic measure of national economic well-being and progress by introducing measures of environmental degradation and resource depletion. The costs of environmental degradation and resource depletion would be subtracted from the GDP.

The Canadian Institute of Chartered Accountants raised the issue of including all costs and liabilities in corporate accounting with their ruling that environmental liabilities must be charged against assets in preparing financial statements for corporations.

The OECD, the Government of Canada, and many other government agencies in Canada and abroad are working on the problem of developing proposals for and making changes in the international agreements governing systems of national accounting; that is, adjusting the GDP to give a more realistic measure of economic well-being and progress.

New systems of accounting are important because it is difficult to determine costs and potential savings from effective environmental management, and one cannot allocate scarce resources without total cost accounting. Full cost accounting is important at the micro level: it is no longer acceptable for organizations to impose costs on the environment because those costs will be paid sooner or later. Similarly, at the national level, allocation of resources and development of effective policies must include the negative effects of pollution or resource depletion.

EDUCATION AND TRAINING

Obviously, ongoing education and training programs on the theory and practice of the use of the environmental management tools, individually and in sets, is very important.

Because the tools are constantly being improved on the basis of the continuous improvement model, education and training programs for employees in corporations, government, and other institutions will be essential.

Figure 11.13 shows how state of the environment reports (SOER), new systems of national accounting (NSNA), and environmental audits could contribute to better and less expensive environmental impact assessments. Training and education should show how tools could work in sets to complement one another. Figure 11.14 shows how the planning process is assisted by strategic

FIGURE 11.13
The Environmental Impact Assessment Process, Showing Relationships with Environmental Audits, SOER, and NSNA

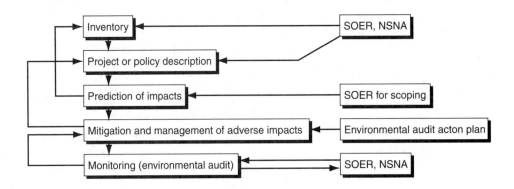

environmental assessment, environmental impact assessments, environmental audits, and state of the environment reports.

APPLYING ENVIRONMENTAL MANAGEMENT TOOLS

The use of the environmental management tools allows institutions to anticipate and avoid problems in a proactive rather than reactive way. They assist with analysis and reporting of performance and with day-to-day management, which requires timely feedback to make appropriate adjustments. The tools are important for the allocation of scarce resources.

The use of these tools is often characterized by a high level of concern and commitment, but without a similar level of understanding of the specific applications. There is a good deal of confusion about some terms and definitions, which will be partially resolved by the publication of guidelines by national and international standards organizations. There is a wide diversity of approaches that is slowly being narrowed. The Canadian Standards Association (CSA) and the International Organization for Standardization (ISO) are playing very important roles nationally and internationally in developing environmental management tools and pollution prevention guidelines. Figure 11.15 shows seven of the ISO's subcommittees (SCs) and the working groups (WGs) preparing documents on various subtopics for environmental management.

FIGURE 11.14
Integration of Environmental Management Tools

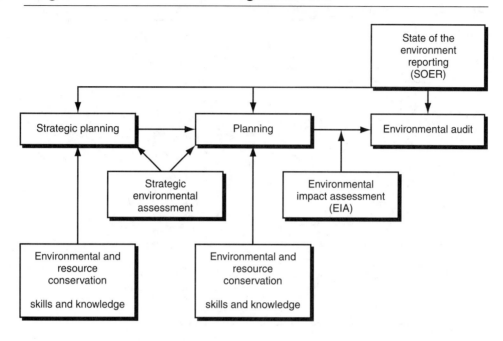

Terms and methodologies must be harmonized if the advantage of universal application, regardless of the jurisdiction, location, environment, or resource involved, is to be achieved. The parallel environmental accord to NAFTA between Canada, Mexico, and the U.S.A. commits the three partners to the harmonious development and application of most of the tools.

The very rapid increase in the application of the tools poses a problem: it is now difficult to keep up with the advances. However, that problem is preferable to earlier development stages when there was a very slow acceptance of the need for such tools and a long transition period of moving from theoretical models to practical and cost-effective application of the tools.

Part of the reason for change is a wide acceptance of the continuous improvement model. The tools are being used in spite of their imperfections and their incomplete development—with the understanding that the users of the tools are learning how to use them and how to improve them. The continuous improvement model dictates that change will be the norm, and that both individuals and institutions will have to be continually improving their skills and knowledge.

This is why environmental scientists must not only continue to refine their scientific skills and knowledge, but also to develop their management skills.

FIGURE 11.15
**Subcommittees and Working Groups That Are Part of the International
Organization for Standarization (ISO)**

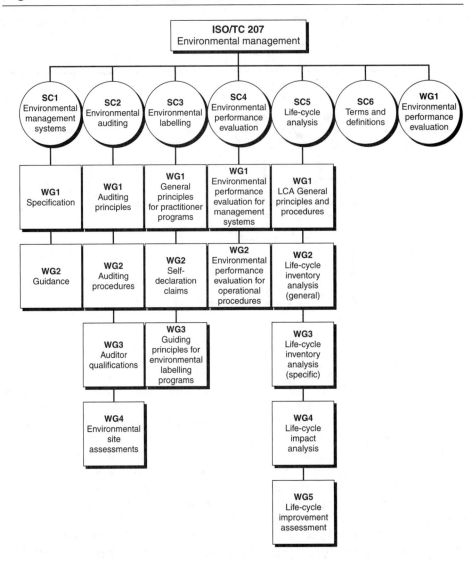

Source: With the permission of the Canadian Standards Association, material is reproduced from CSA Standard, Z760-94, Life Cycle Assessment, which is copyrighted by CSA, 178 Rexdale Blvd., Etobicoke, Ontario M9W 1R3. While use of this material has been authorized, CSA shall not be responsible for the manner in which the information is presented, nor for any interpretations thereof. This CSA material may not be updated to reflect amendments made to the original content. For up-to-date information, contact CSA.

They will need to be able to synthesize the results of research and data gathering from various disciplines; to integrate that information into the social, political, and economic context; and then to clearly communicate the results of the synthesis and integration to the decision-makers. This is too important to leave to nonscientists.

NOTES

1   Criminal prosecutions take place when laws are broken. Proof must be beyond a reasonable doubt, but in many cases of environmental infraction, a due diligence defence is possible. Due diligence means that you must be able to use the environmental tools described on page 228 ff. to prove that you have been duly diligent in environmental management. Civil liability means that corporations and institutional decision-makers can be sued in civil court when they are responsible for damages imposed on other parties. The burden of proof is only to the level of balance of probabilities and a due diligence is not possible.

REFERENCES

Newsletters and magazines
Newsletters and magazines are important sources of information in a rapidly changing field like environmental management.

BATE—Business and the Environment, a newsletter produced by Cutter Information
    Corporation, 37 Broadway, Arlington, Md., 02174 5539.
    1-800-888-1816
    http://www.cutter.com
EM Air and Waste Management Association, One Gateway Center, 3rd Floor, Pittsburgh,
    Pa. 15222.
Enviroline, 222 Riverfront Ave., Calgary, Alta. T2P 0A5. E-mail enviroca@cadvision.com
Environmental Update, Canadian Standards Association, 178 Rexdale Blvd., Etobicoke, Ont.
    M9W 1R3.
Gemi News, 2000 L Street N.W., Suite 710, Washington, D.C., 20036.
Hazardous Materials Management, 951 Denison St., Unit 4, Markham, Ont. L3R 3W9
    Internet address: *http://www.io.org/~hzmatmg*
    E-mail: hazmatmg@inforamp.net
Impact Assessment, International Association for Impact Assessment, North Dakota State
    University, Institute for Business and Industry Development, Hastings Hall, P.O. Box
    5256, Fargo, N.D., 58105 5256.

SOE Bulletin, State of the Environment Directorate, Environment Conservation Service, Environment Canada, Ottawa K1A 0H3.

Books

de Andrace, Roberto, and Ken F. McCready. 1994. *Internalizing Environmental Cost to Promote Eco-Efficiency*. Business Council for Sustainable Development, World Trade Centre Building, 3rd Floor, Geneva.

Global Environmental Management Initiative. 1993. *Total Quality Environmental Management: The Primer*. Washington, D.C.: GEMI.

Schmidheiny, Stephan. 1992. *Changing Course*. Cambridge, Mass.: MIT Press.

Thompson, Dixon, and Serena van Bakel. 1995. "A Practical Introduction to Environmental Management on Canadian Campuses." National Round Table on the Environment and the Economy, Ottawa.

QUESTIONS FOR DISCUSSION

1. Define "management" and discuss how each part of that definition can be assisted with the application of some of the environmental management tools.

2. Discuss the driving forces that are requiring corporations and institutions to introduce environmental management systems. Discuss how you would use that list of forces to convince a corporation or institution to start to be more environmentally responsible.

3. List the environmental management tools and discuss their application, considering whether each is primarily a tool that is applied to anticipate and avoid problems (e.g., environmental impact assessment, product and technology assessment) or whether it is applied to assess problems and set priorities for action (e.g., life cycle assessment, environmental audits, state of the environment report, indicators, new systems of national accounting).

4. For each of the environmental problems described in other chapters, discuss how the environmental management tools might be applied to help solve those problems.

Green Politics and the Rise of the Environmental Movement

Robert Paehlke

Department of Environmental and Resource Studies
Trent University

INTRODUCTION

This chapter considers the origins, evolution, and possible future of the environmental movement in North America, with some emphasis on Canada and on what has recently come to be called green politics. Green politics goes beyond the particular and immediate concerns of the specific organizations within the environmental movement and its historical antecedent—and now collaborative partner—the conservation movement. Green politics is, in a sense, the means by which the concerns of conservationists and environmentalists are integrated into the wider political debates of contemporary society—especially in relation to matters such as economic well-being, social equity, and international relations.

The chapter begins with a brief assessment of the rise of the conservation movement, a development that dates from the late 19th century. This opening section also discusses the rise of the environmental movement in the late 1960s and contrasts its goals and style with those of the conservation movement. The second section of the chapter looks at the evolution of the environmental movement through the 1960s, 1970s, 1980s, and early 1990s. This assessment emphasizes and contrasts what I call the two waves of environmental concern (1968–1976 and 1986–1994). The chapter concludes with speculation on the future of the environmental movement and green politics.

■—————■

THE CONSERVATION AND ENVIRONMENTAL MOVEMENTS

Significant North American conservation organization and activities date back more than a century now. The thought that underlies these efforts precedes these organizations by some decades and would include the writings of such prominent 19th-century American figures as George Perkins Marsh, Henry David Thoreau, and John James Audubon (Paehlke, 1989). Marsh, a physical geographer, has been credited by some with creating the modern concept of ecology. His masterwork, *Man and Nature; or, Physical Geography as Modified by Human Action* (1864), surveyed the negative environmental effects of human economic activities such as mining, forestry, agriculture, and settlement. Thoreau articulated the virtues and joy of living modestly in close daily contact with nature, and Audubon captured the beauty and importance of nature, in both pictures and words. Thoreau asserted that "in Wildness is the preservation of the World," and Audubon wrote that "the greedy mills told the sad tale, that in a century the noble forests ... should exist no more."

In the 19th century and since, the conservation movement often went hand in hand with the establishment of national parks. Yellowstone National Park was created in 1872 (Curlee, 1995). Yosemite National Park required a more significant campaign led in the 1880s by John Muir and Robert Underwood Johnson. Meetings in San Francisco in 1889 led to the formation of the Sierra Club, formally established in 1892 with John Muir as the first president. Its goals are clearly articulated in its articles of incorporation: "To explore, enjoy, and render accessible the mountain regions of the Pacific Coast; to publish authentic information concerning them; to enlist the support and cooperation of the people and the government in preserving the forests and other natural features of the Sierra Nevada Mountains" (Allin, 1995b; Cohen, 1988). A century later exploration and preservation remain the dual goals of the organization, but the membership and effort is now continent-wide.

In Canada the earliest national parks—Banff was the first, in 1885—were not so much rooted in a conservation movement wresting them from competing uses as created to encourage tourism on the new Canadian Pacific Railway. In both the United States and Canada the motives were mixed and varied from park to park, but in time conservation and preservation came to require an ever more attentive and politically oriented effort on both sides of the border. Additional conservation organizations were continuously created throughout the ensuing years and today span the globe, as do national parks.

The term "conservation movement" is said to have originated among U.S. President Theodore Roosevelt's natural resource advisors in 1907 (Allin, 1995a). By that point conservation had both ascended to political prominence in the United States and become divided within itself. The movement included those who sought "preservation" and those who would prefer "wise use." This latter approach might today be called "multiple use" and would be typified by continued logging in Algonquin Park or controlled hunting on public forest lands. The debate over what is appropriate within each wilderness or quasi-wilderness location is continuous and ever-changing.

Major conservation organizations in the United States now include the Sierra Club, the National Audubon Society, the Wilderness Society, the Izaak Walton League, the World Wildlife Fund, the National Wildlife Federation, Defenders of Wildlife, and the League of Conservation Voters. Several of these organizations have memberships in excess of one million individuals and families, and collectively they have budgets in the hundreds of millions of dollars. They publish, lobby, educate, organize, and conduct and fund scientific research. In Canada major conservation-oriented organizations include the Canadian Nature Federation, the Federation of Ontario Naturalists (and many other provincially based organizations), the Sierra Club of Western Canada, the Western Canada Wilderness Committee, the World Wildlife Fund, and the Algonquin Wildlands League.

The Canadian conservation movement, as a mass-based movement, generally came later than that in the United States. For example, the Canadian incorrect!

X/Nature Federation, the oldest national conservation organization, was not founded until the 1930s (McNamee, 1995). There are many reasons for this. Settlement came later, we are less organization-oriented than are Americans, population densities have all along been sharply lower—there is, or we could imagine that there was, more wilderness. The Canadian government provided alternatives—royal commissions on forestry practices, especially in the 1920s, and the federal Commission on Conservation (founded in 1909 and disbanded in 1921, in part because it was too effective). It might be suspected that many Canadians still believe that our "empty" spaces and "our resources" are limitless.

Beginning in the late 1960s a new set of issues and new sets of organizations came to the fore—the environmental movement was born. Some date the origin of the environmental movement to the publication of Rachel Carson's *Silent Spring* in *The New Yorker* magazine in 1960 (Carson, 1962). While this book was concerned about nature and wildlife, the threat was pesticides and bioconcentration, not loss of habitat. The problem was pollution and the cure involved changes in industrial practices and products, not improved wilderness preservation and resource management. Both the problem and to some extent the impacts were deeply rooted in urban life and the core of industrial society. It was not long before many other pollution problems gained prominent attention.

New organizations sprang up rapidly in the late 1960s and early 1970s, including Environmental Action, Natural Resources Defense Council, Friends of the Earth, Pollution Probe, and the Environmental Defense Fund. Public concern was widespread and growing. In this period governments created new agencies (Environment Canada and the U.S. Environmental Protection Agency) and passed new legislation and regulations regarding air pollution, water pollution, and environmental impact assessment. New publications also emerged including, in the U.S., *Environment* (in 1959), and *Environmental Action* (in 1970) and, in Canada, *Alternatives* and *Probe Post*. The new environmental issues and organizations spurred many older conservation organizations to broaden their range of concerns. The Sierra Club was one of the most adaptive.

Fast on the heels of rising societal concern with pollution issues was the energy crisis of 1973 (followed by another in 1979), an event anticipated in part by Earth Day (1970), and by the publication of the widely read book *The Limits to Growth* (1972). The first Earth Day—April 22, 1970, marked by mass demonstrations throughout North America—emphasized public education about pollution, resource depletion, and the waste of a consumer-oriented society. *The Limits to Growth*, based on early computer simulations of pollution, population, and resource use, predicted that industrial society would be in deep trouble if ways were not found to radically improve air and water quality, to slow population growth, and to manage our renewable and nonrenewable resources more soundly. This latter concern later came to be captured by the term "sustainability."

The energy crisis shook, perhaps for the first time, mass confidence in the sustainability of the industrial/consumer society. Just as the Great Depression fostered doubts about the economic and social capabilities of industrial capitalism, the energy crisis of the 1970s, combined with growing evidence about pollution and toxic chemicals, caused many to wonder whether the earth itself was up to the challenges posed. Several important differences between the concerns of the conservation movement and the concerns of the new environmental movement began to emerge. The environmental movement focused on more urban-oriented problems, concerns seemingly more likely to pique the interest of the North American majority than were the wilderness concerns of the conservation movement (see Figure 12.1).

Moreover, many within the environmental movement saw these new concerns as carrying fundamental challenges for capitalism or industrial society, or both. There seemed to be little room for "wise use" solutions and even the "preservation" of nature seemed to some a quite insufficient way to conceptualize the problems we faced. Some early environmentalists looked at the conservation movement as outdated and not oriented to the monumental and disparate problems of the day. Preserving a small wetland, or the habitat of a "minor" species, seemed trivial when we were faced with a toxic planet and the near-imminent collapse of industrial society. Some environmentalists in the early 1970s had a definite apocalyptic tone and sensibility. Many individuals in the United States and Canada chose to abandon cities and "return to the land." Some organizations were less concerned with lobbying government for new policies than with sounding the alarm and rejecting the fundamental values of contemporary society.

FIGURE 12.1
Environmental Movement

Combines 'Traditional' Conservation Concerns ...
Loss of habitat
Overexploitation of forests
Endangered species
Water management and allocation
Scenic preservation and quality recreational spaces
Biodiversity and ecology

... with More Urban-Oriented Health and Sustainability Concerns
Air and water quality
Occupational and environmental health
Hazardous wastes
Municipal solid waste disposal
Resource dependancy
Global warming, ozone depletion, acid precipitation

However, other, more moderate or even conservative voices were also heard from within the environmental movement as it developed. The Science Council of Canada (later eliminated by the Mulroney government) published *Canada as a Conserver Society* in 1976. This important work urged Canadians to "do more with less" and welcomed the use of "market mechanisms" to foster renewable energy, recycling, reuse, and pollution abatement. Energy Probe, established as part of the Toronto-based Pollution Probe in 1973, has advocated the privatization of public utilities as a means of promoting a greater emphasis on decentralization and diversification of supply sources and of advancing efficient use of electrical energy.

Other new organizations sought a global, multi-issue constituency. One such organization, Greenpeace, was founded in 1971 in British Columbia but rapidly moved to a global scale. Greenpeace was founded to protest the Amchitka, Alaska, nuclear weapons tests. In this it, in a sense, followed the earlier protests of atmospheric nuclear tests that preceded, and some feel established a future audience for, Rachel Carson's ideas. Greenpeace has been instrumental in internationalizing environmental concerns and in integrating the concerns of the conservation movement, the environmental movement, and the peace movement. Greenpeace uses media masterfully and grew rapidly throughout the 1980s. The organization has nearly five million members worldwide, including two million in the United States.

The environmental movement has faced many challenges in its short history. In some ways the energy crisis was a challenge as well as a boost. In the early and middle 1970s environmentalists appeared to oppose all means of overcoming the rapid rise in energy prices and the political challenges to Middle Eastern oil supplies—offshore oil drilling was opposed, as was the strip-mining of coal and all aspects of the nuclear fuel cycle. Only with the articulation of the so-called soft energy path by Amory Lovins and others did the sense that environmentalists were nothing but negative oppositionists subside (Lovins, 1977). The economic difficulties of the late 1970s and early 1980s, and the political changes that emerged at that time, posed an even more serious challenge to the environmental movement.

Until neoconservatism came along environmentalism was a "motherhood" issue that almost no one would openly and publicly oppose. Ronald Reagan changed all that, presumably forever. He denied the very existence of acid precipitation and asserted that if one had seen one redwood, one had seen them all. His reduction of the scale and role of government started with the enforcement of many key pieces of environmental legislation. But, interestingly, his radical shift in tone restored and accelerated the growth in environmental organizational membership and strength. This was the case in the early 1980s despite the low ebb for environmental issues in opinion polls and in media coverage. The mass public had turned to unemployment and inflation as their first concerns, but a smaller activist public would not let government roll back pollution and resource management to the pre-environmental movement days. Neither of

Reagan's early antienvironmental appointees (James Watt and Anne Gorsuch Burford) survived his first term in office (1980–1984).

TWO WAVES IN THE HISTORY OF ENVIRONMENTALISM

Thus far there have been two distinct waves of environmental concern in North America (Paehlke, 1992). These waves could be measured by high ranking of environmental issues in public opinion polls, media attention, or attention from public figures. Between the waves are troughs where other issues, usually economic and/or social, are dominant. I would place the first environmental wave from 1968 through 1976 and the second from 1986 until quite recently, perhaps 1994. The late 1970s and early 1980s witnessed serious economic dislocations and the rise of neoconservatism. The recession of the early 1990s, combined with massive governmental debt levels, has also distracted attention from the second wave of environmental concern and, in the United States especially, has again opened environmentalists to direct political attack from the likes of Rush Limbaugh and others.

The distinctions drawn here between the two waves of environmentalism are impressionistic, matters of different emphases at different times; they are differences of degree, not kind. All through this period as a whole (from the 1960s through to the present) environmentalism has been nothing if not intellectually complex. Some individuals and organizations proceed from comprehensive ecological and political analyses, others simply oppose a particular project or projects. The environmental movement is as much an analytic tool for observers as self-conscious entity. I would assume that many of those acting within that movement would not be members of any organization, just people who had changed their everyday behaviour or were doing their jobs in government, at a scientific field station, or within a trade union. The notion of a movement signifies a wide variety of activities and, *in toto,* considerable societal change.

Figure 12.2 and Figure 12.3 set out some of the major issues and characteristics that have been prominent in each of the two waves of environmental activity. Other analysts and environmental activists might compile somewhat different lists. Several observations about my particular lists are worth noting here. Second-wave issues are noticeably more often international or global in character. Most notable in this regard are climate warming, ozone depletion, acid precipitation, and the threats to tropical (and temperate) rain forests. As well, the second wave includes a resurgent concern with wilderness, nature, ecology, and biodiversity—the hallmarks of the conservation movement. In the second wave these became (and remain) "cutting-edge" issues where they were of lesser concern to many 1970s environmentalists. Finally, many first-wave

FIGURE 12.2
Prominent Environmental Issues during and First and Second Waves

First Wave (1968–1976)
Air and water pollution
Energy crisis
Offshore oil drilling, oil spills
Nuclear power
Population
Resource depletion
Urban neighbourhood preservation

Second Wave (1986–1994)
Climate warming
Ozone depletion
New wilderness and habitat concerns, including
old-growth forests, tropical rain forests, and animal rights
Waste recycling, landfill siting, recycling
Hazardous wastes, carcinogens
Fisheries, forests, and biodiversity
Oil-tanker spills
Urban planning, automobiles, land use
Indoor air quality

concerns remain prominent and thus the total list has grown considerably from one decade to the next.

Not only are the issues different, but the environmental movement of the 1990s has a tone and a character different from those of the 1970s. There was, in 1970 more frequently than now, even more of a sense that as an environmentalist one was thoroughly out of step with one's society. There was a sense that that society was not viable and that its impending decline need not be mourned. Some aspects of the early movement were millennialist and some were even, at times, apolitical.

Some organizations and publications within the environmental movement sought to counter these tendencies, to discourage the illusion that fleeing the cities to grow vegetables was an appropriate response to pollution and resource depletion. But these more politically oriented and sophisticated environmentalists were not so successful in countering the policies of 1970s decision-makers. These policies were, in hindsight, for the most part "high stack dispersal and/or end-of-the-pipe" approaches induced almost exclusively by regulatory instru-

FIGURE 12.3
Characteristics and Emphases of the First and Second Waves

First Wave (1968–1976)
Tendency to alienation, detachment from social, political, and economic order
Antitechnological inclinations and attitudes
Tendency to millenialism
Regulatory "end-of-pipe" solutions favoured by decision-makers
Building awareness of problems

Second Wave (1986–1994)
Re-emergence of "preservationist" issues
Globalized focus of concern
Acceptability of some environmental ideas within political
and economic elites
Professional character of major environmental organizations
A multiple-tools approach

ments negotiated in their detail behind closed doors. Some such measures may have been necessary, but collectively they were far from equal to the task at hand then or now.

Second-wave environmentalism is very different. Many environmental organizations have matured and professionalized (though the creation of newer, more radical ones has been ongoing as well). Some of those newer groups have very radical analyses (e.g., deep ecology or anarchist bioregionalism), others have more conventional political analyses but utilize extreme tactics (e.g., "monkey-wrenching") (Taylor, 1995). All serve as a counterpoint to the general turn to professionalism and compromise within now large and established environmental organizations. During the second wave the movement as a whole connected more frequently and in more ways with the normal political processes of the wider society.

In one sense the movement became less millennialist: it was more widely accepted that individual/group "escapes" are virtually impossible and that the collapse of industrial society is not a viable solution. In another sense environmentalism may have become more profoundly millennialist: the new global issues suggest that we really may now be dealing with the ecological viability of the planet as a whole. Even if that is taken to be the case, the solutions advanced by the environmental movement (technology transfer, carbon taxes, a greater dependence on public transportation) are highly practical and compromise-oriented.

Perhaps the most strikingly different aspect of second-wave realities is that environmental ideas had come to be widely held (or at least asserted) within North American and global political elites. For a time in the late 1980s and early 1990s even George Bush and Margaret Thatcher claimed to have green roots and inclinations—a remarkable change indeed. In the 1970s most municipal governments barely tolerated volunteer-staffed recycling depots. Almost no corporate leaders imagined that environmentalism had anything to do with business, save perhaps as a nuisance. For individuals within the political and corporate elites of Canada and the United States, environmentalism was perhaps interesting, perhaps silly, but had nothing to do with one's working life other than as a source of regulations that one sought to avoid or comply with.

The second wave of environmentalism advanced in a more complex political climate. A series of events and scientific findings spurred a strong surge of pro-environmental opinion, especially in the late 1980s: climate warming, the growing ozone hole, the Exxon *Valdez*, the PCB fire at St. Basile le Grande, the visits by rock stars to the Brazilian rain forest, the radon scare, and second-hand tobacco smoke findings all contributed to the mood. As noted, elites appeared to be onside, and they consulted rather than derided environmentalists; but at the same time they raised very sophisticated arguments about the compatibility of economic growth and environmental protection and the need to integrate environment and economy. Sometimes such a perspective is altogether appropriate, but not always.

A gulf opened within the environmental movement itself, between those whose values and views were informed by an ecocentric view (including deep ecology) and those who favoured sustainable development. People with solid environmental credentials were on both sides of the gulf. Neither concept had been widely articulated before the second wave of environmental concern.

An ecocentric view asserts that humans are but one species among many, that nature and nonhuman species are no less valuable in their own right than are humans (Fox, 1990, 1995; Devall and Sessions, 1985). In the deep ecologist's view, wild nature must, in some instances, be chosen over human habitat and human well-being. In contrast, the concept of sustainable development, in its classic statement (World Commission on Environment and Development, 1987), gives priority to *human* needs, and many of its advocates assert that we can simultaneously achieve continuing economic growth and improved environmental protection.

An emphasis on sustainable development is in a sense less green than an emphasis on deep ecology values, but, to the extent that win–win options are available, there can be points of agreement between these two perspectives. Moreover, sustainable development has provided a context within which enthusiasts of economic growth, environmentalists, and advocates of greater equity can enter a "trialogue." Many first-wave environmentalists and some deep ecologists have allowed little scope for, and paid little attention to, opportunities for social change, incremental public policy steps, or product or process improvements. Advocates of sustainable development have focused on these things perhaps too exclusively and too narrowly.

There is, thus, room for mutual learning. The practical components of contemporary (second-wave) environmentalism could usefully be informed by the insights of deep ecology. Can we, one might ask, move from green products like phosphate-free detergents to green products like compact urban form and public transportation systems? Only within a dialogue about the details of everyday economic and social life and about the environmental values that are most important can necessary changes be understood, let alone achieved. Achieving change will also likely require as well a sense of the political and intellectual role of environmentalism and green politics within a post–Cold War, post-communist world. Such considerations move us from the history of environmental organizations to the realm of ideas and politics at the ideological level (Paehlke, 1989).

ENVIRONMENTALISM IN A POST-COMMUNIST WORLD

The speed with which the euphoria over the demise of communism and the Cold War has faded is astonishing. There are many reasons for this: a variety of unexpected outcomes, including the wars in Bosnia and elsewhere; the global recession and jobless growth that followed rapidly in the wake of the change; the economic plight and political instability of the former Soviet Union and Eastern Europe; and perhaps—one might add—the loss, for some in the West, of a psychologically and economically important enemy. One might even speculate that the demise of communism and anti-communism has undermined something of the sense of solidarity and collective purpose that they provided. Ideology can be ugly, but it is not without positive (integrative) functions.

The end of history leaves everyone adrift—there is at present no widely held vision of the future, no coherent prospect for positive change. The widespread seeming demise of a left perspective leaves many to wonder what, if anything, remains of the predominant intellectual/political perspective of the past century or more. The decline of left ideas as a coherent perspective on the world is a result of more than the fall of communism. It is also a function of the accelerated globalization of political economy and the decades-long rise of governmental indebtedness in many nations. Governments everywhere, the leading source of new employment for more than four decades, no longer have a capacity for additional growth. A left perspective seems somehow pointless in the face of that reality. Left governments in power seem, and are, even less different from right governments than they used to be.

Within this context the prospects of environmentalism as an emerging ideology must be evaluated. The moderate left, which has had ideological and organizational links with environmentalists, has served vital—now unfilled—functions within capitalist liberal democracy. These would include creative and balancing functions. The current weakness of the left throughout the world, both electorally and intellectually, is highly problematic for a number of reasons. First and foremost, industrial capitalism may well no longer be capable of generating enough jobs. The public sector has been the principal source of new employment for decades. There is little to suggest that even interest rates near zero and worldwide free trade will generate global gains in employment in the present context; they may not even produce sustained economic growth.

It is possible that the tenacious problem of jobless growth cannot be resolved without a creative ideological tension that is presently lacking (Aronowitz and DiFazio, 1994). There is at present no serious political challenge to the rule of economic technocrats, who share an ideology that presumes the necessity of a particular form of economic growth. Growth, in this view, is sought with but minimal regard for either equity or environment.

The environmental movement, without allies, is not an adequate political match for neoconservative economism on any but a small number of relatively minor questions and issues. Moreover, accelerated consumer spending within the rich nations—the goal of the neoconservative economists who dominate public policy—is, to say the least, environmentally doubtful. It is also highly challenging to achieve in the face of high unemployment, economic instability, and the recent debt experience of most consumers. For this latter reason it is possible that ideological competition may well return in the coming years and one should consider the possibility that environmentalism and the environmental movement will play a central role.

I have argued elsewhere (Paehlke, 1989) that environmentalism is itself inherently neither left nor right. On the question of jobless growth, environmentalism offers an interesting counterpoint: the possibility of an explicit advocacy of growthless jobs. That is, environmentalists argue that work opportunities should be more equitably shared lest the quest for adequate employment through unrestrained economic growth impose unacceptable levels of environmental damage. Expanding economic activity almost inevitably imposes environmental costs, and some environmentalists contend that even present levels of economic activity are not sustainable.

Other environmentalists, however, advocate sustainable development and believe that we can and must have both economic growth and environmental protection. This is perhaps the central tension within the contemporary environmental movement. It is the basis for a potential split between those environmentalists inclined to cooperation with the remnants of the ideological left and those who would go with what might be termed the greening of capitalism. These are not, of course, mutually exclusive intellectual options. Environmentalists might simultaneously press labour and the left for wage and hours restraints in exchange for greater employment security and simultaneously promote the employment opportunities associated with public transportation, recycling, and green consumer products.

Another of the central political differences within the contemporary environmental movement—varying views as to who is at fault as regards environmental harm—reveals a further left/right tension within the movement. But, as further evidence of the left/right neutrality of environmentalism, the environmental movement as a whole is decidedly ambivalent on this question. Some environmentalists are certain that environmental damage is a "crime" of corporations and economic and political decision-makers. Others argue that we are all complicit in the many harms that are imposed on nature.

Implicit in these competing perspectives are conclusions on how government and society ought to proceed on environmental protection. One's answer determines the character of one's environmental politics. Should the emphasis of environmental policy be on changing the behaviour of most individuals within the marketplace? Or should attention be focused primarily on those individuals or organizations who impose on nature most severely? That is, is the problem primarily overconsumption (possibly linked to human population levels), or is it primarily wrong-headed extraction and production decisions? Environmentalism is neither left nor right in part because there are many and varied views within the movement on this question.

This tension within environmentalism about the attribution of blame distinguishes environmental politics from "self-interested" politics—all politics as ordinarily understood. Environmentalism allows at least the possibility that we are all to blame for some of the important problems that we face. Left/right divisions, regional divisions, gender divisions, ethnic divisions, and sectoral divisions all direct blame elsewhere and all are economically self-interested. Someone else—capitalists or welfare mothers or deadbeat dads or ethnic minorities or majorities—is always at fault for the condition of both society and one's group within that society.

That does not necessarily prove that nonenvironmental (or even anti-environmental) politics are always on a lower moral ground. The self-interestedness of human groups is sometimes and to some extent important to moral and social progress. As well, environmental divisions are in some instances economically self-interested conflicts (as between often-prosperous wilderness advocates and loggers, for example). Nonetheless, environmental politics as often as not are politics argued on behalf of nonhumans, on behalf of as yet unborn generations, or on behalf of values that are not easily translated into economic values. Environmental politics do not have a constituency so automatic as that of economically interested, "everyday" politics.

The tension within environmentalism between "we are all at fault" and "we are all imposed upon by a few environmental despoilers" is not likely to be resolved. There is too much truth on each side. What is not, however, commonly appreciated is the irony that may attend on this tension. The view that we are all of us the source of environmental problems would seem to be appropriate to a right-of-centre environmentalism, a focus on corporate despoilers appropriate to a left-of-centre environmentalism. The former would seem to urge mild collective impositions on all, the latter to call for more stringent impositions on economic elites—regulations and criminalization, for example. Ironically, capitalism as an institutional structure could be more profoundly impacted by a widespread conclusion that the environment can be protected effectively only if we, all of us, make do with less by way of material possessions and/or find ways to reduce human numbers.

The political significance and future of environmentalism is bound up in considerations of this sort. Is it a movement that will make common cause with the right? Is it a political movement that will make common cause with the left (or even supplant the left as the leading threat to the contemporary ideological hegemony of corporate capitalism)? Or is environmentalism more likely to remain so purist and sectarian that it has no more than a passing influence on partisan politics as we know it? These questions require a further consideration of the varieties of contemporary environmentalism.

Right environmentalism has gained considerable visibility in recent years. Previously, the political right was content to simply dismiss or ignore environmental problems. The strength of the second wave of environmentalism (1985–present) has been too great for attempts at accommodation and integration to continue to be forgone. Right environmentalism can be seen as having four principal tenets:

1. Human population levels require continued increases in wealth and economic development, though they must now take environmental constraints into account.
2. The blame for environmental harm is universal.
3. Unconstrained markets can and will lessen that harm.
4. Environmental harms are not so serious as they are asserted to be by environmental "extremists."

The preferred policy options of right environmentalism are multi-stakeholder consensus-seeking forums, the removal of government subsidies from environmentally harmful activities, and voluntary initiatives of all kinds.

Left environmentalism would agree with right environmentalism on the first tenet, the need for continued economic growth, but would disagree on how this might be achieved. Few on the left have recently had much that is distinctive to say, however, about how this desired economic growth might be achieved. Left environmentalism is, however, more consistent than right environmentalism in allowing that environmental problems are indeed serious. It offers an explicit view that multinational corporations are to blame for most, if not virtually all, environmental damage. Parallel to the old Marxist notion of "false consciousness," left environmentalism takes marketing and advertising to determine and control the material desires of individuals. Only the elimination or control of market forces and corporations can, in this view, lessen environmental harm.

Centrist environmentalism may well be more purely, or militantly, environmentalist than are either of the other two perspectives. Environmental harms are not only serious, but may determine the future existence of humans and all other species. Such views can drift into millennialist lunacy in some cases. In political and policy terms, however, this view is potentially more pragmatic and moderate than either of the other two. Human population levels are a problem, but are not so all-determining as they tend to be for the right. All are to blame, but some are perhaps more guilty than others—the views of left and right are thus compromised and balanced. The implication of this is that market-based policy tools are essential, but so too is regulation. The market can be a useful tool, but so can governmental intervention. Economic growth and environmental protection can, in this view, be achieved concurrently, but often they conflict, and when this is the case environmental values should prevail. Both the left and the right, for opposite distributive reasons, would have difficulty with this assertion.

These are each typified perspectives. In the real world they rarely exist in pure form. But they are internally consistent views and each has a familiar ring within the contemporary debates on environmental issues. Two variants are particularly common within the contemporary debates in environmental policy. These variants might be called centre/left environmentalism and ecoentrepreneurialism. Centre/left environmentalism (hereafter called progressive environmentalism) would balance blame for environmental harm between corporations and individuals. Ecoentrepreneurialism would not wait, for example, for the market to solve resource shortages through higher prices for raw materials. It actively produces green products.

All of these perspectives make more sense if one dispenses with a conventional view of left and right. Politics might be seen, alternatively, as having three poles: environment (green), equity (left), and economy (right). The virtues of the market economy are articulated by capitalists, conservatives, and economists. Equity is advanced in sometimes conflicting ways by labour, minorities, feminists, and the left. Environmental protection is stressed by environmental organizations, environmental scientists, and environmentalists. Few individuals operate exclusively within one of these perspectives (capitalist, left, green), though some may try hard to do so. Most of the contemporary political terrain remains open to views that are combinations of these three perspectives or that shift among them depending on the particular issue at hand.

Post–Cold War ideology could come to be dominated by shifting coalitions that combine two of these three poles. These coalitions might be called ecoentrepreneurs, progressive greens, and the growth coalition (see Figure 12.4). Ecoentrepreneurs occupy the ground between capitalism and environmentalism; progressive greens, the ground between the left (equity advocates) and environmentalists. The growth coalition—and many examples of this formation have been visible over the past several decades—links labour and capital in opposition to environmental protection. The political potential of this latter coalition is obviously formidable; it carries easy access to all nongreen governments.

The politics of the future may belong to the growth coalition. As resource stocks decline and/or human population levels continue to rise, scarcity issues

FIGURE 12.4
Shifting Coalitions in Post–Cold War Ideology

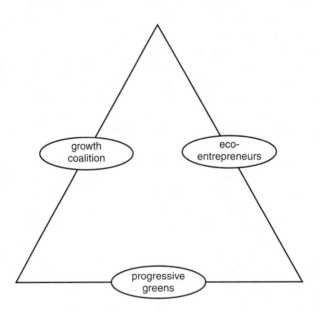

will arise more frequently. Conflicts will intensify over uncut forest lands, as-yet-untapped (environmentally risky) energy supplies, and land use disputes of all sorts. In a context of high unemployment (a result of globalization and automation), the growth coalition and a politics of environmental denial may be in a strong position. Many people might accept the somewhat ascetic alternatives of environmentalism, but it is harder to imagine a popular majority engaged politically in active pursuit of what could be caricatured by the growth coalition as shared poverty.

If politics were ever to come to a straight fight between growth advocates and environmentalists, even assuming a ecoentrepreneurial and progressive green alliance (see Figure 12.5), the outcome would seem doubtful for environmental protection. The best prospect for pro-environmental politics within this plausible future may hinge on two issues. First, greens require a broadly acceptable means of resolving, at least partially, the question of jobless growth. Second, a balanced view regarding blame for environmental harm must be established and maintained allowing a green coalition of progressive greens and ecoentrepreneurs.

Unequivocal attacks on capital are problematic in an age of maximized capital mobility. (This is not to say that such attacks should never be raised, but rather that they will not easily succeed in the present context.) Equally, any undue emphasis on "we-are-all-to-blame" themes opens environmentalists to

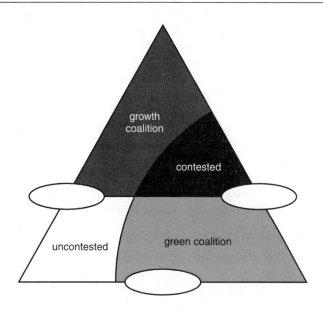

labels of elitism by growth advocates posing as populists. Such accusations are already commonplace and the irony associated with their origins is all too frequently missed.

JOBLESS GROWTH, ENVIRONMENTALISM, AND POLITICS

Jobless growth would appear to be a central characteristic of both contemporary and future political economy. It is a new enough phenomenon that its political and ideological importance has not yet been widely appreciated. Its causes are multiple: industrial automation, office automation, governmental deficits (causing employment reductions in the one realm not fully subject to automation: human services), massive and growing poor-nation labour pools continuously draining skilled industrial jobs from North America and Western Europe, and the reduced need for management layers as communications technologies advance. Products are produced less expensively, but fewer and fewer in the rich nations have stable full-time, skilled employment. Youth unemployment is very high—there is now a "lost" generation without an economic depression—and both voluntary and involuntary early retirement are increasingly the norm.

Productivity increases; labour costs decrease. Prices are stable; interest rates are low. But there is high unemployment and higher underemployment. Economic growth is very slow, so low that jobless growth may be something of a misnomer on a macroeconomic level, employment instability preventing a restoration of consumer confidence. But jobless growth is highly visible at the microeconomic level: from the faltering economic giants (IBM, GM, the airlines) to the economic success stories (Northern Telecom, Apple Computers, Bell Canada). Neither is immune to massive downsizing and/or layoffs. Even firms with spectacular growth in recent years (Hewlett-Packard, Microsoft) have not hired many. There are many new engines of economic growth, but few, if any, engines of employment. There especially are few new full-time, relatively permanent jobs that are neither menial nor low-paying. There is no replacement for the steel or auto industry on the horizon, no new mass employer of well-paid workers.

These things are well-known. What is not appreciated is the potential environmental and ideological significance of this new reality. Environmental protection initiatives can threaten jobs. Usually (Paehlke and Vaillancourt-Rosenau, 1994), there is no net threat to employment. In the case of producing paper from postconsumer waste or selling soft drinks in refillable containers, for example, more jobs are gained than lost. But existing jobs are threatened, and in a world of jobless growth and high unemployment those jobs will be defended vehemently. Thus Clinton and Gore allow cutting in the old-growth remnants of the Pacific Northwest; the government of British Columbia permits logging in Clayoquot Sound. These are governments with relatively strong environmental empathy. Others that follow may be inclined to leave nothing standing.

Jobless growth and its implications for environmental protection is, in my view, the issue on which environmentalism will succeed or fail as a political movement. To succeed politically in the 1990s and beyond, environmentalism must do nothing less than provide for the 1990s what John Maynard Keynes offered to the 1930s: simple, workable, even if partial, economic solutions. It would appear that no other political perspective has sufficient inclination or intellectual capacity. Two promising policy possibilities have been advanced thus far—one is reduced work time in patterns and outcomes that are widely acceptable; the other is a taxation structure that shifts the burden from income, property, and sales to something like the throughputs of energy and virgin materials. Both initiatives may be necessary to simultaneously achieve environmental protection goals and a modicum of economic justice.

One alternative that has been widely advanced is various taxes on pollution, but that is far too complex to administer in most forms. If simple, such taxes would have perverse economic and environmental effects, as in the case of a carbon tax. A carbon tax is a hidden subsidy to nuclear power. Economically, a carbon tax is regressive and may not be sufficient in itself to, for example, move people from automobiles to public transportation.

Keynesianism was implicitly, if not explicitly, an ideological response to Marxism. The massive and painful flaw in the capitalism of his day, he argued, could be corrected technically by societal and governmental initiatives; revolutionary transformation was neither necessary nor likely to succeed. Few today are calling for rapid and radical change of any sort. Keynes was right on many counts. But capitalism, it would appear, is not self-correcting in matters environmental, nor any longer as regards employment. New forms of intervention on these two fronts would appear to be in order. We should be aware that there will be unintended consequences. We should learn from the ideological past that perfection is unattainable on either front and that all is not the fault of devils, rich or poor or foreign. The simplest solutions technically and economically (as noted above) may be the most challenging to accept culturally and politically.

Working less and distributing equitably what work remains as productivity increases is one obvious solution, but human beings have always defined themselves and their social structures through work. Moreover, the labour market is now decidedly globalized and one cannot easily have sabbaticals-for-all in one country. A few small nations in Asia appear capable of working hard enough and cleverly enough to make almost everything for everyone. Once they own everything it will be hard to find a way to pay for it all. Achieving a simultaneous balance between productivity and environmental protection and between output and equity of employment opportunities, on a global basis, is the principal challenge ahead. It is as much a cultural, psychological, and philosophical challenge as it is an economic and environmental one. Contemporary technical economics seems not to be worried about the problem, let alone to have grasped the level of the challenge.

The effects of environmental protection on employment levels and on economic justice would be first-order concerns. For example, attention would be paid to the uneven effects of energy taxes. The poor spend a higher proportion of their income on energy than do the rich; therefore, unadjusted energy taxes are regressive taxes. Another example arises in a careful consideration of recycling. Recycling initiatives produce more jobs than are lost, but those new jobs are less likely to be unionized. New employment is often located in urban regions and is lost in poorer hinterland regions where there are fewer, if any, employment options. The broad point is that considerations of this sort have to date been given insufficient attention by the environmental movement.

GLOBALIZATION, TRADE, AND ENVIRONMENTAL PROTECTION

A progressive environmental politics might well also be open to an expanded application of criminal law to some kinds of environmental harm. However, the trend to economic globalization poses a real threat to the prospects for this or any other interventionist environmental initiatives. On one level the truth of this latter assertion is obvious. One cannot criminalize institutions that are both perceived to be essential and in actuality globally mobile. But more than that, globalization of corporations and capital, without a corresponding level of globalization of environmental organizations and political power, produces a variety of more subtle threats.

One very daunting threat is the international levelling of environmental policy, including regulations, combined with the absence of enforcement in some jurisdictions. That is the principal environmental threat implicit in NAFTA. Just as the former Soviet Union had impressive environmental and occupational health statutes on the books, so too in many areas does Mexico. But there is only a minimal enforcement apparatus and less interest in actual enforcement. This situation, combined with low wages enforced by an anti-union government, places continuous pressure on Canadian firms to press for lower standards and enforcement here. It may well be the case that individual managers would prefer not to do so. But their operations, in most cases, will continue to exist only if their cost structures are lower than equivalent operations in Mexico and elsewhere.

The existence of comparable legislation and standards in Mexico makes it difficult to challenge the situation on the grounds of unfair trade practices. The nonlevel playing field can be demonstrated only through continuous and detailed observations within another quasi-sovereign nation. This is a sovereignty of convenience. Making an effective legal case against polluters is difficult enough within one's own state, as other authors in this volume make clear. It is all but impossible elsewhere. Anecdotal evidence and impressions will not suffice within trade condition enforcement panels. One should be clear here as well that it is both Canada and Mexico that resisted attempts by the United States to achieve stronger internationalized enforcement of environmental standards.

But whether or not some advances are made on this particular front, globalization in general, independent of comprehensive trade agreements, threatens environmental protection in other, more subtle and indirect, ways. The first is through the acceleration of jobless growth. Jobless growth in turn affects the control of environmental harms in three ways. First, high unemployment creates political pressures to allow economic activities that are patently destructive. Second, it undermines efforts at mitigation, planning, and regulatory enforcement by placing other demands on a declining pool of public funds. Third, a climate is created in which the more stringent and interventionist public policy tools, such as criminalization, are off-limits on a one-nation basis. There can be no environmentalism-in-one-nation within a globalized world. Let us look at these effects in a bit more detail.

Over the past two centuries Canada has cut an astonishing proportion of a forest more than 8000 kilometres long and hundreds of kilometres wide. There is now increasing evidence that the biodiversity of this forest is lost even when the forest-as-timber is replaced effectively. How much of the remaining old-growth forest will be preserved? In a world of jobless growth how much stronger are the pressures to cut if and when it becomes clear that the Canadian forest industry must otherwise be significantly downsized for the several decades before sufficient second-growth is available? Even at the local level, when there are hundreds or thousands out of work, how valuable is a particular wetland that could be a supermarket? How many will oppose a new mine in a pristine wilderness or risky offshore drilling in the Beaufort Sea?

Jobless growth is the result of globalization combined with both the removal of management layers made more technically feasible by computers and the automation of manufacturing processes. Both of the latter are accelerated within the wealthy nations by globalization. If a firm has a higher wage structure than a competitor in a poor nation, it must make do with fewer employees. The acceleration of this combination of factors in recent years has now put massive pressure on the leading source of employment opportunities over the past 40 years: the public sector. Public sector management layers will now also be eliminated and operations increasingly automated (e.g., with driver's licence-issuing machines).

Governmental deficits also ensure that there is no effective oversight of local planning decisions at the same time that the pressures on local governments to approve all development proposals intensifies. These local pressures stem from the need to protect employment and to generate the additional tax base necessary to cover local government revenue shortfalls. Pollution abatement is also less effectively enforced because there are fewer inspectors.

Finally, innovative and distinctive initiatives on environmental protection are all but foreclosed. No jurisdiction is likely to further criminalize pollution when the polluter is a model citizen compared to his competition in other nations. As well, tax and subsidy regimes must be harmonized, lessening the prospects for the innovative use of market-based tools as well. The decision on softwood lumber in favour of Canada suggests that subsidies to extraction may somehow be more acceptable than export restraints (which are explicitly disallowed in the case of energy in both the FTA and NAFTA). What of product bans? Canada was instrumental in blocking the attempt by U.S. EPA to block the import, sale, and use of asbestos. Such gumption may be politically possible only when a hazardous material or product is an imported material or product. Internationalized trade regimes foreclose even this opening.

Indeed, internationalized trade institutions may themselves prove to be the single greatest threat to the reduction of corporate environmental harm. This is a matter that is on one level over and above the question of jobless growth. Environmentalism historically has been characterized by attempts to force more open governmental decision-making processes against the ordinary inclinations of the administrative state and corporate capitalism (Schrecker, 1984). That is what environmental assessment, for example, is all about. In addition, most major environmental legislation in both the U.S. and Canada contains public participation provisions.

In fact, the distinction between the conservation movement and the environmental movement turns on this very point (Paehlke and Torgerson, 1990). Conservationists trusted the state to recognize and protect the public interest. Environmentalists argued that the environmental bureaucracies must be forced to make decisions in public. Trade panels are for the most part closed operations. Has, it is fair to ask, globalization undermined both the power and legitimacy of the nation state and democracy itself?

ENVIRONMENTALISM AS A FORCE FOR CHANGE

There are possibilities that have not yet been advanced by environmental organizations. One ensures a falling-out between environmentalists and the left, and indeed the overwhelming majority of North Americans. But it needs mention in any case: globalization asserts a downward pressure on wages in the rich nations—a change that could have, environmentally, some positive effects. This is another of the ironies of the present situation: the bad news economically is at least in part good news environmentally. If North Americans could no longer afford to consume there would be, for example, less waste to manage. But the price, of course, is the acceleration of the joblessness- and deficit-based risks to the environment identified above. There are also, however, other possibilities for breaking out of this vicious circle.

Environmentalists could more aggressively pursue the removal of all anti-environmental subsidies: to nuclear power, indeed to all energy supply, to automobiles, to air travel, to mining, forest extraction, and elsewhere. Second, they could, in alliance with labour, seek reductions in work time and thereby move nearer to full employment. They could also seek revisions of trade agreements to permit pro-environmental subsidies. Alternatively, third, they could explicitly seek international subsidy regimes for renewable energy, recycled materials, and nontoxic replacements for toxic products. They might also pursue multinational shifts in tax patterns from income to energy and materials throughputs. If mindful of the equity effects of the new tax patterns, this too could be a measure that could gain popular support. Finally, to offset the tendencies of globalization to weaken protection against corporate environmental harms, environmentalists could seek international agreements on definitions of corporate environmental crime anywhere within a trading zone.

Obviously, none of these four options would be achieved easily, but it would seem that all would require the greater internationalization of environmental organizations. This is true whether or not NAFTA comes to fruition. Without such action environmental harm will accelerate in the future. The range of policy options will contract and the political options will be restricted, at best, to those to which right environmentalism is inclined. Labour in that context would increasingly be propelled toward the growth coalition.

Environmentalism as an ideological current could be a force for change as were liberalism and socialism in their time. Many of those older ideas, of course, remain with us despite the demise of communism having been institutionalized that the liberal democracies that may now replace the old regimes in the East. It was the trade union movement, and peaceful popular uprising—two mainstays of socialist ideology—that, after all, produced the change and the end of the Cold War. This remains the most dramatic political change of this century, perhaps in all of history. Change never occurs, however, without competing ideas and some political tension—here green politics may be a significant part of the future.

THE FUTURE OF ENVIRONMENTALISM

The end of communism and the Cold War opens the opportunity for the human race to improve its condition on a global basis. Given the environmental and economic challenges that face us the opportunity did not present itself too soon. What triumphed by attrition was not, however, pure capitalism—the victory was not one of market over government. What succeeded was democratic capitalism—market tempered by majority wisdom developed in a context of ideological diversity and struggle. C.W. Mills's marketplace of ideas and what it produced may have been more important than Adam Smith's marketplace for goods. Even if that wasn't true in the past, it is true in the new era where ecological constraints meet forms of production that demand ever fewer human producers.

REFERENCES

Allin, Craig W. 1995a. "Conservation Movement." In R.C. Paehlke, ed., *Conservation and Environmentalism: An Encyclopedia.* New York: Garland, 149–51.

———. 1995b. "Sierra Club." In R.C. Paehlke, ed., *Conservation and Environmentalism: An Encyclopedia.* New York: Garland, 587–89.

Aronowitz, Stanley, and William DiFazio. 1994. *The Jobless Future.* Minneapolis: University of Minnesota Press.

Bosso, Christopher J. 1995. "Greenpeace." In R.C. Paehlke, ed., *Conservation and Environmentalism: An Encyclopedia.* New York: Garland, 330–31.

Carson, Rachel. 1962. *Silent Spring.* New York: Houghton Mifflin.

Cohen, Michael P. 1988. *The History of the Sierra Club, 1892–1970.* San Francisco: Sierra Club Books.

Curlee, Anna Peyton. 1995. "Yellowstone National Park." In R.C. Paehlke, ed., *Conservation and Environmentalism: An Encyclopedia*. New York: Garland, 703–4.

Devall, Bill, and George Sessions. 1985. *Deep Ecology: Living as if Nature Mattered*. Salt Lake City: G.M. Smith.

Fox, Warwick. 1995. "Deep Ecology: Meanings." In R.C. Paehlke, ed., *Conservation and Environmentalism: An Encyclopedia*. New York: Garland, 165–67.

———. 1990. *Toward a Transpersonal Ecology: Developing New Foundations for Environmentalism*. Boston: Shambhala.

Lovins, Amory B. 1977. *Soft Energy Paths: Toward a Durable Peace*. Cambridge, Mass.: Ballinger.

Marsh, George Perkins. 1864. *Man and Nature; or, Physical Geography as Modified by Human Action*. New York: Charles Scribner.

Meadows, Donella H., et al. 1972. *The Limits to Growth: A Report for the Club of Rome's Project on the Predicament of Mankind*. New York: Universe Books.

Paehlke, R.C. 1989. *Environmentalism and the Future of Progressive Politics*. New Haven: Yale University Press.

———. 1992. "Eco-History: Two Waves in the Evolution of Environmentalism." *Alternatives: Perspectives on Society, Technology and Environment* 19(1): 18–23.

———, and Torgerson, D.T., eds. 1990. *Managing Leviathan: Environmental Politics and the Administrative State*. Peterborough, Ont.: Broadview Press.

———, and P. Vaillancourt-Rosenau. 1994. "Environment/Equity: Tensions in North American Politics." *Policy Studies Journal* 21: 672–86.

Science Council of Canada. 1976. *Canada as a Conserver Society*. Ottawa: Science Council of Canada.

Taylor, Bron R. 1995. "Radical Environmentalism." In R.C. Paehlke, ed., *Conservation and Environmentalism: An Encyclopedia*. New York: Garland, 539–40.

World Commission on Environment and Development. 1987. *Our Common Future*. New York: Oxford University Press.

QUESTIONS FOR DISCUSSION

1. How would you distinguish between the conservation movement and the environmental movement? Give Canadian examples of organizations of each type.

2. How do the two waves of environmentalism differ?

3. Is the environmental movement on the political left or the political right (neither or both)? Give reasons for your assessment.

4. How might such economic policy concerns as global trade and unemployment affect the quality of environmental protection?

5. Will environmentalism play a significant role in Canadian politics in the future?

Turning the Medicine Wheel: Aboriginal Land Claims and the Environment

Thomas Fleming

Department of Sociology
University of Windsor

This is not to say that in Canada land claims based on aboriginal rights were only recently invented. The Native people had never abandoned their land claims or their claim to aboriginal title; but for a long time such claims were mistaken for the rhetoric of powerlessness.

– Thomas Berger (1991:141)

INTRODUCTION: SURVIVAL AS DISTINCT PEOPLES AND THE LAND

It is only in recent years that Canadians have begun to understand something of the complexities and uniqueness of aboriginal cultures. Aboriginal Canadians are the first peoples of Canada, those who lived upon and worked the lands that this country now occupies for thousands of years before the arrival of European pioneers. However, even though events like the Mohawk–Canada crisis at Oka (O'Reilly-Fleming, 1994; York and Pindera, 1991) or the activities of the National Chief of the Assembly of First Nations, Ovide Mercredi, are well known to large numbers of Canadians, far fewer are cognizant of the legacy of despair that successive federal and provincial governments have created in native communities.

The list of problems that confront aboriginal Canadians living on reserves is long and overwhelming. On these small tracts of land set aside for aboriginal Canadians, typically in rural and often remote areas, conditions are often unthinkable. Alcoholism, violence, the sniffing of gasoline and other substances on rags, suicide, disease, lack of education, few jobs, and involvement with the criminal justice system are common features of many reserves (York, 1990; Ratner, 1990). After touring several reserves, Archbishop Desmond Tutu compared the conditions suffered by many aboriginal Canadians to those suffered by black South Africans in the apartheid homelands. If this were not enough for aboriginal Canadians to endure, there were concerted attempts by the federal government in the 1970s to assimilate aboriginals into the mainstream, dominant white culture (Weaver, 1981). Though aboriginal peoples were self-governing communities before the arrival of the first Europeans, their calls for self-government, which were most forcefully expressed during the 1980s debates on the Canadian Constitution, were given superficial attention by the federal government but did not result in an entrenchment of native rights to self-determination in legislation.

It is in this light that we must begin any serious discussion of the relationship between native land claims, various levels of government, the courts, corporate developers, environmentalists, and the environment. This chapter is going to look at these actors and their actions in a drama that will have significant impact on the present and future use of large tracts of land in Canada.

We will discover that the history of this problem stretches back several centuries but has evolved into a series of debates over the most appropriate use of the resources. Our attention will be directed to a specific legal case involving thousands of acres of land in British Columbia that was at the centre of a dispute between aboriginal Canadians and the provincial government. This famous case, known as the *Delgamuukw* decision, will provide us with insights into how various parties acted in this dispute and the environmental implications such legal decisions have for aboriginal communities, and eventually, for wider society. To a lesser extent we will also explore some ancillary cases that have garnered much media attention, including the cutting of primeval forest in Clayoquot Sound in British Columbia.

ABORIGINAL AND ENVIRONMENTALIST PERSPECTIVES

Certainly the central issue with which environmentalists have concerned themselves, in terms of the use of lands where there is disputed ownership involving aboriginal Canadians, is the preservation of the natural environment in a state devoid of development, exploitation, or damage to ecosystems. The philosophy of environmentalists favours the retention of unspoiled wilderness both as a natural resource for present and future generations and for the inherent ecological values reflected in its preservation. Environmentalists struggle to preserve natural animal and plant species that can easily be in danger of extinction in the face of modern industrial development in previously undisturbed areas. The plight of the grizzly bear in British Columbia, whose numbers have shrunk to some 8000 animals, is one example of the rationale that environmentalists would point to in fighting against what they view as the exploitation of Canada's national resources, which are often irreplaceable, by greedy multinationals.

In their efforts, environmentalists have aligned themselves with a view of aboriginal culture that focuses upon what are often loosely described as "aboriginal values," "the native way," a "relationship with mother earth," or "respecting the land." All of these generalized views are predicated upon select perceptions of aboriginal beliefs. They are often unrelated to the views of aboriginal peoples, whose lives are impacted by governmental and corporate partnerships that exploit environmental resources on their ancestral lands. These views, generalized or not, have inherent value, but they do not represent the views of all tribes, nor, I will argue, are they consistent with any one tribe.

Aboriginal values cannot be equated with the dominant culture's often sentimental view of native philosophy. Native philosophies are not readily discernible, nor are they consistent across various groupings. We have been acutely aware of native culture in specific forms since the 1970s when various authors explored the genocide practised by successive American governments in clearing lands for waves of immigrant settlers by displacing aboriginal peoples (Badcock, 1976; Miller, 1991; Ponting, 1986). But what sense can be made of native views of the environment? As we shall discover in the next section of this chapter, native peoples have historically enjoyed a close relationship with the land and animal and fish life, since their survival depended on a knowledge and constructive use of these resources. Modern native views are more complex. While many natives advocate both in religious and practical terms their connection to the living environment, many also believe the land can be both preserved and turned to good use for aboriginal peoples. This involves developing the commercial potential of natural resources, making a trade-off between total preservation and the provision of employment and capital for aboriginal stakeholders. Conservation and resource use are not seen as incompatible.

The term "environmentalist" is also one that deserves clarification in terms of defining this issue. In Canadian society we associate environmentalism with efforts to preserve forests, fish stocks, and wildlife. Scientists, most notably David Suzuki, are well known for their efforts to raise our environmental consciousness through television and books. But there are many different groups of environmentalists. Greenpeace, the World Wildlife Fund, the Sierra Club, the Jane Goodall Institute, and Pollution Probe are all well-known groups with both national and international membership. Each focuses upon different environmental problems using unique forms of tactics to pressure governments and corporations in sensitive environmental issues. Some groups advocate peaceful civil disobedience in the manner of the Reverend Martin Luther King Jr. Greenpeace, for example, uses an oceangoing ship, *The Rainbow Warrior*, to launch dinghies to protest against the taking of whales and, in July 1995, France's planned discharge of a nuclear bomb in the Pacific. These groups are often engaged in internal conflict over tactics and causes.

GOVERNMENTS AND THE LEGAL SYSTEM

The actions of governments and courts are often inextricably linked, according to both social theorists and legal analysts (Foucault, 1977; Mandel, 1996). Mandel (1996) argues that judges are merely lawyers for the status quo, ensuring that the powerful of society retain as much power and influence as possible (Fleming, 1985; Turk, 1985). Certainly in the issue of native land claims there is much at stake. If natives could resolve outstanding land claims in their favour, they would have control of a great deal of Canada's lands. This would mean that governments that gave natives too much could well wind up experiencing a "legitimization crisis" as described by Jurgen Habermans, wherein the electorate loses faith and votes them out of office. Governments within Canada have thus traditionally been very reluctant to grant native land claims, and nowhere more so than in British Columbia. The analysis to be developed later in this paper will demonstrate the long history of resistance to acknowledging even the term "aboriginal right" in native land claim cases.

CORPORATE DEVELOPMENT

Corporate developers view land as a source of resources and revenue that are easily exportable to multinational coffers. Early in the 1980s, Canadian researchers began to predict the infiltration of both American and multinational corporations into the arena of resource harvesting in this country (Laxer, 1989). Corporations support government claims to disputed lands for obvious reasons, but they have popular support amongst labour factions in Canada also. While environmentalists might wish to save natural habitat as undisturbed wilderness, forestlands, and wetlands, there are many who view resource harvesting as a source of income and have a dim view of efforts to exclude corporations from such practices as "clearcutting" trees and strip-mining, or indeed any intrusion into Canada's natural habitat. Corporations in one view could be seen to be creating well-paid employment in areas where jobs are scarce as well as employment in many related ancillary industries.

'AT THE PLEASURE OF THE CROWN'—THE HISTORY OF NATIVE LAND CLAIMS

It would be impossible in one chapter to outline the entire history of land claims involving conflicts between federal and provincial governments and aboriginal peoples. However, in this section we will explore some of the key legal and political developments. Aboriginal land rights have a longer history than any other human rights question in Canadian history. While all provinces have been involved in long-standing cases of aboriginal rights, none has a longer or more active history than that of British Columbia and its native peoples. The Nishga are one of the tribes of northwestern British Columbia who now cluster in four villages in the Nass River valley. In the 1850s the population of natives in this region numbered 50 000. By 1900, only 10 000 remained (Berger, 1981: 229). Smallpox, tuberculosis, and alcohol all contributed to their decimation. British Columbia also abolished their religious heritage by banning the potlatch, the central ceremony of their religion. Aboriginal Canadians were powerless to resist since they were granted the right to vote only in 1949.

When the Europeans arrived, native culture was thriving in British Columbia. Tribes recognized that certain lands belonged to others because they had inhabited them for several thousand years. Europeans recognized that aboriginal peoples retained an interest in the lands they had occupied as the original residents. This was to be referred to as "aboriginal title" or "Indian title" (Berger, 1981: 221; Tennant, 1991). For Europeans to gain use of lands to which aboriginals held title, they made treaties with them, paying out goods and money. When, for example, land was needed for settlements or as access routes for the national railway system, the government signed treaties with native groups (Berton, 1973). Readers should understand that the Canadian experience with aboriginal peoples is different from that of America, where wars of extermination were waged against native tribes to conquer and force them from their lands (Vescey and Venables, 1980). Canadian native leaders have often pointed out that they have never surrendered title to their lands either through treaty or defeat in a war. The document that established the British approach in Canada to treaties was contained in the Royal Proclamation of 1763.

The settlement of British Columbia can be said to have only begun in earnest after 1849 when Vancouver Island became a Crown colony. Neither the original government of this area, nor the settlers who arrived looking to homestead, nor the British government would provide funds for negotiating treaties. Soon, there were few who would even acknowledge the existence of aboriginal title. The attitude of Joseph Trutch, the chief commissioner of lands, reflected a popular view of native title in 1867:

The Indians have really no right to the lands they claim, nor are they of any actual value or utility to them, and I cannot see why they should either retain these lands to the prejudice of the general interests of the Colony, or be allowed to make a market of them.

His view was not much different from that expressed over 125 years later by government representatives and corporate officers after a decision that extinguished aboriginal title to thousands of square miles of land (*Financial Post*, March 9, 1991, p. 1).

The approach of the British Columbia government of the time was to set aside reserves for aboriginal peoples without bothering to consult them on where these should be located. This meant that native territories that predated the arrival of settlers by thousands of years were ignored. Natives were often moved from these lands, and the most fruitful lands taken from them. When the 1887 provincial royal commission into northwest coast Indians solicited interviews with native leaders, Chief David MacKay said this about land rights:

How can they give it when it is our own? ... They have never bought it from us or our forefathers. They have never fought and conquered our people ... it has been ours for generations ... for thousands of years.

By 1909, Premier Richard McBride commented, "[I]t would be madness to think of conceding to the Indians' demands."

The Nishga Land Commission was formed in 1913, and in 1916 the tribes were joined by others in the Allied Tribes of British Columbia, forerunners of modern native organizations. They petitioned Ottawa to have their claims adjudicated and title established. The Crown sidestepped the issue of title and instead awarded a form of welfare payment of $100 000 a year. It was not until 1967, in the Cultural Revolution that spawned feminism, prisoners' rights, and civil liberties legislation, that a new legal case was launched by the Nishga in the B.C. Supreme Court. Their claim was simple: Indian title had *never* been extinguished in British Columbia. The case went on to the B.C. Court of Appeal, where it was determined that Canadian law did not recognize aboriginal title and the Nishga had no legal interest in the land. One of the trial judges reflected the racist sentiments of the court in saying the Nishga were "a very primitive people with few of the institutions of civilized society, and none at all of our notions of private property." Since the Nishga did not have a system of written deeds for land and all land was owned communally, the legal system would not acknowledge their claims. White law had by virtue of its written nature achieved ascendancy over oral native law passed down through thousands of years. Paralleling views of African culture, the courts and broader society did, and unfortunately do, view native peoples in terms of crafts, carvings, dance ceremonies, and drinking. This is a misguided view of peoples whose culture had been compared anthropologically in the mid-1800s to advanced Chinese society.

The Nishga finally took their case to the Supreme Court of Canada in 1971, where they lost by a vote of 4–3. But Justice Emmett Hall, on behalf of three of the judges, found that aboriginal title to their lands had never been lawfully extinguished. In 1981 these words were added to the Canadian Constitution: "The aboriginal rights and treaty rights of the aboriginal peoples of Canada are hereby recognized and confirmed."

DELGAMUUKW V. BRITISH COLUMBIA

However, it is not accurate to think that these various forms of recognition have led governments and the courts to settle land claims cases. One glaring example is the case of *Delgamuukw v. B.C.* In 1991, the fifty-one hereditary chiefs of the Gitskan and Wet'suwet'en peoples asserted their claim to more than 22 000 square miles of land in northwestern British Columbia. This land is rich in minerals and forests, and the harvest of these resources would result in profits calculated in billions of dollars. The native plaintiffs had to assemble a staggering amount of oral history as well as scientific evidence from numerous sources to make their claim. The trial judge, Chief Justice McEachern, made much of the archaeological evidence presented, but dismissed most of the oral evidence as "not literally true." In discussing the evidence of native elders and tribe members, he commented that "very often they were recounting matters of faith which have become fact to them.... I have a different view of what is fact and what is belief." The judge's view of the evidence could reasonably be argued to have been flippant, to have failed to accord due weight to their claims. McEachern further found that the natives' contemporary way of life was not an aboriginal life, thus invalidating their own assessment of their lifestyle. The land claims of the natives were dismissed by McEachern with this amazing statement: "[O]ur Courts of law ... labour under disciplines which do not always permit judges to do what they subjectively think (or feel) might be the right or just thing to do in a particular case." Readers might consider, "If judges will not do the right thing, who will?" We might further ask, "Why don't they do it?"

The ruling in this case has been appealed to the Supreme Court of Canada (1993). The hearing will not be for several years since the volume of evidence each side has to amass is a daunting task. In the interim, native land rights in this region remain unsettled.

ENVIRONMENTAL IMPACTS IN CANADA

Our understanding of the environmental impacts of corporate development on disputed territory to which aboriginals lay claim cannot be understood by reference to one land claim dispute. Certainly the amount of land involved in each of these disputes is often unfathomable to the average city dweller. The potential environmental problems that flow from development of these lands have both a local and global significance. In this section we consider several examples of the direct environmental impacts of development. One of the most significant is that of Hydro Quebec in its building of the Great Whale power project dams on Cree lands. These dams not only displace large numbers of native peoples from their ancestral homelands but would flood 5000 square kilometres of land necessary for the creation of hydro power. While the corporate position is that courts have upheld that the company has respected the rights of aboriginal peoples, this is not the consensus of those affected by the flooding. Richardson (1976) views these developments not only in terms of the destruction of massive segments of untouched forest lands, animals, and plant species, but in its effects on aboriginal culture.

The Kemano case involves attempts by Alcan Aluminum Limited to divert the waters of the Nechako River into the Kemano River system. While the federal and provincial governments had both agreed to let the company proceed with the development in 1987, this was despite the objections of the Carrier Sekani Tribal Council and a coalition of fishing, environmental, and labour groups opposed to the project. While the provincial government had ordered an environmental review in 1993, the development was still allowed to continue while the review was being done. Alcan had spent almost half a billion dollars on the project by the time the review was ordered. However, readers should be aware that under the Environmental Protection Act in Ontario most infractions involving large companies are settled by voluntary compliance rather than prosecution. At the same time a different point of view was reflected in the policies of the Canadian Aboriginal Miners Association. The association wanted to see more development and the involvement of increasing numbers of native peoples in mining to stimulate growth in stagnant Far North economies.

Similarly, the dispute over attempts to allow logging in the Temagami wilderness (Bray and Thomson, 1990; Hodgins and Benidickson, 1989) has pitted the Teme-Augama Anishnabai against the Ontario Ministry of Natural Resources (MNR), which want to allow cutting of the pine forests of the region. The MNR's policies emphasize production based upon a 50-year rotation of forest cutting; that is, one in which it is estimated that the forest will regenerate every fifty years. By 1990, protests against logging had generated seven court decisions and 124 arrests.

What then are the environmental and ecological effects of logging, deforestation, and the flooding of large tracts of forests and wildlands? We live in an era when the demands of our society for energy and natural resources are unmatched at any time in history (Brundtland, 1987: 33–34). The World Commission on Environment and Development has indicated that in Canada we are reaching thresholds that endanger the basic integrity of our ecosystems.

The greenhouse effect poses a serious threat to life-support systems on Earth and arises largely from the cutting and burning of forests. Global warming is directly related to the accumulation of CO_2 in the atmosphere. The effects include rising sea levels that could submerge low-lying coastal cities and river deltas around the world. It could also drastically harm national and international agriculture and trade. Since Canada has the greatest natural forest reserves in the world, much of which lie on land whose title is disputed by aboriginal peoples, the enormous significance of land claims settlements is readily apparent.

Forest loss and the destruction of wild lands and wetlands by deforestation and flooding extinguish innumerable species of plants and animals. As a result, future generations cannot benefit from this genetic diversity to improve crop varieties—for example, to make them more impervious to insect attack, drought, extremes of weather, and wind. Since these areas contain many species and subspecies that are unknown or unstudied, their scientific values will never be known. The potential medical and industrial benefits of these species and plants are lost forever in the face of large-scale developments in areas of natural reserve.

Deforestation and flooding have a variety of effects, including soil erosion, sedimentation, changes in water quality, siltation of rivers, streams, and lakes; changes in water temperature, which can affect crop production and create the potential to increase health and water-related diseases; destruction of fish spawning grounds; reduction in tourist and recreation visits worth millions of dollars to the area; increased runoff, accelerating soil erosion; the loss of wildlife and biodiversity; the need for resettlement of peoples, and the destruction of traditional economies.

The risks and impacts that we have reviewed above have effects that are local as well as global in nature. All of us on earth share the risks of the destruction of large-scale reserves of undisturbed forest since we not only have clear evidence of the present and future danger such projects present, but we are also unaware of the potential losses we may suffer due to our lack of knowledge of deep forests. In fact, it may be truly stated, "The risks increase faster than do our abilities to manage them."

We must also be aware that environmental degradation can dampen or reverse economic development in our country. Environmental stresses are inextricably linked to one another. Deforestation can impact on agriculture, recreation, the atmosphere, and people. In the Temagami region, the cutting of the old pine forest trees, some of which have been dated at 375 years of age, will destroy not only healthy tree stands but also snags (standing dead trees), deadfalls, and thick floors of organic materials that have been evolving for over 500 years.

The settlement between the Cree Indians and the Quebec government in the James Bay project is an example of a predicament native bands across the country face because of large-scale developers. The 6000 Cree of Quebec, many of whom still lived in a traditional hunting lifestyle, agreed to a $150 million payment from the province in exchange for large parcels of land needed to develop the project and for certain future protections. In total, the Cree and Inuit received title to 65 300 square miles of territory, some 60 000 of which they retained hunting, fishing, and trapping rights to, but not the right to stop mining and development. The aboriginal groups lost 80 000 square miles of the Mistassini hunting territory, which shrank to 7000 square miles. Clearly, the massive flooding required to produce hydroelectricity has had an immense impact on the environment and traditional lifestyle of the Cree and Inuit. The fate of other aboriginal peoples is unlikely to be different, given that governments and a legal system promote a compromise system that permits the legal seizure of unbelievably large tracts of northern lands.

SOCIO-LEGAL IMPACTS: PEOPLE AND POLITICS

The failure of successive governments to recognize native land rights is understandable. Native groups, in hundreds of outstanding land claims, have an interest in large portions of the country we call Canada. For natives, the right to use or preserve the resources on these lands is a matter of simple survival of their culture. Without a land base, no culture has been able to survive in the modern world. Further, the aboriginal peoples understand that these resources would make them independent both economically and politically from various forms of government. Aboriginal peoples, under the leadership of Ovide Mercredi and others, have fought hard to institute native self-government. There has been little government effort to accept either the ability of natives to govern themselves or live under their own laws. Native uprisings like that at Oka are a direct result of governments ignoring the land rights of natives and treating them as if they were children incapable of handling their own affairs. Oka focused world attention on Canada's treatment of its native peoples. When the army and police surrounded Oka and denied medicine, food, water, legal counsel, and media access to the natives under siege, the action evoked a swift and highly negative response from the United Nations. In fact, Canada has been accused of more human rights violations by its indigenous peoples than any other signatory to the UN Treaty. Without control of their own lands, aboriginals seem condemned to an apartheid-like existence on many reserves across this country.

It is not surprising that governments do not wish to acknowledge, other than in a superficial manner, the legitimacy of native land claims. Governments and corporate interests have a close relationship in modern society. If native land claims were settled in favour of aboriginal groups, the potential economic loss to the government and corporations seeking to exploit land resources would be inestimable. Governments, like those in British Columbia, have shown a marked reluctance to thwart corporate plans for exploitation even when irreplaceable resources are involved.

CLAYOQUOT SOUND

Come, ye brave men of Clayoquot,
Come, ye bold women too.
There is a fire burning on the mountain,
The sting of smoke that fills the air.
Hear the shriek of the whistle,
Hear the snarl of the chain,
Hear the crackin' in the heartwood,
Hear it again, and again, and again.

– Bob Bossin, 1995

The best example of this clash of interests is in British Columbia's Clayoquot Sound. This area is a pristine rain forest, one of the few remaining in the world. International logging interests want to clearcut this area, a process that takes out all of the trees and leaves only stumps. It irrevocably damages the ecological systems that are supported by forests, as landslides and mudslides abound once the trees are gone. It destroys completely and forever the habitat of the wildlife.

Given the fragility of many species of mammals, birds, and fish and their declining numbers, this may result in the disappearance of species and/or the non-identification of unknown species. Only a massive campaign involving celebrities, millions of people worldwide, environmental groups, and native groups caused British Columbia to back away from clearcutting on July 6, 1995. Readers should be aware that several regions in this area have already been clearcut. Robert Kennedy Jr. commented on this international concern: "We're here for our own sake.... We are protecting the trees because we believe the trees are more valuable to humanity standing than if they are cut down."

Interestingly, native views should not be presumed to coincide with those of environmentalists. In fact, while there is some degree of convergence between the two, natives often view environmentalists as being as single-minded as the government. Francis Frank, Chief of the Tla-o-qui-aht, expressed this clearly when he stated: "For some time, we kept hearing what those people do not like. As time wears on, that argument wears a little thin.... We wanted to hear what was acceptable." While environmentalists do not want any intrusion that would result in the cutting of timber stocks, native groups are leery of arguments that sustainable forest practices are practical or possible. While natives wish to preserve certain forest areas, they also live in the contemporary world where their economic considerations are central to decision-making. It may be that they will sign an agreement with International Forest Products Limited that will permit logging. The comforting, romantic notion of native Canadians and their culture that prevailed over a century ago no longer holds. They are a part of the contemporary world and their views on their land will be their own, not those of others.

RESOLUTIONS AND RAMIFICATIONS

Given the diversity of interests involved, there is no magic solution to the protection on traditional native lands and the environments and the ecosystems they support. Native leaders have indicated that they seek solutions that are ideal in nature—that is, ones that balance the need for economic development, native interests, and the protection of the environment. The legal history of resolution has not favoured native Canadians, despite clear evidence that the international community frowns on Canada's management of its forest reserves and its treatment of aboriginal Canadians (Reid, 1992). An Angus Reid poll of 5000 residents of 17 countries, found that most held a negative image of the Canadian government's policies toward its forests.

The pressure to sustain economic growth and development arises largely out of the Canadian context in a world that is hungry for natural resources. However, as I have argued, there is a close relationship between protection of the environment and economic growth. It is not only our natural resources that are fragile but also our economy, which can crumble in the face of exploitation and mismanagement. The impacts of our decisions, if they do not protect our forests, ecosystems, and wildlife, will have not only local and national consequences, but also global ramifications for generations yet unborn.

REFERENCES

Abele, F., and J. Friesen, eds. 1991. *Aboriginal Resource Use in Canada: Historical and Legal Aspects.* Winnipeg: University of Manitoba Press.

Abele, F., and D. Stasiulis. 1989. "Canada as a White Settler Colony: What about Natives and Immigrants?" In W. Clement and G. Willams, eds., *The New Canadian Political Economy.* Kingston: McGill–Queen's University Press, 240–76.

Asch, M. 1984. *Home and Native Land: Aboriginal Rights and the Canadian Constitution.* Vancouver: University of British Columbia Press. (Originally published by Methuen, Toronto).

Badcock, W.T. 1976. *Who Owns Canada? Aboriginal Title and Canadian Courts.* Ottawa: CASNP.

Berger, Thomas. *1991. A Long and Terrible Shadow: White Values, Native Rights in the Americas, 1492–1992.* Toronto: Douglas and McIntyre.

———. 1985. *Village Journey: Report of the Alaska Native Review Commission.* New York: Hill and Wang.

———. 1981. *Fragile Freedoms.* Toronto: Clarke, Irwin.

———. 1977. *Northern Frontier, Northern Homeland: Report of the Mackenzie Valley Pipeline Inquiry.* Ottawa: Department of Supply and Services Canada.

Berton, P. 1972. *The Last Spike.* Toronto: McClelland and Stewart.

Bray, A. 1990. *Temagami: A Debate on Wilderness.* Toronto: Dundurn Press.

Brody, H. 1991. *The Peoples Land.* Toronto: Douglas and McIntyre.

Brundtland, G.H. 1987. *Our Common Future: The Final Report of the World Commission on Environment and Development.*

Cassidy, F., ed. 1991. *Reaching Just Settlements: Land Claims in British Columbia.* Lantzville, B.C.: Oolichan.

Chamberlin, J.E. 1975. *The Harrowing of Eden: White Attitudes toward Native Americans.* New York: Seabury Press.

Cohen, A. 1991. *A Deal Undone: The Making and Breaking of the Meech Lake Accord.* Toronto: Douglas and McIntyre.

Delgamuukw v. British Columbia. 1991. B.C.J. no. 525. Smithers Registry no. 0843.

Duff, W. 1965. *The Indian History of British Columbia.* Vol. 1, *The Impact of the White Man.* Victoria: Queen's Printer.

Fleming, T., ed. 1985. *The New Criminologies in Canada: State, Crime and Control.* Toronto: Oxford University Press.

———, (with L. Visano). 1983. *Deviant Designations: Crime, Law and Deviance in Canada*. Toronto: Butterworths.

Foucault, M. 1977. *Discipline and Punish*. New York: Pantheon.

Friederes, J.S. 1983. *Native People in Canada: Contemporary Conflicts*. Scarborough, Ont.: Prentice-Hall.

Havemann, P., et al. 1985. *Law and Order for Canada's Indigenous People*. Regina: Prairie Justice Research, University of Regina.

The Indian Act. Revised Statutes of Canada, 1970, Vol. IV, Chapters 1–6.

Krotz, L. 1992. *Indian Country: Inside Another Canada*. Toronto: McClelland & Stewart.

Laxer, G. 1989. *Open for Business: The Roots of Foreign Ownership in Canada*. Toronto: Oxford University Press.

Little Bear, L., and M. Boldt, eds. 1988. *Governments in Conflict? Provinces and Indian Nations in Canada*. Toronto: University of Toronto Press.

MacLaine, C., and M. Baxendale. 1990. *This Land Is Our Land: The Mohawk Revolt at Oka*. Toronto: Optimum.

Mandel, M. 1996. "The Dialectics of Constitutional Repression." In T. O'Reilly-Fleming, ed., *Post-Critical Criminology*. Scarborough, Ont.: Prentice-Hall, 252–314.

Miliband, R. 1969. *The State in Capitalist Society*. London: Wiedenfeld and Nicholson.

Miller, J.R. 1991. *Sweet Promises: A Reader in Indian–White Relations*. Toronto: University of Toronto Press.

O'Connor, J. 1973. *The Fiscal Crisis of the State*. New York: St. Martin's.

O'Reilly-Fleming, T. 1994. "The Mohawk–Canada Crisis: Native Peoples, Criminalization and the Justice System." In D. Baker, ed., *Reading Racism and the Criminal Justice System*. Toronto: Canadian Scholars' Press, 233–42.

Ornstein, T. 1973. *The First Peoples in Quebec*. Montreal: Thunderbird Press.

Ponting, J., ed. 1986. *Arduous Journey: Canadian Indians and Decolonization*. Toronto: McClelland & Stewart.

Ratner, R.S. 1990. *Child Welfare Services for Urban Native Indians*. Report to the United Native Nations. May.

Reid, A. 1992. Poll. Winnipeg, Man.

Richardson, B. 1976. *Strangers Devour the Land*. Douglas and McIntyre.

———, ed. 1989. *Drum Beat: Anger and Renewal in Indian Country*. Toronto: Summerhill Press, The Assembly of First Nations.

Shorten, J. 1991. *Without Reserve*. Edmonton: NeWest.

Tennant, P. 1991. *Aboriginal Peoples and Politics: The Indian Land Question in British Columbia, 1849–1989*. Vancouver: University of British Columbia Press.

Turk, A. 1985. "Law, Conflict and Disorder: From Theorizing toward Theories." In T. Fleming, ed., *The New Criminologies in Canada: State, Crime and Control*, 254–70.

Vecsey, C., and R. Venables, eds. 1980. *American Indian Environments: Ecological Issues in Native American History*. New York: Syracuse University Press.

Weaver, S. 1981. *Making Canadian Indian Policy: The Hidden Agenda, 1968–1970*. Toronto: University of Toronto Press.

York, G. 1990. *The Dispossessed: Life and Death in Native Canada*. London: Vintage.

———, and L. Pindera. 1991. *People of the Pines: The Warriors and the Legacy of Oka*. Toronto: Little, Brown.

QUESTIONS FOR DISCUSSION

1. What are the views of aboriginal people on the issue of land claims versus that of the courts?

2. Why have governments been reluctant to acknowledge native land claims?

3. What were the issues in Delgamuukw from the viewpoint of the various participants?

4. Do you think that Clayoquot Sound should be preserved as it is, or should natives be free to sell parts of the rain forest?

5. What would you consider a fair way to settle native land claims in the future?

6. What kinds of damage does clearcutting do to the environment?

Is Sustainable Forestry Community Forestry? A British Columbia Perspective

Duncan Taylor

Department of Environmental Studies
University of Victoria

AN INDUSTRY IN CRISIS

Without question, Canada possesses one of the world's largest forest industries. With some 453 million hectares of forestland, it has about 10 percent of the earth's commercially productive forests and approximately 25 percent of the international forest market. Within Canada, about half of the total volume of timber comes from British Columbia and one-third of Canada's direct forest jobs. In 1990, for example, there were about 85 000 direct industry jobs accounting for some $3 billion a year in wages. Indeed, forestry is responsible for about one-quarter of the province's gross domestic product (GDP) (Travers, 1990).

Yet by the early 1990s, the provincial forest economy was facing a serious crisis. Jobs were rapidly disappearing due to a high Canadian dollar, a North American economic recession, and a rapidly diminishing supply of old-growth timber. Consequently, in an effort to remain globally competitive, vast quantities of timber were sold abroad at what critics claim remains well below the real market value. In turn, B.C. forest companies have tried to cut costs by shutting down unprofitable mills and by increased mechanization—both of which have resulted in a reduced labour force. For example, in 1950, 1000 cubic metres of timber generated two jobs; in 1989, it generated one. Indeed, employment in the B.C. timber industry has been dropping at a rate of approximately 2000 jobs a year. By comparison, in 1984, Switzerland was able to generate 11 times the number of jobs per thousand cubic metres of timber; New Zealand, five times the number; and the United States, 3.5 times the number (Hammond, 1991a: 78–80).

These disparities continue despite dramatic increases in harvest levels. Since 1911, British Columbia has logged some 2.5 billion cubic metres of wood, but half of this has been cut down since 1977. The annual cut was 74.3 million cubic metres on Crown forestland, well above the provincial government's own estimated long-run sustained yield target of 59 million cubic metres a year (Travers, 1992: 39). This figure jumps to 89 million cubic metres if timber harvested on private lands is also taken into account. Moreover, this figure is only the wood that has been accounted for or "scaled." It does not cover the vast amounts of timber damaged during harvesting and then left on the forest floor, for which government records do not exist.

In 1992, a federal report on the state of the environment noted that on the coast of British Columbia, which is the most productive timber area, only 16 years of accessible old growth remained at current industry cutting rates (Environment Canada, 1992). Industry representatives were quick to deny this figure, claiming that Environment Canada obtained much of its data from environmental groups such as the Sierra Club of Western Canada. However, the

---

ongoing removal of the ancient temperate rain forests and the current attempt to replace them by industrial tree farms has intensified the growing conflict among competing interest groups: environmentalists, loggers, forest companies, and indigenous people. Consequently, for an increasing number of British Columbians and other Canadians, the current forest practices are both environmentally and socially unsustainable.

ENVIRONMENTALLY UNSUSTAINABLE

The forest industry has been treating forestry as a single-sector industry and has focused almost exclusively on economic profits to the detriment and virtual exclusion of other forest values, including the myriad forest-dependent species and the ecological processes that created the trees.

SOCIALLY UNSUSTAINABLE

Many of British Columbia's 103 forestry-dependent communities have been subjected to the cycles of boom and bust common to single-industry towns; as well, increasing mechanization of mills and equipment has led in recent years to massive job layoffs.

CRITICISMS AND CONFLICTS: HISTORICAL RELATIONSHIPS IN FORESTRY

These criticisms of B.C.'s forest industry are not new. Since 1970 the system of forest management has been under intense fire from several directions. The state agencies and forest corporations that control the province's forests have faced stiff criticism from environmentalists protesting against destruction of wilderness, from native Indians asserting their rights over traditional territory, and from forest industry workers concerned about the impacts of government and company policies, on jobs. Although these critics share a number of complaints, they have not generally presented a harmonious front. Some of the most bitter conflicts seen in the province in recent years have pitted forest industry workers against environmentalists or native–environmentalist coalitions. Intensely committed advocates of wilderness preservation have waged a long series of vigorous anti-logging campaigns, linking up in a number of instances with native communities determined to assert control over traditional territories. In response to these and other pressures, many forest industry workers and their families have joined pro-logging "share" groups. These aggressively promote the view that the industry is jeopardized and its employees belittled by urban environmentalists disconnected from the economic realities of the province. Not surprisingly, with individuals' feelings of identity and belonging at stake, emotions run high. A number of local forest land use conflicts have led to blockades, and a few have produced acts or threats of physical violence.

THE CASE FOR COMMUNITY FORESTRY

By their very nature, forestry issues involve the need to somehow reconcile conflicts arising from the interaction of human social systems with biophysical systems. Throughout Canada, these conflicts have tended to pit environmentalists against forestry workers or those who argue for the need to "preserve" intact ecological systems against those who argue for economic stability and job protection. For both camps, the *status quo* is not the way of the future. In the pages ahead, we shall examine one set of reform proposals that appears to have some potential to bring together those opposed to "business as usual" management of the forests. This is the idea that forest management responsibility should be devolved to local communities. The decentralist, community forest board model has been embraced by groups and individuals from the native Indian, forest industry worker, and environmentalist camps. Endorsements have come from individuals as disparate as Paul George, one of the founders of the province's largest wilderness preservation group, and Patrick Armstrong, a leading spokesperson for the share group movement (Drushka and Doyle, 1991: 60). Indeed, a number of groups and individuals have advanced detailed community control proposals. These proposals comprise an impressive body of grassroots democratic theory. It will be argued, however, that they leave some important questions unanswered.

The focus of this chapter is British Columbia, Canada's largest forestry province. And while this province has unique forms of forest tenure system and political institutions, the problems its communities are faced with have much in common with those of other forest-based communites throughout Canada. Indeed, the growing desire of communities to control their own destinies crosses provincial borders. For example, the planned conversion of much of Alberta's boreal forest to tree plantations has already resulted in court challenges and demonstrations by First Nations people whose communities have historically depended on the forests for their game, fish, berries, herbs, and spiritual values. In turn, Ontario has also been the focus of major confrontations. Not only have there been environmental demonstrations over the liquidation of one of Canada's last remaining old-growth red and white pine forests in the Temagami region, but throughout Northern Ontario communities have felt the economic hardships of pulp mill closures with the depletion of accessible mature conifers (Cooperman, 1993: 57–59). As such, the experiment for community forestry, now being tried in British Columbia, deserves to be studied on a wider geographical basis.

As already noted, dissatisfaction with forest management performance has intensified significantly in recent years. Much of the opposition has focused on adverse environmental impacts. A diverse assortment of groups concerned with wilderness preservation and environmentally sensitive forest practices have coalesced to challenge everything from clearcut logging to the stumpage system that governs the pricing of Crown timber (Wilson, 1990). The environmental movement has established important alliances with native Indians determined to resist further liquidation of old growth on territory within land claim areas. Native people have played a key role in struggles for preservation of areas such as South Moresby, the Stein valley, and Clayoquot Sound (May 1990; Broadhead, 1989; M'Gonigle and Wickwire, 1988), and have begun to challenge decisions of tenure holders and the Ministry of Forests (MOF) in a number of other parts of the province. More recently, in an attempt to pressure the British Columbia government to change current forestry practices, provincial environmental groups working with their counterparts in the United States and Europe have lobbied for an end to clearcut logging and a boycott of B.C. forest products. For example, in January 1993 a full-page ad in *The New York Times* called for a halt to old-growth logging in Clayoquot Sound on the west coast of Vancouver Island. One year later, the campaign against clearcutting in B.C. had been taken across Europe by members of Greenpeace. Indeed, they were successful in persuading a number of publishers to look to "clearcut-free" sources of pulp.

Dissatisfaction with industry–MOF stewardship has also increased among the industry's workforce. Worker disenchantment intensified as it became apparent that the end of the early 1980s recession would not bring a return to prerecession employment levels. Instead, the industry continued to march through a traumatic shakeout, closing numerous mills deemed obsolete while instituting modernization and "rationalization" strategies at other mills and operations. These changes sharply reduced the job benefits of each cubic metre of wood harvested (Travers, 1991: 37), meaning that despite increasing the harvest, the industry slashed its workforce by 12 000 direct jobs between the peak employment years of 1979 and 1989 (Peel, 1991: 5). IWA coastal employment levels in 1990 stood at about 50 percent of 1980 levels (Wood, 1990: 11). The impacts of these cuts have naturally been felt most strongly in the dozens of communities outside the Vancouver–Victoria area that rely on the forest industry as the primary employer. For example, Port Alberni lost over 2000 direct jobs during the 1980s and, according to one analysis of its prospects, would likely lose over 1300 more in the early 1990s (Wood, 1990: 1). In turn, a recent study prepared for the federal government, entitled *Canada's Forest Industry: A Strategy for Growth*, recommends laying off some 20 000 B.C. forest employees to foster global competitiveness.

Some workers accept industry arguments that "environmental withdrawals" from the forest land base have been a major cause of job loss. A more balanced attribution of blame would cite factors such as increased competition from areas of the world enjoying lower labour costs and faster growing timber, competition-driven attempts to lower production costs through shutdowns and plant modernization, and an apparent shift in investment emphasis from the (relatively) labour intensive solid wood sector to the more capital intensive pulp sector (IWA–Canada, 1990; Truck Loggers Association, 1990 and 1990a; Marchak, 1988 and 1991).

These problems and symptoms naturally lead a growing number of British Columbians to question whether the province's forest economy is either environmentally or socially sustainable. Gloomy predictions about the industry's future abound. As a result, groups dissatisfied with management of the province's forests have explored a variety of policy alternatives. Most reform proposals leave control in the hands of the ministry–industry axis, offering everything from suggestions for tenure system change to recommendations regarding the "rules of the game" that guide the conduct of logging. On a more radical plane, some critics have challenged the entire structure of centralized control, contending that the changes necessary will not be achieved unless a significant amount of power to determine forest use is transferred to the community level.

In the next section, this decentralist vision will be introduced by looking at how a number of proposals have contributed to a model of community forest board control. Following this, there will be a critical examination of this model and some speculation about the solidity of the worker–native–environmentalist alliances that have coalesced in its support. In developing this commentary the authors drew upon observations offered by about 60 community leaders from the Alberni and Cowichan areas of Vancouver Island who were interviewed in the summer of 1991.

THE COMMUNITY FOREST BOARD MODEL

Those dedicated to decentralization of forest management authority have produced an extensive literature over the past two decades. The seminal work is the oft-cited report of the Slocan Valley Community Forest Management Project. Presented in 1975, it has remained a powerful manifesto for community control. Its influence can be seen in later proposals from individuals and organizations like Herb Hammond, Michael M'Gonigle, the Tin Wis Coalition, and the Village of Hazelton. All these proposals flow from the grass roots, from individuals intensely involved with the management of forests near their communities. All reflect a current of citizen resistance to precepts of globalism that imply that it is not possible or reasonable for communities to control the way their human and natural resources are used by international capital. All contend that local citizens can do a better job of promoting economic and environmental health than corporate and state decision-makers located far from the resources they are managing.

Like most of the other proposals considered here, the Slocan plan for devolution is set in the context of a much broader blueprint for forest policy reform. After diagnosing the local forest economy as afflicted by unsustainable rates of cut, excessive waste, and too little investment in silviculture, it developed a comprehensive alternative vision. Among other things, it called for a system of intensively managed rural woodlots, greater use of selective logging, reduced cuts based on ecologically sound plans for each major watershed, and the development of new milling capacity to enhance the amount of value added at local manufacturing facilities. At the centre of this blueprint was a proposal that management authority for the area's natural resources should be transferred to a resource committee made up of six members elected by the local community, and six representatives of provincial government agencies.

In turn, the Tin Wis Coalition is an alliance of native, labour, and environmental organizations. Its model of community control is set out in a detailed draft Forest Stewardship Act (Tin Wis Coalition, 1991). The draft legislation leaves the provincial Ministry of Forests and other ministries with important functions and seems to assume considerable continuity in the tenure system. But the command structure governing provincial agencies and licensees would be significantly altered. The new regime would involve a provincial Forest Resources Board along with Community Forest Resources Boards in each of the forest districts. The provincial board would set forest practices minimum standards and would serve as the appellate body where community board decisions were contested. The local boards would assume responsibility for a range of important regional planning and management tasks, including forest use zoning, the supervision of licensees, the preparation of management plans, and the approval of the allowable annual cut recommended by the province's Chief Forester. Each of the community boards would consist of 13 members, with seven elected and six appointed by cabinet. The provincial Forest Resources Board would also have 13 members, with community boards to elect six regional representatives and cabinet to appoint the remainder.

The Village of Hazelton's "Framework for Watershed Stewardship" was released in 1991 following vetting of an earlier draft by environmental groups, industry organizations, and local government authorities. It proposes that stewardship of natural resources be devolved to "Watershed Authorities." The provincial government and each authority would negotiate a devolution contract establishing the spectrum of sustainable management practices open to the local managers. Local planning decisions would be subject to provincewide standards designed to promote goals such as biological diversity, forest industry accountability, reduced corporate concentration, increased processing in the local area, and the preservation of biological diversity. Reinvestment in planning and management would be guaranteed by provisions giving the Watershed Authority first call on resource revenues generated in the region. Board members would be "chosen by a combination of election, and appointment by Judges sitting in the local region" (1991: pt. 1.2).

COMMUNITY FOREST BOARD MODEL—DECENTRALIZED DEMOCRACY

What impact would adoption of a decentralized, community forest board model have on the character of B.C. democratic institutions? We begin with a closer examination of how the various proposals would define the community and represent community citizens on the new forest boards.

Most proposals favour using watershed features to define community boundaries. Each of the Watershed Authorities proposed in the Hazelton plan would be responsible for a portion of a large river basin or for a smaller watershed. According to the plan, adoption of this scale would carve out regions such as the Nechako basin, the Queen Charlotte Islands, East Vancouver Island, etc. (1991: pt. 1–2). Hammond (Hammond and Hammond, 1985: 9) proposes that watershed boundaries be the basis for the new units, arguing that "because watersheds link all parts of the forest ecosystem, forest management by watershed units will permit use and protection of all forest values. Watershed management units provide for regionally based decisions which are truly integrated with consideration of the entire ecosystem and the needs of all people in the region." Hammond (1990: 45) also suggests that consideration be given to the boundaries of what used to be a key provincial Forest Service administrative unit, the forest ranger district. The Tin Wis proposal uses current Forest Service boundaries, proposing a Community Forest Board for each of the 43 Forest Districts presently in place.

On the issue of how Community Forest Board members should be selected, the consensus favours a system that would combine election and appointment. In Hammond's (1990: 44) mind the combination method is consistent with the principle that "all forest user groups are represented in an equitable way," and would help to neutralize problems that might appear if the board were entirely elected or appointed: an elected board might "be subject to control by the strongest special interest group," while an appointed one might "be exposed to the risk of patronage appointments." In its justification, the Tin Wis plan (Tin Wis Coalition, 1991: IV–3) adopts a more elitist tone, suggesting that the elected members would represent the grass roots, while "the appointed members will serve as a check to remind the boards of the overall purposes and policy of forest stewardship. Appointments allow knowledgeable and thoughtful people who might not run for elections to serve, and to provide stable longer-term leadership if they do a good job."

The Tin Wis proposal gives the appointment power to the provincial cabinet, while as noted, the Hazelton plan (1991: pt. 1.2) delegates it to the judiciary. The Tin Wis draft (Tin Wis Coalition, 1991: IV–4) adopts the popular notion of the "stakeholder," proposing that the six individuals appointed to each board should represent the following stakeholder categories: (1) First Nations peoples; (2) non-timber-related business persons (tourism operators); (3) timber-related workers; (4) environmentalists and non-commercial forest users; (5) timber-related licensees, forest land owners, independent logging contractors; (6) non-timber-related resource users (guide outfitters, trappers, commercial fishers, etc.).

It is perhaps unfair to nitpick over proposals that are merely formative and conceptual. The parts of the community forest board constitution just considered do, however, raise some troublesome questions.

Initially, there is the question about the demarcation of community boundaries. If real power over the province's forests—for example, power to zone forestland and determine the level of cut—were at stake, could the province's hinterland communities be expected to amicably divide the province into community forest board fiefdoms? This is doubtful. Any exercise in territorial demarcation would likely boil down to a debate about whether boundaries should be ecologically or economically defined. Some would argue for boundaries based on watersheds or other geographical features, contending that only those living within the area so defined should be granted the rights of community citizens. Others would argue that people living outside the watershed area who depend economically on its resources should also be entitled to be treated as part of the community. A version of this debate has been played out over the past few years in discussions over membership on two advisory bodies struck to develop sustainable development plans for the Clayoquot Sound area on the west side of Vancouver Island (Darling, 1991). In this case the study area was defined in terms of the natural boundaries of the area under examination. But in putting together the study teams, the provincial government rejected the argument that decisions about the area should be made only by people in the communities encompassed by these boundaries (Tofino and some Indian communities), choosing instead to also represent two "outside" communities that are economically dependent on the forests of Clayoquot Sound (Port Alberni and Ucluelet). This case illustrates the slippery slopes that would confront those trying to draw forest board boundaries. If Port Alberni were entitled to representation on the Clayoquot Sound board would it not also be entitled to be on boards governing numerous other areas within the broad region from which Port Alberni mills draw wood fibre? If communities like Port Alberni could claim a right to representation on the forest boards of areas in their hinterlands, could the same claim not then be made by communities further "downstream" in the chain of economic dependence?

The problems and uncertainties foreseen by many of those interviewed are summed up by a Tofino resident who has been intensively involved in the Clayoquot Sound experience.

> I think part of what we're having trouble with here in Clayoquot Sound is that the loggers don't live here. The loggers may live in Ucluelet, some of them live in Port Alberni.... So suddenly it's a pulpmill worker in Port Alberni that I have to be thinking about and that's hard. That's been hard from the start and in fact right at the beginning we said "Forget it, we're not going to worry about a pulpmill worker in Port Alberni, that's too far

away basically for it to be considered part of our community, part of the community of decisions." But there really is an interdependency that has to be recognized so we do have to give some thought to those jobs far away. But it has made it harder, it has meant that we're not working just at that community level, it's not me sitting down with my local logging community member and trying to sort this out. It's trying to deal with people that I don't know.

It is easy enough to see the dilemmas that would quickly become apparent. Boards based on strict ecological boundaries might find it difficult to establish the degree of broader legitimacy necessary to effectively design and execute forest use decisions. But any attempt to encompass wider areas of economic interdependency would result in sprawling areas, with the "communities" so defined unlikely to be characterized by (or capable of fostering) the kind of responsibility for the "place" so integral to the philosophy of community control advanced by Hammond and others.

Turning to another part of what has emerged as the consensus community forest board constitution, we also have concerns about proposals that representation be granted to certain "stakeholder" groups. Not enough consideration has been given to the question of which interests deserve to be "privileged" with the stakeholder designation. This oversight may indicate a natural tendency on the part of those drafting proposals to avoid difficult questions. Or it may reflect the belief that questions about the designation and weighting of different interests would be rendered irrelevant by the adoption of a "consensual" approach to community decisions. That is, some proposals imply that if "everyone" can be brought to the table, then it should be possible to locate a community consensus.

Just as it may be naive to assume that community forest boards would always be able to rely on consensual decision-making, perhaps it is unrealistic to believe that it would be possible to avoid difficult questions about the details of the appointment process. Which interests should be designated as stakeholders? How much weight should be given to different groups? Who should do the appointing? If the boards did possess important forest management powers then the political assumptions implicit in positions on questions like these would soon become very explicit. Interviews (Hutcheson and Maki, 1992: 69–74) indicate that a range of conflicting definitions of stakeholder would quickly surface. In many areas the politics surrounding these important constitutional decisions could be expected to be nasty enough to undercut the prospects of the board ever achieving legitimacy.

Leaving these concerns aside, we can consider whether a community forest board system would, overall, represent a more democratic way of managing the province's forests. The answer must be a qualified yes. Unquestionably a community forest board scheme would significantly reverse a situation in which, in the words of the Slocan report (1975: 5–1), "local people are rarely included in the resource policy decision making processes, nor are they considered in the policies which manipulate our environment, jobs, and quality of life." Ordinary people would have more say in important forest policy decisions. The community forest board would provide a site for a more discursive democracy, one likely to promote fuller discussion of how "development" should be defined and pursued. As a result, ordinary people would have much greater opportunities to learn about and control the forces influencing their futures.

Adoption of the forest board model would, however, involve some redistribution of power from metropolitan to hinterland communities. Not all of the province's ordinary citizens would gain a greater say. Just how much the voice of citizens of the Vancouver–Victoria area would be reduced would depend on how much power would be left with provincial authorities. There is some vagueness in the proposals on this point, but all make it quite clear that decisions of the local boards would be subject to provincewide standards established in legislation and enforced either by the provincial government or by an agency like the Tin Wis Coalition's provincial forest board. All seem to agree with M'Gonigle's notion of the double veto, that is, with a system that would allow residents of the metropolitan area to continue influencing forest policy through their leverage on the provincial government.

EVALUATING THE ARGUMENTS FOR COMMUNITY CONTROL

Community empowerment is the prerequisite to all other changes. The existing pattern of resource over-exploitation has evolved and been maintained because local communities have had virtually no control over their local resource base. (Michael M'Gonigle, 1987:4)

Given the forces that have beset B.C.'s forest economy in the last decades, it is not surprising that there is still a widespread perception that resource-dependent communities have very little influence over the decisions that most affect them. Local people mention that they are rarely consulted about policies, and indicate that when they are invited to participate in a public forum or task force, the major decisions usually end up being made elsewhere. As one Tofino resident put it:

[There is] the sense that whatever you say right now to the Forest Ministry, it is completely at their discretion as to what they do with it. And there is a definite sense from people who've been saying stuff to the forest industry for years that nothing has changed, and that there's got to be a better way—what is the point. You're saying the same thing year after year to these various planning processes and no changes are happening. (Hutcheson and Maki, 1992: 27)

Indeed, despite an increasing number of opportunities for public participation in the forest policy process, there remains a deep sense of scepticism as to their overall value. This scepticism has fuelled arguments for a greater community control over the resource base. Increasingly, we hear the argument that a "top down" approach should be rejected in favour of approaches that "empower" local communities. As a member of the Lake Cowichan community remarks:

I think it has to come from the local people. It has to come from the bottom up. I have never seen anything really work that's been somebody in Victoria or Ottawa saying "this is the way it should be" because something happens to it between the time it gets from there to here. Well generally it's disappeared. It has to be the will of the local people. (Hutcheson and Maki, 1992: 27)

ARGUMENTS FOR COMMUNITY CONTROL

Arguments for community control are interrelated but they fall into several categories:

1.   Community dependence on exports of a single resource leaves the local economy vulnerable to external market variations. Long-term stability requires diversification and investment in the local economy. Local residents are best able to devise and implement imaginative and effective development strategies. Moreover, greater community control of local forests would enable those people who are most knowledgeable about their own area to have a meaningful impact on the decisions that most affect them. As one Lake Cowichan resident noted:

[A] lot of times you know those local people have a lot more knowledge of what's going on than that logging company ... than the guy who's sitting up in the 23rd floor of the Bentall building in Vancouver who happens to be vice-president. [The local person] knows where the waste is ... because he's working with it. (Hutcheson and Maki, 1992: 30)

A closely related argument is that the community forest board form of management would be more likely to be sympathetic to entrepreneurial small businesses, and that these are often better at adapting to changing and specialized market requirements than are large organizations (M'Gonigle, 1986).

2. Outside control of the local resource base often results in surplus revenues being redirected elsewhere. Companies tend to be reluctant to purchase from local suppliers, invest in local manufacturing, and locate management and research facilities in the community. It is argued that a community forest board structures would keep a larger share of revenues within the region. Revenues from timber could be used to offset taxes and provide funding for local social, business, and recreational projects. Wages now drained off by outside bureaucracies would be more apt to stay within the community, thus providing for a range of indirect benefits.

3. Community forest boards can best protect the wide range of forest economic and environmental values. For example, community-based enterprises are more apt to be sensitive to the protection of water supplies, fish and wildlife habitat, and esthetic values. They are also more likely to enhance opportunities for tourist and recreational enterprises. Moreover, it is argued that the community board would be better placed to deter waste and encourage production of a wider variety of specialized wood products through intensive management (M'Gonigle, 1986: 182). It would promote "site-specific" management practices and the use of a variety of harvesting procedures consistent with "wholistic," environmentally sustainable forestry (Raphael, 1981; Hammond, 1991).

4. Community boards will be well-positioned to exhort residents to make the changes and sacrifices necessary for social and economic transformations. A shift of responsibility to the community level has the potential to create a real sense of community spirit and solidarity. Locally controlled structures should be more responsive to the changing needs, values, and lifestyles of the local population. Control over one's resources promotes a feeling of greater control of one's life. In turn, when local people are more in control of the decisions that affect their lives, they will be more likely to take care of the local environment. Indeed, the imperative of self-interest should dictate a more responsible approach to the needs of both the community and the environment (Dunster, 1989: 12).

Are the assumptions underlying the arguments for community forest boards realistic? Any discussion here must be very speculative since the performance of any board would be influenced by a host of factors, many of which would be specific to local circumstances and most of which cannot be anticipated from this vantage point. In the long run, the challenge for those managing the province's forests in the years ahead will be to bring about a major transformation in the nature of the province's forest economy. In turn, this is likely to depend on achieving a major transformation of values. The question, then, is whether community forest boards would be able to do a better job (than the current management regime) of guiding the province through this multifaceted transformation. As we have suggested, much would depend on whether community forest boards were able to achieve a high level of political legitimacy.

ALLIANCES WITHIN FOREST POLICY REFORM

We have already alluded to the question of political legitimacy in our discussion of the community forest board constitution. As noted, problems to do with the definition of the community and the selection of members might result in boards whose legitimacy is impaired. Approached differently, the legitimacy problem can be seen as integrally related to the challenge of maintaining alliances among groups that have traditionally espoused conflicting goals, but that have come together in organizations such as the Tin Wis Coalition to support community control.

In a broad sense, questions about the durability of these alliances call into focus the diversity of interests that have come together in support of the concept of sustainable development. Supporters of this concept have tended to cluster around one of two antithetical world views, each with its own set of assumptions about knowledge and values, and its own vision of the proper human–environment relationship. These may be referred to as the Expansionist World View and the Ecological World View—the latter still emerging and not yet fully developed (Taylor, 1992). The former is rooted in the Enlightenment idea of progress through scientific and technological mastery over nature for human ends, and in the Gifford Pinchot model of "wise management" conservation. This position is reflected in mainstream economic theory and in positions favouring the ongoing growth and globalization of commodity markets—in short, in an adherence to "sustainable economic growth." The Ecological World View, on the other hand, stresses "developing environmental sustainability." Rooted in a Counter-Enlightenment and Romantic tradition, it views nature and humans as a systemic web—each of the parts is related to the larger whole and possesses intrinsic and non-utilitarian values, as well as life-support and utilitarian ones. Asserting the need for limits to current forms of human and economic growth, it emphasizes the preservation of biological diversity and wilderness areas.

In the current debates over sustainable development strategies these two positions tend to emerge into stark relief. This tension was clearly evident in the acrimonious debates among environmentalists, IWA, and forest industry representatives on the Clayoquot Sound Sustainable Development Task Force Process. In the end, the task force was unable to develop a consensus-based negotiation process and failed. The parties resorted to traditional value perspectives and positional bargaining—"trees versus jobs." Environmentalists accused the process of being hampered from the outset by a forestry "log and talk" agenda imposed by the province (Darling, 1991). We have to question whether community forest boards in other parts of the province would have any more success in bringing about a productive working relationship between local representatives of the two world views.

As noted earlier, Michael M'Gonigle and other members of the environmental community have begun to stress the need for larger regional environmental standards and legislation. In part, this is a response to what is regarded as a lack of meaningful provincial forestry and environmental regulations. As we saw, it also reflects a concern to retain for outsiders a position that would allow some control over the kind of resource development policies pursued by community boards. But inasmuch as it represents a reaction to logger antipathy to "outside" interference by urban environmentalists, this latter point underscores an ongoing weakness in the mainstream environmentalist position. North American environmental groups may be criticized for failing to assess the socioeconomic and political dimensions of wilderness and resource issues, and consider the extent to which environmental degradation is predicated on existing political and economic structures (Thrupp, 1989). (Such criticisms are currently being directed at environmentalists by people in various parts of the world who feel that they have lost control over their futures.)

We would argue that the long-term durability and transformative potential of worker–environmentalist alliances will depend on whether environmentalists are willing to develop and act upon a broader critique of structural and social equities. Without a proper critique of existing socioeconomic structures and strong advocacy on behalf of potentially viable alternatives for the members of resource-dependent communities, the environmental movement will remain an easy target for those whose interests are tied to the status quo. Indeed, the rise of anti-environmentalist "community" coalitions under the banner of "share" or "wise use" groups underscores the way in which the environmental position can be set in opposition to the public's need for economic and social stability (Emery, 1991). Given the problems environmentalists have had in linking their goals to the goal of a healthy and fair economy, it is perhaps not surprising that, according to public opinion polls, support for environmental protection fell as Canada entered the early-1990s recession.

What has often been ignored by environmental organizations is the centrality that social justice and equity issues play in the Brundtland Report's interpretation of strategies for sustainable development. The report reminds us that, in the long run, the ability of community forest boards to preside successfully over the transformation of local forest economies may very well depend on the extent to which they can deal with such issues:

> Physical sustainability cannot be secured unless development policies pay attention to such considerations as changes in access to resources and in the distribution of costs and benefits. Even the narrow notion of physical sustainability implies a concern for social equity between generations, a concern that must logically be extended to equity within each generation. (43)

And again:

> New approaches must involve programmes of social development, particularly to improve the position of women in society, to protect vulnerable groups, and to promote local participation in decision making. (38)

These concerns were recently brought to the fore by the British Columbia Round Table on the Environment and the Economy. It noted that "achieving social equity, and therefore social sustainability, means having access to: the decision-making processes affecting the sustainable community; equal opportunities for education and training; adequate recreational opportunities, health care, social support services, and housing; a quality of environment; and an opportunity to earn a livelihood" (British Columbia Round Table on the Environment and the Economy, 1991: 7).

This statement underscores a growing recognition that the environmental, socioeconomic, and political dimensions must all be accounted for in discussions of strategies for community survival and environmental protection (Prince, 1992). Moreover, it raises the need for debate over the extent to which current trends toward a global liberal trade policy and a North American economic market fly in the face of the ability of resource communities to maintain themselves.

Such concerns were addressed at the Tin Wis conferences in Tofino in 1989 and Port Alberni in 1990. What is perhaps most significant in the Tin Wis position is a recognition that any meaningful pursuit of environmental sustainability must be linked to an analysis of current corporate control and political–economic decision-making. As one writer notes: "While the coalition has been sympathetic to those who work to immediately stop environmental destruction, the focus of Tin Wis and other similar groups has been not to act to protect various aspects of the environment, but to take part in the ecological project of creating fundamental cultural, economic, and political change that will sustain the natural world" (Cholette, 1991–92: 12).

THE TRANSFORMATION OF FOREST MANAGEMENT

In the long run, the challenge of trying to guide the province through a transition from a first-growth forest economy to a sustainable second-growth one would no doubt prove to be a daunting one for community forest boards. The arguments on their behalf do, however, point to some compelling reasons why boards would be well-placed and well-constituted to develop transformation policies that were imaginative, effective, and sensitive to community needs. But obviously the challenge will be to create alternatives that are both economically and environmentally viable. Moreover, success will depend on an ability to initiate and sustain the necessary transformations. Boards would need to appeal to the community's long-term "enlightened self-interest" and a common set of concerns in order to maintain the support of disparate groups and individuals.

In the short term, community forest boards would have to confront a number of immediate problems. If most analysts of the province's forest industry are correct, whoever is responsible for allocating and managing the province's forests in the decades to come will be presiding over a declining industry. Faced with increasing numbers of unemployed workers, community forest boards would likely be under considerable pressure to develop retraining and economic diversification schemes as well as programs to rebuild the forest base. A transfer of revenue gathering power to the local level might put some boards in a strong position to finance such transformation policies. But what about boards that would inherit resource bases so decimated that they would be incapable of producing the revenues needed to fund the rebuilding job? Where would they get the money needed to retrain workers, support those forced into early retirement, build a sustainable and competitive second-growth industry, and subsidize new, nonextractive enterprises? We suspect that, in the short term, boards in many parts of the province would require infusions of provincial and/or federal money. Such transfers might well be seen as long overdue and perfectly justifiable given the wealth that has been drained out of the province's hinterland with liquidation of old-growth forests. But that point aside, forest communities would have to compete with an increasing demand from other publicly funded services, such as schools and hospitals, for fewer and fewer dollars. And they would have to do so at a time of increasing worries about the size of government debts and deficits. In an era of fiscal restraint Canadians may not be willing to put their finances into community social and environmental concerns.

SENSITIVE FOREST PRACTICES: PROPOSALS FOR CHANGE

The proposals examined in this paper reflect strong currents of grass roots support for democratization of political–economic structures and strong doubts about the economic policy agenda of the last decade. As noted, these proposals also reflect a healthy degree of citizen resistance to the notion that, in the era of economic globalism, it is not legitimate or possible for communities to control the way their natural and human resources are used by transnational corporations. Whether or not these proposals lead to radical political restructuring, they have markedly enriched the debate over the province's future. Indeed, they raise important questions for the future role of resource-based communities, not only in British Columbia, but throughout Canada. They have introduced into the arena of public discourse important challenges to practices and assumptions that have come to be taken for granted. They have expanded the debate over impacts on the environment to include arguments about social equity and the meaning of real democratic health.

REFERENCES

B.C. Forest Resources Commission. 1991. *The Future of Our Forests.* Victoria: Forest Resources Commission.

B.C. Ministry of Forests. 1984. *Forest and Range Resource Analysis.* Victoria.

B.C. Ministry of Forests and Lands. *Annual Report,* 1986–87. Victoria.

British Columbia Round Table on the Environment and the Economy. 1991. "Sustainable Communities." Victoria: B.C. Round Table on the Environment and the Economy.

British Columbia Round Table on the Environment and the Economy. 1992. "Towards a Strategy for Sustainability." Victoria: B.C. Round Table on the Environment and the Economy.

Broadhead, John. 1989. "The All Alone Stone Manifesto." In Monte Hummel, gen. ed., *Endangered Spaces: The Future for Canada's Wilderness.* Toronto: Key Porter.

Bulkley Valley Community Resources Board. 1992. "Agreement." *Forest Planning Canada* 8(1): 7–10.

Cholette, Kathy. 1991–1992. "Tin Wis: An Ecological Project." *The New Catalyst* 21.

Cooperman, Jim. 1993. "Cutting Down Canada." *Clearcut: The Tragedy of Industrial Forestry.* San Francisco: Sierra Club Books and Earth Island Pres.

Darling, Craig R. 1991. *In Search of Consensus: An Evaluation of the Clayoquot Sound Sustainable Development Task Force Process.* Victoria: UVIC Centre for Dispute Resolution.

Drushka, Ken. 1985. *Stumped: The Forest Industry in Transition.* Vancouver: Douglas and McIntyre.

———. 1987. "B.C.'s Forests: Condition Critical." *The Truck Logger,* Dec. 1986/Jan. 1987: 11+.

———. 1990. "The New Forestry: A Middle Ground in the Debate over the Region's Forests?" *The New Pacific* 4: 7–24.

Drushka, Ken, and John Doyle. 1991. "Defenders of the Faith." *The Truck Logger,* Dec./Jan.: 52–60.

Dunster, Julian. 1989. "Concepts Underlying a Community Forest." *Forest Planning Canada* 5(6).

Emery, Claude. 1991. *Share Groups in British Columbia.* Ottawa: Political and Social Affairs Division, Research Branch, Library of Parliament.

Environment Canada. 1991. *The State of Canada's Environment.* Ottawa: Minister of Supply and Services.

———. 1992. *State of the Environment Report.* Ottawa: Minister of Supply and Services.

Forest Resources Commission. 1991. *The Future of Our Forests.* Victoria: Forest Resources Commission.

Hammond, Herb. 1989. *Public Forests or Private Timber Supplies? The Need for Community Control of British Columbia's Forests.* Winlaw, B.C.: Silva Ecosystem Consultants Ltd. (Submission to the B.C. Round Table on the Environment and the Economy).

———. 1990. "Community Control of Forests." *Forest Planning Canada* 6(6): 43–46.

————. 1991. *Wholistic Forest Use*. Winlaw, B.C.: Silva Ecosystem Consultants Ltd. (Submission to the B.C. Round Table on the Environment and the Economy).

————. 1991a. *Seeing the Forest among the Trees—The Case for Wholistic Forest Use*. Vancouver: Polestar Press Ltd.

Hammond, Herb, and Susan Hammond. 1985. "Sustainable Forest Planning and Use." *Forest Planning Canada* 1(4): 8–10.

Hammond, Herb, and Brian Egan. 1989. *Initial Analysis of Forest Use in Clayoquot Sound*. Winlaw, B.C.: Silva Ecosystem Consultants Ltd.

Hutcheson, Sarah, and Tim Maki. 1992. "Bringing 'Community' to Forestry: A Discussion with Community Leaders in the Cowichan Valley and Alberni–Clayoquot Regional Districts." (Unpublished paper for the Sustainable Communities Initiative, University of Victoria).

IWA–Canada, Canadian Paperworkers' Union, and the Pulp, Paper and Woodworkers of Canada. 1990. Brief to the British Columbia Forest Resources Commission.

Loomis, Ruth, with Merv Wilkinson. 1990. *Wildwood: A Forest for the Future*. Gabriola, B.C.: Reflections.

M'Gonigle, Michael. 1986. "From the Ground Up: Lessons from the Stein River Valley." In Warren Magnusson et al., eds., *After Bennett: A New Politics for British Columbia*. In Vancouver: New Star Books: 169–91.

————. 1987. "Local Economies Solve Global Problems." *The New Catalyst*, Spring.

————. 1989–90. "Developing Sustainability: A Native/Environmentalist Prescription for Third-Level Government." *B.C. Studies* no. 84: 65–99.

M'Gonigle, Michael, and Wendy Wickwire. 1988. *Stein: The Way of the River*. Vancouver: Talonbooks.

Maitland, Alice. 1990. "Forest Industry Charter of Rights." *Forest Planning Canada* 6(2): 5–9.

Marchak, M. Patricia. 1991. "For Whom the Tree Falls: Restructuring of the Global Forest Industry." *B.C. Studies* no. 90: 3–24.

————. 1988. "Restructuring of the Forest Industry." *Forest Planning Canada* 4(6): 18–21.

May, Elizabeth. 1990. *Paradise Won: The Struggle for South Moresby*. Toronto: McClelland & Stewart.

Pearse, Peter H. 1976. *Timber Rights and Forest Policy in British Columbia*. Report of the Royal Commission on Forest Resources, 2 vols. Victoria: Queen's Printer.

Peel, Sandy. 1991. "The Future of Our Forest." *Forest Planning Canada* 7(6): 5–7.

Pinkerton, Evelyn W. 1993. "Co-Management Efforts as Social Movements: The Tin Wis Coalition and the Drive for Forest Practices Legislation in British Columbia." *Alternatives: Perspectives on Society, Technology and Environment* 19(3).

Prince, Michael J. 1992. "Sustainable Development: Its Meaning and Implications for Canadian Social Policy." Paper presented at the conference The Path to Brazil '92: Global Issues and the Environment, University of Victoria.

Raphael, Ray. 1981. *Tree Talk: The People and Politics of Timber*. Covelo, Calif.: Island Press.

Slocan Valley Community Forest Management Project. 1975. Final Report.

Sterling Wood Group Inc. 1989. *Forest Management Audit of Tree Farm Licence 46 and Its Predecessors Tree Farm Licences 22 and 27*. Victoria: Sterling Wood Group.

Taylor, D.M. 1992. "Disagreeing on the Basics: Environmental Debates Reflect Competing World Views." *Alternatives: Perspectives on Society, Technology and Environment* 18(3).

―――. 1994. *Off Course: Restoring Balance between Canadian Society and the Environment.* International Development Research Centre, Ottawa.

Thrupp, Lori-Ann. 1989. "Politics of the Sustainable Development Crusade: From Elite Protectionism to Social Justice in Third World Resource Issues." *Energy and Resources Group.* Berkeley: University of California.

Tin Wis Coalition. 1991. *Community Control, Developing Sustainability, Social Solidarity.* Vancouver: Tin Wis Coalition.

Tin Wis Coalition Forestry Working Group. 1991. *Draft Model Legislation, Forest Stewardship Act.* Vancouver: Tin Wis Coalition.

Travers, Ray. 1990. "Economic and Social Benefits from B.C.'s Forests." Notes for a presentation at the Transition to Tomorrow: Community Options Forestry Conference, February 1991, University of Victoria, Victoria, B.C.

―――. 1991. "Comparative Data Charts." *Forest Planning Canada* 7(3): 32–45.

―――. 1992. "History of Logging and Sustained Yield in B.C., 1911–90." *Forest Planning Canada* 8(1): 39–48.

Truck Loggers Association. 1990. *B.C. Forests: A Vision for Tomorrow (An Overview).* Vancouver: TLA.

―――. 1990a. *B.C. Forests: A Vision for Tomorrow.* Working Papers. Vancouver: TLA.

―――. 1990b. *Options for the Forest Resources Commission: Review, Reconsideration, Recommendations.* Vancouver: TLA.

Village of Hazelton. 1991. *Framework for Watershed Management* (formerly the *Forest Industry Charter of Rights*). Hazelton, B.C.: The Corporation of the Village of Hazelton.

Wagner, Bill. 1988. "An Emerging Corporate Nobility? Industrial Concentration of Economic Power on Public Timber Tenures." *Forest Planning Canada* 4(2): 14–19.

Wilson, Jeremy. 1987–88. "Forest Conservation in British Columbia, 1935–85: Reflections on a Barren Political Debate." *B.C. Studies* 76: 3–32.

―――. 1990. "Wilderness Politics in B.C.: The Business Dominated State and the Containment of Environmentalism." In William D. Coleman and Grace Skogstad, eds., *Policy Communities and Public Policy in Canada.* Mississauga, Ont.: Copp Clark.

Wood, Robert S. 1990. *An Analysis of the Forest Industry Employment Situation in Port Alberni.* Report prepared for Douglas Kerly, Provincial Job Protection Commissioner. Victoria: Sterling Wood Group Inc.

World Commission on Environment and Development. 1987. *Our Common Future.* Oxford: Oxford University Press.

Young, Cameron. 1987. "B.C.'s Vanishing Temperate Rainforests." *Forest Planning Canada* 3(6): 12–14.

QUESTIONS FOR DISCUSSION

1. Define sustainability. What factors have affected the economic and the social sustainability of the forestry industry in British Columbia?

2. There are strong arguments on both sides of the forestry debate in British Columbia. Identify the key arguments and decide which you find more persuasive, and why.

3. Evaluate the community forest board model. What factors must be present for the model to work in practice?

4. Discuss the case for and against community control of forestry.

5. How can some of the lessons learned and policies developed in British Columbia be generalized to forestry policy in other parts of the country?

CHAPTER 15

New Directions in Environmental Concern

Melody Hessing

Department of Sociology
Douglas College

CONTEMPORARY PERSPECTIVES ON THE ENVIRONMENT

New directions in environmental concern have developed in response to increased understanding of the complexity of environmental systems, the dependence of human beings on the biophysical environment, and the escalating and negative consequences of our actions on the quality of that environment. These new approaches reflect the increasing number of stakeholders, growing frustration with existing institutional perspectives and strategies, and accelerating social conflict over proposed solutions to contemporary environmental problems. Wilderness protection, energy policy, and forestry practices, for instance, have become increasingly contentious issues not easily resolved by political debate and traditional initiatives. Moreover, the emergence of new technology, the dynamics of demographic increase and mobility, and shifts in political and economic regimes continue to change the context in which we approach environmental issues.

The current development of new perspectives of the environment is a continuation of a process by which humans have explored the universe and their place in it. All human cultures have held perspectives of their physical environments, and these have evolved with the social organization and use of technology. Humans have progressed from hunting–gathering, to agricultural, and more recently, to industrial societies. Each of these ways of life has brought about different relations between people and the natural environment. Nomadic hunter and gathering groups, for instance, were directly dependent on natural environments for their survival. The development of agricultural society brought about greater social complexity as well as an increase in human manipulation and control of the biophysical environment (Harper, 1996, p. 42).

The Industrial Revolution further transformed the relations between humans and the physical environment, and contributed to the formation of activities and attitudes that continue today. Industrial production, enhanced by continuing technological innovation and the emergence of a market-based capitalist economic system, accelerated the impact of humans on the biosphere by increasing the pace and scale of *withdrawals* from the environment, such as the depletion of the fishery, as well as the *additions* to it, such as pollution and toxic wastes (Schnaiberg and Gould, 1994). The industrial culture reflects a perspective of the environment that Catton and Dunlap have labelled the "human exemptionalism paradigm" (1980). According to this model, humans perceive themselves as unique among species because their cultural capacity (including their ideas, values, and technology) allows them to use and to harness their biophysical environments.

In the industrial era this cultural capacity reflects two primary themes: an anthropocentric, or human-centred, perspective of both human society and natural systems, and the belief in the desirability and utility of market-based economic systems. These are reflected in a *dominant social paradigm* that has the following characteristics:

1. The environment is an open-ended resource system for human use.
2. Nature is valued only in market terms, and devalued for its own sake.
3. Growth, consumption, and the accumulation of wealth are valued.
4. There are no real limits to growth.
5. Science and technology deal effectively with social and environmental problems. (adapted from Harper, 1996, p. 323)

While concern has been increasingly directed to the conservation of natural systems, this has taken place within the parameters of this paradigm. The development of "resource management" policies at the turn of the century reflects recognition of the rapid depletion of natural resources, and the necessity for stewardship of natural systems through the implementation of these principles. Over the course of the century, resource conservation has grown "beyond concern for a mere husbanding and efficient use of nonrenewable resources to include both environmental quality and renewable resources" (Oelschlaeger, 1991, p. 284). Yet the limitations of mainstream institutional approaches to resource management, and changes in the composition and interplay of ecological and social factors, have led to the generating of alternative approaches.

ENVIRONMENTALISM: ALTERNATIVE APPROACHES

Bramwell traces the growth of "the ecology movement" to the integration of scientific knowledge with changes in esthetic and moral values that have accompanied the development of modern industrial society (1989). The ecological significance of human activity on the integrity of natural ecosystems has been recognized for well over a century (Marsh, 1874). In the late 1800s and early 1900s, conservation movements developed in North America in response to the rapid destruction of forests and wilderness by the lumber industry (Harper, 1996). Yet while conservationists advocated the protection of nature for utilitarian purposes, a preservationist approach increasingly promoted the protection of nature for its own sake, as well as for nonconsumptive human use. Organizations such as the Audubon Society and the Sierra Club over a century ago recognized the importance of preserving biodiversity and protecting wilderness areas from development.

By the second half of the 20th century environmentalism had escalated into a full-fledged social movement, reflecting a diversity of perspectives, concerns, and issues. The climate of economic prosperity and growth in the 1960s, and the early stages of a transition to a service-based economy, provided a material basis from which to focus on noninstrumental, nonproductive issues, although continuing economic expansion created additional environmental problems. Urbanization, the increased scarcity of natural resources, the physical limits of the North American frontier, an increase in outdoor recreation, as well as a climate of social activism, were among the factors that contributed to the development of this new wave of environmentalism.

In addition, scientific evidence pointed to the detrimental health effects of exposure to radiation and toxic chemicals. The publication in 1962 of Rachel Carson's *Silent Spring*, which documented the toxic effects of pesticides, mobilized public concern about pollution, while Paul Ehrlich's *The Population Bomb* (1968) addressed the present and future consequences of overpopulation. Barry Commoner (1971) identified technology and corporate power, ranging from the hazards of nuclear wastes to pollution, as major environmental issues. The mobilization of public support for environmentalism was triggered by international incidents like the Chernobyl and Three Mile Island nuclear accidents, the Bhopal chemical disaster, and the Exxon *Valdez* oil spill. Media reports of these and other events alerted public opinion to the potential severity and long-term impacts of many industrial practices and to the ineffectiveness of regulatory regimes.

From these varied incidents and approaches a new environmental paradigm has emerged, capable of addressing a range of applications or issues. This *new ecological paradigm* emphasizes the embeddedness of human society in natural systems (Catton and Dunlap, 1980, p. 34). This model recognizes the existence of a finite biophysical environment and ecological laws governing natural and social systems. Accordingly, human beings are perceived as interdependent with other species in the biosphere, but exceptional in their cultural capacity to impact this environment.

This new ecological paradigm reflects the emergence of the contemporary environmental movement. Within this movement, different conceptual approaches reflect a variety of ways of explaining the character of the relations between human society and the biosphere. These "environmentalisms" include deep ecology, social and socialist ecology, ecofeminism, and global ecology, as well as an antienvironmental countermovement. These perspectives identify divergent sources of and solutions to environmental problems, some of which seek simply to reform present institutions, while others require more dramatic changes. This chapter will discuss the contributions, the interconnections, and the limitations of these and other approaches.

ENVIRONMENTAL ISSUES, SOCIETY, AND THE BIOSPHERE

DEEP ECOLOGY

Deep ecology attempts to replace the the dominant anthropocentric perspective of our culture with a biocentric or ecocentric approach. The term "deep ecology" was coined in 1972 by the Norwegian philosopher Arne Naess and has been widely disseminated (Naess, 1973; Sessions, 1988). Deep ecology situates humans within the natural environment as one species among others, and thus reflects both our dependence and impact on natural systems. Deep ecology "refers to finding our bearings, to the process of grounding ourselves through fuller experience of our connection to earth" (Devall, 1988, p. 11). Deep ecologists argue that we as human beings must recognize our own connections to natural systems rather than regarding the biosphere as simply a resource for and backdrop to human history.

Deep ecology was inspired by a number of crosscurrents: rapid declines in wilderness and open space; dramatic increases in population; a recognition of the limitations of technological development, science, and rationalism; and the increased North American popularity of Eastern religions. The complexity of ecological explanation and the spiritual character of human relations to other forms of life are reflected in this approach. Deep ecologists adopt a holistic approach to the understanding of human society and natural systems, looking at the interconnections among all systems. In contrast to focusing the viewfinder of our cultural camera on the "people" icon, deep ecologists would refocus attention on the entire content and context of a picture of contemporary society.

The emergence of deep ecology has contributed to the development of numerous strategies designed to reconfigure the relations between humans and the environment. Some deep ecologists look for cultural alternatives to our industrial-era relations with nature, often offering the lifestyles of indigenous peoples as a guideline for our own practices. Others have studied Eastern philosophies, such as Zen Buddhism and Taoism, for ways of integrating human spirituality with nature. The concept of *voluntary simplicity,* introduced by Bill Devall, suggests countering consumerism and workaholism by minimizing material consumption and emphasizing self-sufficiency and an appreciation of nature. Other deep ecologists have stressed the psychological aspects of our connections with nature, emphasizing the potential of interconnectedness and self-realization (Mathews, 1991).

Among the strategies endorsed by deep ecologists are those emphasizing the protection of natural systems as a means of preserving biodiversity and recognizing the significance of wild spaces not only for other species, but for human well-being. A preference for *appropriate technology,* typically low in eco-logical impact and oriented to specific and local needs rather than large-scale use, is also consistent with the deep ecologist concern for environmental protec-tion. In contrast to megaprojects like large-scale hydro generation projects (such as James Bay, the Columbia River, and the Peace River), smaller-scale and "soft," non-fossil-fuel projects are preferred. The use of solar energy, wind gener-ators, and thermal energy, with smaller impacts and costs, are promoted to min-imize impacts on ecological systems.

Deep ecologists are dissatisfied with mainstream political institutions that are large-scaled, bureaucratic, and geared to anthropocentric goals. *Decentralization,* made popular by Shumacher's *Small Is Beautiful* (1973), considers locally based technology appropriate to environmental protection because it is more respon-sive and adaptable to local requirements. Many deep ecologists adopt nonvio-lent strategies for change, such as political protests, and often encourage *direct action,* methods of opposing projects like logging and dam construction through an on-site protest of development activity. *Bioregionalism* integrates an ecological perspective with the rationale for decentralization, arguing that present institu-tions are based on bureaucratic, rather than ecological, or even human, needs. Accordingly, political and economic decisions do not reflect the particular and unique characteristics of an area. For instance, a political riding may include portions of the coastal rain forest as well as an interior arid zone, while the forestry and agricultural policies developed for one may be inappropriate for the other. Decisions regarding the allocation of timber licences, the siting of pulp mills, and the zoning of land would more adequately support and protect local needs if they are made by residents rather than shareholders of a corporation or remote political representatives.

Yet deep ecology is criticized from all sides, attacked for being too dangerous and radical, as well as for being unachievable, idealistic, and naive. As an embodiment of the radical spirit of deep ecology, activism is sometimes decried for its terrorist tendencies, which include the spiking of trees to prevent logging and the Sea Shepherd Society's sinking of whaling vessels. In fact, tactics of activist groups typically range from direct action like the blockade of logging trucks at Clayoquot Sound to political lobbying, research, and public education. Some critics suggest that ecoradicalism fuels the antienvironmental counter-movement by dampening potential public support (Lewis, 1994). For others, however, more radical approaches are necessary to widen the horizons and boundaries of potential change.

Others take issue with the central ideas of deep ecology itself. Some argue that from a perspective of "biospheric egalitarianism" (Lewis, 1994, p. 28) all forms of life would have intrinsic value and humans would be neither greater nor lesser than other species. This would grant humans the same value as snails, burrow-ing worms, or badgers, ignoring the fundamental differences between humans and "others," and ignoring the intellectual and technical capacity of human beings. Deep ecologists also have a Luddite reputation of antitechnology and primitivism for their endorsement of appropriate technology and decentralization (Schnaiberg and Gould, 1994). Furthermore, decentralization's potential reinforcement of existing localized economic and political interests over ecological interests is viewed as a strategic problem by many environmentalists. The abstract and ideological tendencies of deep ecology are also resented by those who wish to find immediate and pragmatic solutions to environmental issues.

Deep ecology challenges the apparent neutrality of the concept of environmental stewardship by recognizing that the majority of our environmental actions are "human interest stories." Yet its universalism, idealism, and abstraction have prompted numerous responses, not only from critics of environmentalism, but from other environmentalists. The tendency of deep ecologists to focus on univeral aspects of the human/nature connection ignores the specific social, economic, and institutional roots of domination, which other environmental perspectives explore in greater depth.

SOCIAL AND SOCIALIST ECOLOGY

Social ecology

Social ecology, perhaps best known in the work of Murray Bookchin (1972; 1981; 1990), excavates the foundations of anthropocentrism to identify the social origins of human domination. Bookchin notes that humans have been dominated by one another—the young by the old, women by men—through institutions like patriarchy and slavery through most of human history. He argues that "the domination of nature first arose within society as part of its institutionalization ... that placed the young in varying degrees of servitude to the old and in patriarchies that placed women in varying degrees of servitude to men—not in any endeavour to 'control' nature or natural forces" (1990, pp. 188–89).

While Bookchin argues that early forms of human society were more egalitarian and that humans lived more harmoniously with natural systems, he observes that human society has been increasingly characterized by social inequality and domination. We cannot easily harmonize our relations with nature while we condone the unequal distribution of rewards and the unequal use of power among one another. Furthermore, these inequalities do not just stem from individuals' desire for control and power, but are rooted in material systems in which some profit by others' domination.

Bookchin's solution to anthropocentrism is to eliminate the human forms of domination that underlie and characterize it. His alternative to a society based on hierarchy is one based on equality, which he identifies as "ecological anarchism." Bookchin, like many other ecological observers, is critical of large-scale bureaucratic institutions. His vision is summarized by Carolyn Merchant as directed to an "ecological society to be achieved through reliance on the resources and energy of the local bio-region, face-to-face grass-roots democracy ...

---

linked together in a confederation, and the dissolution of the state as a source of authority and control" (1994, p. 9).

Central to Bookchin's vision of an anarchic society is the rejection of central forms of power, whether political, economic, or social. Social ecologists, like deep ecologists, prefer a decentralized form of political and social organization, a theme central to the social democratic traditions of anarchism. A decentralized approach is viewed to promote greater citizen participation in government, foster greater knowledge of and commitment to local and regional ecosystems, and develop a greater sense of community self-sufficiency. The process of consensual decision-making is further endorsed as a rejection of hierarchically based management and government.

Yet, while social ecology has a strong and loyal following, it has remained less well-known than other environmental perspectives. Social ecology is primarily associated with the writings of Murray Bookchin, with relatively little additional input by other writers, which has restricted the cross-fertilization and dissemination of the literature. His decentralized and egalitarian alternatives appear, like those of deep ecologists, rather utopian in an era in which large-scale corporations and governments continue to flourish through bureaucratic organization and economies of scale.

Socialist Ecology

Socialist ecologists, or "red greens," as they are more informally called, share social ecologists' concern with social inequality, but direct their critique to market-based capitalist economies and their legacy of social and ecological disorganization. Some observers have attempted to use this position to establish an ecological niche for a Marxian analysis, identifying the ways in which the processes and products of natural systems are compatible with a Marxian agenda (Dickens, 1992). Others have applied the socialist tradition of the Marxian literature to a range of contemporary environmental issues (O'Connor, 1989; Ophuls, 1977) and to the ecological consequences of contemporary market economics.

Socialist ecologists thus understand the structural requirements and social dynamics of capitalist economies to exploit both social and natural environments. A socialist ecology explores the ways in which the industrial capitalist economic system, and especially the relations among corporations, the state, and economic elites, contribute to the process of environmental as well as social degradation. In an industrial capitalist society, the private ownership of production and the drive to accumulate surplus value (as profits) are enhanced through the exploitation of labour and nature. Both natural and social resources (labour, trees, fish) are purchased or sold cheap to maximize productivity and profitability. Markets are geared to short-term transactions producing immediate profits, while the long-term social and ecological consequences of these transactions— the erosion of hillsides and sedimentation of streams from logging and mining, the poor health of miners and socioeconomic instability of resource communities—are economically invisible. This "externalization" of environmental and social costs means that products are cheaper, and thus contributes to corporate profits and the prosperity of the market-based economic system.

Socialist ecology is perhaps one of the least well-known of the "new" environmentalisms. This is understandable given the overwhelming success and power of market economies, the recent dissolution of "socialist" states, and the poor record of environmental stewardship under these latter regimes. Furthermore, the political and economic power vested in upholding the capitalist system deters resistance and restricts an alternative vision of economic activity. A socialist approach would replace a privately owned system of production with a collective one. This would provide a more equitable means of distributing wealth and would reject principles of profit and growth in favour of a more stable and sustainable economic base. While the failure to implement the principles of socialist ecology may be due in part to the hegemony of contemporary capitalism, smaller examples of cooperatively owned and operated ventures have been successful, especially in less developed countries.

Social and socialist ecological approaches thus have in common a number of themes that counter the tenets of deep ecology. They tend to place less emphasis on the potential of individuals in changing the world through alternative beliefs, (low-) consumer patterns, or karma than do deep ecologists. Their primary orientation to concerns about social inequality reflects a continuing anthropocentrism. While social and socialist ecologists are also critical of technological innovation, they are more likely to address their concerns to its ownership and control than to an inherent distrust of the medium. They share with deep ecology a distrust of the state, and understand the potential for its perpetuation of social hierarchy and control.

Ecofeminism

The ecofeminist literature encompasses a number of different perspectives, which have in common two basic principles: the affinity of women to the natural environment due to their common productive and reproductive functions, and their mutual subordination and control by patriarchal, or male-based, systems of power. Ecofeminism was forged through the experience of women in the feminist and the peace movements, and fuses feminist critiques of power, militarism, and technology with environmental concerns.

Among ecofeminist positions, a radical approach recognizes the parallel contributions made by women and nature to the support of social and ecological systems. Women perform both reproductive and productive labour: they give birth and nurse their young, socialize and care for children, support and nurture family members, and do most domestic work. Women's responsibility for the mechanics of daily subsistence makes them more familiar with and sympathetic to the caretaking roles of other species. Not only the congruence between natural and domestic systems, but nature's provision of an infrastructure—oxygenation, water purification, soil enrichment—on which human life is dependent, contribute to the ties between women and environment. This complements women's dependence on and stewardship of ecological systems, especially in less developed countries where they engage in subsistence economies. For these women, responsibility for maintaining food supplies means knowing what crops to grow, when to plant and harvest, and how to maintain optimal conditions for future production. This common engagement in the maintenance of life support systems provides a link in the work done by women and nature.

A spiritual branch of radical ecofeminism has its roots in early cultures and religions extolling the contributions of women and nature. Many embrace the concept of a Goddess religion, whose pagan roots celebrate the female force in natural life cycles (Eisler, 1987; Starhawk, 1986). The "natural" cycles of women, including menstruation, pregnancy, and childbirth, are associated with the cycle of natural events—the waxing and waning of the moon, the seasons, birth, and death. Women's power in reproduction and in productive work are celebrated, rather than diminished, and much of this celebration is directed to a ritualization and ceremony designed to elevate and to honour these contributions.

While radical ecofeminism celebrates the contributions of women and nature to survival, it also recognizes their joint oppression by patriarchy as the primary source of their subordination. The control of women's reproductive rights by the church and the state, and the low wages and poor working conditions experienced by women, reflect their oppression in the interests of men. Patriarchal control over women's bodies is paralleled by the management of nature in practices ranging from predator control to trapping and hunting and the commoditization of wild animals.

Radical ecofeminists advocate numerous strategies for change, many of which are consistent with those identified earlier in this chapter. Among them, a feminized decentralization process would contribute to the production of more representative and informed decisions, as well as to the empowerment of women. The ideal ecofeminist enterprise would also be cooperatively owned and operated, based on principles of consensual decision-making, and sensitive to ecosystemic needs.

While the radical ecofeminist approach is that most frequently identified as ecofeminism, its essentialist tendencies, especially the biological association of women with domestic responsibility, are problematic for many feminists. Rather, the ways in which women nurture and support others are viewed as the product of social organization as well as socialization into gendered roles. A liberal ecofeminist position is geared towards the dual project of empowering women and protecting the environment by changing these socialization patterns, as well as by promoting institutional change. Liberal ecofeminists accept the existing institutional framework of a market economy situated within a democratic political system as a context amenable to women's full participation. The underrepresentation of women in environmental decision-making, from the corporate boardroom to government agencies, is remedied by affirmative action campaigns and education.

The more critical socialist ecofeminist position argues that women's choices are limited by the larger context of social class and gender inequality, products of a capitalist economic system. The dual subordination of women and nature reflects the combined power and advantage of patriarchal and capitalist systems, and the benefits that accrue to them. The patriarchal benefits from women's domestic work complement men's advantage in the labour force, while corporations and a male elite benefit from the low wages paid the female workforce. Both families and corporations benefit from the activities of natural ecosystems, not only through the provision of raw materials, but from the maintenance of an environment—air, water, soil—on which all human life is based. Accordingly, socialist ecofeminists argue that only significant structural change—the shift from capitalism to a socialist, commonly owned and operated economy, the shift from patriarchy to a feminist society—can bring about gender equity as well as environmental preservation.

Socialist ecofeminism also is increasingly directed to the analysis of global perspectives. Maria Mies (1986), Vandana Shiva (1988), and others have explored the ways in which women and natural environments are exploited not only through traditional patriarchal institutions such as the church and the family, but through the global extension of capitalism and its alliance with development, agencies. Development processes have been especially injurious to women, as male ownership of increasingly privatized land and transitions to market-based agriculture have further eroded women's status. Moreover, Shiva links the exploitation of women and nature through the global expansion of development, which has "destroyed women's productivity both by removing land, water and forests from their management and control, as well as by the ecological destruction of soil, water, and vegetation systems so that nature's productivity and renewability have been impaired" (1990, p. 191).

Global Ecology

The context in which we conduct trade, watch television, harvest resources, exchange information, and conduct politics has become increasingly globalized, and the scope and amount of this activity is having additional consequences for the character of both human society and natural systems. Ever-growing levels of resource consumption and environmental degradation are spurred by the demands of burgeoning populations and free range transnationals, while socio-economic disparities increase both within and among nations. The increasingly international scale of institutional transactions encourages both convergence and conflict among different actors—banks, corporations, and governments, while it has ramifications for the environmental systems on which they are based.

The increase in our knowledge about the global implications of environmental change has contributed to a new level of concern for the necessity of global cooperation in environmental protection. A global approach views the acceleration in the scope and pace of economic activity, human population trends, ecological disorganization, and social polarization as interrelated. Many of the issues discussed in the preceding chapters of this book are inherently global: population growth, ozone depletion, pollution, global warming, and threats to biodiversity. Global ecological perspectives are linked to an understanding of social differences, although their theoretical integration is still in the formative stage.

Sustainable Development

Among the contributions to the formation of a global ecological perspective has been the popularization of the concept of sustainable development. Sustainable development has been identified as "that development that meets the needs of the present without compromising the ability of future generations to meet their own needs" (World Commission on Environment and Development, 1987, p. 43). This concept recognizes several issues: the social and environmental limitations of the current trajectory of development, the need to consider social and environmental concerns in an integrated fashion, and the international scope and character of social inequalities as a feature of continuing development.

The issue of sustainable development requires us to address the ways in which we will be able to support human and other forms of life over future generations. Studies in recent decades have indicated that present rates of population growth and resource consumption are not viable over the long term. Present as well as projected patterns of production and consumption exceed the carrying capacity of the planet (Catton, 1980; Meadows et al., 1972). Since the 1970s, social inequality has been growing both within and between nations. While affluence has increased at the upper end of the social spectrum, increases in unemployment and poverty are among the indicators of trends to social polarization. On a global basis this gulf between rich and poor continues to increase, propelled by the movement of production to less developed countries with cheaper sources of labour and by technological advances in production that have reduced the demand for labour.

Increased polarization between developed industrialized countries in the Northern Hemisphere and their less economically developed neighbours in the Southern Hemisphere is problematic not only on ethical and political, but on environmental grounds. There are differences not only in the ways that rich and poor experience environmental degradation, but also in their impacts on natural systems. Lower socioeconomic classes and racial minorities, for instance, "live in zones more threatened by toxic wastes of all kinds, and landfills and waste repositories are more likely to be built in the ... communities where they live" (Harper, 1996, p. 251). Postel states that environmental quality is impacted by extremes of wealth and poverty:

[P]eople at either end of the income spectrum are far more likely than those in the middle to damage the earth's ecological health—the rich because of their high consumption of energy, raw materials, and manufactured goods, and the poor because they must often cut trees, grow crops, or graze cattle in ways harmful to the earth merely to survive from one day to the next. (Postel, 1994: pp. 5–6)

Differences in social as well as geographical location contribute to different patterns of environmental impact. As Harper states, "[T]he affluent ... damage the environment because of the volume of energy and material they consume. The poor do so because whatever they consume is likely to have a greater per unit environmental impact" (1996, p. 252). The poverty caused by the elimination of traditional subsistence lifestyles and the entry to market-based waged labour also contributes to the deterioration of people's immediate environments in their quest for survival. Inequalities in the distribution of wealth among countries detract from the ability of the south to determine its own future, constrain communication and interaction between global citizens, destabilize the political and the economic climate, and contribute to even greater environmental degradation.

The global dimensions of both ecological and social systems, literally a "whole earth system," is increasingly identified as both the content and framework of analysis. The *gaia hypothesis* identified by James Lovelock (1976) addresses the natural systems component of this analysis. Lovelock perceives the earth as a self-regulating set of chemical and physical systems. From this perspective, he argues that environmental problems can be reduced through the development of our technological capacity so that it reflects the organic wholeness of the world's biophysical systems. Lovelock's approach offers an organic and holistic approach to environmental problems, while appealing to technological solutions to ease current problems. Yet the addition of social factors to the analysis of global biophysical systems is an even more complex and difficult task.

Sustainable development is generally addressed in terms of its social ramifications, but *development* and *dependency* models approach it in very different ways. The *development* model for reducing international social inequality was generated in the postwar years and continues to be the dominant approach to sustainable development today. It assumes that the provision of economic aid, technology, and education to undeveloped countries will lead them on the same path of prosperity as the more affluent nations have followed. The industrialization of the less developed countries will contribute to a modernization process that will curtail population growth while encouraging employment and a better standard of living. High fertility rates in the less developed countries are viewed as a primary contributor to poverty and environmental degradation, while birth control and increased access to education are stepping-stones to affluence. The infusion of international financial aid through agencies like the International

Monetary Fund and the World Bank, as well as massive transfers of technology, will further enable the less developed countries to mature into global economic players.

The social and political mechanisms for achieving sustainability assume the continuing priority of market economics and the adaptation of existing social institutions. The dissemination of market-based instruments for environmental protection, such as tax incentives, technological development, green consumer alternatives, and industrial self-regulation contribute to a greater climate of environmental protection. The internalization of environmental costs becomes the basis for corporate competition. As a means of establishing the long-term security of resources, regulatory compliance, and the enhancement of public relations, corporations will adopt efforts to enhance environmental protection. Our cultural values and lifestyles must also be adapted so that they are less costly, both financially and ecologically. Localized forms of production and social organization, and a renewed emphasis on community, have also been identified as cornerstones of sustainability (Daly and Cobb, 1989).

Yet critics of mainstream development models argue that the economic foundations of contemporary society are structurally responsible for the ecological and social damage we have sustained, and that these must be fundamentally reshaped. In contrast to the dominant development approach to social inequality, *dependency* theory identifies the increasing gap between rich and poor countries as the product of the historical and economic forces of industrial capitalism. Rather than perceiving this gap as short-term and resolvable, modernization (through traditional methods of colonization and industrialization) is seen to perpetuate the development of "underdevelopment."

The dependency model described by Frank (1967) comprises the centre (composed of urban, industrial, and developed areas or nations) and the periphery (which includes a rural hinterland, the source of resources). The relations between these two—the engine of growth at the centre consuming resources from its hinterland—are structurally unequal. Traditionally, industrial powers provided capital and technology, while less developed countries provided a cheap and abundant source of resources, and a market for imported, manufactured products. Today the more developed countries continue to profit from the under-development of the south, not only as a creditor, but through the continuing exploitation of the land and labour it controls. As the success of the centre is based on its exploitation of the periphery, the system is resistant to change. The south cannot catch up to the north through existing efforts, as the two are locked in a position of powerful to powerless, lender to debtor, rich to poor, from which there is little material incentive for the north to extricate itself.

Global economic inequality is thus a product of uneven patterns of development that emerged through relations of colonialism and imperialism and are perpetuated in contemporary economic systems of ownership and control. For dependency theorists, the problem of development lies with the more developed countries and the economic institutions they control. This approach requires more extensive changes, such as the nationalization of industry in an effort to gain local or national control, a difficult task in a global marketplace dominated by large transnational corporations. Furthermore, although dependency theory is a means of identifying the limitations of mainstream development, it has yet to explore ecologically sustainable alternatives to market-based systems.

Thus, those engaged in the very substantial project of sustainable development must accommodate the requirements of both social and natural systems, and must acknowledge and transcend the historical and structural limitations of mainstream development approaches. The standard development approach attempts to achieve social change through the adaptation of existing institutions. But disproportionately high levels of consumption and pollution among the more developed nations raise concerns about the potential development of those less developed. In recent years, the possibility has been suggested of trading the underdevelopment of the less developed countries for the overindustrialization of the more developed. The debt of the less developed countries, some suggest, could be traded in the form of tax pollution credits, or forgiven in exchange for its protection of natural areas, which would work to reduce the legacy of underdevelopment.

However, there is still little indication that these kinds of activities can resolve the more fundamental levels and differences of inequality that have been produced over time. Furthermore, the debate, as ever, retains an anthropocentric bias, attending more directly and immediately to social than to ecological concerns. The "dependency" of both less and more developed countries on the biosphere remains invisible and unresolved in much of the contemporary sustainability discourse.

NEW DIRECTIONS

Recent economic and political changes have implications for environmental protection. Increased degradation and scarcity—both environmental and economic—have provoked contradictory moves, on the one hand to antienvironmentalism, but on the other to an expanded constituency and social concern for environmental protection. The "restructuring" of the economy has included technological innovation and the offshore movement of capital that have resulted in the downsizing of corporations, displacement of workers, and cutbacks to state budgets, restricting potential for the administration of both social and environmental welfare. Free trade and other international provisions for trade have also heightened concern, as the competition of a free market implies cost-cutting that may counter and curtail regulatory efforts. These current trends signify for some the necessity for increased environmental vigilance.

The representation of environmental interests in policy formation is also being revisited, within the context of economic and political pressures. The participation of multiple stakeholders in the production of environmental decisions and the funding of environmental groups may be increasingly limited in times of tight budgets. The emergence of a conservative New Right and an anti-environmental movement is additionally problematic for environmental protection. The disaffection of larger sectors of the population due to increased unemployment and taxes has produced a reaction to government and other forms of collective activity, and promoted a move to privatization and fiscal conservatism. Industry's self-identification as an "environmental" interest is illustrated by the "wise use" movement or the Forestry Alliance in British Columbia. Thus, the increased climate of economic restraint will require new approaches for addressing changing ideological frameworks as well as emerging environmental issues.

Another major approach to environmental issues is the incorporation of indigenous peoples in the perceptions and processes of environmental protection. Cultural diversity in such approaches is significant to how we recognize and deal with environmental issues. Environmental racism—the location of environmentally destructive activities such as mercury contamination in Grassy Narrows, or the siting of toxic waste sites adjacent to groups either desperate for income or least capable of resistance—is a problem for indigenous and other marginalized peoples. Indigenous peoples play a unique role, both in terms of their relations with natural environments and in their social and economic subordination within mainstream cultures. Indigenous peoples experience social marginalization and have been largely excluded from industrialization through geographic isolation as well as educational and cultural discrimination.

Another issue related to aboriginal entitlement is that of the construction of megaprojects, especially the building of large dams and subsequent harnessing and export of energy. The James Bay hydroelectric project in Quebec illustrates some of the problems around development, social inequality, and environmental degradation. The construction of the James Bay project in the late 1960s, to create electrical power exported to the United States, raised a number of problems, not just about ecological, but about cultural survival. The construction of the dam destroyed habitat for moose, elk, and other species on which aboriginal peoples depended for subsistence, and of course introduced other cultural values. The positions of aboriginal people illustrate to some extent the larger questions around development. What are the long-term costs and benefits of development to indigenous peoples? Are the objectives of indigenous peoples necessarily compatible with those of environmentalists? Does development by indigenous peoples reflect a position of environmental sustainability? These questions need to be addressed more critically by emerging perspectives.

Indigenous peoples are frequently held up as exemplars of environmental stewardship. Their belief systems directly refer to and honour the natural landscape, while traditional lifestyles have been directly dependent on natural systems for physical survival. Moreover, ownership of large tracts of land is increasingly contested by indigenous people, who claim that they have lost title to the land through force, intimidation, and other unjust methods of appropriation. Throughout Canada and in other countries, aboriginal land claims currently create problems about land ownership and development. While indigenous issues are manifested in national terms, they are a global issue as well. They illustrate the differential social impact of environmental actions, while both countering the simplicity of a north-south dichotomy and embodying it on a local and national basis.

Issues of economic development and environmental degradation are becoming increasingly the basis of international politics as nations compete over the control of scarce resources. Other international disputes such as the early 1990s Gulf War between Iraq and U.S.-led forces represented conflict over the continuing supply of oil to the West. During the Newfoundland cod crisis of 1995, a Spanish trawler was apprehended by Canadians for fishing the Grand Banks, illustrating the inadequacy of international law. Not only has there been little agreement on an international legal code, but the institutional basis for policing and the judicial process remain both contentious and undeveloped.

A CONTINUING VIGILANCE

In summary, then, new and alternative approaches to environmental issues provide innovative and diverse ways of understanding the relations of humans to the natural world. Environmental issues have become central to contemporary discourse—in the media, in government, in law, and in education. Regulatory standards have been increased, protected areas have been legislated, remediation projects have been successful. Yet, as we have seen, increasing pressure on natural environments requires continuing vigilance.

Canada's unique geographic and social positions are keys to the articulation of new environmental approaches. We have the largest land mass of any nation on earth, and are the second least developed of any country, which means that we have considerable potential for the protection of environmental quality. We also inhabit a country that is northern, sparsely settled, and vulnerable to impacts, but historically dependent on resource extraction. This provides us with a unique opportunity to study the impacts that humans have on the earth, and to protect, preserve, and mitigate both past and future ecological disruption. The natural environment, either directly or indirectly, provides us with a living, and defines the character and quality of our lives. It is also interesting that no one alternative is prevalent in Canada, largely due to its vastness. The power and choice of approach to the environment is a deeply personal conviction of individuals, irrespective of location or environmental situation. This allows us great freedom to pursue different approaches and ideas. The diversity of our national community opens up many possibilities to solving our environmental problems and defining our unique Canadian environmental approach.

In Canada, the lack of ecological awareness among most contemporary urban dwellers enables us to lose our "natural" heritage while being unaware of and often complacent about this loss. The cultural malleability that enables us to adapt to living in concrete buildings also makes us strangers in our own land. We are a country with a diversity of both indigenous and cultural populations, yet we have not adequately identified the character of these diverse and multiple relations with the landscape. The approaches we have reviewed in this chapter are germane to the resolution, not just of conflict, but of our relationship with the environment. We need to combine our unique geographic and historical legacy, and our strong commitment to collective well-being, to include a variety of both natural and social approaches. We need to continue to generate and to implement alternatives—better, wiser ways of being on and of the earth.

REFERENCES

Bookchin, M. 1990. *The Philosophy of Social Ecology: Essays on Dialectical Naturalism.* "Thinking Ecologically: A Dialectical Approach." Montreal: Black Rose Books.

———. 1981. *Toward an Ecological Society.* Montreal: Black Rose Books.

———. 1972. *Post-Scarcity Anarchism.* Montreal: Black Rose Books.

Bramwell, A. 1989. *Ecology in the 20th Century: A History.* New Haven: Yale University Press.

Brown, L.R., et al. 1984–95. *State of the World: A Worldwatch Institute Report on Progress toward a Sustainable Society.* New York: W.W. Norton and Company.

Catton, W.R. 1980. *Overshoot: The Ecological Basis of Revolutionary Change.* Urbana: University of Illinois Press.

Catton, W.R., and R. Dunlap. 1980. "Environmental Sociology: A New Paradigm?" *The American Sociologist 13:* 41–49.

Commoner, B. 1971. *The Closing Circle.* New York: Knopf.

Daly, H.E., ed. 1973. *Toward a Steady-State Economy.* New York: W.H. Freeman and Co.

Daly, H.E., and J. Cobb. 1989. *For the Common Good: Redirecting the Economy toward Community, the Environment, and a Sustainable Future.* Boston: Beacon Press.

Devall, B. 1988. *Simple in Means, Rich in Ends: Practicing Deep Ecology.* Salt Lake City: Peregrine Books.

Dickens, P. 1992. *Society and Nature: Towards a Green Social Theory.* Philadelphia: Temple University Press.

Eisler, R.T. 1987. *The Chalice and the Blade: Our History, Our Future.* San Francisco: Harper & Row.

Frank, A.G. 1967. *Capitalism and Underdevelopment in Latin America.* New York: Monthly Review Press.

Harper, C.L. 1996. *Environment and Society: Human Perspectives on Environmental Issues.* Upper Saddle River, N.J.: Prentice-Hall.

Lewis, M. 1994. *Green Delusions: An Environmentalist Critique of Radical Environmentalism.* Durham, N.C.: Duke University Press.

Lovelock, J. 1976. *Gaia: A New Look at Life on Earth.* Oxford: Oxford University Press.

McNeely, J.A., K.R. Miller, W.V. Reid, R.A. Mittermeier, and T.B. Werner. 1990. *Conserving the World's Biological Diversity.* Washington, D.C.: International Union for Conservation of Nature and Nature Resources, World Resources Institute, Conservation International, World Wildlife Fund–U.S. and the World Bank.

Marsh, G.P. 1874. *The Earth as Modified by Human Action.* New York: Scribner and Armstrong.

Mathews, F. 1991. *The Ecological Self.* London: Routledge.

Meadows, D., D. Meadows, J. Randers, and W. Behrens. 1972. *The Limits to Growth.* New York: Universe.

Merchant, C. 1994. *Ecology: Key Concepts in Critical Theory.* Hawthorne, N.J.: Humanities Press.

Mies, M. 1986. *Patriarchy and Accumulation on a World Scale.* London: Zed Books.

Milbrath, L. 1989. *Envisioning a Sustainable Society: Learning Our Way Out.* Albany, N.Y.: State University of New York Press.

Naess, A. 1973. "The Shallow and the Deep, Long-Range Ecology Movement." *Inquiry* 16: 95–100.

O'Connor, J. 1989. "Political Economy and Ecology of Socialism and Capitalism." *Capitalism, Nature, Socialism* 3: 33–57.

Oelschlaeger, M. 1991. *The Idea of Wilderness: From Prehistory to the Age of Ecology.* New Haven: Yale University Press.

Ophuls, W. 1977. *Ecology and the Politics of Scarcity.* San Francisco: W.H. Freeman and Co.

Postel, S. 1994. "Carrying Capacity: Earth's Bottom Line." In Lester Brown et al., *State of the World 1994: A Worldwatch Institute Report on Progress towards a Sustainable Society.* New York: Norton.

Schnaiberg, A., and K.A. Gould. 1994. *Environment and Society: The Enduring Conflict.* New York: St. Martin's Press.

Sessions, G. 1988. "Ecological Consciousness and Paradigm Change." In M. Tobias, *Deep Ecology.* San Marcos, Calif.: Avant Books.

Shiva, V. 1990. "Development as a New Project of Western Patriarchy." In I. Diamond and G.F. Orenstein, *Reweaving the World: The Emergence of Ecofeminism.* San Francisco: Sierra Club Books.

———. 1988. *Staying Alive: Women, Ecology and Development.* London: Zed Press.

Shumacher, E.F. 1973. *Small Is Beautiful: Economics as if People Mattered.* New York: Harper & Row.

Starhawk. 1986. *The Spiral Dance: A Rebirth of the Ancient Religion of the Great Goddess.* San Francisco: Harper & Row.

Wolf, E.C. 1987. *On the Brink of Extinction: Conserving the Diversity of Life.* Washington, D.C.: Worldwatch Institute.

World Commission on Environment and Development. 1987. *Our Common Future*. New York: Oxford University Press.

QUESTIONS FOR DISCUSSION

1. Describe, in brief, the *source* of environmental degradation according to each of the following perspectives: deep ecology, social and socialist ecology, radical ecofeminism, globalization (dependency theory).

2. What are the *solutions* to environmental degradation offered by each of these approaches?

3. Name one constraint, or limiting factor, in implementing each of these approaches.

4. In what ways is deep ecology compatible with radical ecofeminism? Is it possible to be a deep ecologist and an ecofeminist? Why or why not?

5. Which of the environmental approaches reviewed in this chapter was most appealing to you, and why? Identify two limitations of this approach.

6. Give an example of a contemporary environmental issue in your region (such as wilderness protection, forestry practices, energy megaprojects, pesticide use, endangered species) and briefly discuss it within the context of one of the above environmental approaches. What are the sources of the problem? What are the solutions?

7. Imagine that you are living in the year 2050. Identify the worst environmental issue of that time (feel free to invent it). Then discuss which of the current alternative approaches are valid in explaining the persistence of this problem. If none of them is, identify a new approach that may be more relevant to explain the issue. What are its basic principles? Solutions?

CONTRIBUTORS

Alistair J. Bath is an assistant professor in the Department of Geography at Memorial University of Newfoundland, where he teaches natural resource management. He has focused much of his research on the human dimensions in wildlife resources management, in particular the management of large carnivores. He has been involved with wolf reintroduction in Yellowstone National Park and with wolf management in Riding Mountain National Park. He has completed polar bear research in Churchill, Man., and has current projects under way in Europe and the U.S.

Monica Campbell is the environmental health specialist with the Metro Toronto Teaching Health Units (c/o North York Health Department). There she participates in applied research and provides continuing education to public health staff. Previously she worked for the City of Toronto Environmental Protection Office. She is assistant professor in the Department of Preventive Medicine and Biostatistics and an adjunct professor at Ryerson's School of Environmental Health. She holds a doctorate in toxicology and conducts research on soil contamination, drinking water, lead, pesticides, state-of-the-environment reporting, and air quality.

George H. Crowell received his B.A. at Princeton University in 1963 with honours in history. He received his Ph.D. in 1966 at Union Theological Seminary in New York City. He taught religion at Lake Forest College in Lake Forest, Ill., until 1968, and from then until his retirement, in January 1996, he taught religious studies at the University of Windsor. Throughout his life he has been involved with social, political, and peaceful organizations and actions.

Nancy C. Doubleday has been involved with Arctic issues on behalf of Inuit organizations from the community level to the international arena. She is trained as a biologist and lawyer and has dealt with many issues—land claims, political development, environmental protection, harvesting rights, and Arctic contaminants. She is a member of the Department of Geography at Carleton University, and her current research focuses on paleoecological investigations in the High Arctic and on Arctic contaminants policy.

Thomas Fleming has been involved in environmental issues for more than two decades. He has taught at many Canadian universities, including York, University of Toronto, and University of Alberta, and he currently teaches at Windsor. A respected teacher, he has been nominated for both provincial and institutional awards of excellence.

F. Kenneth Hare is University Professor Emeritus at the University of Toronto in the Department of Geography. He is also former Provost of Trinity College. He was the first chair (1979–1990) of the Climate Program Planning Board of Canada, and has chaired inquiries in Canada and elsewhere. He is a Companion of the Order of Canada and holds the Order of Ontario. He is also a Fellow of the Royal Society of Canada and holds the International Meteorological Organization Prize as well as the Patron's Medal of the Royal Geographical Society (London).

Isobel W. Heathcote holds a B.Sc. from the University of Toronto and an M.S. and Ph.D. in physical limnology from Yale University. Her work experience encompasses employment in consulting, government, and teaching. She is currently on the faculty of the School of Engineering and the Faculty of Environmental Science at the University of Guelph, where she also holds the position of Director, Institute for Environmental Policy. Her research interests centre on integrated water management and watershed restoration, waste minimization in small industrial facilities, and environmental policy development.

Melody Hessing is a sociologist who specializes in the study of environmental and feminist issues. She lives in Vancouver, where she teaches sociology at Douglas College and holds appointments as adjunct professor in Criminology at Simon Fraser University and research associate in the Sustainable Development Research Institute and the Centre for Women's Studies and Gender Relations, University of British Columbia. Her publications address issues in ecofeminism and sustainability, the regulatory state and environmental protection, and Canadian environmental policy. Her current research centres on the integration of social and natural sciences and the social construction of natural environments.

Doug Macdonald teaches environmental politics and policy at Innis College, University of Toronto, and the Faculty of Environmental Studies, York University. He is the author of *The Politics of Pollution: Why Canadians Are Failing Their Environment* (1991). In 1994 he co-authored the study *Taxation and User Fees as Potential Policy Instruments in the Emerging Regulatory Regime of Solid Waste Diversion*.

Ian MacQuarrie, a lifelong Islander, lives on a small farm in central P.E.I. In 1996 he retired from the University of Prince Edward Island, where he taught Ecology, Environmental Science, and Natural History courses for more than 30 years. He has been involved in many aspects of land and resource use: impact assessments, studies on sustainable agriculture, soil erosion, and ecological reserves. In addition to farming, he devotes his time to writing about the natural history of the island.

Robert Paehlke teaches at Trent University in Peterborough, Ont. He is the editor of *Conservation and Environmentalism: An Encyclopedia* and author of *Environmentalism and the Future of Progressive Politics*. He has published articles on environmental policy in the *International Political Science Review, Society, Canadian Public Administration, Environmental Ethics,* and *Administration and Society*. He was the first editor of the journal *Alternatives: Perspectives on Society, Technology and Environment,* now published at the University of Waterloo.

Raymond A. Rogers is an assistant professor in the Faculty of Environmental Studies at York University. He is the author of *Nature and the Crisis of Modernity: A Critique of Contemporary Discourse on Managing the Earth* (1994) and *The Oceans Are Emptying: Fish Wars and Sustainability* (1995). His current project is a book entitled *Solving History: The Challenge of Wildlife Conservation.*

Duncan Taylor is a professor of environmental studies at the University of Victoria, where he was instrumental in developing the interdisciplinary environmental studies program. His current area of research is community forest initiatives in British Columbia as well as cultural and environmental restoration in western Scotland. He is a director of the Ecoforestry Institute Canada and has recently authored a book on Canadian environmental issues and policies entitled *Off Course: Restoring Balance between Canadian Society and the Environment.*

Dixon Thompson teaches environmental management and has a continuing research program with graduate students that examines the development of environmental management systems and tools, including environmental assessment, environmental management structures, environmental impact assessment, environmental policies, environmental audits, technology assessment, life-cycle assessment, and new accounting systems. He also teaches and researches in the areas of water resources management and product and technology assessment and waste minimization. Since 1986 he has done research and published extensively on trade and environment issues, especially as they relate to NAFTA and development issues.

G. Keith Warriner is an associate professor of sociology at the University of Waterloo who specializes in environmental sociology. In addition to work on environmental public involvement, his research has included studies of agriculture, the commercial fisheries, energy conservation, and environmental attitudes. Over the past three years he has been a co-investigator to a large interdisciplinary project examining sustainability in the the Grand River watershed in Ontario. In other current research he examines grassroots environmentalism, the toxic waste movement, and developments in green political thought.

INDEX

Abbey, D.E., 117
Aboriginal Canadians
    environmental protection and, 328
    living conditions, 276
    megaprojects and, 328
    traditional attitudes to environment, 277
Acid aerosols, 118
Agricultural diversity, 50
Agroecosystem profile, 80
Air quality
    asthma, 106
    automobile, effects of, 108–9
    exercise, negative effects of, 106
    exposures, 106
    heating residences, effects of, 111
    industry, impact on, 111–12
    particulate levels and the elderly, 117
    strategies for improvement of, 124
    urban, 106, 120
Allin, Craig W., 253
Almond, Gabriel, A., 175, 176, 177
American Lung Association, 118
Arctic
    DDT in, 89
    emissions and effluents, 87
    history as viable ecosystem, 88–89
    toxic chemical contaminants, effects, 87
    transportation of atmospheric pollutants, 89
Arnstein's ladder
    citizen empowerment, 188
    elements of, 189–90
Arnstein, S.R., 186, 187
Aunan, Lauri, 212

Bachrach, Peter, 177
Badcock, W.T., 278
Ballantyne, E.E., 19
Bata case, 226
Bauer, M.A., 118
Bear
    bait stations, 36–37
    encounters with humans, 37
    hunting, 36
    illegal killing of, 33
    populations in Canada, 33
    populations in Europe, 33
    trapping, 33
Berger, Thomas, 179, 276, 279, 280
Bidleman, T., 93
Bio-Integral Resource Centre, 126
Biotechnology
    intellectual property rights and, 166
    negative consequences of, 166–67
    role in agriculture, 166
Bookchin, M., 319, 320
Bounty systems
    poisoning, 18
Brat, A., 283
Bruton, Jim, 172
Burch, William R., 181
Burnett, R. 115
Brundtland, Harlem, 145, 283

California Air Resources Board, 109
Canada–U.S. BOREAS project, 143
Canadian Centre for Policy Alternatives, 165
Carnivores
    large, 16
    public knowledge, 37
    worldwide attitude toward, 30
Carson, Rachel, 49, 90, 254

Catton, W.R., 316, 323
CELA, 210
Chang, T.Y., 125
Checkoway, Barry, 184
Cherniavsky, Ben, 203
Cholette, Kathy, 306
Citizen participation
    definition of "the public" and,
        185–87
    efficiency, 178–80
    equity issues, 181
    limitations of, 180–81
    objectives of, 176
    problems of, 178
    profiles of participants, 182
    representativeness, 184
    reviews of, 173–76
    theories of, 176
    womens' involvement in, 182
Cizek, Peter, 189
Clayoquot Sound, 285, 299
Climate, 134
    Canadian government, lack of
        response to change, 144
    climatic models, 136
    models using atmosphere and
        ocean, 137
    prediction of short-term changes,
        136
Cluff, H.D., 19
Cohen, David S., 212
Cohen, Michael P., 253
Cole, Richard, 177
Coleman, Daniel A., 194
Commission of Planning and
    Development Reform (Ontario),
    124
Commoner, Barry, 316
Condon, 95
Connor, Desmond, 172
Conservation
    meaning of, 9
    "trees versus jobs," 304
    "wise management" system, 304

worker–management alliances,
    305
Contaminants, 89–91
    competing interests in Arctic,
        98–99
    economic disbenefits, 96
    education of public, 100
    effects on Arctic traditional diet,
        95
    global implications, 94, 101
    government role, 97
    international responses, 98
    journey through ecosystem, 98
    management, 97
    "market basket" studies, 96
    media reporting of, 94
    policies, southern Canada, 100
    sources, in Arctic, 92
    traditional food sources and, 92
    travelling, effects of, 93
Cooperman, Jim, 294
Corporate development, 279
Coward, H., 144
Creighton, James L., 180
Curlee, Anna, 253
Curtis, James, 181

Dahl, Robert, 177, 180
Daly, H.E., 326
Daneke, Gregory, 177
Darling, Craig R., 298, 304
Deep ecology
    bioregionalism, 318
    decentralization, 318
    defined, 317
Deforestation, 283–84
Delgamuukw decision, 277
Dependency theory, 326
Devall, Bill, 260, 317
Dickens, P., 320
Disposal facilities
    Keele Valley and, 209
    siting of, 208
Dockery, D.W., 117

Dotto, L., 144
Dunlap, Riley, 181, 191
Dunster, Julian, 303

Earth Day, 191
Eckersley, Robyn, 191, 192, 193, 194, 195
Ecocentric view
    defined, 260
Ecofeminism, 321–23
Ecological citizenry
    elements of, 191
    participation, 191–92
Ecologo system, 239
Ecology movement, 315
Ecosystem
    desert margin and, 142
    health of, 122
    Pacific coast rain forest and, 143
    tropical rain forest and, 142
    working models of, 142
Ecosystem planning
    policy responses, 6
Eisler, R.T., 322
Emery, Claude, 305
Emissions
    air, 210
    international control efforts, 146
    levels, 146
    non-vehicle sources, reducing, 126
    reduction of vehicle emissions, 125
    strategies, 125–26
Energy Probe, 256
Environment
    dominant social paradigms and, 315
    new perspectives on, 314–16
Environmental audits, 237–38
Environmental impact assessment, 232
Environmental indicators, 241–44
Environmentalism
    alternative approaches, 315

defined, 262
future of, 264
history of, 192–94
jobless growth and, 267
politics and, 265
post-communism, 261
strategies for change, 272
Environmental issues
    complexity of, 3
    decision-making, 2, 172, 187, 188
    developed countries and, 9
    undeveloped countries and, 9
Environmentalist
    defined, 278
Environmental law, 226
Environmental management
    application of, 246–49
    definitional issues, 221–23
    education and training, 245
    forces affecting, 225
    scientists' roles in, 223
    strategies, 229–30
    structures to facilitate, 230–32
    tools for, 223–24, 228–29
Environmental movement
    divisions in, 263
    history of, 253–56
    neoconservatism and, 256
    perspectives on, 263
    two historical waves of concern, 257–59
Environmental policy
    Canadian, 270
    international, 270
    Mexican, 270
    Vorsorge, 71
Environmental problems
    round-table approach, 8
Environmental protection
    economic justice and, 269
    policies and, 268
    threat to jobs, 268
Environment Canada, 121
Exxon Valdez, 260

Farming
    dangers of, 53
    diversification, 55
    economy and, 53
    effects of corporations, 165
    family, 164–65
Fleming, Thomas, 278. See O'Reilly-
    Fleming, Thomas
Food production
    ecosystem and, 46–47
    effects of, 44
    farmland, 45
    history of, North America, 46
    intensive production, 46
Forestry
    clearcut logging, 295
    community control, 302–3
    decentralization of management,
       296
    environmentalists vs. foresters,
       294
    environmental withdraws, 296
    history of, in British Columbia,
       293
    selection of forest board members,
       298
    stakeholders, 300
Forests
    economy, 292
    harvest levels, 292
    public views, 286
Foucault, M., 278
Fowler, C., 168
Fox, Warwick, 260
Frank, Chief Francis, 286
Freeman, M.M.R., 95
Free Trade Agreement. See NAFTA
French, H.F., 121, 122
Freudenberg, William R., 176, 181

Gaia hypothesis, 325
Galtung, Johan, 194
Genetic engineering, 49

Gentrification, 123
Gilbert, Roger, 210
Gillies, J., 176
Global distillation, 91
Global ecology, 323
Globalization
    jobless growth and, 271
Global warming
    effects of, 138–41
    history of, 134
    response to in Canada, 145
Goodlad, J., 94
Gottlieb, Robert, 181
GRAND Canal System, 163
Great Whale Project, 282
"Green Dot" system, 212
Greenhouse effect
    gases, sources of, 126
    natural, effects of, 135
    stabilization of, 146
Greenpeace, 256
Green Plan funding, 99
Greens
    political beliefs of, 266
Green theory
    green politics and, 194
    relationships with nature, 195
Griffiths, Len, 213
Grizzly bear
    behaviours, 22
    population distribution, 23
    status as endangered species, 23

Habermas, J., 278
Hammond, Herb, 298, 303
Hare, Kenneth F., 142, 147
Harper, C.C., 326
Harper, C.L., 314, 315
Hays, S.P., 181
Hazelton Plan, 298
Heilbroner, Robert, 193
Hewitt, G., 17
Horstman, D., 115

Howell, Robert E., 180
Hurtig, Mel, 154
Hutcheson, Sarah, 300, 302, 304

Incineration, 209
Industrialized agriculture
    effects of, 165
IPCC findings, 138
IWA-Canada, 296

Johnson, Donald E., 175
Jurisdictional gridlock, 6

Keeling, C. David, 135
Kemano case, 282
Kennedy, Robert, Jr., 286
Kolenosky, 198

Langton, Stuart, 173, 175
Latour, Bruno, 183
Laxer, Gordon, 279
Lewis, M., 318
Life cycle assessment, 240
Life cycle costing, 240
Linton, 164
Lipset, Seymour Martin, 176
Lopez, Barry, 16, 17
Lorimer, James, 181
Lovelock, J., 325
Lovins, Amory B., 256
Lucas, Alistair R., 186

McCloskey, Michael, 181
Macdonald, Doug, 212, 213, 214
McEachern, Chief Justice, 281
MacKay, Chief David, 280
Mackenzie Valley Pipeline Inquiry,
    179
McRoberts, David, 205
"Mad cow disease," 54
Makuch, Zen, 212
Mandel, M., 278
Marchak, M. Patricia, 264
Marsh, George, 252

Matthews, F., 317
Meadows, D., 323
Mercredi, Ovide, 285
Metropolitan Toronto Planning
    Department, 109
M'Gonigle, Michael, 300, 302, 303
Michels, Robert, 177, 183
Mies, M., 322
Milbraith, Lester, 181
Mill, John Stuart, 177
Miller, J.R., 278
Mills, C. Wright, 185
Mitchell, Bruce, 7, 137
Mitchell, T.R., 175
Molfino, N., 115
"Monkey-wrenching," 259
Montreal Protocol, 144
Morrison, Denton, 181
Mountain lion
    behaviours, 23
    natural recovery, 29–30
    trapping of, 21
Mulroney, Brian, 145
Mumme, S.P., 121

Naess, Arne, 317
NAFTA (North American Free Trade
    Agreement)
    dispute settlement mechanisms,
        162, 168–69
    enforcement of, 158
    environmental legislation, 157
    Environmental Side Agreement,
        155
    impacts, 152
    incomprehensible nature of con-
        sidered, 153
    laying of charges under, 156
    public advocacy and, 74
    public opinion and, 154
    regulatory frameworks, 81–82
    treaties under, 156
    United States interest in Canadian
        resources, 159–161

water diversion, 76
water resources, control of, 162
National Environmental Policy Act, 172, 176
Native land claims
    Canadian constitution and, 281
    history of, 279–81
Newman, P., 109
Nisbet, Robert, 180
Nishga tribe, 279
Nitrogen dioxide, 118
Northern Badger Case, 226
Novek, Joel, 189

O'Connor, J., 320
OECD, 203
Oelschlaeger, Max, 315
Oka (Quebec), 285
OMOE, 205
OMOEE, 122
Ophulus, W., 320
O'Reilly-Fleming, Thomas, 276. See Fleming, Thomas
O'Riordin, Timothy, 195
Ostro, B.D., 119
Ozkaynak, A., 116
Ozone
    ground level type, 116
    hospital admissions and, 115

Paehlke, Robert C., 252, 256, 261, 262, 272
Paquet, 30
Parenteau, Rene, 189, 193
Pateman, Carole, 173, 175, 177
PCBs, 90
Peel, Sandy, 295
Peirce, John C., 172
Peoples' Food Commission, 165
Pesticides
    contamination, 50
    effects on wildlife, 47
    effects on Arctic, 91
    health effects on humans, 48

organochlorine compounds (DDT, DDE), 90
pests' resistance to, 48–49
Poaching
    policies, 17
    wolves, 19–20, 38
Policy-making, 3
    perspectives on, 4
    public participation in, 9
    responses to, 7
    See also Water policy
Pollution
    air, social impacts, 123
    changes in air pollution levels, 112–13
    control efforts, 121
    "criteria pollutants," 115
    effects of human activity, 67
    "hands-off" policy, 78
    non-point, 77–78
    street drainage, 78
    types of in air, 114–15
    water quality and, 66
Ponting, Rick, 278
Population management, 20
Press, Daniel, 173
Prince, Michael, 306
Product and technology assessments, 239

Ratner, R.S., 276
Recycling, 205–6
    costs, 207, 213–14
    market demands for after products, 211–13
    product stewardship, 214
Remedial Action Plans (RAPs), 80
Renewable resources
    ecosystem impact, 141
    human values, effects, 14
    large carnivores, 14
    species management, 14–15
Resistance
    seed banks, 168

Resource management perspective
fishing industry, 5
Restructuring, 327
Richardson, B., 282
Richardson, Mary, 183
Risk management, 244
Rizzo, B., 143
Rodney, W., 19
Rosenbaum, Nelson M., 175, 177, 188
Royal Commission on the Future of
Toronto Waterfront, 125

Satori, G., 175–77
Scarce, Rik, 175
Schnaiberg, Allan, 183, 314, 319
Schumpter, J.A., 175, 177
Schwartz, J., 117
Science Council of Canada, 55
Searle, R., 144
Sears, Paul, 195
Seguin, R., 19
Selznick, Phillip, 177
Sessions, George, 317
Sewell, Derrick, 177
Shiva, V., 322
Smit, B., 144
Social ecology
defined, 319
ecological anarchism and, 319
Socialist ecology
defined, 320
"red greens," 320
Soil degradation, 52
Solid waste
amount generated, 203
economic goals and, 202
history of regulation, 204
municipal forms, 203
principles of, 4 "R's," 204–5
See also Hazardous waste
Spry, J.M., 19
Stankey, G.H., 180
Stardom, 19
Starhawk, 322

Starke, L., 114
Stouffer, R.J., 137
Sulphur dioxide, 177
Supply management, 54
Suspended particulates, 116–17
Susskind, Lawrence E., 187
Sustainable development, 324
conflicting views of, 262
Swenarchuk, M., 158
Syme, G.J., 180

Taylor, Bron, 194, 259
Taylor, D.M., 304
Temagami (Ont.), ix, 283
Tennant, F., 280
Tester, Frank J., 189, 190, 191
Thrupp, Lori-Ann, 305
Thurston, G.D., 119
Tin Wis Coalition, 297
Tokar, Brian, 194
Tompa, F.S., 19
Toronto, City of, Department of Public
Health, 114, 116, 117, 118,
120, 125, 126
Toronto, City of, Special Advisory
Committee on the
Environment, 126
Toxic substances
bioaccumulative potential, 76–77
in air, 119
persistence of, 76
toxicity, 77
trace toxics, 119
Travers, Ray, 295
Truck Loggers Association, 296
Tseng, R.Y., 117
Turk, Austin, 278

UNEP/WHO, 122
Urban Development Sectoral Task
Force, 124
Urbanization
effects on air quality, 107
history of, 107–9

Urban planning
    ecosystem-based, 124
    ideal structures, 127

Vanderzwaag, David, 186
Van Liere, Kent D., 180
Verba, Sidney, 175, 177
Vincent, Andrew, 175

Walker, Jack, 177
Wania, 91
Washington, 137
Waste generation
    landfills, 205
Water conservation, 60
    Canadian water policies, 60
    quality, 61
    sewage treatment, 61
    waste, in Canada, 60
Water exports
    to United States, effects of, 163–64
Water management
    barriers to, 72
    conflicts, 73
    decision-making, 82
    Great Lakes Basin and, 73
    sewage disposal, 65
    watershed, 71
Water policy, Canadian, 74–75
Water quality
    industry discharges, effects of, 68
    inorganic pollutants and, 68
    nutrients and, 67
    physical condition/appearance
        and, 67–68
    toxic organic chemicals, effects of,
        68-69
    toxics management policy, 69–70
Water resources
    Canadian, 61
    Canadian Constitution and, 81
    chlorination, 64–65
    cholera epidemics, 63
    history of in Canada, 63–64

    in Mexico, 81
    in United States, 81
    piped water systems, 64
Weaver, S., 276
Wein, E.E., 95
Wengert, Norman, 186
Wernette, D., 123
Wildlife management
    political influences, 35
Wildlife resources
    effect on economy, 35
    human dimensions, 34
    stakeholders, 34
Wildlife sustainability
    endangered species legislation, 15
    management, 15
    prey–predator relationships, 15
Willeke, Gene E., 185
Wilson, Jeremy, 295
Wiltse, 19
Wind erosion, 52
Winfield, Mark, 212
Wolf
    aerial shooting of, 19
    control programs, 26–27
    recovery, Montana, 31
    recovery, Yellowstone, 31–32
    recovery and persecution, Europe,
        32–33
    social organization, 21–22
    tourism and, 35–36
    traffic and, 28
Wong, M.P., 89
Wood, Robert S., 295
World Commission on Environment
    and Development, 270
World Council of Churches, 144

Yearly, S., 183
York, G., 276

Zehr, Stephen C., 183
Ziegenfus, R.C., 114, 117

A COMMUNITY OF LEARNING SOLUTIONS

Nelson County

library · nelson canada · metropolis · thomson.com · t.c · college campus · school house · the edge · the burbs

Visit us on the Web at **http://www.nelson.com/nelson.html**
You can send your comments to us by e-mail at **college_arts_hum@nelson.com**

To the owner of this book

We hope that you have enjoyed *The Environment and Canadian Society,* and we would like to know as much about your experiences with this text as you would care to offer. Only through your comments and those of others can we learn how to make this a better text for future readers.

School _____ Your instructor's name _____

Course _____ Was the text required? _____ Recommended? _____

1. What did you like the most about *The Environment and Canadian Society?*

_____
_____
_____

2. How useful was this text for your course?

_____
_____
_____

3. Do you have any recommendations for ways to improve the next edition of this text?

_____
_____
_____

4. In the space below or in a separate letter, please write any other comments you have about the book. (For example, please feel free to comment on reading level, writing style, terminology, design features, and learning aids.)

_____
_____
_____

Optional

Your name _____ _____ Date _____

May ITP Nelson quote you, either in promotion for *The Environment and Canadian Society* or in future publishing ventures?

Yes _____ No _____

Thanks!

You can send your comments to us via e-mail at
college_arts_hum@nelson.com

PLEASE TAPE SHUT. DO NOT STAPLE.

FOLD HERE

I(T)P® Nelson

an International Thomson Publishing company

MAIL ▶ POSTE

Canada Post Corporation
Société canadienne des postes

Postage paid	Port payé
if mailed in Canada	si posté au Canada
Business Reply	Réponse d'affairess

0066102399   01

0066102399-M1K5G4-BR01

ITP NELSON
MARKET AND PRODUCT DEVELOPMENT
P.O. BOX 60223 STN BRN 8
TORONTO ON M7Y 2H1